ILLION PEOPLE:

graphic Dilemmas and World Politics

s by Georges Tapinos and Phyllis T. Piotrow

MIDDLE EAST IN THE COMING DECADE:

Wellhead to Well-being?

s by John Waterbury and Ragaei El Mallakh

JCING GLOBAL INEQUITIES

s by W. Howard Wriggins and Gunnar Adler-Karlsson

AND POOR NATIONS IN THE WORLD ECONOMY

*s by Albert Fishlow, Carlos F. Diaz-Alejandro, Richard R. Fagen,
oger D. Hansen*

ROLLING FUTURE ARMS TRADE

*s by Anne Hessing Cahn and Joseph J. Kruzel, Peter M. Dawkins,
cques Huntzinger*

RSITY AND DEVELOPMENT IN SOUTHEAST ASIA:

oming Decade

s by Guy J. Pauker, Frank H. Golay, and Cynthia H. Enloe

EAR WEAPONS AND WORLD POLITICS:

atives for the Future

*s by David C. Gompert, Michael Mandelbaum, Richard L. Garwin,
hn H. Barton*

A'S FUTURE

n Policy and Economic Development in the Post-Mao Era

s by Allen S. Whiting and Robert F. Dernberger

RNATIVES TO MONETARY DISORDER

by Fred Hirsch and Michael W. Doyle and by Edward L. Morse

EAR PROLIFERATION:

tions, Capabilities, and Strategies for Control

*by Ted Greenwood and by Harold A. Feiveson and
re B. Taylor*

RNATIONAL DISASTER RELIEF:

a Responsive System

n Green

1980s Project Studies/Council on Foreign

STUDIES AVAILABLE

COLLECTIVE MANAGEMENT:
The Reform of Global Economic Organizations
Miriam Camps, with the collaboration of Catheri

SOVIET-AMERICAN RELATIONS IN THE 19
Superpower Politics and East-West Trade
Studies by Lawrence T. Caldwell and William Di

INDUSTRIAL POLICY AS AN INTERNATIO!
William Diebold, Jr.

GROWTH POLICIES AND THE INTERNATIC
Lincoln Gordon

CHALLENGES TO INTERDEPENDENT ECO!
The Industrial West in the Coming Decade
Studies by Robert J. Gordon and Jacques Pelkmc

SHARING GLOBAL RESOURCES
Studies by Ruth W. Arad and Uzi B. Arad, Rach
Jose Piñera, and Ann L. Hollick

AFRICA IN THE 1980s:
A Continent in Crisis
Studies by Colin Legum, I. William Zartman, and
Lynn K. Mytelka

BEYOND THE NORTH-SOUTH STALEMATE
Roger D. Hansen

ENHANCING GLOBAL HUMAN RIGHTS
Studies by Jorge I. Dominguez, Nigel S. Rodley,
Richard Falk

OIL POLITICS IN THE 1980s:
Patterns of International Cooperation
Øystein Noreng

SIX
Dem
Stud

THE
Fror
Stud

REI
Stud

RIC
Stud
and

CO!
Stud
and

DIV
The
Stud

NU
Alt
Stud
and

CH
Fou
Stud

AI
Stud

NU
Mc
Stud
Th

IN
To
Stud

Collective Management

Collective Management

THE REFORM OF
GLOBAL ECONOMIC ORGANIZATIONS

MIRIAM CAMPS

With the Collaboration of
CATHERINE GWIN

1980s Project/Council on Foreign Relations

McGRAW-HILL BOOK COMPANY
New York St. Louis San Francisco
Auckland Bogotá Düsseldorf Johannesburg London Madrid
Mexico Montreal New Delhi Panama Paris São Paulo
Singapore Sydney Tokyo Toronto

Robert Valkenier was the editor of this book for the Council on Foreign Relations. Thomas Quinn and Michael Hennelly were the editors for McGraw-Hill Book Company. Christopher Simon was the designer and Teresa Leaden supervised the production. The book was set in Times Roman by David E. Seham Associates, Inc.

Printed and bound by R. R. Donnelley & Sons, Inc.

Library of Congress Cataloging in Publication Data
Camps, Miriam.
Collective management.

(1980s project/Council on Foreign Relations)
Bibliography: p.
Includes Index.
1. International economic relations.   2. International
Bank for Reconstruction and Development.   3. International Monetary Fund.   4. United Nations—Economic assistance.
I. Gwin, Catherine, joint author.   II. Title.
III. Series: Council on Foreign Relations.   1980s
project/Council on Foreign Relations.
HF1411.C335   337   81-394

                        AACR1

123456789   RRD RRD   898765432 1

ISBN 0-07-009708-9

ISBN 0-07-009709-7 PBK.

Contents

Foreword: The 1980s Project

Few people dissent from the proposition that better ways must be found to manage collectively the problems that can no longer be handled by states acting independently. Yet there is little consensus in today's world on how international institutions should be reorganized and strengthened to meet this need. This book examines the main functions that will need to be performed during the next decade or so by global intergovernmental institutions if the international economic system is to operate in an efficient, orderly, and equitable manner. To this end, it suggests changes in policies, in principles, and in organizational structures in four main areas: the relief of poverty and the provision of basic support; trade and production; the management of money and the coordination of macroeconomic policy; and development and the international transfer of resources.

The book is one of the concluding volumes in the series of studies produced by the 1980s Project of the Council on Foreign Relations—studies dealing with issues likely to be of international concern during the next 10 to 20 years. The ambitious purpose of the 1980s Project was to examine important political and economic problems not only individually but in relationship to one another. Some studies or books produced by the Project primarily emphasize the interrelationship of issues. In other, more specifically focused studies, considerable efforts have been made to write, review, and criticize them in the context of more general Project work. Each Project study is thus able to stand on its own; at the same time it has been shaped by a broader perspective.

The 1980s Projects had its origin in the wide recognition that many of the assumptions, policies, and institutions which have characterized international relations during the past 30 years are inadequate to the demands of today and the foreseeable demands of the period between now and 1990 or so. Over the course of the decade, substantial adaptation of institutions and behavior will be needed to respond to the changing circumstances of the 1980s and beyond. The Project sought to identify those conditions and the kinds of adaptation they might require. It was not the Project's purpose to arrive at a single or exclusive set of goals. Nor did it focus upon the foreign policy or national interests of the United States alone. Instead, it sought to identify goals and to suggest courses of action that are compatible with the perceived interests of most states, despite differences in ideology and in level of economic development.

The published studies of the Project are aimed at a broad readership, including present or potential policy makers and those who would influence the policy-making process, but are not confined to any single nation or region. The authors of project studies were asked to remain mindful of interests broader than those of any one society and to take fully into account the likely realities of domestic politics in the principal societies involved. All those who have worked on the Project, moreover, have tried not to be captives of the status quo; they have sought to question the inevitability of existing patterns of thought and behavior that restrain desirable change and to look for ways in which those patterns might in time be altered or their consequences mitigated.

The 1980s Project was at once a series of separate attacks upon a number of urgent and potentially urgent international problems and also a collective effort to bring those separate approaches to bear upon one another and to suggest the kinds of choices that might be made among them. The Project had more than 300 participants from the United States and abroad. A small central staff and a steering Coordinating Group defined the questions, and nearly 100 authors, from more than a dozen countries, worked on the studies. Ten working groups of specialists and generalists were convened to subject the Project's studies to critical scrutiny and to help in the process of identifying interrelationships among them.

The 1980s Project was the largest single research and studies effort in the history of the Council on Foreign Relations, comparable in conception only to a major study of the postwar world, the War and Peace Studies, undertaken by the Council during the Second World War. At that time, the impetus of the effort was the discontinuity caused by worldwide conflict and the visible and inescapable need to rethink, replace, and supplement many of the features of the international system that had prevailed before the war. The discontinuities in today's world are less obvious and, even when occasionally quite visible (as in the abandonment of gold convertibility and fixed monetary parities), only briefly command the spotlight of public attention. That new institutions and patterns of behavior are needed in many areas is widely acknowledged, but the sense of need is less urgent—existing institutions have not for the most part dramatically failed and collapsed. The tendency, therefore, is to make do with outmoded arrangements and to improvise rather than to undertake a basic analysis of the problems that lie before us and of the demands that those problems will place upon all nations.

The 1980s Project was based upon the belief that serious effort and integrated forethought can contribute—indeed, are indispensable—to progress toward a more humane, peaceful, productive, and just world. And it rested upon the hope that participants in its deliberations and readers of Project publications —whether or not they agree with an author's point of view— may be helped to think more informedly about the opportunities and the dangers that lie ahead and the consequences of various possible courses of action.

The 1980s Project was made possible by generous grants from the Ford Foundation, the Lilly Endowment, the Andrew W. Mellon Foundation, the Rockefeller Foundation, and the German Marshall Fund of the United States. Neither the Council on Foreign Relations nor any of those foundations is responsible for statements of fact and expressions of opinion contained in publications of the 1980s Project; they are the sole responsibility of the individual authors under whose names they appear. But the Council on Foreign Relations and the staff of the 1980s Project take great pleasure in placing those publications before a wide readership both in the United States and abroad.

The 1980s Project

1980s PROJECT WORKING GROUPS

During 1975 and 1976, ten Working Groups met to explore major international issues and to subject initial drafts of 1980s Project studies to critical review. Those who chaired Project Working Groups were:

Cyrus R. Vance, Working Group on Nuclear Weapons and Other Weapons of Mass Destruction

Leslie H. Gelb, Working Group on Armed Conflict

Roger Fisher, Working Group on Transnational Violence and Subversion

Rev. Theodore M. Hesburgh, Working Group on Human Rights

Joseph S. Nye, Jr., Working Group on the Political Economy of North-South Relations

Harold Van B. Cleveland, Working Group on Macroeconomic Policies and International Monetary Relations

Lawrence C. McQuade, Working Group on Principles of International Trade

William Diebold, Jr., Working Group on Multinational Enterprises

Eugene B. Skolnikoff, Working Group on the Environment, the Global Commons, and Economic Growth

Miriam Camps, Working Group on Industrial Policy

1980s PROJECT STAFF

Persons who have held senior professional positions on the staff of the 1980s Project for all or part of its duration are:

Richard H. Ullman was Director of the 1980s Project from its inception in 1974 until July 1977, when he became Chairman of the Project Coordinating Group. Edward L. Morse was Executive Director from July 1977 until June 1978. At that time, Catherine Gwin, 1980s Project Fellow since 1976, took over as Executive Director.

PROJECT COORDINATING GROUP

The Coordinating Group of the 1980s Project had a central advisory role in the work of the Project. Its members as of June 30, 1978, were:

Until they entered government service, other members included:

COMMITTEE ON STUDIES

The Committee on Studies of the Board of Directors of the Council on Foreign Relations is the governing body of the 1980s Project. The Committee's members as of January 1, 1980, were:

Acknowledgments

This book was planned and for the most part written by Miriam Camps. Catherine Gwin's major contributions were Chapter 7, International Resource Transfers, and much of Chapter 4, Poverty and Basic Support. But we exchanged ideas on all parts of the book, and we both subscribe to the general approach as well as the main proposals. It is difficult to collaborate across an ocean, and perhaps even more difficult to do so across a generation. The book may have lost something in consistency from the fact that we look at some problems through different lenses and have sought to compose our differences. But, for the most part, we think this double vision has been stereoscopic, adding depth rather than blurring.

None of the other 1980s Project studies were commissioned or written with the needs of this book in mind. A surprising number of them, however, contributed importantly to our thinking, as is apparent from the footnotes. Four of them—by William Diebold, Jr., Albert Fishlow *et al.*, Lincoln Gordon, and Øystein Noreng—should be singled out for special mention, for we are conscious of having drawn on them very directly.

A number of people read and commented on the entire manuscript (or substantially all of it), and we should like to record our particular thanks to them: Robert Asher, Carlos Díaz-Alejandro, Lincoln Gordon, Gerald Helleiner, Alfred C. Neal, Joseph S. Nye, Oscar Schachter, and Paul Streeten. Most of them also attended a special review meeting of the manuscript held in mid-

January 1980. Many important, last-minute improvements in the manuscript were made in response to their suggestions. The errors of fact or judgment that remain are all of our own making.

Many other people read individual chapters at various stages along the way or were of particular help to us in clarifying our thoughts or in prompting new ones. To them, too, we are most grateful and happy to record our thanks: Hollis Chenery, Charles Cooper, Charles Frank, Peter Kenen, Michael Kuczynski, Edwin M. Martin, Edward L. Morse, Margaret Potter, Gustav Ranis, Tom de Vries, and Marina v.N. Whitman. Lincoln Gordon did double duty, reading several chapters several times; and he also enabled Miriam Camps to try out some of her ideas in March 1979 on a session of the Salzburg Seminar, of which he was the chairman and organizing genius. Robert Asher and Paul Streeten were also of much help to us along the way as well as stimulating critics at the final stage.

Most of the central ideas in the book were outlined to a small international conference held at the Seven Springs Conference Center in Mt. Kisco, New York, in June 1979 to mark the formal conclusion of the 1980s Project. Those attending the conference were: Tatsuo Arima, Karl Birnbaum, Hedley Bull, Miriam Camps, William Diebold, François Duchêne, Albert Fishlow, David C. Gompert, Catherine Gwin, Roger D. Hansen, Pierre Hassner, Stanley Hoffmann, Girilal Jain, Kim Kyong-Won, Lim Bian Kie, Winston Lord, Charles W. Maynes, M. Thierry de Montbrial, Edward L. Morse, Joseph S. Nye, Andrew Pierre, John Ruggie, Justinian Rweyemamu, Luciano Tomasini, Richard H. Ullman, William Wallace, and Ross Wilson. Their questions and criticisms came at a crucial stage in the writing of the book. But neither those who participated in that conference nor those who have read and commented on sections of the book should be assumed to share our views or to support in any way any of our specific proposals. Some of them would, we know, at points dissent quite sharply.

Many people in addition to those we have already mentioned helped shape our thoughts. Some of our biggest debts are owed to those whose writings we have plundered, not least the nameless writers of reports for the institutions on which we have concentrated. As with the list of people thanked above, so with our bibliography: both could easily be twice as long, yet both would still be incomplete.

Robert Valkenier, the Council's editor, helped shape our prose, pruning away the redundant and clarifying the confusing; to him, too, our thanks. And our thanks go as well to other members of the Council staff, notably Patricia Berlyn for her skillful preparation of the index, and Debra De Palma, Janet Rigney and others in the Library, Grace Darling, and the many typists of many drafts.

Finally, we should like to acknowledge our particular debt to William Diebold, Senior Research Fellow at the Council. We have trespassed on his time remorselessly and have drawn on his apparently limitless knowledge without scruple.

We finished writing this book in February 1980 and assumed that it would be published during the fall. For reasons beyond our control, publication was delayed, and some up-dating, mostly of facts and figures, was done during the fall of 1980. Had we been aware at the time of writing of the delays that lay ahead, doubtless some of the exposition would have been framed a little differently. But our analysis seemed to us to remain valid and was not altered.

Miriam Camps
Catherine Gwin

Abbreviations

ASEAN	Association of South East Asian Nations
BIS	Bank for International Settlements
CFF	Compensatory Financing Facility
CGIAR	Consultative Group on International Agricultural Research
CIEC	Conference on International Economic Cooperation
Comecon	Council for Mutual Economic Assistance
C-20	Committee of Twenty
DAC	Development Assistance Committee
ECA	Economic Commission for Africa
ECOSOC	Economic and Social Council
ECU	European Currency Unit
ECLA	Economic Commission for Latin America
ECWA	Economic Commission for Western Asia
EMF	European Monetary Fund
EMS	European Monetary System
EPU	European Payments Union
FAC	Food Aid Convention
FAO	Food and Agriculture Organization
G-5	Group of Five
G-10	Group of Ten

G-24	Group of Twenty-four
GAB	General Arrangements to Borrow
GATT	General Agreement on Tariffs and Trade
GNP	Gross National Product
IAEA	International Atomic Energy Agency
IBRD	International Bank for Reconstruction and Development
ICA	International Commodity Arrangements
IDA	International Development Association
IDB	Inter-American Development Bank
IEA	International Energy Agency
IFAD	International Fund for Agricultural Development
IFC	International Finance Corporation
ILO	International Labour Organisation
IMF	International Monetary Fund
ITO	International Trade Organization
ITU	International Telecommunication Union
LDCs	Less-Developed Countries
MDB	Multilateral Development Bank
m-f-n	Most Favored Nation
MTN	Multilateral Trade Negotiations
NATO	North Atlantic Treaty Organization
NICs	Newly Industrializing Countries
NIEO	New International Economic Order
OAPEC	Organization of Arab Petroleum Exporting Countries
OAS	Organization of American States
OAU	Organization of African Unity
ODA	Official Development Assistance
OECD	Organization for Economic Cooperation and Development

OEEC	Organization for European Economic Cooperation
OPEC	Organization of Petroleum Exporting Countries
PTO	Production and Trade Organization (proposed)
SDRs	Special Drawing Rights
UN	United Nations
UNBSP	United Nations Basic Support Program (proposed)
UNCTAD	United Nations Conference on Trade and Development
UNDP	United Nations Development Program
UNDRO	United Nations Disaster Relief Office
UNESCO	United Nations Educational, Scientific and Cultural Organization
UNFPA	United Nations Fund for Population Activities
UNICEF	United Nations Children's Fund
WFC	World Food Council
WFP	World Food Program
WHO	World Health Organization
WP-3	Working Party Three of the Economic Policy Committee of the OECD

Collective Management

Introduction

In recent years, questions of international institutional reform have assumed a prominence they have not had since the end of World War II when the main lines of today's system were put in place. Shifts in power relationships, the proliferation of new states, the multiplication of linkages of many kinds and the resulting awareness of interdependencies, the heightened expectations and changing attitudes about the roles of government and the goals of international action, the intransigence of some old problems and the emergence of some wholly new kinds of problems—all these and many other factors have raised questions about the adequacy of existing international institutional arrangements to help governments deal with problems that can no longer be dealt with simply on a national basis.

This book is about the need for improved intergovernmental economic institutions at the global level. Our concentration on global institutions does not mean that we believe them to be the only ones which need improvement, nor that we consider the global level the most important one for the "management" of many problems, nor, indeed, the appropriate one for many purposes. But we do think that in the 1980s rather more of the weight of the "management" of the international economic system should be borne by global institutions. Our reasons for thinking so are partly empirical and partly normative, for reasons we explain in our first two chapters.

1

We have not looked at all the functions now performed by intergovernmental institutions at the global level but have concentrated on what seem to us to be the essentials of the system, those functions and those instrumentalities that provide the bony structure supporting an international economic system capable of advancing the normative concerns discussed in Chapter 2. We have been less concerned with organizational details than with substance, that is to say, with the ends that should be pursued through collective action and the content of the rule systems that should be sought. But *how* rules are made affects their content, and *how* decisions are reached frequently determines their acceptability. Organizational arrangements are no substitute for policies, but they can undermine or enhance them. We have, therefore, looked at organizational structures as well as at the substantive ends we feel should be pursued.

Although we are concerned more with the policies and processes that institutional arrangements should encourage than with strictly organizational questions, in Chapter 4 (Poverty) and Chapter 5 (Trade and Production) we put forward some rather detailed organizational suggestions. We do so with many misgivings, for our bias is against anything smacking of organizational blueprints. We are well aware that in both instances we are opening ourselves to the charge of building castles in the air, that neither set of proposals, however "sensible" it may be in the abstract, would be negotiable. This may well be true. Nevertheless, we think that in both cases there is merit—as a way of giving greater precision and concreteness to our general argument—in sketching out what an organization designed to serve the purposes under discussion might actually look like. Moreover, in both cases, the proposals contain ideas that may stimulate thinking about "practical," incremental steps. In the case of the proposed Production and Trade Organization, enough statements have been made about the need for thinking about a "new ITO"—albeit usually couched in very general terms—to make it time for someone to attempt an outline. (Before long, others will doubtless do a better job than we do.)

Just as it is a mistake to be complacent about the way relationships are now ordered, so too is it a mistake to feel that no substantial institutional improvements can be made unless the whole slate can be rubbed clean and new structures built again from scratch. We have tried to take an overall view, but that has not led us to propose sweeping reforms everywhere. In some cases, the process of evolution simply needs nudging along. In other areas, the institutional fabric seems to us to have serious gaps, places where fairly radical reforms are needed. In one sense, we are, of course, outlining our own prescription for a New International Economic Order. But we would not describe what we are trying to do in just those terms. The debate over the NIEO is a sterile one. The international economic order—the relationships among states and the institutions needed to support them—is constantly changing. It is different today from what it was when the Group of 77 laid down their barrage of demands at the Sixth Special Session of the General Assembly in the spring of 1974. Further evolution is needed. Our purpose has been to try to look a little farther down the road from where we are to-day, and to look at the needs of the system as a whole, not at the "deals" required to settle an obsolescent debate.

Our approach is, quite deliberately, a normative one. But this is not a cookbook full of tested recipes. Some of our cakes would doubtless fall, our bread fail to rise. It is intended simply as a contribution to what must be a continuing process of discussion and debate on how to make the international economic system function rather more efficiently, rather more equitably, and rather more predictably.

Many of the changes that we recommend thinking about in the 1980s run directly counter to what seemed to be the dominant trends in world affairs as the decade of the seventies came to an end. (And when we wrote this book.) The sense of loss of control at the national level in most modern industrialized states was almost palpable. For the most part, it was leading to responses that reflected a tendency to turn inwards, to give priority and lend respectability to ways of thinking about national needs and purposes that are a far cry from the perspectives we advocate: ones that give more weight to systemic concerns and more meaning to the concept of global welfare. In a world in which the deliberate destruction of life has taken place in Kampuchea,

3

something very close to mob rule has prevailed in Iran, and the term "Cold War," rather than sounding like an echo from the past, has seemed an all-too-likely description of the future, are we deluding ourselves when we see glimmerings of an awareness of belonging to a global community? Are we simply straining our eyes when we see the beginnings of a global economy? Given the way democracies must function, are we indulging in wishful thinking when we believe the United States, or any other country, can pursue policies that give more weight to the needs of the system? Why, in today's world, waste effort trying to improve "collective management" at the global level? Would it not be better to "face facts," batten down the hatches, cooperate with the "like-minded"—where that is easy (or unavoidable)—and wait for better times?

The arguments of Hobbesian "political realists" are always especially beguiling when the world is out of joint, as it so visibly is at the start of the 1980s. "Interdependence" has become a cliché, a much overworked and rather boring term. But, like most clichés, it underlines a fact. Interdependence is a multifold process that could be reversed by truly cataclysmic events, but not for long by lesser happenings. And, in today's world, many of the signs of turmoil that seem to mock the concept of global welfare also underline the impossibility of returning to a world in which time and space were useful buffers and national boundaries set the perimeters within which economic problems could be solved. Does turmoil in Iran suggest that there is no need to knit the rapidly industrializing countries into the fabric of international economic relationships? Does continuing stagflation suggest that national governments have all the answers and all the tools? Does the changed economics of energy suggest that cooperation with the "like-minded" is all that is needed? Does the sky-rocketing price of gold suggest that no thought should be given to "man-made" reserve assets?

The times may be unpropitious for some of the kinds of action we suggest and some of the shifts in perspective that we think are needed. But it is worth recalling that one of the most creative periods of thought about institution-building came during the darkest period of World War II and that another came during the frostiest years of the Cold War. The latter yielded not just defense pacts and arms races, as the revisionists would have us believe, but also a new awareness of the economic benefits to be gained from shifting the focus from the national unit to a larger one: the European Community for some purposes, the OEEC/OECD area for others.

Much of the new thinking that is now needed draws on these two streams of thought and action. The first is what might be called the "Bretton Woods" stream. In brief, this was the recognition of the need for widely accepted rules to avoid "beggaring neighbors" and to enable market forces to point to efficiencies internationally in much the same way as they do nationally. It also recognized the need for mechanisms to transfer resources among countries when, for various reasons, commercial markets failed to supply the credits needed for some of them to realize their potential for recovery from war or for economic development. The second is what might be called the "integration" stream. This involved the realization that the nation-state is not the right unit, the efficient scale, in which to view and to cope with many economic problems. Both streams, the Bretton Woods and the integration streams, now need to be carried further, adapted to changing facts and changing needs, and blended together in new ways.

The Bretton Woods conception assumed a different universe of states, a concentration of economic power, and a far less intense interaction among economies than we have today. The integration concept acknowledged this interaction but was concerned with the consequences of interdependence only for relationships among the advanced industrialized countries where the interactions were most pronounced. It also, of course, had political overtones and objectives, although these were weaker in the OEEC/OECD than in the European Community.

The relevance of the integration conception for institutional needs at the global level is not only that it stressed the importance of closer coordination of policy as a consequence of market integration (financial as well as commercial) but also that it emphasized the need to shift the perspective in formulating certain policies from the nation-state to a larger unit. We are not

5

suggesting that one can or should think about global institutional needs during the 1980s as though market integration on a global basis approached that within the European Community. Nor are we assuming that there is, or can be in this decade, more than a very rudimentary sense of world community, that is, of belonging to a common society. There is no global political compact from which obligations can be derived, no social structure to support much sense of belonging to a world community. What we do suggest is that, increasingly in the years ahead, some problems should be thought about and dealt with in ways that give more weight to considerations of "global welfare" and to systemic effects than has been the case in the past. Our reasons are partly normative, but, mainly, they derive from our perception of the way the world is moving.

ONE

A Changing World

A few years ago, it seemed to many observers of the international scene that the picture of the world which most policymakers carried in their heads bore surprisingly little resemblance to the complicated mosaic that in fact existed. And it seemed to many policymakers that most academic writers on international affairs had surprisingly little understanding of the constraints restricting policy choices and that they had a rather touching belief that governments were monoliths, capable of pursuing clear and consistent policies.

Many of the more simplistic assumptions about the nature of the world and about the capabilities of the principal actors on the global stage now lie buried under an avalanche of recent analysis.[1] Something like a new consensus on the nature of the world in which we live seems to be emerging. Descriptions which even a few years ago seemed fresh and revealing now read like hackneyed statements of the obvious. The fact that we live in a pluralistic world with cross-cutting relationships and interdependencies of many kinds—psychological and social as well as ecological and economic—running not only among states but among subgroups within separate states and among enterprises and other non-state actors; the fact that, although the United States and the Soviet Union still dominate the strategic equation, the world is no longer rigidly bipolar but marked by new

[1]See the bibliography.

centers of power and centers of new kinds of power; that power has become diffused, and that the distribution of political power and economic power do not fully coincide; that the heterogeneity of states has become much more marked with the emergence to nationhood of a host of new states whose basic structures are still unformed; that nationalism, which for a time seemed in decline, has had a renascence, not only in the new states, as was anticipated, but even in old, established states; that states are not the only "actors" on the global stage and are, in some respects, less influential than other entities—all this and much more forms part of today's corpus of assumptions. Similarly, the curious belief that flourished for a time—in policy-making and academic circles alike—that economic problems were separable from other issues of policy and best kept that way, has been overwhelmed by the reality of the politics of oil prices and the economics of arms races, to cite but two familiar examples. Political economy has, once again, become respectable—and inevitable.

That the world of the 1970s was different from the world of the 1950s was a message which by the end of the decade had been absorbed by analyst and policymaker alike. But it is worth asking whether this now-familiar picture will hold through the 1980s. Which features of today's world are likely to become more important and which less important? What attitudes that we now take for granted may well change in significant ways?

Radical discontinuities, by definition, cannot be foreseen, and a surprise-free future would be a most unusual future. But, if one looks at the main characteristics of today's world, some trends seem likely to become more pronounced, some others may well have peaked and seem likely to flatten out, and some concerns seem likely to grow while others diminish or change as we move through the decade of the eighties.

In the eighties, as in the seventies, the strategic stand-off between the United States and the Soviet Union seems certain to remain the dominant concern in the realm of security. Efforts to find safer and less costly ways to manage the central balance are likely to continue, despite some recent signs that the superpowers' efforts to "cap" their arms race have come to a dead end and another costly upward twist is in prospect. Perhaps, as the decade wears on, new ways of slowing the competition will be found. But a vastly improved security picture in the area of central confrontation seems unlikely. So, too, does a major deterioration into war.

China will become a more active player and a more important factor in the calculations of both superpowers. But, again, the crude balance of the seventies seems likely to hold, a balance that is not really triangular, and certainly not pentagonal, although both Japan and Western Europe are important factors, as, too, are some of the newer powers. It would be a mockery to call this balance a framework of peace, yet today, and probably for this decade, there is a stable enough stand-off so that people and their governments, in all but a handful of tormented states—Kampuchea, the Lebanon, Iran—can give a low enough probability to truly cataclysmic events to proceed in planning their futures in fairly conventional ways.

In the fifties and early sixties both superpowers regarded their competition as worldwide: gains for one were more or less automatically regarded as losses for the other. In the late sixties and early seventies, the United States, at least, took a more differentiated view. It took steps to disengage from some parts of the world where its direct interests were hard to define and the exercise of its power appeared to create problems rather than to bring either peace to the region or useful influence to itself. Certain assumptions were implicit in this process of disengagement. There was considerable hope that the process of disengagement would be a mutual one and that both superpowers would pursue a policy of restraint in areas like Africa where their direct interests were marginal. There was also an expectation that in some parts of the world other friendly powers would play a more dominant role and, with a little material help, that local balances would tend to preserve the peace.

Recent developments in Africa, in the Middle East, in Southeast and Southwest Asia have led to new questions. If the withdrawal of United States power is not matched by a similar policy on the part of the Soviet Union, what then? With the emergence of some strong local powers and new drives by them to exert

9

influence in and over the area, can regional situations be left to regional settlement? And how is the picture altered if some of these new regional powers acquire nuclear weapons? Having rejected the concept of a universal security role for the United States and having decided to accept a higher level of violence in various parts of the world, will we find that peace is not "divisible" after all? Will we find that the pressures toward interdependence, which today so visibly limit autonomy in the economic sphere, critically circumscribe the ability to pursue a rather different pattern of interstate relations in the security field?

These questions will be examined in detail elsewhere.[2] The point here is that, as we move into the eighties, the trend toward United States' disengagement, which for a time appeared to characterize the seventies and to set it apart from the two preceding decades, seems likely, for some new reasons, to become again a subject of debate. It is not a trend that can be extrapolated with any confidence.

DIFFERENTIATION IN THE SEVERAL "WORLDS"

The greater importance of some regional powers in the security equation is one aspect of an already apparent broader trend which will gain in significance: the increasing differentiation that is occurring among groups of states which we have tended to lump together. Particularly conspicuous in what used to be called the Third World, this growing differentiation is becoming apparent in the other "worlds" as well. It is a trend with inevitable consequences for the cohesion of these groupings and one which will affect the way relationships among states can best be "managed" or institutionalized.

During the seventies, one was struck by the surprising cohesion of the "Group of 77," that is, of the 115 or so developing countries which acted together in the United Nations and other forums to push the claims of the less developed countries

[2]Richard H. Ullman, *International Security Issues and American Foreign Policy*, McGraw-Hill, for the Council on Foreign Relations/1980s Project: New York (forthcoming).

(LDCs) for a new international economic order. The very fact that the world was astonished by the continuing cohesion of the group reflected the very real differences within it. Signs of strain were visible by the end of the decade, but, for some years to come, strenuous efforts will doubtless be made to maintain a common front. And probably they will be largely successful. Certainly, outside attempts to split the group are foredoomed and will only serve to cement an improbable coalition. But cohesion seems bound to erode over time. For the present, the "77" are demandeurs, and agreements are far more easily found on what to ask than on what to give. Yet, as some of their demands are met, as others are dropped, and as still others become the subject of active negotiation, cohesion will become more difficult. The needs and real interests of countries like Brazil, Mexico, and South Korea, which are becoming powerful industrial states with large and growing modern sectors, are very different from those of other countries, like many in Black Africa, that remain precariously balanced on the edge of disaster. Already, of course, the Organization of Petroleum Exporting Countries (OPEC) at one end of the spectrum and the poorest "Fourth World" countries at the other are identifiable subgroups, and, for some purposes, they claim and receive separate treatment. The process of fission is bound to continue.

It is possible that as the LDCs become more aware of their differences, and as these differences in fact become more pronounced, and common prescriptions lose validity, some LDC regional groupings will tend to grow in importance, both as areas within which resources are mobilized to mutual advantage and as bargaining groups within wider forums. But the increasing differentiation among the LDCs may also tend to strain the cohesion of some of the larger regional systems like the Organization of American States (OAS) and the Organization of African Unity (OAU), although the OAU may continue to be held together by common animosity to South Africa. Smaller, subcontinental groupings, like the Andean Group, may prove more durable and more effective, sometimes also acting as a counterweight to a growing regional power. Thus, as one looks ahead, some growth in LDC regionalism does, indeed, seem probable, although not necessarily where, today, it looks the strongest. And, it is unlikely that substantial powers will be vested in regional authorities because "nation-building" will—almost everywhere in the developing world—continue to be the overriding priority.

What about the cohesiveness of other groupings? The breakup of OPEC has been wished for, sought, and prophesied for some years. Thus far, although some disagreements about price-setting have occurred, the organization has held together. And, again, the surest way to keep it together is for outsiders to try to play on the differences. Yet, in looking a decade or so ahead, one of two broad lines of development seems probable. Either the United States, Western Europe, Japan, and a few other important oil-importing countries, through a combination of energy saving and the development of new sources of energy, will substantially reduce their dependence on imported oil, or they will fail to do so. If they succeed in reducing their dependence, the price of oil is unlikely to fall appreciably because other sources of energy are unlikely to be any cheaper.[3] Nor will energy be so abundant that oil cannot be sold without resort to drastic price-cutting. In short, even if the major importing countries belatedly adopt sensible energy policies, the cartel may not break apart. But it may become a much less important factor on the international scene, no longer a force to be feared and respected by outsiders and also no longer the focal point of a relationship among a particular group of countries.

Somewhat paradoxically, the cohesion of the cartel might be strained to the breaking point if the importing countries fail to adopt sensible energy policies. In that event, one can foresee toward the end of the decade the possibility of a mad scramble for oil in which different tactics vis-à-vis the main oil producers might be followed by the three main competing groups—the United States, Western Europe, and Japan—each using a combination of carrots and sticks to win or to force favors from the producers they have the means to woo or harry into a deal. Barring this kind of breakdown (an avoidable one, given sensible

---

[3]Perhaps this statement should be qualified. To judge by events in 1979, the spot price may, at times, be bid up to ridiculously high levels from which there will be some falling back.

policies), OPEC does not seem to be a natural grouping for any purpose other than fixing oil prices, and one would therefore expect it to wane in importance as the global adjustment to higher energy prices is made. For this reason, among others discussed later, the recent innovation in setting up the International Fund for Agricultural Development (IFAD) of using OPEC as one of the constituencies from which representation is drawn does not look like a desirable or compelling precedent.

If preoccupation with national identity and growing divergencies in real interests arising from differing natural endowments and stages of development seem likely to erode the cohesion of the Group of 77 and to complete the elimination of Third World from the vocabulary of contemporary international relations (although not, unfortunately, the elimination of poor countries from the reality of international life), what can one foresee for the Second and First Worlds?

In the Second World, the smaller countries of Eastern Europe and, to an extent, the Soviet Union itself are today caught up in the dilemmas that confront, in an acute form, the countries of the First World and, to an ever-growing degree, those of the Third: how can a nation capture the advantages of a high degree of interaction with other nations without sacrificing more control over its own destiny than is politically acceptable? In the smaller countries of Eastern Europe, the tug from the West is strong, and the benefit of fuller participation in the international economic system a constant lure. Stressing the need for a better international division of labor has become a respectable "socialist" way of pushing not only for wider access to Western markets but also for more two-way interaction with the international economy. The need for technology and the pressures from consumers—which become particularly difficult to ignore when mixed with nationalist pressures—have combined to yield considerable Soviet tolerance for an expansion of economic relationships between Eastern Europe and the West, just as they have also increased the Soviet Union's interest in expanding its own trade and other commercial undertakings.

To look no further than the decade ahead, it would be optimistic to expect any drastic change in the cohesion of the Second

World. Even the present slow trend toward somewhat easier economic and human relationships within countries and with the West could be reversed. But the cost of cutting the links with the outside world rises as the links multiply and thicken. The costs that must be calculated if the Soviet Union sought to turn back the clock include not only the disruptions to the economies of the smaller Eastern European countries and the strains this would put on their relations with the U.S.S.R., they also include the way these highly unpalatable actions would interact with other forces within Soviet society which are pushing for a more open, less highly controlled system.

The Second World will certainly remain a more cohesive and a more distinct group than will the Third World, with far less diversity than exists within the other "worlds." Nonetheless, diversity within the group seems likely to grow rather than to diminish, with consequences for the way each country sees its own interests affected by broader international arrangements. Hungary's experiments with market prices seem likely to be followed by other moves taking it further away from the more orthodox system of its socialist neighbors. The GNP per capita of the German Democratic Republic already places it high on the global income scale, above some of the founder members of the First World and embarrassingly distant from some of its closest Second World partners.

On turning to the First World here, too, more rather than less differentiation within the group seems probable, although conflicting pressures are at work, some making for more cohesion, some for less. The First World, unlike the Second, is not an easily identifiable group of countries. Although membership in the Organization for Economic Cooperation and Development (OECD) is frequently taken as the test, it is not a very satisfactory one. All the highly industrialized market-economy states are members of the organization, but so too are states like Portugal and Greece which have more in common with many Third World countries. Among the core of a dozen or so highly industrialized, market-economy countries, "spontaneous integration" has gone very far; the web of interconnectedness is uniquely dense, both by historical standards and by comparison with the links running between the core and other countries. As a result of the revolution in transportation and communications, the progressive relaxation of controls over trade, payments and other transactions, and the speed and ingenuity with which enterprises took advantage of these new developments, the economies of this group of countries are now not only very interconnected but also highly vulnerable to one another. Once this process of integration is underway, it tends to feed on itself, for the very vulnerabilities that the process creates tend to push governments to seek to manage collectively what they can no longer handle separately. Yet, at the same time, the process sets up counterpressures: collective management is difficult, it erodes national autonomy, and it leads to demands to loosen existing links and to find ways to avoid further enmeshment.

Even within the most clearly identifiable inner group of First World countries there are subgroups, most notably the European Community, which at times pull against the cohesion of the larger group. So, too, in a rather different way, do the summit meetings of the six or seven most powerful OECD countries. And so, too, does the fact that the economic performance of the old, industrialized, market-economy countries is tending to diverge rather than to converge. Again, although too much can easily be read into per capita GNP figures, the fact that the figure for the United States is about twice that of the United Kingdom has an effect on the self-images of the two countries and also on the way some institutional arrangements need to be thought about in the future.[4]

It is already hard to think of Portugal, an OECD country, as a rich, industrialized country and of Brazil, a leading member of the Group of 77, as a poor LDC. As we move through the eighties, the reality for many purposes seems likely to be closer to a continuum than to a set of separate worlds. Whatever the scale of measurement, it will be fairly easy to identify which states lie at the two extremes: which are very rich, which very poor; which highly industrialized, which barely started on the road to development. There will be clustering, but also much

[4]Perhaps of more importance in terms of "self-image" is the fact that the United Kingdom now comes well below Japan in the GNP league table.

overlapping, and states will not remain fixed in their rank ordering but will shift about. Not only will the universe of states look more like a continuum than it does today, but even the key countries will change with the subject being addressed, very few of them being key countries at all times.

This is not to say that the fault lines that today divide "North" from "South" and "East" from "West" will disappear in this decade. They will not. But, in many ways, these geographic labels and the familiar division into "worlds" are likely to look increasingly arbitrary and to become increasingly meaningless categories for many purposes. Institutionalizing relationships at the global level by using as constituent groups the First, Second, and Third Worlds (sometimes with OPEC, sometimes with the Fourth World separately identified) is unlikely to be for long the right prescription.

One factor which, almost everywhere, has contributed both to the erosion of these separate "worlds" and to the questioning of the adequacy and, perhaps, relevance of many of today's institutional arrangements is the resurgence of nationalism. It was a conspicuous trend in the seventies. Will it continue? Many different attitudes and forms of behavior are frequently lumped together under the general heading of "nationalism," and the reasons for, and the implications of, nationalism vary, depending on the part of the world being considered.

In many of the LDCs, nationalism is an almost inescapable part of nation-building, and its prevalence is scarcely remarkable. Nor is it surprising to find in the ex-colonial territories that form the bulk of the new nations born in the fifties and sixties an exaggerated and anachronistic insistence on unfettered national freedom of action and absolute sovereignty. But insistence on self-reliance, independence, and sovereignty is not only a predictable reaction to the previous situation of political and economic dependence, it is also a form of protest against an international system that seems to many of the new nations to be rigged in favor of the old, developed countries. To some extent, it is a bargaining device for obtaining changes in that system. "Interdependence" in the context of the present system is rejected as simply another form of "dependence." Frequently, the implication is left—occasionally it is made explicit—that if the international economic system were different, the insistence on complete national freedom of action might be less absolute and cooperative arrangements of various kinds easier to find.

The more extreme arguments of the "dependencia" school have already lost their appeal in many LDCs, and the belief that the only road to salvation lies through cutting all links with the international system has given way to more selective approaches to delinking and to more emphasis on the need to change the rules.[5] Some changes in the system have already been made to give the LDCs a more effective voice in rule-making. More modifications seem in prospect. But much remains to be done to bring the LDCs into the management of the system and to make it more responsive to their needs. (Later chapters suggest ways in which this might be done.) Once this process is felt to be securely under way, some manifestations of LDC nationalism that run counter to the obvious need for more cooperation and that have seemed to be both short-sighted and out of tune with the realities of today's world should diminish. At the same time, the emotional and patriotic rhetoric of nationalism that is the natural accompaniment of nation-building seems likely to continue to be strong in most of the new nations. Probably it will become more pronounced in some as they acquire more of the traditional symbols of national power, like armies, navies and airlines.

In the countries of Eastern Europe, nationalism is partly a protest against the dominance of the Soviet Union: the slogans of the LDCs about full respect for sovereignty and unfettered control over natural resources are imbued with a special meaning. The Soviet Union has encouraged the LDCs in some of their more extreme condemnations of the inequities and iniquities of the existing international economic system, echoing LDC charges that it is largely a system designed for (and participated in by) the market economies of the industrialized West. But many of the words and expressions that are now part of the

[5]See the study by Carlos F. Diaz-Alejandro, "Delinking North and South: Unshackled or Unhinged?" in Albert Fishlow et al., *Rich and Poor Nations in the World Economy*, McGraw-Hill, for the Council on Foreign Relations/1980s Project: New York, 1978.

stock-in-trade of most LDC politicians at international meetings become double-edged when used by representatives of the smaller countries of Eastern Europe.

Nationalism in the Soviet Union itself is also a form of protest and dissent, and one that is particularly worrying to the Soviet leadership. Even the most casual visitor to Moscow feels at the center of an empire, not simply of a very large country, and, to judge by the faces one sees, an empire in which the European Russians are a minority, albeit very clearly the ruling minority. Nationalism as protest, both in the smaller countries of Eastern Europe and in the Soviet Union, can be expected to endure and probably to grow. The safe assumption for the future is that the Soviet leadership has the means to keep the pot from boiling over, and will use them if necessary, but that the "nationalities problem" within the Soviet Union and similar pressures coming from Eastern Europe will continue to pose problems for the leadership. Perhaps this may make the Soviet Union more cautious in supporting liberation movements elsewhere.[6]

In the seventies, many nationalist movements were also fed by a strong new interest in, and desire for, identification with ethnic groups, a trend particularly conspicuous in the old established nations of the Western World. It is hard to tell how much of the glorification of ethnic identity is real and lasting and how much of it is a transient, trendy phenomenon. Some of it is undoubtedly a facet of the current, and probably lasting, concern over basic human rights, a logical concomitant of the drive to abolish discrimination for racial or other ascriptive reasons. Some of it is one manifestation of a more general reaction against overcentralization, against bigness, against the fact that, in most modern states, too many decisions over individual life are made by centers that are remote from the individual. "Small is beautiful," independence for Quebec, Scotland, Brittany, and

[6]See John C. Campbell's introductory essay, "The Role of the Soviet Union in World Politics in the 1980s," in Lawrence T. Caldwell and William Diebold, Jr., *Soviet-American Relations in the 1980s: Superpower Politics and East-West Trade*, McGraw-Hill, for the Council on Foreign Relations/1980s Project: New York, 1981.

a new interest by scholars in minor and hitherto neglected ethnic groups in distant regions of the world are all, in some measure, reactions against the impersonality and the remoteness of the control points of modern life and the homogenizing tendencies that have accompanied economic growth.

Will some of the old existing states break up? Probably not, *provided* the process of devolution which is already in train in most of them is fast enough, for strong incentives for organizing economic functions on a large scale are pulling against the separatist pressures. Thus, somewhat paradoxically, pressures from ethnic groups within states seem likely to continue to combine with demands from other groups to produce policies at the national level that are nationalistic or neomercantilistic.[7]

In the old established states, we have not seen the "end of the nation state" that some people in the early fifties were hoping for and some were prophesying as the logical consequence of the growing irrelevance of frontiers in a world of rapid transport, almost instantaneous communication, and awareness of the advantages to be gained by pushing certain kinds of decision-making to higher levels of government. Although the European Community has continued slowly to modify in various ways the character of the economic (and political) relationships among its member states, the heady days of institution-building experienced by the "Europeans" in the early fifties are now only memories and seem unlikely to come again. In Western Europe, as in the rest of the industrialized world, the nation state is not "well," but it is very much alive. Everywhere it is still the level of government that produces most of the direct, short-term, visible benefits and public goods all people want. And in the seventies, nurtured by the increase in energy prices and by the stagflation that was in part, but only in part, the consequence, economic nationalism in the form of a kind of neomercantilism was everywhere apparent.

---

[7] On the other hand, separatism in Scotland has probably been strengthened by U.K. membership in the Common Market. Similarly, the proximity to the U.S. market probably makes independence more thinkable for Quebec.

NEOMERCANTILISM

It is worth taking a closer look at this trend toward neomercantilism, for it is a strong current today. Its causes, strength, and character affect—sometimes positively, more often negatively—many of the shifts in policy and ways of institutionalizing relationships advocated in later chapters.[8]

Particularly since World War II, all of the highly developed industrialized countries have greatly expanded their health, education, and welfare programs and now provide extensive services and recreational and cultural amenities designed not only to protect and to contribute to the social and economic well-being of their people but also to enrich their lives. Governments are likewise expected to maintain high levels of employment, stable and inflation-proof currencies, and constantly expanding standards of living.

There is a strong temptation all of the time for all governments to export economic problems rather than to meet them through internal adjustments. And, in democratic countries, this temptation is strengthened by the need to meet the demands now placed upon them. It is both more popular electorally and usually cheaper in direct budgetary costs to protect an industry threatened by competition by restricting imports than it is to pay unemployment benefits and retraining costs, particularly in periods of low growth when alternative employment may be hard to find. Thus, much of the protectionism or neomercantilism that has come to the surface in the last few years differs in origin and in objective from old-fashioned mercantilism, although in policy terms it finds expression in many of the old-fashioned ways, e.g., in restricting imports, either directly or by pressure on foreign exporters to hold down their exports, and by manipulating exchange rates.

[8]See the introductory essay by Edward L. Morse and Thomas Wallin, "Demand Management and Economic Nationalism in the Coming Decade," and the study by Jacques Pelkmans, "Economic Cooperation among Western Countries," in Robert J. Gordon and Jacques Pelkmans, *Challenges to Interdependent Economies: The Industrial West in the Coming Decade*, McGraw-Hill, for the Council on Foreign Relations/1980s Project: New York, 1979.

All the advanced industrialized countries believe that some industries (e.g., steel) are essential for security. And prestige remains a strong incentive for protective action in other industries (e.g., automobiles). But today, far more than in the past, protectionism and other manifestations of economic nationalism are less often closely associated with the pursuit of national power and more often the consequence of concern for domestic welfare and of awareness of the verdict at the polls if expectations are not met. Frequently, however, the short-term welfare of particularly vocal, politically strong groups seems more compelling than the long-term interest of the country as a whole. The role of the nation-state in modern societies has not diminished, but it has changed as the expectations attached to governments have grown and as some power has shifted from governments to well-organized groups within societies. Much today is demanded of governments, but that very fact has imposed new limits on the ways governments can move to meet these new demands.

It is all too plain that governments of modern democratic states find it difficult to take the long view and that too often the national interest is little more than the sum of parochial interests. In the eighties, even more than in the seventies, the contradictions between the pressures on goverments to let this kind of calculation inform their policies and the need for them to take a longer view, one which gives more weight to the needs of the system as a whole, seem bound to become more glaring. Whether attitudes will change enough to reduce the contradictions to tolerable levels is an open question. But unless electorates are given a better understanding of what the now commonplace rhetoric of global interdependence implies and are ready to accept those implications, the outlook for the adoption of policies that match needs is bleak.

INTERDEPENDENCE

A growing awareness of the oneness and finiteness of the world we live in was one of the most marked differences between the seventies and the fifties. The view of the earth from the moon, the worldwide ramifications of the sudden increase in oil prices, the series of global conferences on population, the environment, food, and habitat—all, in different ways, carried the same message of global interdependence and finite limits. A spate of studies and reports in the early seventies prophesied doom in measurable time unless steps were taken to curb the exponential growth of both population and the use of resources and unless many questions were viewed and acted upon as interconnected global problems, not as congeries of more or less unrelated national problems. Despite, or perhaps because of, the controversy it provoked, the Meadows' report, *The Limits to Growth*, sponsored by the Club of Rome, was by far the most influential of the popular reports, although the short book *Only One World*, written by Barbara Ward and René Dubos before the Stockholm conference on the environment, ran it a close second.

For a time, global interdependencies of all kinds and the fragility and exhaustibility of "spaceship earth" were, perhaps, in danger of being exaggerated. Some of the more alarming predictions of overshoot and collapse rested on shaky assumptions and sloppy analysis, and these were soon exposed.[9] The dramatic change in life-styles and in "global consciousness" that some anticipated as a result of the new awareness of environmental and other "one world" problems proved to be confined to a tiny minority: neither the "greening of America" nor the "greening of the world" was a widespread phenomenon.[10] But although exaggerated claims inevitably bred their own debunking, the pendulum could not swing all the way back: some global problems have to be handled globally; problems and peoples are linked and interconnected in new ways; mindless growth does spell disaster. As one looks ahead to the eighties, one can safely predict that concern with questions related to growth will persist, that awareness of the global dimension of many problems

[9]Carl Kaysen, "The Computer that Printed Out W/O/L/F/," *Foreign Affairs*, July 1972, pp. 660–68.

[10]Charles A. Reich, *Greening of America: How the Youth Revolution Is Trying to Make America Livable,* Random House: New York, 1970; Tom J. Farer, "The Greening of the Globe: A Preliminary Appraisal of the World Order Models Project (WOMP)," *International Organization,* Winter, 1977.

will continue to grow, and that the feed-back effects of living in a closed system will become increasingly apparent.

Concern with growth will be fed by several factors: higher-cost energy and the prospect of a shortage of energy in the mid-eighties; pressure on food supplies and perhaps a recurrence of the prospect of an absolute shortage (as seemed in prospect in the early seventies); increased prices and at least temporary supply problems with some other raw materials; continuing environmental problems ranging from various kinds of pollution to, perhaps, some climatic changes; and all the consequences of crowding that will become everywhere more apparent with the inevitable increases in population. But it also seems probable that there will be no recurrence of the overly simplistic calls for no growth, or zero growth, that occurred in the early seventies. Stagflation in the advanced countries and the difficulties it has caused have underlined the dependence of those countries as well as of the developing countries on continued economic growth. The concern in the eighties will be with *kinds* of growth and *patterns* of growth: how to get enough of the right kind of growth in the right places while avoiding too rapid consumption of scarce resources. The need to shift to new kinds of growth and to adjust to what today seems the safe prediction of lower rates of growth in the old industrial states promises to pose some of the most difficult problems in the years ahead.

In the eighties, the desire for greater autonomy will continue to vie with the pressures making for greater interdependence. Facile assumptions that interdependence was almost always "good" in world-order terms and that closer relationships between states and societies in themselves promoted more civilized behavior are no longer fashionable. Today, in contrast, there is much emphasis on the costs of interdependence and much analysis of the nature and consequences of its various forms and of other types of interconnectedness among states and other entities. Meanwhile, the networks multiply and thicken. And it is difficult to see how the trend toward more interaction between states might be reversed, short of some cataclysmic event such as general war. In the last decade, efforts have been made to create "buffers" and to reduce vulnerabilities. And a

23

few states may succeed in substantially reducing their linkages with others. But, today, the only "closed system" is the world, and the trend toward a more intensive interaction among the units into which it is subdivided seems inevitable, although the trend line will doubtless be a jagged one and will not be the same for all countries.

Today and for many tomorrows, we shall live in a mixed system. We are caught in the process of transition between two modes of thinking about and of dealing with many problems, gradually and erratically moving from what might be called "international economics and politics" to what might be called "world economics and politics." Usually we think and operate in the first mode, but occasionally we use the second. When acting in the first mode, we are seeking a more or less frictionless interaction between the external sectors of 150 or more national economies and polities, trying to facilitate the pursuit in harmony of separate and frequently conflicting national goals. When acting in the second mode, we are trying to do something rather different and to promote the efficient functioning of a closed global system, to optimize, to use the economists' term, on a world basis. Most of our attitudes, most of our assumptions, most of our tools derive from the first mode. Many of our difficulties arise because in some respects, although by no means all, objective facts require a shift to the second mode. The difficulties of living in this mixed system, part "international," part "world" or "global," seem bound to grow. And the lack of congruence between the economic and scientific dimensions of many problems and our political and social structures is certain to become more acute, making it more difficult to find acceptable solutions.

In purely economic terms, it often already makes sense to think of the world as the unit for which the most efficient use of resources is being sought. Many multinational enterprises are truly global entrepreneurs. Computers work in "real time." As John von Neumann pointed out twenty-some years ago, after a certain point, speed in communications does not enable things to be done more rapidly but expands the area over which the same thing can be done.[11] In some ways, it is also easier in moral and philosophical terms to take the goal of optimizing welfare on a global basis as the ultimate objective of political and social action than it is to take that of any smaller unit.

But for the present, and for the future with which we are here concerned, we know that our political and social structures will not support what might be economically most efficient or normatively most desirable. The sense of global community is still very weak—in some places and in some people it does not exist. The welfare demands of those nearer to hand and of those who share common social and political goals almost always rank higher than do the demands of those farther away and less like-minded. Moreover, we do not yet have the political skills required to manage many problems as global problems and on a global basis, even when objective facts and moral imperatives already make it the obvious thing to try to do. The shift in perspective and in prescription will be slow and erratic. But we can anticipate continuing pressures—some from the logic of objective facts, some from the implications of normative goals such as the elimination of poverty—to make the shift. And we can anticipate continuing tension between the two modes of thinking and acting in many areas of concern.

Implicit in the concept of global or world community there are the ideas not only that the world's welfare is to be optimized, (rather than that of a particular state or group of states), but also that it is the individual rather than the nation whose interests are of primary concern. Again, this is not a concept that commands general support today: it is openly attacked in some societies and honored more by words than by deeds in most societies. Almost everywhere, the nation-state is still the political and social structure that commands the most loyalty and disposes of the most power. Nevertheless, although the claim of the individual rather than the state to be the essential component of the world system will not become widely accepted in the years ahead, there is a detectable shift in the way individual claims are

[11]Quoted in *Encounter,* June, 1977.

regarded today as compared to the situation even a relatively few years ago. This has become conspicuous recently in the new attention given to human rights and in the emphasis put on re-shaping assistance to the developing countries to ensure that the basic needs of the poorest people within those countries are met.[12]

We live in a time of many contradictions, most of which show every sign of continuing throughout the eighties. On the one hand, we have new demands placed on governments. On the other, we have a pervasive distrust of governments—a dualism characterizing the international as well as the national sphere. At the international level, the problems of governance become compounded by the further contradiction that despite the em-phasis on the new need for collective management there is little willingness to delegate any power to international or suprana-tional agencies. Some of the more ambitious attempts to do so, such as the European Community, are in conspicuous difficulty. The new emphasis on the need to give reality to the concept of the world as a community by accepting an obligation to organize international relationships to meet the basic human needs of all people coexists with insistent demands for recognition of the sanctity of unfettered national action. Diversity, resurgent na-tionalism, and the proliferation of entities called states but shar-ing few common characteristics create a sense of a more frag-mented world. Yet the evidences of the global cobweb of interconnectedness in which we are all caught up are every-where about us.

By definition, no one can predict unforeseeable changes. Events in the eighties will doubtless pose new challenges and

---

[12]The following quotation from a speech by Secretary of State Vance to the OECD ministerial meeting, June 24, 1977, is also indicative of the shift: "We are in transit to a new era of cooperation and common action. In practical terms our journey will involve going beyond new directions for industrial de-mocracies, new discourse with state-trading nations, and new relationships with developing countries. It will take us to a firmer focus on people. It is the individual and collective hopes of people, their rights and their needs that de-serve the fullest measure of our dedication." Official text issued by U.S. Infor-mation Service, June 24, 1977.

alter, or render irrelevant, some of the approaches that today seem worth exploring if we are to deal more effectively with those problems we already know we face. Some problems are very old and intractable, some of them are very new and only now beginning to be understood. But it is safe to predict that one of the biggest tasks will be to broaden the understanding of the need for change—in assumptions, in attitudes, in modes of thinking, in institutional arrangements—if the political process is to evolve to match the world we live in. Heightened expectations and the social demands on all governments, but particularly on democratic governments in modern societies, make any policy requiring short-term sacrifice for long-term gain or the setting aside of a strongly felt particular need for a less directly experienced general interest difficult to pursue. Yet it is policies of this kind that the successful management of change in a closely packed, elaborately interconnected, "closed" system increasingly requires.

TWO

Goals and Values

In recent years, "world order" studies have burgeoned. They have covered a broad spectrum, ranging from skeptical scholarly studies of the characteristics of the contemporary international system or order and the likelihood of change in that order to radical calls for drastic redistribution of power and wealth and the adoption of new norms of international behavior.[1] Several collective transnational efforts at defining new goals, new norms for international behavior, and new institutional arrangements have also been made. Two of the most ambitious were the World Order Models Project, sponsored by the Institute for World Order, and the RIO (Reshaping the International Order) Project, sponsored by the Club of Rome and the Dutch government and coordinated by Professor Jan Tinbergen. A third transnational effort—more prestigious but more narrowly focused than the other two—was that by the Independent Commission on International Development Issues (the Brandt Commission). And, at the level of governments, aspects of the debate over the "new international economic order" (NIEO) have, of course, dominated the agenda of virtually all international economic discussions.

[1] Recent books and journal articles (cited in the bibliography) by Hedley Bull, Oran Young, and Robert Tucker illustrate the first; those by Johan Galtung, Richard Falk, and the Hammarskjold Foundation illustrate the second.

Anyone who has even a cursory acquaintance with the recent outpouring of analytical and prescriptive studies, official and unofficial, highly scholarly or frankly "committed," must be struck by the enormous diversity of views about the relative importance of the problems we confront, about the kinds of change in governmental policies and in international institutional arrangements we should be seeking to encourage or discourage, and about what results particular acts or conditions can be expected to produce.[2] Individual value systems are far apart, and even intellectual consensus is hard to find. Yet it is perhaps not straining the evidence to suggest that certain propositions, although they might not command universal support, are very widely shared. Thus, although views vary greatly on the amount and rate of change that is feasible and desirable, even those who are most apocalyptic about the world's condition do not believe that the ideal world can be blueprinted and built to specification. Instant Utopias are everywhere out of fashion. Most people who think, write, and negotiate about improving the international order stress the need to encourage or promote processes of change: changes in the attitudes of individuals, changes in the behavior of states and other international actors, and changes in the institutional arrangements that underpin, lubricate, insulate, or govern relationships at the interstate and transnational level.

To encourage change, however, implies some consensus on goals. And goals reflect values. We live in a world characterized by diversity and by the absence of any dominant culture or ethos; indeed, we live in a time when the very concept of a dominant culture is repugnant to many people. Yet, despite the wide diversity in diagnosis, in outlook, in standards, and in values, there would probably be an impressive consensus about many of the characteristics—the conditions which should exist and the processes which should be under way—in what would be widely perceived to be an "improving international order" and a

[2]See Edward L. Morse and Thomas Wallin, "Demand Management and Economic Nationalism in the Coming Decade," in Gordon and Pelkmans, *Challenges to Interdependent Economies:* op. cit.

broadly acceptable order, albeit an international order or system that would fall well short of anyone's view of Utopia.[3]

In the first place, there are some widely recognized, near-absolute conditions of an acceptable order. The conditions can best be indicated by their contraries—things that if they were to occur would be considered by virtually everyone to represent a serious deterioration in the existing order: nuclear war, any war involving two or more of the main centers of power (the United States, Western Europe, the Soviet Union, China, Japan), a major nuclear catastrophe, a major ecological or environmental disaster, or widespread economic chaos. An improved system, by definition, would strengthen the safeguards against the occurrence of any of these.

In addition, it would be surprising if there were not very widespread agreement on a second list of "bads," that is, things that ought not to happen and that in an improved order would be much less likely to happen: wars, genocide, gross abuses of human rights, starvation and other forms of severe economic deprivation, terrorism, nuclear blackmail, major ecological and environmental deterioration, and uncontrolled growth of population.

And fairly ready agreement could probably be reached that in an *improving* order some things should be happening, that is, some processes should be in train: progress toward disarmament, more efficient use of human and material resources, improvement in the living standards of the disadvantaged, more resolution of disputes by peaceful means, steady advancement of human rights, and improvement everywhere in the quality of life.

Once one moves beyond the comparatively short list of near-absolutes, the consensus becomes more tenuous. One is then in the realm of trade-offs, of more or less, and the degree of consensus will be directly related to the way the general proposi-

---

[3]We are here using the words "order" and "system" interchangeably, and more loosely than many scholars would consider appropriate, to describe the totality of defining characteristics of whatever it is we are discussing, e.g., the world, some part of the world, money, trade, etc.

tions are stated. Thus, for some, although terrorism is bad, it is not as bad as the denial of civil rights to a minority. Everyone accepts the goal of advancing human rights, but there are sharp disagreements on what the words mean. "Severe economic deprivation" is defined variously at different times and places.

It is hardly surprising that it becomes increasingly difficult to reach consensus on goals and objectives as one begins to define them more sharply, moving from a general statement to the definition of the policies, procedures, rules, and attitudes required to achieve or to promote them. Not only do different groups attach different weights to goals that are frequently in competition, but differences over values and normative principles—freedom, equality, justice—frequently underlie the different priorities accorded to competing goals. These value preferences almost always complicate the process of rule-making and policy prescription. Even within fairly homogeneous national societies, differences over the weights to be given to widely accepted goals that nevertheless compete for claims on national resources—like welfare and defense—and over the priority to be given to promoting normative principles that may at times conflict—like freedom and equality—are the very stuff of domestic politics. The difficulty of translating the pursuit of any generally agreed-upon objective, such as the improvement in the standard of living, into specific policies obviously increases with the heterogeneity of the society. And as one moves to the global level, it is tempting to say that value systems are so various, and so at odds, that no appreciable improvement in existing arrangements is possible because once one moves beyond the level of rhetoric and the most general objectives, the essential minimum of consensus needed to sustain collective action will evaporate.

We think there is a little more to build on than that bleak assessment would suggest, although the diversity of today's world—the heterogeneity of states and the wide variations in what they "need" from the system and in their power to affect it—clearly limits the kinds of arrangements it is useful to envisage.

Today, four main normative principles (or perhaps, more precisely, simply desiderata) attract strong support when considering the procedures, rules, and other institutional arrangements that should govern economic interaction at the international level. For short, these desiderata can be called efficiency, equity, autonomy, and order (not in the sense of "system" but in the sense of predictability, stability, and reliability). Tension and incompatibility among the four instantly appear if any one of them is given an overriding importance, and much of the argument in international forums today arises because countries differ on their relative importance. It seems clear enough that rules and procedures needed at the global level will not command sufficient support to be widely honored unless they go some way toward satisfying each of these rather different desiderata. It is therefore worth looking more closely at some of the arguments each attracts.[4]

EFFICIENCY

The rules and other institutional arrangements that governed the trade and payments of the central system for most of the period since World War II were designed to reduce friction among states by providing certain "rules of the road." Beyond that, they were intended to facilitate the expansion of trade and thus to promote a better international division of labor and a more efficient use of resources. To achieve these positive goals, they relied explicitly on market forces. Both the goal of "efficiency" and the reliance on the market are today being challenged.

If one puts aside for the moment the question of how much reliance can or should be placed on market forces and focuses first on the goal of the most efficient use of the world's resources, acceptance of this goal clearly assumes a world that is far closer to being a global community than in fact it is. We do not have today, nor are we likely to have soon, the political infrastructure and the social attitudes that would make strict allegiance to the principle of comparative advantage a realizable

[4]Obviously, states desire other things as well, such as increasing their power and influence over others.

goal in the foreseeable future. How is it, then, that it could have been the implicit if not the explicit goal of the postwar trade and payments system?

There are at least three reasons why, until recently, the most efficient use of global resources has seemed, like peace, a blameless goal. In the first place, like peace, it was regarded as a remote goal, not an achievable target. The Bretton Woods system dealt in relatives, not absolutes: *freer* trade and payments, not *free* trade and payments. And in the context of the highly protected system of the late 1940s and 1950s, reducing barriers tended to expand trade without posing serious problems of adjustment. Second, although the international trade and payments system was conceived of as a global system, the system was fully operative for the most part only for the industrialized, market-economy countries. Thus, although "efficiency on a global basis" was the norm implicit in the rules, the "universe" to which the rules really applied was far more restricted. For the most part, it was a "universe" of reasonably homogeneous states in terms of living standards and social and economic outlook. In the third place, the General Agreement on Tariffs and Trade (GATT) and the International Monetary Fund (IMF) provided ways of slowing down the process of removing barriers if a country suffered from the process—that is, if structural changes were, in fact, probable—but there were few provisions to encourage adjustments to new situations and nothing beyond reliance on market forces to bring about change.

Today, the situation is very different. The efficient use of resources on a global basis, which was endorsed by the developed market-economy countries when it was simply a remote goal without much operational significance, has become unacceptable to them when application of the principle means domestic hardship. Even holding to present levels of liberalization is difficult precisely because larger shifts in production patterns than can be easily accommodated now seem likely to follow. The goal of a better international division of labor has—at the rhetorical level—changed hands and become a slogan of the Group of 77.[5]

---

[5]It has also become a slogan in some of the smaller countries of Eastern Europe but, again, with a selective application.

But the LDCs interpret the goal in a highly selective way, invoking other principles when their own very high tariffs and other restrictive measures come under scrutiny. They want a new international division of labor, but they would be even more unwilling than the advanced countries to see comparative advantage be the only test.

Today, there are two main objections to basing global rules *simply* on the norm of the efficient use of global resources. The first is the unwillingness of any country really to accept the heterogeneous world of today as the unit for which welfare is to be optimized. The second is the equally pervasive unwillingness to accept the most efficient use of global resources as an overriding goal. Many LDCs would put a different distribution of the world's wealth and production capacity well ahead of "efficiency," and most developed countries would insist that shifts to patterns of international production which would reflect a more efficient use of resources on a global basis should be slow enough so that the problems of adjustment could be handled without provoking substantial social unrest or economic hardship.

Yet, if one is to have any *global* trade and payments rules, the universe for which they are designed must, by definition, be the globe. And few, if any, governments would deny that encouragement of a more efficient use of resources should be *one* objective, indeed a central objective, of the rules system.

In addition to the objections to giving an overriding priority to the norm of efficiency, today we hear much criticism of the further assumption underlying the postwar trade and payments system that the way to achieve efficiency in the use of resources is by removing barriers and putting one's faith in the market. Perfect markets exist in textbooks but seldom in real life. Sometimes markets are distorted or deliberately rigged by monopolies or oligopolies; sometimes they are interfered with by governments to serve other ends, such as defense, social welfare, environmental protection; and sometimes they are simply inadequate and do not accurately reflect social and other costs.

Most of the authors of the postwar trade rules had rather less faith in the perfection of markets than some of the present criticism would suggest: the International Trade Organization (ITO) Charter reflected great awareness of the distortions caused by concentrations of economic power. But increased social demands and the acceptance by most governments of a greater responsibility for general welfare have inevitably led to more use of subsidies, taxes, and similar measures, sometimes designed simply to ensure that markets take into account social, environmental, and other costs, but frequently to produce results different from those that would result from a "perfect" market. Similarly, although multinational enterprises are not new phenomena, their ability to distort markets or to strengthen their own competitive position in ways not open to others has been greatly increased by the revolution in communications. Nevertheless for most tradable goods, market competition is a stimulus to efficiency—as the increase in the use of markets by the planned economies of Eastern Europe testifies—and it is usually the best guide we have to comparative advantage. The prevalence of distortions, intentional and unintentional, and of governmental intervention to further desired social, economic, and political purposes does not mean that markets are no longer useful, but, rather, that the maintenance of truly competitive markets frequently requires not a policy of laissez faire but one of positive intervention to eliminate or offset distortions. This is true at both the national and the international levels. Like the norm of efficiency, so the instrument of market guidance needs to be supplemented, not abandoned. More is said about these problems in Chapter 5.

EQUITY

Equity is a poor shorthand term, because, as recourse to a dictionary shows, it can mean either "fair" or "equal," two different concepts. It has become a portmanteau term covering several things, all of which, as different groups argue with varying degrees of intensity, the international economic system should provide. In addition to the term's dual meaning, the demands that international economic arrangements should be more "equitable" use the concepts of equality and of fairness to apply sometimes to relationships between states, sometimes to relationships between people. It may be useful, therefore, to begin by unpacking the many different things that are frequently bundled together under this heading.

The easiest objective to agree upon need not detain us long: the international economic system should be fair in the sense that the rules, procedures, and so forth that govern international economic intercourse should not be biased—intentionally or unintentionally—against poor or weak countries, or indeed against or in favor of any country or group of countries. This principle would seem to need no elaborate justification.

Difficulties soon arise, however, because views differ about what constitutes bias and about the criteria that should govern the weights accorded to countries in the management of the institutions. For example, views differ about how far the same rules applied to countries that are very differently endowed are biased in their result if not in their intent. Some argue that only a system built upon the principle of one state, one vote is equitable; others, that only a system in which voting strength corresponds to some measure that more accurately reflects the true weight of the country in the system, or is more representative of the numbers of people involved, is truly equitable. We return to both types of problem in later chapters when we discuss institutional needs in particular fields.

Another kind of "equity" that, during the last decade or so, has become of central concern has to do with the issue of how the world's goods are distributed, both as among states and as among people. Here, much of the recent argument has focused on the emotive issue of growing gaps. Not surprisingly, the gap in the levels of per capita GNP between the rich countries and the poor, and the "unfairness" of a situation in which countries with about 25 percent of the world's population consume about 75 percent of its resources, have figured most prominently in statements by representatives from the LDCs. In contrast, it is the gap between the incomes of the rich and the poor within countries—particularly within the developing ones—and the "unfairness" of transfers which sometimes seem to result in the poor in the rich countries helping the rich in the poor countries that receive most of the emphasis in the rich nations.

37

It may well be that a pattern of income distribution which narrows the differentials between rich and poor within countries is a necessary ingredient of programs designed to eliminate abject poverty and to promote national development. But as a definition of the "equity" that should characterize or be a norm of the international economic system, the narrowing of gaps in personal incomes within states or across national boundaries goes well beyond what most people have in mind or would be prepared to advocate. The concept of equity as applied to welfare, rather than to fairness in decision-making, is used very loosely and broadly. Normally, it embraces the need for an improvement in the living standards of the poorest people and the raising of the GNPs of the poor countries to a level that would enable them to provide, without further outside help, an adequate standard of living for their peoples. But because some would define adequate as being not grossly dissimilar from what is enjoyed by the rich countries, we are back once again on the treacherous and emotive ground of gaps.

The necessity of providing for the poorest and most disadvantaged section of domestic society is one that all the advanced, industrialized, democratic states, and a good many others, today accept. In part out of conscience, in part as a result of the pressures that the disadvantaged can apply, in part because growth and affluence have made it relatively painless to do so, there has been a marked expansion in the roles governments are expected to play, not only in putting floors under poverty but in seeing to it that the floors are rising ones and that the means are found, through education, housing, medical care, etc., to increase the opportunities for a satisfying life for all their citizens. Nevertheless, distributional arguments remain at the center of the political process in all countries. Normally, political bargaining keeps the tensions within more mature societies within acceptable limits, but occasionally they flare into open confrontation. One of the defining characteristics of a viable modern society is its ability to find a rate of social change and of redistribution that is acceptable to most of its citizens most of the time.

Clearly, many of the same forces that have produced domestic change are present today on the international scene: conscience, powerfully assisted by television, and pressure, powerfully assisted by the new experience of the vulnerability of the rich "advanced" societies. But although the forces making for change are there, the crucial element, the sense of belonging to a common society, is, as yet, woefully weak, and no global political compact exists from which to derive rights and obligations.

The difficulties of agreeing on how equity goals should be defined, on what instruments should be used to promote them, and on how divergent and conflicting views should be mediated are daunting. Perhaps, as we suggest in Chapter 4, it will be possible to agree that international arrangements should exist so that the worst forms of abject poverty can be eradicated during the next decade, that is, that the resources needed to do so should be made available by the international community if the governments concerned are prepared to try.

The quest for equity with all its ambiguities will undoubtedly continue. Pushed to an extreme, the demands for fair shares can, at times, produce the perverse result of smaller amounts. But if it is ignored, the result is not only hardship but usually a poorer society. Although equity will be a more ambiguous and controversial norm than efficiency, in many parts of the world it is likely to be a more powerful one. Equity must be pursued, but, like efficiency, it will never be fully attained. And, like efficiency, although it must be one test of the adequacy of any regime or system, it cannot be the sole test.

AUTONOMY

Until fairly recently, it would have seemed odd to list what has come to be called "autonomy" for nation-states among the characteristics that the international economic system must possess if it is to be widely acceptable. The ability of a state to exercise effective control over its own destiny and to "be itself" was assumed to be in the natural order of things, to be close to a definition of statehood. Today the interlinked processes of modernization and growing interdependence have created a new situation.[6] Governments, particularly in advanced industrialized societies, are expected to provide a wide array of benefits to their peoples, yet it is becoming increasingly difficult for them to do so unless the international environment is congenial and other countries are pursuing compatible policies.

Interrelatedness and the dependence of states on the action of others take many forms. There is an "international public goods" element to the satisfaction of many domestic needs. Security is a domestic public good in all societies, that is, it is something that can neither be supplied to nor withheld from one individual without doing the same for all members of the society. An analogous situation holds among the states within the North Atlantic Treaty Organization (NATO). So, too, with many questions having to do with the environment or the economy. The "good" in question—clean air, monetary stability, etc.—can only be supplied by a number of states acting collectively, and it cannot easily be denied one state without denying it to others at the same time. In other cases, the ability of a state to pursue its own interests may be eroded by the actions not of other states but of non-state actors. Investment plans, taxation policies, balance-of-payments calculations can all be affected by the actions of multinational enterprises. Television undermines the abilities of governments to control attitudes and links consumption standards in ways that create demands many governments cannot meet.

Not exactly a goal or a norm in the sense that economic efficiency and the various kinds of equity are goals to be pursued or norms against which actions or rules can be tested, autonomy is something that all states want up to some point, and if it is encroached upon beyond that point, the existence of the state itself is called into question. Where the line is drawn differs with the

---

[6]See Robert O. Keohane and Joseph S. Nye, *Power and Interdependence: World Politics in Transition,* Little, Brown: Boston, 1977; and also Edward L. Morse, *Modernization and the Transformation of International Relations,* The Free Press: New York, 1976.

state and with the time. General de Gaulle's France drew the line in one way, the France of Giscard d'Estaing in another. Moreover, there are clearly some qualitative differences between the autonomy that is regarded as important by an advanced country and autonomy as it is conceived by many of the new, developing countries. Most of the advanced countries are old, established states with strong cultural and political traditions that give them a sense of national cohesion. Many of the developing countries are new states—some are more or less artificial constructs of the colonial period—still searching for a sense of national identity.

With their strong cultural traditions, old, established states, whether they be modern states or non-modern, like India or China, obviously have less to fear from a loss of autonomy in some kinds of decision-making than do the newer states, or an entity like the European Community whose existence depends on the right to exercise powers within a very narrow compass. But governments in democratic states have a political concern unconnected with the preservation of statehood: to the extent that their ability to provide the wide array of benefits now expected of them by the electorate is impeded by the action of external forces beyond their control, they may stand to suffer at the polls.[7] This factor not only feeds other forces pushing states toward neomercantilism, it also encourages them to search for ways to reduce the constraints on their freedom of action, either by loosening the links that bind them to international networks or by insulating themselves as best they can from external events. The resort to floating exchange rates is an example of loosening, the imposition of import controls would be an act of insulation.

Today's preoccupation with autonomy has an old-fashioned, nationalistic side. But it also has another, more modern and practical side having to do with the need to find new ways to pursue policies when the political span of control is not congruent with the economic dimensions of the problem. Finding better ways to reestablish control through cooperation, rules, or other

[7]For an extended discussion, see Jacques Pelkmans, "Economic Cooperation among Western Countries," in Gordon and Pelkmans, *Challenges to Interdependent Economies,* op. cit.

forms of collective action at the international level is a recurrent theme of this book.

ORDER

Order, like autonomy, is hardly a novel desideratum. Indeed, some people would argue that order is the defining characteristic of any system, and that to say the international economic system should promote order is simply to utter a tautology. We use the term *order* here to mean that the rules, institutions, and conventional forms of behavior should provide certainty and predictability to states and other international and transnational actors, and they should reduce and, if possible, eliminate certain kinds of disruptive actions.

There has been a tendency in the debate over the need for a new distribution of power and wealth for both those who advocate and those who resist change to equate order with stability and to confuse stability with the maintenance of the status quo. Order is also sometimes defined to mean the maintenance of a given hierarchy (or ordering) of states. There is nothing inherently inconsistent between order, as the term is used here, and change, in rules or in hierarchies. In an imperfect world, conflict is probably inescapable between the quest for autonomy, in the sense of national freedom of action, and the desire for order or predictability. It is possible to conceive of perfect autonomy and perfect order coexisting, but perfect order—of any kind—is unattainable this side of Utopia. Like the other desiderata, order is something all states want, although some attach a higher value to it than others. The main disagreements come not over the desirability of rules and other guarantors of order but over the content of the rules, that is, the ends to be sought and the means to be used.

From this brief review it should be clear that these four purposes, goals, or norms are not wholly parallel and cannot really be described accurately by any collective noun more precise than desiderata. They are competitive in the sense that sometimes—although perhaps less often than at first appears—trade-offs must be made between them: more of one can only be had at the expense of less of another. And states and individuals value them very differently. But unless pushed to an extreme, they need not be irreconcilable, and a system that provides enough of what is wanted under each of the rubrics need not be an impossible dream.

THREE

Institutional Patterns and Principles

For many years, the dominant theme in much of the thinking and writing about the international system, or world order, was that the global polity, like a national polity, needed central governance if it was to enjoy peace, prosperity, justice, and other widely esteemed attributes of the "good society." World government was generally regarded as unattainable in any time period that one could usefully think about. Yet, at the same time, in much of the thinking about international organization, the implicit analogue was something akin to a federal government. More transfer of power from the national and regional levels to the world level, with, of course, more efficient and more powerful global institutions, was the standard solution.

Recent times, however, have seen a pronounced swing away from this kind of thinking. Today, the stress is on the obvious dangers in too much concentration of power, the inefficiencies and unresponsiveness of the central structures, the conspicuous lack of consensus about goals to be sought, the sheer difficulty of institutionalizing relationships among more than 160 highly dissimilar states, and the loss of the pleasures of diversity, as well as of the safety valves it provides. The emphasis now given to the advantages of the diffusion of power, pluralism, decentralization, a plethora of cross-cutting relationships, different hierarchies of power in different issue areas undoubtedly reflects the fact that the study of international relations and organization has become more rigorous than it once was. It reflects, as well, past disappointments with the League of Nations and with the more ambitious United Nations (U.N.). But it also reflects a tendency to make a virtue of necessity—that is the kind of world in which we live.

In thinking about the institutional arrangements likely to be needed, not just today but during the next decade or two, it is clearly desirable to discard facile and deceptive parallels with the nation-state and to be well aware of the dangers and the difficulties of seeking too much institutionalization at the global level. Yet, like the earlier enthusiasm for world government and universal prescriptions, the emphasis on decentralization, on pluralism, on separatism can be carried too far. A system with very little global management and which denies the reality of economic interdependence is attractive to those in the LDCs who argue for an extreme course of national autonomy and "de-linking." But such a system also denies the legitimacy of a concern with global welfare. It is therefore attractive as well to those in the developed world who, alarmed at the pressures of population on resources and fearful for their own future well-being, advocate the *triage* strategy of the battlefield and the adoption of policies toward poor countries that amount to reserving the lifeboats for the able-bodied.

Many people who would, rightly, condemn both extremes nevertheless harbor a desire for more decentralization, more national or group autonomy, less global surveillance and collective management than seems likely to be required if we are to move toward an improved international system characterized by the conditions and the processes discussed in Chapter 2. Although it would be a mistake to underestimate the pressures for separatism and the pragmatic attractions of a policy of simply letting those countries which want to cooperate get on with it without trying to work out more embracing arrangements, it would also be a mistake to underestimate the extent to which it is now becoming necessary to deal with certain problems as truly global problems, despite the difficulties in doing so.

We have become accustomed to the fact that environmental pollution does not respect national boundaries or, sometimes, continental limits; that unrestrained population growth anywhere is bound, over time, to affect the conditions of life everywhere; that the oceans are the earth's last "commons" and that all countries have an interest in the rules agreed upon to govern their use. The concept of global interdependence has become a cliché. But we do not yet fully comprehend the depth and nature of the many kinds of interconnectedness in which we are caught, such as the transmission of inflation. Nor do we really comprehend the implications and the consequences in policy terms of living in a closed global system.

In one sense, of course, we have always lived in a closed system because the world is finite. But, until recently, it was a very large world, and there was always a dumping ground somewhere "out there." Today, and even more tomorrow, density, interconnectedness, and feedback, particularly in the environmental and economic systems, mean that problems can no longer be avoided by being exported. In a number of ways, as pointed out in Chapter 1, we are moving, albeit gradually and erratically, from a situation that lends itself to analysis and prescription in terms of *international* politics and economics to a situation more accurately described as *world* or *global* politics and economics.

Implicit in the concept of a global economy are the ideas not only that it is the world's welfare, rather than that of any state or group of states, that we should seek to optimize, but also that it is the individual rather than the nation whose interests should be of primary concern. Indeed, reason suggests that only at the two ends of the spectrum—in the individual and in the global community—will the units to match the problem sometimes be found. But the world is far from ready for heroic leaps into a new system based on these perceptions. For the period with which we are concerned, we shall live in a system that will be part international, part global; part state-centric, part people-oriented. For many years to come, the weight will continue to fall on the first concept in each of these pairs. Moreover, many other units will continue to compete for loyalty and allegiance with the individual and the state: families, villages, tribes, religious groups, labor unions, professional associations. The list is long.

47

And other actors, such as banks and enterprises, not nation-states, will continue to be the ones that most strongly push the system toward something like a global economy.

It will sometimes be desirable when building institutions, codifying behavior, agreeing on procedures, etc., to try to anticipate the future and to do what can be done to enhance the still rudimentary consciousness of global community by shifting the focus and taking the world as the unit of analysis. But human nature and national policies will militate against going very far, even when empirical facts and the difficulties of dealing with the problem in the conventional international way point strongly in this direction. Similarly, although the claim of the individual, rather than the state, to be the essential component of the world system will not often be explicitly recognized, it should not be wholly set aside. Shifting the focus from states to individuals may, at times, offer the only satisfactory way of handling problems that have distributional implications.

Short of a radical shifting of perspective, the larger good—global welfare—and concern with the individual can be given weight in institutional arrangements in many ways. The staffs of global institutions routinely analyze problems from a world perspective, although they do not often base their analysis on any very rigorous view of what optimizing welfare on a global basis would really entail lest they be accused of unrealistic projections. And people-oriented poverty programs are today the focus of much attention, although, again, political realism severely limits the extent to which any of these programs in fact make people rather than states the recipients of aid. Some further steps that might be taken in both directions are suggested in the following chapters.

It is the thesis of this book that in the years ahead more attention should be given to strengthening a few key institutional arrangements at the global level. But this does not mean that there should be a presumption in favor of action at that level at all times. On the contrary, institutional arrangements should normally be at the lowest level adequate to deal with the problem. Not only is cooperation easier and the institutionalizing of relationships much more manageable among small groups of like-minded and closely interdependent states than it is on more inclusive bases, it is also surely a wise principle of administration that, wherever possible, problems should be dealt with at the level closest to the individual.

Today, however, governments are frequently driven by the pressure of events, by the attitudes of the key actors, and by the sheer difficulty of organizing collective management beyond the circle of states most necessary to the accomplishment of any particular task to ignore, or at least to play down, the interests of those not easy to include. And they avoid confronting the implications in institutional terms of their now standard rhetoric of interdependence and global community. But when thinking about the changing nature of many problems—the increasing inability of even the largest states to provide autonomously the many benefits now expected of them, the way shock waves from increased oil prices or erratic currency movements are transmitted throughout the system—it is difficult to avoid the conclusion that in the years ahead more, not less, attention will have to be paid to arrangements at the global level.

The institutional arrangements needed at the global level do not, of course, all conform to a common organizational pattern, for they serve many purposes. In some cases, they simply provide information required for intelligent policy formation at the national level, and in other cases, they provide public goods that cannot be supplied in any other way.

The main reasons that global institutions—indeed, most international institutions—are needed can be grouped under four main headings, although, like most classifications, this one is rather arbitrary. First, the high degree of interaction between states, groups of states, and other international actors, such as multinational companies, means that "rules and procedures" of various kinds are frequently needed simply to reduce friction, provide certainty, and enable mutually beneficial and generally desired interactions to take place as smoothly and efficiently as possible. Examples of the need for this type of rule-making abound. The resulting rules, procedures, surveillance arrangements, and simple forms of "management" are the staples of such old, established, functional international organizations as the Universal Postal Union and the International Telecommunications Union. But rule-making and enforcement of this kind, designed to eliminate or reduce friction by regulating the processes of interaction, is also a conspicuous aspect (although not the only aspect) of the work of the GATT and the IMF. The need for such regulation can be expected to grow at the global level and other levels as interactions multiply and as more countries become part of the many networks that link economies, societies, and polities.

Second, institutional arrangements at the global level are needed because many results that are widely desired can only be achieved by some kind of collective action. Today, much of the work of the specialized agencies and of the U.N. system as a whole is concerned with the collective task of relieving misery and assisting the process of development. But sometimes there is a need for coordination or harmonization of domestic policies among a particular group of countries rather than for the extension of assistance from one group of countries to another. Coordination of policies as the path to benefits that cannot be achieved simply by unilateral action has, until now, been more characteristic of limited-member institutions, such as the OECD or the European Community. But as we discuss in Chapters 5 and 6 (concerned with trade and production and with the management of money), more coordination of policies now needs to take place, if not among all countries, at least in a context which reassures all countries that the global interest is being taken into account.

This second category overlaps and merges with a third one. Global-level institutions are needed to provide public goods or to control public "bads" on a global level in much the same way as a national government provides and controls them on a national level. On both levels, certain measures for "law and order," public health, and environmental protection have to be supplied collectively if they are to be supplied at all. The World Health Organization (WHO) provides a public good on the global level, that is, virtual control of smallpox. On a less than universal but potentially global basis (in the sense of being open-ended), the International Atomic Energy Agency (IAEA) provides another, in this case, protection against diversion of nuclear materials. The need for global public goods will grow as more countries become modernized and networks multiply and thicken. Indeed the orderly functioning of an intricately interconnected and increasingly integrated global economic system is itself becoming a necessary global public good that seems likely to be adequately supplied only if improvements are made in the global institutions concerned with trade, money, investment, and resource transfers.

Various arrangements that would today usually be considered as falling within the second group (that is, they are designed to promote cooperation among states to achieve some agreed-upon ends) may come to be looked at in a new way, somewhat analogous to the provision of public goods. Therefore, some tasks may, in time, be regarded not as intergovernmental tasks, depending as now on discrete and reversible government decisions, but as something the system should provide, more or less automatically. For example, just as the state in all advanced societies today undertakes an obligation toward its poorest citizens and in various ways "puts a floor under poverty," so it seems desirable (as we argue in Chapter 4) to encourage the acceptance of a "global obligation" for meeting certain very basic human needs. Widespread acceptance of the need for the global system to be able to fulfill such an obligation would extend beyond anything that exists today, although the U.N. system of disaster relief is a tentative step in that direction.

This need for global institutions capable of providing certain global public goods and of fulfilling a few global obligations is analogous to a fourth category of institutional needs. For certain purposes, institutional arrangements are required on a global basis because either there are no fixed property rights in a resource of global concern or there is a widespread acceptance of a common global jurisdiction. The number of cases where a true "commons" exists because there are no fixed property rights is small and, clearly, likely to diminish rather than to grow. Decisions reached at the as yet unfinished Law of the Sea Conference have already diminished substantially the area of the oceans that will, in fact, be treated as "common." At best, only the oceans beyond the 200-mile limit will remain a commons in which no property rights are fixed and for which global jurisdiction is accepted. In contrast, it seems probable that on a subglobal basis there may, over the years, be a few new commons areas established by agreement; that is, states will give up their national rights and put some areas under common jurisdiction.[1] The prospect for true global jurisdiction is likely to be limited to the oceans beyond the 200-mile limit, outer space, rights to the frequency spectrum, and, possibly, part of Antarctica.

It is easy enough to define categories of purposes for which global institutions are needed in other ways, and to add categories. For example, forum functions, like those provided by the General Assembly of the United Nations, might be viewed as a weak form of the second group or as a separate group. The collection and dissemination of information is a necessary adjunct of almost every other function, but it could also be a category on its own. The intention here is not to provide a complete, watertight typology but simply to illustrate the main reasons that institutional arrangements at the global level are required and to suggest why the need is likely to increase rather than diminish in the years ahead.

For many of the purposes for which institutions are needed at the global level, similar institutions are also necessary at the regional level, and sometimes also among groups of countries that are linked not primarily by geography but by common interests or by common problems. Where this is true, differences of view tend to exist about the nature of the relationship that should be established between the various levels of management, about which level should be paramount, and about the need for and locus of leadership within the system as a whole. Three broad patterns of relationship—each with variants—are frequently seen to be in competition.

One pattern that, for obvious reasons, attracts much support in the highly developed, non-Communist, industrial world is that of concentric circles. Sometimes the innermost circle is the tri-

[1]Oran Young, *Resource Management at the International Level,* Nichols Publishing Co.: New York, 1977.

lateral combination of North America (that is, the United States and Canada), Japan, and the European Community; sometimes it is a more limited group of the four, five, six, or seven most powerful industrial, market-economy countries. The second circle is usually the OECD group of countries, bringing in Australia, New Zealand, and the other Western European countries. But sometimes it is suggested that the second circle should be the OECD group plus some newly rich or rapidly industrializing countries. Saudi Arabia, South Korea, Israel, Brazil, Mexico, and, until recently, Iran are the most often-mentioned candidates for inclusion. Sometimes, as in the case of money, the most inclusive circle is an organization like the IMF, which is global in the sense that its membership is open to all countries that accept its rules but is not truly universal. At other times, the most inclusive circle is a more nearly universal organization, like the United Nations, in which all countries, with very minor exceptions, participate. Under the concentric circles concept, the innermost group, by virtue of its high degree of interdependence and weight in the international system, both undertakes close coordination of key policies among its own members and provides the leadership for the wider universe of countries. Frequently, it is seen as, in effect, setting the rules for the system as a whole.

A second pattern, periodically advocated, is that of a world divided into several blocs, with essential rule-making done within each bloc and global institutions acting mainly as forums for the brokerage of differences between blocs. Again there are variants. Sometimes, although rather less often today than in the past, the competing groups or blocs are continents or other geographic regions.[2] At other times, they are groups based on stage of development and ideology, such as the familiar First, Second,

[2]See, for example, Ernest H. Preeg, *Economic Blocs and U.S. Foreign Policy,* Report No. 35, National Planning Association: Washington, D.C., 1974. A variant of this conception can be detected in proposals that the way for Europe, Japan, and North America to secure access to raw materials is to make special arrangements with particular groups of LDCs on a more or less continental basis, i.e., Japan with Southeast Asia, Europe with Africa, the United States with Latin America.

and Third Worlds, a tripartite division which, as we saw in Chapter 1, has already become anachronistic in many ways.

A third pattern puts global institutions in the central place, gives paramountcy to global rules, and regards other arrangements, both regional and functional, as ancillary or subordinate.

One can find examples of each pattern in today's arrangements. Thus, money conforms more or less to the first pattern, although events are pushing us toward a three-bloc system centered on the dollar, the mark, and the yen. The way bargaining is normally carried on in the United Nations Conference on Trade and Development (UNCTAD) is a variant of the second, as is the IFAD.[3] The handling of trade rules is an illustration of the third, although a rather weak one because the primacy of the global institution—GATT—is questioned by some countries and the rules are strained or distorted by others.

Just as in today's world one finds examples of all three patterns, so, in thinking about the future, elements of each pattern will and should be present; for in institution-building, as in less metaphoric kinds of architecture, form should follow function.

Increasingly, however, global rules and procedures should set the controlling standards and provide the guidelines within which groups of countries requiring more intensive modes of co-operation can carry the process further and within which the special needs of countries can be accommodated.

Broad political reasons, as well as reasons arising from the character of the problems, seem to us to underline the importance of working toward a single international economic system rather than one characterized by a number of separate "worlds" based on geography, ideology, or stage of development. The

[3]IFAD, which was established in 1977, goes further than any other existing international organization in formalizing group constituencies. The advanced industrialized countries, the OPEC countries, and the non-oil-producing LDCs each have, as a group, the same number of votes and the same number of representatives (six) on the Executive Board. How votes and seats are distributed within the three groups is left to the groups to decide. Cuba is a member of Group III (LDCs), but no Eastern European country belongs to the organization. Nor does China.

positive political benefits of economic links and of common participation in institutions regulating those links can easily be exaggerated. Indeed, in many cases, closer involvement clearly intensifies rather than reduces friction. But the hardening of the divisions between North and South, East and West, which would accompany a conscious turning away from the efforts to treat global problems in global terms and to give greater content to the rhetoric of interdependence and global community would almost certainly increase political rivalry and heighten tensions.

Although the changing nature of today's universe of states and the nearly worldwide character of many economic networks point to the need for more global-level management than today exists, the proliferation of universal, one-country, one-vote institutions provides no answer. On the contrary, the need is for far more radical pruning and restructuring of the central global institutions than is today being contemplated. There is little to be said for the kind of inefficient universalism toward which we seem to be heading. It is costly and wastes the scarcest resource the world commands—skilled manpower. It bears hardest on the poor and small countries which are, nevertheless, its strongest advocates since otherwise they see themselves as unrepresented and their interests neglected. And it encourages the rich and powerful to resort to arrangements among themselves, giving rise to complaints that there is one rule for the rich, another for the poor.

All states, except those that deliberately cut themselves off from economic intercourse with the rest of the world, have a legitimate interest in what might be called the bony structure of the international economic system, that is, the rules and standards that are accepted as controlling or paramount, and the procedures which basically determine how the system operates—how money is created and managed, how trade and markets are regulated, how, and for what purposes resources are transferred. Yet the nature of their interest varies enormously as does their ability to affect the functioning of the system, either positively or negatively. Moreover, some countries are far more willing than are others to accept the disciplines and constraints that are implicit in any form of collective action, and some countries are far more able than are others to translate such commitments into policies and actions.

If global rules and procedures are to be widely acceptable, there must be more awareness than there has been in the past of the need to provide for participation in the making of rules and in the operation of procedures of all countries that are affected by them. Yet, at the same time, there needs to be more acceptance of the fact that the right to participate carries with it certain responsibilities. It is, indeed, odd that the banal observation that countries should play a greater or lesser role in particular institutional arrangements depending on their importance to the issue in question (and its importance to them) is regarded as a controversial statement. In any organization that is more than a forum for airing views, the one-nation, one-vote rule is almost always inadequate, and some form of participation that matches "voice" with needs, responsibilities, and weight is inescapable if the purposes the institution is designed to serve are to be met.

There must also be more acceptance of the fact that some of the most highly industrialized, market-economy countries must cooperate more closely and regulate more things in common than it is necessary for many other countries to do. But, at the same time, this close cooperation must not become a way of simply shifting problems on to those who are not participating. The need for closer cooperation is partly a matter of self-interest on the part of those countries whose economies are most closely interlinked; but it is also a matter of broader concern, for they carry great weight in the international economy and how they manage their own affairs affects directly the health of the system as a whole. A willingness of countries not in the "inner group" (and membership of any "inner group" will change with time) to see these core members collaborate more closely should be matched by the acceptance by the "inner group" members of the fact that their weight carries the obligation to supply certain kinds of public goods to the system as a whole. Accordingly, their policies should be designed not simply with their own national needs in mind but should be informed, as well, by a systemic or global concern.

A brief look at the recent institutional innovation of "Summitry" is appropriate here because some people see in the further development and institutionalization of the periodic meetings among the heads of government of the six or seven largest, highly industrialized, market-economy states the best way to give the international economic system the steering and the leadership the United States supplied in the first two decades after World War II. The argument for organized "Summitry" is a double-barrelled one. The United States can no longer alone play the role it played in the fifties and sixties as the leader and steerer of the system. The reasons are interrelated: the diffusion of economic power in the international system, a general restlessness and dissatisfaction with American leadership, a loss of will on the part of the American people, and an American unwillingness to run its economy to suit the larger purpose of global stability now that the United States itself has become much more open and vulnerable to external events. In this situation, the six or seven governments whose leaders have been meeting fairly regularly since 1975 should become the surrogate for U.S. leadership.[4] The economies of these countries are so closely interconnected and, collectively, they command so much of the world's effective economic power that only if they can harmonize their policies in a mutually reinforcing way will they be able to handle efficiently their own economic problems. Given their preponderance in the international economic system, it is essential that they do so, not just for their own prosperity but for the health of the system.

Clearly, this line of argument has some validity. For a time, fairly regular meetings by the leaders of this group of countries undoubtedly strengthened their collective will to resist dealing with their acute domestic economic problems by beggar-my-neighbor policies and probably resulted in some useful harmoni-

---

[4]As of the summer of 1980 there had been six summit meetings. More is said about Summitry in Chapter 6.

zation of policies, or, at the least, in a greater awareness of each other's problems and policy choices.[5]

The governments of countries whose economies are highly interdependent will always need to consult more intensively and to go further in coordinating their policies than is necessary more widely. Moreover, if they carry great weight in the system, this process will contribute to the better functioning of the entire system and can give it much of the steering and leadership that it undoubtedly needs for some purposes. But the world of today and tomorrow is clearly not looking for hegemony, whether of one power or of a few. The powerful six or seven can and should, for some—not all—purposes, act as leader, steerer, and motor; they cannot and should not try to be a supreme council sitting at the top of a pyramid. Moreover, they can only play these roles effectively if two conditions are met. The first condition is that their own policies must be informed with a global, or systemic, view. The second is that there must be an adequate global framework or context, by which we mean an effective set of institutions in which the interests of other affected countries are fully represented and fully taken into account. Today, neither condition is adequately met. The countries at the center are too preoccupied with their own immediate problems, and their policies are too much influenced by parochial concerns, too little by the needs of the system as a whole. And the context of effective global institutions is far too weak. The rest of this book deals largely with that context.

One of the virtues in the LDCs' proposals for a New International Economic Order (NIEO) is that they have ranged widely over aid, trade, money, investment, business practices, commodities, and the institutional arrangements that encourage or constrain governmental action in these areas. Yet although comprehensiveness was both unusual and highly desirable, the fact

[5]It is perhaps worth pointing out that, as we are using the term, "harmonization" does not mean the adoption of common policies or similar policies but of policies that complement and reinforce one another, and the avoidance of policies that conflict or cancel out one another.

that the basic documents[6] and the positions taken in the United Nations and other forums have been so sharply focused on demands, frequently couched in rather extreme forms, has meant that no real sense emerged of what a new, more balanced array of institutional arrangements (rules and organizations) might look like. The sense of grievance was clear. So, too, was the general demand for more direct participation, and particularly more weight, in decision-making and for a different distribution of the world's resources and of its productive potential. Unfortunately, but perhaps understandably, the developed countries' response has been to regard the New International Economic Order as a widow's cruse of wants and to assume that as soon as one demand was met another would inevitably take its place. Too much acrimony and too many false starts now surround the various documents that might at one time or another have become the starting point for negotiation.

Reform today should not proceed by claiming that resolutions adopted by consensus but clearly opposed by governments whose agreement is essential if anything substantial is to happen are firm commitments which must be fulfilled. Nor should reform proceed from either the pessimistic assumption that, imperfect though the present system may be, any change is bound to be for the worse or the optimistic premise that a magic, global bargain waits in the wings to be unveiled at the appropriate moment. Rather, we must recognize that much of the charge and countercharge about a NIEO is beside the point. The distribution of economic power in the world is changing, the rules are changing, the problems that should be uppermost on interna-

[6]United Nations, General Assembly, Resolution of the Sixth Special Session, "Declaration on the Establishment of a New International Economic Order," 3201 (S-VI), May 1, 1974; United Nations, General Assembly, Resolution of the Sixth Special Session, "Programme of Action on the Establishment of a New International Economic Order," 3202 (S-VI), May 1, 1974; United Nations, General Assembly, Resolution "Charter of Economic Rights and Duties of States," 3281 (XXIX), December 12, 1974; United Nations, General Assembly, Resolution of the Seventh Special Session, "Development and International Economic Cooperation," 3362 (S-VII), September 16, 1975.

tional agenda are changing—all are today different in many important respects from what they were a decade ago. Further reforms are needed—this will always be true. But the analysis of further reforms should begin from where we are today, not from positions that were first taken a decade or so ago.

Whatever the other shortcomings in the way they set about pushing for a NIEO, the LDCs were right to emphasize the need to look at the whole array of international economic institutional arrangements, for one of the keys, perhaps *the* key, to agreement on major reform is to focus on the overall picture, to be concerned with balance in the system as a whole. That does not mean, of course, that all the pieces on the board must be moved if any one piece is to be moved: rather, the opposite. Frequently, better balance can be achieved by moving very few pieces. But the whole interlocking system of rights and obligations has to be looked at if sensible, and widely acceptable, judgments are to be made about how the interests of individuals, groups, and states are to be adequately and fairly represented in and served by the system as a whole. Today, unfortunately, all the main contestants tend to look at their position in each issue area separately, and too often they resist to the death any arrangement that gives them a position they regard as inferior to that of others or as less advantageous than that which they enjoyed in the past.

So, too, with the four desiderata of order, equity, autonomy, and efficiency. The way in which they are to be satisfied has to be looked at in light of the overall situation, not by seeking to satisfy each objective in the same measure everywhere. For example, it is better for "order" to stand higher in the scale than "autonomy" when considering monetary policies, but for "equity" to outrank "order" when concerned with the transfer of resources. It is better to give "efficiency" a high priority when writing trade rules and to transfer resources directly, rather than to bias the trade rules to bring about needed transfers. If the system as a whole is balanced and is felt to satisfy in reasonable measure the competing desiderata, there should be considerably less pressure to distort any one institution to accomplish purposes that can more appropriately be dealt with by other institutions.

Ideally, one should try to look at the distribution of power and benefits not just in the international economic system as a whole but at their distribution in the political/security system as well, for clearly there is much interaction between the two. Not only are there obvious direct interconnections, such as the competition for resources between the desire for arms and the needs of development, but there are other interactions. For example, a country's feeling of weakness and lack of control over its economic destiny is frequently fed by a real, or perceived, weakness in the political security realm. This is not, of course, seen only in the LDCs. The interaction between political/military dependence and economic policy was very clear in the monetary policy of de Gaulle's France. But because there is a limit to how much can be attempted in one short book, we have had to confine ourselves, in the main, to the welfare area, although we are conscious of the weakness in so doing.

The difficulties of bringing about any change in institutional arrangements in today's world are immense. Difficulties stem from ideological disagreement, from divergent real interests, from intellectual uncertainty, from extreme heterogeneity in the decision-making units, from the lack of congruence between the political, social, and economic dimensions of problems. Added to that daunting catalogue is the purely practical difficulty of overcoming bureaucratic inertia within governments and, perhaps even worse, within international institutions, an inertia frequently fortified by a very energetic bureaucratic interest in holding on to positions of power and influence, or, simply, to sinecures. It is easy enough for any civil servant anywhere to make a persuasive case that any particular function is, if not absolutely essential, at least very useful. Obviously, it would be desirable to prune away much of the unnecessarily lush foliage that has grown up in the shade of the United Nations and to improve many of the specialized agencies, such as the International Labor Organization (ILO), the Food and Agriculture Organization (FAO), and the United Nations Educational, Scientific and Cultural Organization (UNESCO). But to undertake any change is an uphill task, and it is simple sense to concentrate on trying to make more effective the most essential global-level institutions.

The following four chapters discuss in more detail problems and possible prescriptions in four areas that we consider central: the immediate relief of gross forms of economic misery; the regulation of trade and the adjustment to new patterns of production; the management of money and, as a part of that process, the coordination of macroeconomic policies among key countries; and the transfer of resources for development and adaptation to change.

When thinking about the kinds of reform needed to enable global institutions to carry more of the weight of managing the system, it is important to distinguish far more sharply than is frequently done between those global organizations that should have executive or operational functions and those that should not. Except in one important respect, we believe it would be undesirable to make the central U.N. organs more operational or to create new bodies with executive tasks as part of the main U.N. structure. Our exception is a U.N. Basic Support Program which, as described in the next chapter, would be, in concept, an expanded and better funded "UNICEF plus UNDRO."

In looking to the future, we see the main responsibility for rule-making, rule-enforcement, and collective management of today's international economic system and of the coexisting, still embryonic, global economy as resting on a tripod of global-level organizations: improved and reformed versions of today's IMF and World Bank Group and of yesterday's ITO. The major weight of the needed global management cannot be borne by universal one-nation, one-vote organizations but only by organizations in which there is some correspondence between voting strength and economic power, ability to affect the system, and responsibility. This does not mean that small or weak countries cannot be given a larger voice. Dependence on the system, as well as the ability to affect it in a positive or negative way, should be a factor in determining how votes are apportioned.

The right pattern for these key global institutions is along the lines agreed upon at Bretton Woods: any country can join, provided it accepts the basic commitment of the institution; all share in the decision-making process, but that process is a weighted one; and most countries are represented on the principal policy-setting and executive boards on a constituency basis, thus keeping the total number of participants in these bodies to a manageable size. Within this general pattern, improvements are needed in the way votes are distributed and constituencies organized. Each leg of the tripod requires more than modifications in its organizational structure and its procedural arrangements. New ways must be found to deal with new problems, and many problems must be seen in a changed perspective. The world has changed in many ways since Bretton Woods. The constituency of states is larger and more heterogeneous, the networks among states and other actors are denser, and the lines between foreign and domestic concerns are harder to draw. New values, new concerns, and new goals have brought old rules into question and suggested new ones.

The IMF and the World Bank Group have changed over the years although they still need to be reformed in ways that we explore in Chapters 6 and 7. But they have, in most respects, the right basic structure and can, we believe, evolve in ways that are responsive to changing needs. The third leg of the tripod, represented today by an uneasy combination of the GATT and the UNCTAD, is more wobbly, despite the improvements made in the recent multilateral trade negotiations (MTN). As we discuss further in Chapter 5, here it would be better to think in terms of replacement rather than simply repair. We think the time has come to consider a new production and trade organization to replace both the GATT and the UNCTAD, taking over some functions from each but having some new tasks as well.

In the final chapter we discuss briefly some of the other global level organizations that have important roles to play, and the U.N. General Assembly and the ECOSOC are also brought into the picture. A little is said there as well about the role of regional and other intermediate-level organizations. But this book is about needs at the global level, and we have deliberately concentrated on those institutions that seem to us to be critically important if the system is to have the collective management it needs and if some content is to be given to the rhetoric of global community.

FOUR

Poverty and Basic Support

THE PROBLEM OF GLOBAL POVERTY

Had this book been written in the late 1960s, a great deal would have been said about the need for more international attention to the problem of global poverty. It is one of the encouraging developments of the 1970s that the elimination of absolute poverty became so widely accepted as a central concern of the international system. Still, analyses of the problem and recognition of the need have outpaced the changes in policy that are required in both developed and developing countries if global poverty is really to be eliminated or even substantially reduced.

Developing countries have made significant progress in raising standards of living in the last quarter-century. Whether measured in terms either of the growth in GNP or of various social indicators, progress has been unprecedentedly rapid. But it has also been markedly uneven. Despite an encouraging record of economic growth and social change in the developing world as a whole, some countries remain extremely poor, in absolute as well as relative terms. And their economies continue to grow only slowly, when they are growing at all. Within many developing countries, moreover, even where there has been rapid economic growth, little has been done to improve the lot of the people at the low end of the income scale. Enclaves of prosperity and modernity coexist with a situation in which the number of people falling below the poverty line—even minimally defined—remains huge.[1]

According to rough estimates of the World Bank, there were about 800 million "absolute poor" in the developing world at the end of the 1970s. And, if current patterns of economic growth continue, it is expected that there will still be some 600 million people living in absolute poverty by the end of the century.[2] These are people, as Robert S. McNamara described them nearly a decade ago, who live at the very margin of existence, without adequate access to such essential needs as food, shelter, safe drinking water, or health services.[3] The majority of the poor live in rural areas, and the regions with the largest numbers of

[1]A few figures from the book by David Morawetz, *Twenty-Five Years of Economic Development,* The World Bank: Washington, 1978, serve to illustrate these points. The GNP per capita of developing countries as a group grew at an average rate of 3.4 percent a year in the period 1950–1975. This, as Morăwetz notes, was faster than either the developing or the developed countries had grown in any comparable period before 1950 and exceeded both official goals and private expectations. However, while nine countries, with a combined population of 930 million people in 1975, grew at an average annual rate of 4.2 percent or better, and a second group of nine countries with 220 million people grew at between 3 and 4 percent, the large, poor countries of South Asia and many countries in Africa, with a total of some 1.1 billion people, grew in per capita income by less than 2 percent a year between 1950–1975. And, according to Morawetz, though the per capita income roughly trebled for some 33 percent of the people of the developing world from 1950–1975, for another 40 percent the increase in per capita income was only one or two dollars a year. (Summary statistics on pp. 12–14.)

[2]*International Bank for Reconstruction and Development World Development Report, 1978,* The World Bank: Washington, 1978. Those who are counted among the "absolute poor" in World Bank calculations are people with annual per capita incomes of $75 or less or under $200 in 1970 "purchasing-power-parity" dollars—a calculation of "real" average per capita income that seeks to compensate for exchange-rate distortions and structural variations among countries. Obviously, the measure of "absolute poverty" is an extremely rough one, and the lack of information about those living in conditions of dire need is a problem in itself.

[3]See International Bank for Reconstruction and Development, 1972 Annual Meetings of the Boards of Governors, *Summary Proceedings,* Washington: September, 1972, "Annual Address" by Robert S. McNamara, President of the World Bank. Since then there has been an outpouring of studies from the

people living in absolute poverty are in South Asia, Indonesia, and central Africa (where poverty is pervasive but the total numbers are much lower than in Asia because of much smaller populations).[4]

Typically, the absolute poor have weak links, if any, with the organized market economy of their country. They have few of the assets (e.g., land, credit, remunerative jobs) needed to produce income. They are frequently or chronically in poor health because of the conditions under which they live and the absence of health services. And, generally, rates of population growth are high, so that any gains they do make in increasing their incomes are spread thinly.

In the early years of foreign aid, there was an optimistic hope that if the capital resources and the technical expertise that the underdeveloped countries lacked could be made available to them and economic growth accelerated, not only would average living standards improve but mass poverty would be significantly reduced. Unfortunately, the record has not borne out the early optimism. Some countries, including Taiwan and South Korea, have achieved both rapid rates of growth and substantial, broad-based improvements in living conditions. In other countries, notably Sri Lanka and Cuba, living conditions have improved for the mass of the population, even in the absence of high rates of growth. But in the majority of the countries in the developing world, the problem of absolute poverty persists and

---

Bank and elsewhere which document and analyze the problem of poverty in terms both of the maldistribution of income and of absolute poverty and unmet need. For summary descriptions of the dimensions of absolute poverty, see, for example, Morawetz, op. cit.; Gunnar Adler-Karlsson, "Eliminating Absolute Poverty: An Approach to the Problem," in W. Howard Wriggins and Gunnar Adler-Karlsson, *Reducing Global Inequities,* McGraw-Hill, for the Council on Foreign Relations/1980s Project: New York, 1978; and *World Development Report, 1978,* op. cit.

[4]Roughly half of the more than one billion people in the low-income countries of Asia (excluding China) live in absolute poverty. Four large countries—Bangladesh, India, Indonesia, and Pakistan—contain about two-thirds of the world's absolute poor. In sub-Saharan Africa, the situation is more varied, but in few countries in the region are the numbers of absolute poor less than a third of the population. *World Development Report,* op. cit., pp. 38, 47.

may be growing. In large part the problem is one of poor people in poor countries. But there is also a sizable number of absolute poor in many of today's middle-income developing countries where the benefits of rapid growth are not being widely distributed.

Clearly, rapid population growth in the developing world has been a major factor in the failure of economic growth to provide adequate means for widespread improvements in standards of living.[5]

But the determining factor has been the choice of development strategies—in particular, the extent to which national economic policies give explicit consideration to equitable income distribution and to the objective of meeting essential needs. The issue is not, as it is often mistakenly put, that there is a misplaced emphasis on growth. The acceleration of per capita income growth with the participation of the poor—that is, both growth and improvements in the distribution of income—is the first best policy for achieving improved standards of living for all. Particularly in the least developed, low-income LDCs, economic growth must be an essential aspect of any strategy to abolish poverty.

THE BASIC-NEEDS APPROACH

Much of the disenchantment with development assistance that has occurred in the rich countries in recent years, particularly perhaps in the United States, has stemmed from the mounting evidence that in many poor countries aid has not been reaching those people most in need. And, as a consequence, in the last several years much emphasis has been placed on redesigning de-

[5]Despite some recent declines in birth rates in developing countries, gains in real GNP of about 5 percent annually through the 1970s have been seriously eroded by annual population growth rates of 2.5 to 3 percent. Because of the population growth, the number of absolute poor has increased even while the proportion of the population living in absolute poverty in the developing countries has fallen.

velopment-assistance programs so that they will more effectively meet "basic human needs."[6]

The essence of the "basic needs" prescription is, quite simply, that the elimination of poverty and the satisfaction of essential needs should be the explicit, indeed the priority, goal of development; and that only if national development policies are formulated in such a way as to address the poverty problem directly will the number of absolute poor in the world be significantly reduced in anything like a reasonable time.

Beyond these two points, several rather different ideas tend to get bundled together under the rubric of a "basic-human-needs" strategy.[7] First, there is the concept that the world community should not tolerate certain kinds of abject misery, that there is a basic economic "human right" to the means not simply of survival but to something beyond that, although if defined in terms of "rights," there would be no consensus on where the line

[6]This mounting concern is reflected in U.S. aid legislation since the mid-1970s. In 1973, the U.S. Congress passed a foreign aid bill which established "New Directions" for the U.S. bilateral aid program, restricting much of the development loans and grants to agriculture, health, population planning, and other projects designed directly to benefit the poorest of the poor. It also reflected in the annual reports of the late 1970s of the OECD's Development Assistance Committee, most notably in *Development Co-operation, 1978 Review,* OECD: Paris, 1978.

[7]The term "basic-human-needs" strategy gained worldwide currency after a 1976 ILO World Employment Conference. The concluding resolution from that conference stated that: "Strategies and national development plans and policies should include explicitly as a priority objective the promotion of employment and the satisfaction of the basic needs of each country's population." See the preconference report prepared by International Labor Organization, *Employment, Growth and Basic Needs: A One-World Problem,* ILO: Geneva, 1976; and the concluding "Declaration of Principles and Programmes of Action," ILO, World Employment Conference Document WEC/CW/E.1, 1976. In addition, see in particular: the issue of *World Development,* vol. 6, no. 3, March, 1978, which is devoted to a discussion of the basic needs strategy; Roger Hansen, *Beyond the North-South Stalemate,* McGraw-Hill, for the Council on Foreign Relations/1980s Project: New York, 1979; Aspen Institute for Humanistic Studies, *The Planetary Bargain: Proposals for a New International Economic Order to Meet Human Needs,* Report of an International Workshop Convened in Aspen, Colorado, July 7–August 1, 1975.

should be drawn. But all advocates of strategies focused on basic needs mean by this expression something more than the bare minimum that the words themselves suggest. This position is taken partly on humanitarian grounds but also partly because action limited simply to meeting a very basic minimum does nothing to alter the underlying conditions that breed poverty in the first place. The words "basic human needs" are thus usually given a meaning that extends substantially beyond satisfying essential, immediate needs for such things as food, water, shelter, and clothing to providing opportunities for education and employment and, frequently, to measures to promote structural changes in the economy in order to permit a permanent escape from the poverty trap.[8]

Another concept inherent in much of the advocacy of a "basic-human-needs strategy" is that in most developing countries there is a need for and a "right to" much wider participation in the economic and political life of the country. The reasoning is partly that only through broadened participation and more widespread social mobilization is it possible to see how the benefits of growth can, in fact, be spread throughout the country in a way that will endure and be supportive of the goal of self-sustaining development and, perhaps, partly that fuller "participation" has become in recent years an objective on its own in many contexts and in many societies.

Much emphasis is also frequently put on the need to narrow income differentials.[9] As in the case of the emphasis on "participation," some of the emphasis on "equality" is a reflection of

[8]In effect, the basic-needs strategy as articulated by the ILO and others builds on ideas about how to achieve "growth with distribution" and, in particular, the need for a "labor-intensive" approach to development. However, the basic-needs strategy focuses directly on living conditions or meeting basic needs without assuming that the goal will be achieved automatically as a by-product of more labor-intensive growth.

[9]Indeed, some proponents of the basic-needs approach argue that to meet the basic needs of the poor it will be necessary to put ceilings on income—the wealth of the rich—on both a national and international basis. See Adler-Karlsson, op. cit., and the report of the Club of Rome, *Reshaping the International Order,* Dutton: New York, 1976.

the times we live in. But, in many instances, it is difficult to see how the objective not simply of relieving misery but of enabling the "excluded" majorities to attain a decent standard of living is to be achieved unless there is a measure of internal redistribution—of power as well as of goods. This point has particular relevance in the case of middle-income LDCs which could undoubtedly provide a decent minimum for everyone if they had the political will and the administrative means to carry out redistributive programs.[10] In the case of the poorest LDCs, the resources released by substantial measures of internal redistribution would be very small in comparison with the need. Nevertheless, the failure of these countries to move in this direction and to contribute in even a small way to the easing of the poverty problem may increasingly reduce the generosity of potential outside donors. And, more importantly, the growth in many developing countries of "two nations"—a rich cosmopolitan elite that feels itself closer to the world of jet aircraft, computers, and luxury hotels than it does to the poor mass of its own population—is not likely to produce a healthy society nor one that is likely to develop its resources effectively.

Much of the recent advocacy of a basic-human-needs strategy comes down to an argument that national development plans and outside aid—both bilateral and multilateral—should be reshaped so that they rely less on a "trickle-down" strategy of development and focus more directly on improving the lot of the poorest sections of society. The means by which this might best be done obviously vary with the country (and with the expert), but in almost all cases, much emphasis is given to the improvement of public services, to heavy investment in social and eco-

---

[10]It has been estimated that in those middle-income countries with a large number of absolute poor, policies designed to eliminate absolute poverty that focused on increasing employment and policies to increase investment in the assets of the poor need not have a negative effect on overall growth, while more direct measures to provide basic goods and services do entail some trade-off but not a large one. See Marcelo Selowsky, "Balancing Trickle Down and Basic Needs Strategies: Income Distribution Issues in Large Middle-Income Countries with Special Reference to Latin America," World Bank Staff Working Paper, No. 335, The World Bank: Washington, 1979.

nomic infrastructure at the local level—schools, hospitals, water supplies, roads, houses—and to small-scale projects designed to provide employment and improve the productive capacity of the poor in predominantly rural areas, attacking simultaneously the frequently almost untouched problem of rural poverty and the increasing problem of urban overcrowding.

This approach is not, in the minds of those who are now its strongest advocates, one that limits itself to the kind of "welfare" programs that the words, if read literally, might suggest. Rather, it is an approach that clearly intends both to "put a floor under poverty" and to assist the broad process of development. One can go further and say that it is also an approach that redefines development so that progress in satisfying many social indicators ranks equally with more conventional measurements, such as increases in GNP.

Much of this new emphasis is to be welcomed. However, there are problems with the basic-needs approach as a guide for providing international assistance. As spokesmen of developing countries have insisted, rural development and the creation of small-scale, labor-intensive enterprises are not alternatives to broad-based industrialization.[11] And external support for capital-intensive developments in the agricultural, energy, manufacturing, and other sectors will continue to be needed even as some policy shifts are made in both national and international development programs to try to get at the problem of poverty.

[11]This point is forcefully argued by Ajit Singh in the article "The 'Basic Needs' Approach to Development vs. the New International Economic Order: The Significance of Third World Industrialization," *World Development,* vol. 7, no. 6, June, 1979, pp. 585–606: "In industry are to be found not only the increasing returns but also the *dynamic* economies of scale . . . and only industrial development can lead to genuine self-reliance and reduce the technological dependence of the Third World on industrial countries. In many LDCs, furthermore, the key to raising productivity in agriculture lies in mechanizing it, reducing the labor force employed there and channelling it into the more productive industrial sector. . . . Whether or not [the basic needs approach would discourage industrial development,] it is undeniable that the main documents concerned with the BN strategy do not adequately emphasize the positive, let alone the leading, role of industry in bringing about a long-term structural transformation of the economy." (P. 586.)

The fact that "Northern" rhetoric in support of basic needs has not been matched by any significant increase in aid to the South only creates the impression, rightly or wrongly, that the emphasis in the North on meeting basic needs is primarily a cover for declining support for assistance in promoting the long-term, broad process of development.

Moreover, while it is evident that all lower-income countries that have achieved success in meeting basic needs have given priority attention to their poor majorities, conditions in each have varied widely and so have their actual development policies. There is not, in other words, a single strategy that emerges from the different experiences of these countries—nor from the experience of others—that can be said to apply throughout the developing world, even though lessons can be drawn from each.

Also, it is all too easy for a kind of cultural imperialism to permeate the process of determining what is "basic" and what is not. And, because the basic-needs approach to development is centrally concerned with how a country uses its resources at the micro-level and, indeed, how people structure their society, it is almost inevitably a highly interventionist approach. This intrusiveness is one reason that Southern spokesmen have reacted with reserve to the basic-needs strategy and why the enthusiasm for it has come mainly from the North.

It may well be that elites in some developing countries have no intention of doing anything about poverty and that the opposition they have voiced to the basic-needs strategy is only a smokescreen to hide their own lack of concern for their absolute poor. It is our view, nevertheless, that some of the controversy surrounding discussions of "basic needs" could be reduced if it were clearly recognized, in the design of international assistance programs, that *both* a long-term "development function" and a shorter-term "welfare function" are involved in meeting essential needs.

Development necessarily involves structural change. It is a costly, complex, and long-term process. Eliminating absolute poverty in any permanent sense is a function of development and ought to be a key objective. In most poor countries, the achievement of this goal will require accelerated growth as well as effective distributional policies. But if severe deprivation is to be alleviated in the short term, direct and immediate actions are also required, that is, some largely stop-gap measures are needed until the broader processes of structural transformation can take effect. These are not, strictly speaking, "development measures," although they are likely to be most effective if carried out as part of a comprehensive development-with-equity strategy.

Few of the poorest countries can both promote development through productive investment and meet essential needs in the short term through expanded social service expenditures without considerably more external assistance than they now receive. The importance to these countries of *both* long-term development assistance and shorter-term "basic welfare" support is perhaps most clearly illustrated by the problem of malnutrition.

It is now estimated that some 400–450 million people in low-income countries are chronically hungry and malnourished. And, in the time of major crop shortages, as many as 1 billion people may be without adequate supplies of food. About 70 percent of the malnourished live in rural areas, 60 percent in South Asia, and of the total, 40 percent are children.

A frequent response to the problem of malnutrition is one that assumes the problem is principally one of inadequate food supplies and that the solution lies in increasing the production of food. But poverty, not shortage of food, is the core problem. Although 55 percent of the population in the developing world is malnourished (that is, calorie deficient), it has been estimated that it would take only 2 percent of the world's cereal production to meet the minimum caloric needs of today's malnourished poor.[12] In other words, the problem of starvation and malnutrition is not first a food supply problem, although there is a clear need to increase food production, especially in the developing world, to meet a growing *effective* demand for food. Rather, today, malnutrition is largely a problem of too little income to buy,

[12]Shlomo Reutlinger, "Malnutrition: A Poverty or a Food Problem?" *World Development,* vol. 5, no. 8, August, 1977, pp. 715–724.

or to produce, enough food. Any real solution to the problem lies in an increase in the income of the malnourished poor. And in many developing countries—especially today's slow growing, low-income LDCs—the key to better income distribution at increasing per capita levels lies in a much increased emphasis on raising levels of production in the agriculture sector and improving the opportunities for remunerative employment in rural areas. But to wait for incomes to reach a level at which the "calorie gap" could be closed is certain to condemn many people to starvation and acute malnutrition. In the meantime, if the will and the resources were available, there would be much that governments could do—from organizing food subsidy programs to extending basic health services—to increase the number of adequately nourished people.

For governments in poor countries prepared to take immediate short-term measures to alleviate starvation, malnutrition, and other forms of acute deprivation, more adequate "basic welfare support" should be provided by the international community. And, as the rest of this chapter argues, that support ought to be provided in new ways. The assistance needed—to help finance programs designed to provide basic goods (e.g., food) and services (e.g., basic education and primary health care) to those in extreme need—is not an *alternative* but rather a much needed *complement* to financing for development.

A GLOBAL RESPONSE TO SEVERE DEPRIVATION

Today, all modern states recognize that the poor in their societies must be helped in a wide variety of ways. Most modern societies not only shelter the disadvantaged from acute deprivation but, beyond that, have elaborate social welfare schemes to provide free education, health care, and housing, as well as many public services to supply water, sewage, transportation, and so forth. Much of the debate in the domestic policies of these societies turns on how far up the scale of human wants the individual should be entitled to look to the state for help. Dissension ensues when "needs" that are not widely accepted in a society as legitimate are claimed as "rights" that a state has an obligation to meet, particularly when meeting those claims could require measures, such as high rates of taxation, that would have the effect of restricting the freedom of individual choice of large sections of the population. But despite the active and frequently acrimonious debate about the level of wants or needs that the state should seek to satisfy, there is, in all modern societies, a fairly high basic minimum that is beyond dispute.

If the world were a society or a community in any way comparable to a modern nation-state, one could contemplate a system—some form of a global negative income tax, for example—which would underwrite an agreed minimum standard of existence everywhere. As a distant goal, this is not unreasonable. But we do not have that kind of world today, nor are we likely to have such a world in any period worth planning for. Few people feel a sense of obligation toward those belonging to different cultures far away that is in any way comparable to the obligation they accept without question in their own national societies.

Yet a rudimentary sense of global community does exist even on a global scale—what Stanley Hoffmann has referred to as the "flickerings of 'universal consciousness.' "[13] Natural disasters—floods, earthquakes, famines—normally evoke a widespread, if not truly global or especially well-organized, response. And, in the years ahead, it would seem desirable to improve the capacity of global institutions to assist governments to alleviate the worst forms of abject poverty in ways that enhance the sense of global community and the recognition of a global responsibility to meet basic—very basic—needs.

The reason for meeting minimum essential human needs, wherever they exist, seems to us a clear, straightforward, humanitarian one, and the obligation to do so, one that runs not between states but between people. Prudential, as well as humanitarian, reasons for underwriting the essential needs of all people clearly exist globally as they do within national societies.

[13]Stanley Hoffmann, *Primacy or World Order*, McGraw-Hill: New York, 1978, p. 242.

(Simply put, people who are adequately nourished and basically healthy are more constructive members of society than the sick and hungry.) But the main reason for attending to all peoples' essential needs is that if the world is rich enough to abolish forms of misery arising from abject poverty, it has a humanitarian obligation to do so.

The nature of the obligation is somewhat different when one moves beyond the objective of meeting essential human needs. There are still strong humanitarian reasons why the rich countries should assist the process of development of the poor countries, but there is not quite the same kind of obligation. Arguments based on a shared responsibility for individual welfare are weaker, and prudential reasons that derive from the dynamics of interstate relations are more powerful. Thus, if weak states are helped to become more self-sufficient and more capable of providing improvements in the living standards of their own people, they are likely to feel that the international system is more just, and, for that reason, it may be less prone to disruption. Beyond that, systemic reasons deriving from the needs of an increasingly "closed" global economic system point to the advantages all will gain if poor countries are helped to raise their standard of well-being and if all states improve their efficiency in the use of resources.[14]

One should be cautious about drawing too much in the way of implications for international action from the distinction we have made between the humanitarian obligation to relieve human misery and the humanitarian *plus* prudential rationale for helping to accelerate development. But as long as there is severe deprivation on a global scale that cannot be relieved in the short term by

[14]This second point is well made in a recent GATT study on trade and adjustment: "As long as three-quarters of the world's population remain poor it is idle—or perhaps the luxury of the idle—to speak of limits to growth closing in, and of growth impulses being exhausted. The poverty of the vast majority of the world's population indicates not merely the world's need for economic growth but, more directly and more importantly, the world's growth potential." Richard Blackhurst, Nicolas Marian, and Jan Tumlir, *Adjustment, Trade and Growth in Developed and Developing Countries*, GATT Studies in International Trade, No. 6, GATT: Geneva, 1978, p. 67.

national action alone, forms of international assistance will be needed that come more appropriately under the rubric of "basic welfare support" than under that of development financing. And it is the argument of this chapter that, despite the incipient character of the "world community," it would be desirable, in part to nurture and strengthen the sense of community, to have certain "basic support" programs funded in ways that explicitly recognize a global responsibility to relieve the worst forms of economic misery.

In thinking of the decade or so ahead, what, in specific terms, might one try to do? We propose two things. Our most radical suggestion is that a few programs should be accepted as "global tasks" and funded by some form of international tax or by some other non-appropriated money. Not only would the support for these programs not be subject to the whims of legislatures, but, ideally, the amount of money to be spent would not be subject to perpetual rounds of international bargaining. Once the "task" had been accepted and its broad dimensions defined by international agreement, the money would automatically become available. In return for this international acceptance of the "task," recipient governments would have to agree either to the direct administration of activities by an international agency or to adequate international inspection of national performance.

Probably not much, in the course of the next decade, could be accepted as a "global task" and funded in this way. But, as discussed below, perhaps it would be possible to have funded and accepted in this way: (1) a trust fund for emergency relief; (2) one or more programs designed to control certain diseases (such as malaria, sleeping sickness, or river blindness); and (3) a program that helped governments provide immediate and direct relief from starvation and acute malnutrition.

In addition, we propose that a global "basic support program" be established to provide grants to poor countries on a fairly automatic basis for certain clearly defined "basic welfare" purposes. Thus, a country that was poor enough (in today's terminology, the "low-income" LDCs) would have a presumptive right to a grant for a program designed to provide a rather narrowly defined range of basic goods and services (e.g., basic health care, safe water, basic education). We were tempted to propose that both the "global tasks" and the "basic-support-grants program" should be financed from non-appropriated funds, but suggesting that a few specific activities be funded in this way is pushing against the outer limits of the feasible. It would, however, be in keeping with the concept of "global responsibility" for the basic support grants to be financed by a system of assessment based on capacity to pay rather than by voluntary government pledges. An assessment formula based on capacity to pay is also more consistent than is "pledging" with our view that the North-South dichotomy is becoming obsolete and the emerging reality much more nearly that of a continuum of states.

Not only would the source of the financing be different for the "global tasks" and the "basic support grants," but the nature of the obligation that would be assumed would also be different. In the case of the global tasks, the amount of funds that would be made available would depend on the cost of fulfilling whatever task had been accepted as a result of an international negotiation. The total size of the basic support grants program, in contrast, would be set by negotiation among the member countries establishing the program. (More is said below about the way both the funds for the tasks and the basic support grants might be administered.)

The distinction that is being drawn between the method of financing a few internationally agreed "global tasks" and the "basic support grants" is not, of course, meant to imply that some basic welfare activities are more important than others. There really can be no hierarchy among programs designed to underwrite truly minimum needs.

For many years, aid-receiving countries have sought "automatic" resource transfers from non-appropriated sources, partly in the hope of getting more concessional financing, partly as a way of ensuring more certain and continuous financing, partly as a way to avoid the paternalistic odor that clings to donor-recipient relationships, and partly to escape the "strings" and conditions that, one way or another, are usually attached to most transfers, bilateral or multilateral.

Several separate objectives are frequently mixed together: first, a desire for non-appropriated funds; second, a desire for more open-ended commitments of funds; and third, a desire for more "automaticity," in the sense of little donor control over the transfer of funds. The method we are proposing for financing the "tasks" would respond to the first two objectives, and the method proposed for the basic support grants, to the third. It is a good deal easier to envision governments agreeing to greater automaticity in the disbursement of appropriated funds than to an open-ended commitment to finance needs from some non-appropriated source. And any task to be financed in this way would have to be fairly narrowly defined if there were to be any chance of agreement.

A small head tax, exempting those below some minimum per capita income, might be the most appropriate way, conceptually, of raising funds for the agreed "global tasks." Easier to administer would be a "transaction" tax—such as a levy on international mail or international air fares. Alternatively, and in some ways more desirable (in terms of the effect of the tax) would be a tax on the use of non-renewable resources (e.g., oil), on profits from deep sea-bed mining, or on activities that polluted the global commons (i.e., the atmosphere and the seas). Still another possible source of non-appropriated funds for the internationally agreed "global welfare tasks" would be the profits from further sales of IMF gold.[15] Indeed, the profits on the sale of gold represent the only currently available "collective rent." And for that reason they might appear to be the most attractive source of financing. But the gold sales option runs up against arguments having to do with the role of gold in the inter-

[15]In 1976, as part of a broad set of agreements on IMF reforms, member countries authorized the Fund to sell one-sixth of its gold holdings by auction and to put the profits of the sales into a Trust Fund to assist developing countries. Another one-sixth of the Fund's gold was to be returned to member countries in amounts corresponding with their quota shares.

80

national monetary system. Moreover, there is something to be said for underlining the global acceptance of the agreed global tasks by imposing some form of international tax rather than using, for this purpose, what appears to be a "free" source of funds.

A UNITED NATIONS BASIC SUPPORT PROGRAM

In turning from the arguments for accepting certain needs as a "global responsibility" to considering how to give effect to this "obligation" or "responsibility," questions arise about where to house the new programs, how to relate them to other international assistance efforts, and how to administer them.

Anyone who has had much experience in the "world of development" despairs of anything in the nature of radical change in the way multilateral aid is administered: aid bureaucracies are too well entrenched, and each fund or agency has, in addition to a tenacious bureaucracy, its own defenders (as well as detractors) among national governments. For a time, there was a tendency to defend the proliferation of international assistance agencies on the grounds that the more "spigots," the more aid. Today, that argument is seldom heard, and all reports on U.N. restructuring call for some consolidation of funds as well as for better coordination among the many agencies. There is no lack of formal contact among agencies, and better coordination has been a constant quest for many years. Some progress has been made since the first serious examination of the U.N. development system in 1969.[16] But the picture remains one of both vast duplication and inadequate coverage of significant areas. Further tinkering is unlikely to bring the improvements that are needed, particularly because no one seems prepared fully to confront the major institutional issue in the international assist-

[16]United Nations, *A Study of the Capacity of the United Nations Development System* (referred to as the Jackson Report): Geneva, 1969, DP/5.

ance field: the rivalry for primacy between the central U.N. institutions on the one hand, and the World Bank Group on the other. The LDCs, for the most part, favor the United Nations, for there their voting power is dominant, while the advanced countries, in part for the same reason, favor the Bank. We think it is time to grasp this nettle.

Both institutional complexes have important parts to play in the years ahead. But a sharper identification of their respective roles, and some restructuring of both sets of international resource transfer agencies is needed if the two goals of "putting a floor under poverty" and promoting development are both to be met more adequately. The right arrangement, we think, is for the central U.N. agencies, reorganized and streamlined, to take the lead at the "basic support" end of the international assistance spectrum, and for the World Bank Group, collaborating more closely with the regional banks and significantly reformed as well as further strengthened, to be the leader at the development end. Since no sharp distinction can really be drawn between basic support and development assistance, the functions will overlap and the division of responsibility will inevitably remain somewhat blurred.

If efficient operation were the only test, there would be a strong case for putting all resource transfer programs under one agency, for many projects concerned with improving a country's basic infrastructure and productive activities directly serve both purposes. But two reasons persuade us that those programs most sharply focused on the immediate amelioration of the plight of the absolute poor should be located at the center of the United Nations system: the experience of some of the U.N. agencies, most notably UNICEF, in dealing with this kind of problem, and the fact that the United Nations itself is the logical place for programs which are the most visible expression of the acceptance of a global obligation to meet certain very basic, very essential human needs. In Chapter 7, we look at some changes that might be made in the World Bank Group and in procedures for financing development. The remainder of this chapter sketches out some ways the United Nations' basic support activities might be reorganized and strengthened in the light of the above discussion.

The range of today's United Nations' "basic welfare support" is quite broad. The United Nations Children's Fund (UNICEF)—which is essentially a "basic needs" agency—now supplies over $200 million a year in support of nutrition, health, education, and other basic service programs designed to reach children of the rural and urban poor. In recent years the World Food Program has spent over $400 million dollars a year in food aid (that is, cash and commodities) for "food for work" development programs, emergency relief efforts, and special nutrition programs. Though it has only limited resources of its own, the Office of the United Nations Disaster Relief Coordinator (UNDRO) coordinates international relief efforts to countries hit by droughts, floods, or other natural disasters. The United Nations Development Program (UNDP) provides technical assistance financing for a wide range of activities, some of which contribute to meeting basic needs. And, with funds provided largely from the UNDP, several of the specialized agencies—particularly the World Health Organization (WHO), the Food and Agriculture Organization (FAO), and the United Nations Educational, Scientific, and Cultural Organization (UNESCO)—help countries organize programs, some of which are designed to extend basic services (e.g., health care, education, water and sewage facilities) to the poor in developing countries. In addition, in the last 5 to 10 years, many bilateral aid agencies, as well as both the World Bank and the regional development banks, have increased the share of total resource transfers going into programs aimed at meeting basic needs.

Except in the case of UNICEF and UNDRO, much of the basic support assistance now provided by multilateral agencies represents only a very small part of their total programs, and in the case of UNICEF and UNDRO, the assistance provided is limited to groups (mothers and young children in the case of UNICEF) or tied to events (disasters in the case of UNDRO). There is too little effective coordination among the various agencies playing some part in the supply of basic services. Each organization has its own particular focus, policy orientation, and approach. And each agency has not only its own headquarters staff, but often also its own personnel in the field with whom aid-receiving governments must try to deal.[17] As a consequence, much effort is duplicated, and actions, which if taken together could be reinforcing, are too frequently carried out separately.

Better coordination of existing programs is the conventional prescription. But if a significant international effort to meet urgent needs is to be made in the years ahead, it would be preferable to go beyond improved coordination and to combine many of the funds, agencies, and programs into a new United Nations program built on the acceptance of the concept that the relief of acute human suffering is a "global obligation." For illustrative purposes, we are calling this new program (and its administering agency) the United Nations Basic Support Program.

The specific functions of this proposed Basic Support Program would be to offer help in emergencies; to provide grants to poor countries in support of programs designed to provide basic goods and services to people in extreme need; and to organize and oversee the carrying out of certain "global welfare tasks," such as an attack on starvation and acute malnutrition. The proposed UNBSP would take over the functions of and formally supersede UNICEF, UNDRO, and the World Food Program. It might also take over the administration of the United Nations Fund for Population Activities (which now distributes over $100 million for a range of population control programs); assume the work of "mapping" unmet basic needs worldwide that was initiated by the International Labor Organization; and take over most other basic support activities now handled elsewhere in the

[17]There is in each of the countries which receive a good bit of technical assistance from the United Nations, a Resident Representative of the United Nations Development Program who is supposed to serve as the in-country official of U.N. aid programs. But, in most countries, there are also field officers of separate programs. UNICEF, for example, has field officers in 37 countries which serve a total of 126 countries; the World Food Program has offices in 75 countries; and the UNFPA has 30 field coordinators, some of whom cover several countries, posted in the offices of the UNDP Resident Representative as senior advisers on population matters. In addition, the UNFPA has recently established 4 regional liaison offices.

United Nations system, such as small nutrition and primary health care projects now financed by the World Bank.

In many of its aspects, this new Basic Support Program would be an expanded and somewhat modified UNICEF. In past debates on U.N. restructuring, UNICEF has vigorously resisted any suggestion that it be merged with other United Nations programs, fearing that it would lose the strong official support it enjoys, that its unusually good working relations with aid-receiving governments would suffer, and that it would be less successful in attracting voluntary contributions on a worldwide basis. Although in several important respects the UNBSP would operate in new ways, it would be building on and carrying further UNICEF's concern with those in most need, together with its emphasis on self-help and on the provision of basic services, explicitly extending the scope of the program from its present concentration on children and their mothers to all people in extreme need.[18]

As with UNICEF, a major portion of the requests for support from the UNBSP would probably be for technical assistance.[19] Under our scheme, these requests would be met directly by the Basic Support Program. That is, technical assistance would be financed out of the pool of assessed basic support funds,[20] and grants would be made directly to recipient governments, not, as

---

[18]UNICEF itself has found it difficult to deal with problems such as chronic malnutrition, chronic illness, and lack of adequate shelter, water, and sanitation, without involving whole families and communities. Accordingly, in the 1970s, the provision of "community-based services" became a main feature of its assistance effort. For a description of the basic services concept, see Report by the Executive Director, "Basic Services for Children in Developing Countries," UNICEF, 1976. E/ICEF/L. 1342.

[19]Recent UNICEF reports note that since its shift toward more assistance for providing basic services in a way that relies heavily on community involvement and self-help measures, requests by aid-receiving governments for technical assistance (e.g., help in the design and implementation of programs and services) has been growing faster than the requests for supplies and equipment from abroad.

[20]This would mean that assessments on governments for "basic support grants," discussed on pp. 86–90, would replace some of the current voluntary pledging to the UNDP, at present the central fund for U.N. technical assistance activities.

is the predominant pattern today, channeled through the specialized agencies. In this way, recipients would be able to "buy" technical assistance from anywhere, within or outside the U.N. system, although presumably they would often choose to rely on the expertise that can be found in the specialized agencies.

Basic Support Grants

The administration of a new form of financial support—basic support grants—would be the core activity of the new UNBSP. These grants would be allocated directly to poor governments prepared to undertake certain types of programs for providing basic goods and services to those people in most urgent need.

What sort of activity ought to fall within the category of "basic goods and services" to be financed by these grants? For example, should the "basic support grants" finance basic education programs as well as programs to extend health services to the poor and projects to bring safe drinking water to communities? There is no universally accepted list of "basic needs," although, in most of today's discussion, five are most often mentioned: food, water, basic health services, basic education, and sewage facilities. Presumably agreement on this list, or some variant of it, would need to be part of the negotiation on the basic instrument establishing the U.N. Basic Support Program. But the more difficult task of defining just what activities should be eligible for financing within these broad categories would clearly have to be done by the governing board of the new agency.

We would also include family planning programs on the list of activities that should be supported by grants from the UNBSP. It hardly needs to be said that the speed of progress in eliminating or substantially reducing absolute poverty on any lasting basis critically depends on success in reducing birth rates in poor but populous countries and that slower rates of population growth will be, mainly, a function of social and economic development. Since the World Population Conference in 1974, increased attention has been given to population questions by many donor agencies. The assistance program of the United Nations Fund for Population Activities (UNFPA), which is today the main multilateral source of financing for population planning programs, doubled in size between 1972 and 1977. And various assistance programs (including UNICEF and WHO programs in the field of primary health care) now associate family planning activities with other "basic welfare" measures. In bringing assistance for population activities under the U.N. Basic Support Program, the objective would not be to "tie" basic needs assistance to a country's performance in the population field, but rather to facilitate the integration of activities that tend to be mutually reinforcing.[21] Because of the sharp differences of view about family planning, among donors as well as recipients, we would retain a separate fund for the support of population control activities to be fed, as now, by voluntary contributions. But the fund would be administered by the UNBSP in much the same way as the other basic support grants.

Once agreement was reached by the governing body of the UNBSP on the kinds of activities and types of programs that the basic support grants could be used to finance, each aid-receiving country would be largely responsible for the choice, design, and implementation of its own program of assistance. At the time of the establishment of the UNBSP, governments would agree on

[21]The view that essential human needs can most effectively be met by developing a group of interrelated or "mutually supporting" services underlies the approach that UNICEF now follows in its core program of assistance. Its "basic services approach" evolved out of a joint study done by UNICEF and the World Health Organization in the first half of the 1970s. This approach not only emphasizes the interrelationship among certain essential goods and services, it also stresses the importance of community-level involvement in the development of the essential services.

Among those activities that UNICEF now assists through its program of mutually supporting basic services are maternal and child care, family planning, the provision of a safe water supply and sanitation facilities, increased production and consumption of adequately nutritious food, and measures to meet basic education needs. UNICEF, Report by the Executive Director, "Basic Services for Children in Developing Countries," March, 1976, E/ICEF/L-/342. Countries requesting grants from the UNBSP would not be required to ask for this kind of comprehensive approach, although they might well be encouraged to do so. When this was the case, the UNBSP should be even better placed to respond to such requests than is today's more limited UNICEF.

the broad purposes for which countries would be eligible to receive grants. Thereafter, the governing body of the new agency would agree more precisely on the kinds of activities and the types of programs that would qualify and also on certain guidelines that all recipients of grants should comply with, such as using grants only for the assistance of the really poor and in such ways that they did not discriminate against particular ethnic groups. But the recipient countries would themselves determine what kinds of programs within the "approved" categories would be most needed and what methods would be most appropriate. Thus, whether a government used all of its UNBSP grant in one region of its country or another, whether it used it wholly for one activity (e.g., the provision of safe drinking water) or opted for a program of related community services (e.g., whether it decided that basic education was of more importance to it than good sanitation) would be for the recipient country itself to decide, not for the Basic Support Agency to determine.

We suggest that a new grants program operate in this way partly to respond to demands of the LDCs that they be given more voice in the management of resource transfers, partly to increase the likelihood that programs chosen by the recipient governments would be better suited to their special needs and social structures,[22] and partly to underline the fact that, although in one sense these are "welfare" grants, they are "welfare" grants that explicitly accept the right of the recipient government to decide which of its needs are the most urgent and that also assume (until there is evidence to the contrary) that the recipient will put the grant to the general uses for which they are intended.

Each government choosing to receive grants from the Basic Support Program should be required to supply information—or to cooperate with the UNBSP in gathering information—about

[22]The failure to do this has been one of the major shortcomings of recent "aid" programs designed to provide basic assistance directly to the poor. For a discussion of this problem, see OECD, Development Assistance Committee, *Development Co-operation, 1978 Review,* OECD: Paris 1978, pp. 69–78, 85–101.

the dimensions of absolute poverty in its society.[23] Each recipient government would also be required to accept periodic audits by the UNBSP of its grant-financed programs to ensure against misuse of funds, gross inefficiency, or violation of UNBSP criteria or guidelines. Grants would be stopped in case of abuse, but not simply because the UNBSP staff felt a country had not made the best choice in deciding among competing needs.

As discussed above, the grants program would be funded mainly by assessments on countries, calculated according to a formula based on ability to pay. The total size of the grants program for, say, an initial period of five years should be part of the basic negotiation establishing the program, but five-year totals should thereafter be decided by the full membership on the recommendation of the governing body and in the light of the experience with the program. Some governments and some non-governmental organizations might also be encouraged to make additional voluntary contributions to the Basic Support Program.[24] The fund for population control activities would continue to be financed by voluntary contributions. And as discussed further below, there might also be some additional voluntary contributions of food supplies.

All poor countries, that is, all those with an average annual per

[23]Little reliable information now exists on the incidence of malnutrition, on the numbers of people without access to safe water, or adequate health care, or essential shelter. Much of what is now known about the dimensions of absolute poverty is in terms of national averages which do not reveal the real shortfalls in basic needs. Many developing countries have recently begun to make income distribution surveys, to organize various kinds of special antipoverty programs, but few have yet developed the means of keeping under review the extent, nature, and distribution of poverty. Even those that have tried to estimate the number of people living below some nationally determined poverty line have only the most imprecise picture of the conditions under which those people actually live.

[24]Also, some of UNICEF's highly successful way of raising funds should be continued. Its worldwide sale of greeting cards netted over $16 million in 1979 out of a total of $27 million in private contributions. It also received about $33 million in contributions "in kind," i.e., in the form of medical supplies and the like. It would be wholly consistent with the concepts underlying the proposed UNBSP for these kinds of extra, fund-raising activities to continue.

capita income below some "poverty line," say $500, should in our view be eligible to receive "basic support grants." However, the allocation of grants among countries should be weighted in such a way that the poorer the country the higher its per capita share of the funds available.[25] Thus a country such as Chad, with a per capita income of about $120 would receive more assistance per capita than El Salvador with a per capita income of just under $500. In addition, even the poorest countries should put up some matching funds. And some account would have to be taken of the fact that a few very large, very poor countries could, on the basis of absolute need, absorb the bulk of the resources available.

This suggests that there would have to be a ceiling on funds for, say, India, Bangladesh, and perhaps other large, poor countries. There is no good way to set such a ceiling. What is now done in other multilateral concessional aid programs (such as in IDA, the "soft-loan" window of the World Bank) is to limit India—by agreement but not according to any formal calculation of need—to a proportion of the total amount of funds available. And that would seem to be the right approach for the basic support grants program as well, since by any measurement of need, India would qualify for almost any amount of aid-on-easy-terms that the international community is likely to provide.[26]

---

[25]There are obviously problems with using per capita income figures to establish some measurement of need, and there are problems with designating countries on the basis of per capita income levels as "priority countries" for resource allocations. Accurate measures are hard to arrive at, and the same level of income will provide for a different standard of living in different climates and cultures. However, as noted in the OECD, Development Assistance Committee's review for 1979, studies have shown that income per capita data is a fairly good surrogate for other measurements of need in more cases than not. The $500 per capita cut-off point that is proposed for the UNBSP grants includes more than the "least developed countries" as defined by the United Nations and more than the "low-income countries" as defined by the World Bank. But countries near the cut-off point would receive proportionally less assistance than those with per capita incomes far below it.

[26]It should be possible to supplement the resources available from the UNBSP by joining additional, voluntary, bilateral assistance to programs worked out between the UNBSP and its largest client countries. That is, the staff of the

Emergency Relief

Providing and coordinating international emergency assistance would be a second function of the UNBSP. There are obvious advantages to combining the programs—UNICEF, UNDRO, and the World Food Program—that now provide the bulk of the U.N.'s emergency relief. And there are further advantages to having the relief function within the ambit of the agency charged with providing basic support on a continuing basis. Technical assistance for "disaster preparedness and prevention," one of the functions of UNDRO, is very similar to the technical assistance that would be a large part of the other activities of the UNBSP. If the new agency were "tasked" with the global goal of eliminating—or at least, substantially reducing—acute malnutrition and starvation, the arguments would be even stronger. But even if the UNBSP were no more than an enlarged and expanded UNICEF-plus-food-aid program, the advantages in combining the three relief-welfare agencies seem persuasive. Among other things, if relief operations were handled by the same agency that was constantly in touch with the needs and conditions of the poor countries through the basic support program, more knowledge of local conditions should lead to a better tailoring of relief operations to local needs than has always been the case in the past. (The excessive flows of food aid to Guatemala after an earthquake in 1976 that did serious harm to local food producers is the kind of thing that one could hope to avoid.)

The need for emergency relief is greater than intermittent news coverage of famines and earthquakes might lead one to expect. Though disaster-related natural phenomena do not appear to be increasing in frequency, there are indications that the human cost of disaster worldwide will steadily mount through the next decade. One reason is that population increases, combined with the tendency for people to concentrate in urban areas, have increased the human toll of the disasters that do oc-

---

UNBSP might help a recipient government plan programs that exceeded the financing capacity of the Basic Support Program and then help to line up other donors for particular aspects of the program. Some of this type of "multi-bi" collaboration occurs now, but not to a sufficient extent.

cur. Especially in Africa and South Asia, new concentrations of population have arisen without the planning, sanitation, transportation, health services, and other infrastructure developments that usually accompany the growth of cities and towns in wealthier, industrialized societies. The results are populous communities highly vulnerable to massive suffering from such disasters as epidemics, floods, and famines. In the 10-year period 1965–1975, assistance, public and private, from the international community came to $1.6 billion, a substantial amount, but less than one-third of what the countries themselves spent on relief operations alone (excluding the additional amounts they devoted to the more costly disaster preparedness and prevention activities).[27]

In the past, international relief efforts were impeded by understaffing and a failure generally to institutionalize emergency assistance. For example, until 1975 neither the World Food Program nor the World Health Organization had separate, specialized bureaus to handle their constant involvements in relief operations. Major emergencies tended to be dealt with in an ad hoc manner, and there was a general lack of practical coordination among the relief agencies in the field during operations.

Much has been done in recent years to improve the international community's capacity to provide relief to victims of natural disasters and to strengthen the role of the Office of the United Nations Disaster Relief Coordinator (UNDRO) which was established as a focal point in the U.N. system for disaster relief matters. But both lack of clarity in the lines of authority among the many agencies (public and private) that play some part in emergency relief and a lack of funds continue to hamper relief activities. And, as disaster relief studies have repeatedly emphasized, far too little attention has been given to preparedness planning for relief operations. More attention to national disaster

[27]These figures and much of the description of the present disaster relief arrangements come from the study *International Disaster Relief*, McGraw-Hill, for the Council on Foreign Relations/1980s Project: New York, 1977. Its author is Stephen Green, a former official with UNICEF responsible for setting up special relief and rehabilitation projects in Indochina and that organization's famine relief efforts in Ethiopia.

preparedness planning "could alleviate some of the worst of these difficulties and greatly contribute to easing the complex logistical and coordination problems that accompany every disaster."[28]

Today, UNDRO faces difficulties deciding how much of its limited resources to spend on preparedness activities. At the same time, UNICEF is constantly plagued by having to limit its emergency assistance so as not to cut too deeply into its continuing programs. The establishment of a permanent emergency trust fund fed initially and replenished as necessary by the revenues from some form of international tax would ensure adequate money for disaster relief. Funding for disaster preparedness should probably be met from the assessed funds, the decision on how much money should be used in this way to be made by the governing body of the UNBSP.[29]

The recent tragic events in Kampuchea have highlighted a problem that neither private agencies nor intergovernmental organizations have yet found the answer to: how to assist people in desperate conditions if governments refuse to make use of the help that is available or, worse, themselves take actions that intensify the suffering. This is partly a problem that arises in connection with emergency aid in the wake of disasters, but it is also a larger problem. And there is some danger that our shift of emphasis in the basic support grants—placing more of the decision-making about the needs that should be met in the hands of recipient governments—would increase the likelihood that some of

[28]Barbara J. Brown, "An Overview of the Structure of the Current System," in Lynn H. Stephens and Stephen J. Green (eds.), *Disaster Assistance: Appraisal, Reform and New Approaches,* New York University Press: New York, 1979, p. 5.

[29]Currently some $400,000 per year from the U.N.'s regular budget is earmarked for use by UNDRO as immediate assistance in emergency relief operations. In the late 1970s, it was proposed that this emergency trust fund be fed by voluntary contributions, but since few contributions were made, the emergency relief fund has remained an item on the U.N.'s regular budget. Obviously, the $400,000 per year is a small fraction of the amount required to respond to calls for disaster relief. Additional voluntary funds from both governments and private voluntary organizations now provide the bulk of relief assistance.

the worst forms of deprivation will continue despite the fact that resources could be made available to relieve the suffering.

In today's world of sovereign states, there are limits to what can be done to deal with this kind of situation. Public opinion helps, and so, too, may opportunities for groups within states to have channels of communication to international organizations that are not simply through governments. For this reason, it might be desirable for the Chairman of the U.N. Commission on Human Rights to be a member of the governing body of the new UNBSP. Groups, not states, could register complaints with him if, through intent or neglect, any government receiving any form of UNBSP assistance was in effect inflicting unnecessary economic suffering on its people. If, after investigation, the charge was felt to be legitimate, the UNBSP could withhold further funds. This would not, of course, meet the real problem unless the threat to cut off funds and the publicity that would doubtless accompany an investigation prompted the government concerned to take corrective action. But scarce global funds should only be made available to those governments prepared to use them to meet the needs for which they are intended.

The Global Tasks

Where the Basic Support Program would depart most significantly from existing arrangements to help meet immediate short-term needs would be in the carrying out of the internationally accepted global tasks. Indeed, this function of the UNBSP would be the one with the most far-reaching implications in terms of giving meaning to the concept of a shared responsibility for mankind.

Because the concept of "global tasks"—that is, tasks that are accepted as "obligations" by the world community and funded in new ways—represents such a fundamental break with the past, the decision to move in this direction would obviously have to be the product of a special intergovernmental negotiation—initially, of the negotiations establishing the UNBSP. Later, if new tasks were to be agreed to, they would have to result from intergovernmental decisions taken by some prescribed majority laid down in the basic agreement.

Agreeing to designate the control of certain diseases (malaria, river blindness, or some of the major childhood killer diseases that are controllable by immunization) as a "global task" would not be a very large step, although important conceptually and in terms of precedent. A good bit is already being done: the World Health Organization (WHO) serves as the executing agency for a mainly World Bank-financed attack on river blindness, and it is also the lead agency in global immunization programs as well as in a campaign against malaria. Acceptance of these or other, similar disease-control efforts as a "global task" would ensure continuing financial support and put more global commitment behind the programs. As estimated by the World Bank, additional international assistance in the order of $2–3 billion over a five-year period would be needed to give such a task momentum. The UNBSP would formally approve and monitor the programs, but the implementation should, as now, be largely done by the WHO.

The designation of a special attack on starvation and acute malnutrition as a "global task" would be far more important, and it would be a far more difficult step to take. But so much study and attention has recently been given to the problem of world hunger and, rhetorically at least, the goal of eliminating starvation and acute malnutrition has been endorsed so often by so many, that it might not be beyond the realm of the feasible to address at least some aspects of the world hunger problem in this way.

Really to eradicate starvation and malnutrition is a long-term, multifaceted problem, one that is inextricably interwoven with the process of social and economic development. Clearly, the world community is not yet ready to give a long-term, open-ended commitment to accomplish that task through the use of unappropriated funds (or in any other way that is meaningful), desirable though that would be. But it might be possible to gain acceptance for the far more modest objective of agreeing to use revenues from an international tax to meet a substantial part of the cost of national programs designed to deal directly with the most urgent, immediate needs for food. These might be national food stamp or other national food subsidy programs, direct distribution programs, or other measures designed to provide food to the starving and malnourished. Financial assistance might also be given for nutrition-related health and education programs (if needed programs were not adequately covered by the program of basic support grants).[30]

There are several different approaches that governments might adopt. They can, for example, subsidize food purchases by the poor through food ration shops or food stamp programs. Such programs can be hugely expensive if, as in the case of Egypt, governments subsidize food prices generally for the benefit of the urban working classes as well as the very poor. Food subsidy and distribution programs tend also to make heavy demands on a government's administrative capacities. Nonetheless, there are examples of national nutrition programs in developing countries, Sri Lanka's perhaps the most notable among them, which have achieved impressive results in terms of substantially improving the well-being of poor people.

The World Food Council has estimated that it would take some $500–1,000 million in external assistance to mount a major "food entitlement" program on a global scale.[31] This assumes that a major proportion of the total costs would be met by recipients themselves. But, if a decision were made to fund an attack on starvation and acute malnutrition in the way proposed, problems of determining just how large a share of any national program should be covered by the global program and how the total

[30]Overcoming starvation and chronic malnutrition involves not only getting more food to those in need but also attacking health problems directly affecting nutrition. This link between food needs and basic health needs is one of the strongest arguments for bringing the various "basic welfare" programs together under one assistance agency. But because the health-related dimensions of the hunger problem are so extensive (involving the need to provide safe water, sanitation facilities, basic health services, etc.), it is probably not feasible to think of financing a truly comprehensive nutrition-health campaign with revenues from an international tax.

[31]World Food Council, "Toward the Eradication of Hunger: Food Subsidy and Direct Distribution Programmes," United Nations, February 1980, WFC/1980/3. See also James Austin et al., "Nutrition Intervention Assessment and Guidelines," Harvard Institute for International Development, mimeo, 1978; and Marcelo Selowsky, "The Economic Dimensions of Malnutrition in Young Children," World Bank, Staff Working Paper No. 294, October, 1978.

should be apportioned as among countries would certainly have to be answered. As we said, the concept underlying the "global tasks" is that "need" should determine the financing, not the financing the proportion of the need to be met. Logically, therefore, some formula based on estimates of need[32] and estimates of a country's capacity to pay would be required. The poorer the country and the larger its number of acutely malnourished people, the more support it should be entitled to receive. Clearly, this would mean that India would be eligible to receive a very large proportion of the total. Should this matter? By accepting the attack on starvation and acute malnutrition as a "global task," the international community would have accepted the principle that it was "people as members of an incipient global society," not "people as nationals of particular political entities called nation-states" that were to be the focus of the effort. Logically, therefore, so far as the funding of anything specifically accepted as a "global task" is concerned, the fact that a very large share went to one country should be irrelevant. (We said earlier that this principle would not hold for the basic support grant program.) A middle-income LDC with a large number of malnourished poor would, under the formula, be eligible to receive some assistance for, say, an approved national food subsidy program, but support in this case would be limited.[33]

Is this a proposal for an entirely open-ended commitment

[32]In most discussions of the problems of malnutrition, estimates of the problem are based on the level of calorie deficiency as measured against minimum requirements set out in a joint FAO-WHO report, "Energy and Protein Requirements," WHO Technical Report Series No. 522, FAO Nutrition Meetings Report, No. 52: Geneva, 1973.

[33]Obviously, as countries become richer generally, it would be assumed that they would be doing more on their own, through developmental and welfare activities, to reduce the problem of malnutrition. One would not expect the Global Nutrition Program to be paying for the negligence of an upper-income country even if many of its people were malnourished. Therefore, the way the needs formula might work is that below some level of minimum per capita income (say $300) countries would receive assistance based simply on the size of their malnutrition problem. But at successively higher income levels, the weight that was given in the needs formula to per capita income would increase relative to the weight given to the number of malnourished. And at some level of income, a threshold would be reached beyond which international assistance would not be forthcoming.

which publics in rich societies would surely not be prepared to accept? And would it tend to become a program that simply allowed governments in relatively poor countries to "shift the burden" of their poor onto the international community? Limitations and safeguards would be required. First, the kinds of direct support programs that would qualify for assistance would have to be defined as part of the basic decision to undertake the "task," and the extent of the commitment would be controlled, to some extent, in this way. Second, all assistance would be on a matching grant—or, more precisely, a sliding matching grant—basis. This would also exercise a measure of restraint on the total size, and it would help ensure against abuse. Finally, the programs being supported would be reassessed every two or three years or so to determine effectiveness and the continuing need for support.

Undertaking this kind of "global nutrition task" would not eliminate malnutrition and starvation. That will only be possible through longer-term development. But enough studies of direct support programs have been made and enough experts exist to design a "global nutrition support program" that could go well beyond what can now be done by UNICEF and others to feed hungry people.[34]

An attack on acute malnutrition and the eradication of certain diseases seem to us to be the most appropriate "global tasks" for the decade ahead, but others—such as the provision of safe drinking water—might be agreed upon, alternatively or additionally. Once a "task" was accepted and its general scope defined by governments, the responsibility for approving implementing programs, financing them, and monitoring them would rest with the Basic Support Program, although in some cases, as in dis-

---

[34]If the international community were prepared to make a really major attack on world hunger, it is not difficult to outline the main elements of a program of action. Most of the steps that need to be taken were identified by the World Food Conference in Rome in 1974 and have subsequently been refined and added to by the World Food Council. They extend widely over measures to stimulate production of food, to improve food security by a more adequate system of reserves, etc. A UNBSP-administered nutrition support program of the kind described here would be one element, but only one element, in such a program.

ease control, other parts of the U.N. system might be designated as the agency responsible for the design and administration of the program.

Food Aid

It was suggested above that the World Food Program should be one of the programs incorporated into the new UNBSP. If the attack on extreme malnutrition were accepted as a "global task," some part of what the World Food Program now does in providing food aid should be taken over by that program. Despite the fact that the physical supply of food from abroad is frequently a less effective way of coping with widespread malnutrition than are financial transfers that enable countries, and individuals, to buy more food, there are countries that do need assistance in the form of food supplies to meet emergencies and to help during years of poor harvests, and there are "food deficit" countries where food aid provided on a continuous and assured basis can provide essential support to national nutrition programs.

Food aid policies and practices have been severely criticized in recent years for a number of different reasons.[35] In some cases, food aid creates disincentives to agricultural production in recipient countries by depressing food prices, by easing pressures on governments to foster agricultural development, and by creating preferences for foreign "exotic" goods. Thus rice eaters are turned into bread eaters and then into importers of wheat. Moreover, food aid sometimes goes to the "wrong" people within countries, not reaching the hungry by simply providing additional food to those less in need.

Nonetheless, most studies conclude that although the benefits of food aid transfers for the recipient country have sometimes

---

[35]The list of good food aid studies has grown very long in recent years. For a general review of the criticisms made and an assessment of existing food-aid programs, see S. J. Maxwell and H. W. Singer, "Food Aid to Developing Countries, a Survey," *World Development*, vol. 7, no. 3, March, 1979; or the longer report prepared by Singer for the WFP, "Food Aid Policies and Programme: A Survey of Studies of Food Aid," World Food Program: Rome, 1978, WFP/CFA5/5-C. See also Christopher Stevens, *Food Aid and the Developing World*, Overseas Development Institute: London, 1979.

been overstated, the problems are also somewhat exaggerated: the disincentive effects can be guarded against by appropriate food and nutrition policies, and the inefficiencies in many of today's food-aid programs can be reduced.[36] The critical factors in the design of effective food-aid programs are the government's food pricing policy and whether food-aid programs are sufficiently narrowly "targeted" on those most in need. Programs that are not narrowly focused, but instead keep food prices arbitrarily low, either discourage agricultural development or claim an excessive share of government revenues for the subsidy programs.

How much of today's pledged supplies of food aid would be absorbed by the "global nutrition task" would obviously depend on how ambitiously it was decided to define that task. The amounts could be very substantial. Some part, too, of today's food aid will also continue to be needed as a resource for the UNBSP (in its role as the successor to UNDRO) to call on in emergencies.

A question might remain whether, in addition to the amounts used in these ways, there would still be demands from the poor countries which the WFP is today meeting that should, in one way or another, continue to be met by the new UNBSP. And there is the related question of whether the need for the physical transfers of food to poor countries is likely to continue to increase. The answer is probably "yes" in both cases.

Food aid is essentially a form of balance-of-payments support. It provides in kind what countries would otherwise need to purchase from the market. However, it is not simply an alternative form of balance-of-payments support; rather, food aid is an *additional* source of external assistance—the total amount of assistance provided by rich countries to the poor being greater because of food-aid programs than it would be without them. It is for this reason, and really for this reason alone, that there con-

---

[36]For an analysis of the kinds of improvements that could be made, see James Austin et al., "Nutrition Intervention Assessment and Guidelines," op. cit.; and "Nutrition and Basic Needs," prepared by the Agriculture and Rural Development Department of the World Bank, December, 1978.

tinues to be a good argument for the physical transfer of food on a non-emergency basis.

As additional balance-of-payments support, food aid can help to carry countries through years of poor harvest when increased import requirements would otherwise put heavy strains on limited foreign exchange reserves. Food aid provided on a continuous and assured basis can also be an important source of support to countries in which the effective demand for food is rising faster than local rates of production. In particular, food aid can play a critical role in making possible employment-oriented development programs where local food supplies cannot be increased fast enough to keep up with rising incomes and concomitant increases in food demand.

Used in this way, food aid is more closely related to encouraging the process of development than to meeting short-term basic needs. But it would obviously be difficult, and in many ways counterproductive, to have part of the physically supplied food aid handled by the UNBSP and another part by a different agency, for example, the World Bank Group. It is clearly more sensible to merge the total program with the UNBSP than it would be to split it. And it is also clearly more sensible to have the WFP become part of the new UNBSP than to maintain its current uneasy links with the FAO.

Financing and Governance of the UNBSP

There is no really good estimate today of what it would cost to eliminate "absolute" poverty.[37] Another 1980s study, using estimates made by the World Bank, proposed that $10 to 15 billion a

---

[37]The figures most often cited of external resource requirements to meet essential minimum needs come from the World Bank, but as members of the Bank staff responsible for some of the calculations insist: "Investment and recurrent cost estimates can only be arrived at if a large number of assumptions are made on the number of people deprived of basic goods and services, the per capita costs of producing and delivering these to the poor, the economic policies followed by governments, the economic trends in developing countries in the future, etc. As it is unlikely that all such assumptions hold at the same time, the resulting estimates are somewhat arbitrary." Paul Streeten and S. J. Burki, "Basic Needs: Some Issues," *World Development,* vol. 6, no. 3, 1978, p. 419.

year in international aid be provided to ensure that the basic needs of all people were met by the end of the century.[38] This was estimated to be the amount of additional development assistance that would be required annually to develop within countries the capacities to provide on a permanent basis the means for meeting all peoples' basic needs for food, health services, water, sewage facilities, and basic education. The kind of "basic welfare support" that we envisage for the UNBSP is clearly a much more limited objective and nothing like all the external assistance that would be required to achieve the goal of eliminating mass poverty.

Existing "basic welfare" programs of the United Nations (as distinct from assistance for "development" purposes) probably now amount to something less than a half-billion dollars, plus some $400 million in food aid, though the exact amount is difficult to determine because most assistance programs are not sharply focused on meeting essential needs.

We have throughout this chapter cited existing estimates— some made by U.N. agencies, others by the World Bank—of costs of specific basic needs programs. These estimates, as the original reports state, are rather rough. Nonetheless, they provide not-wholly-arbitrary indications of how large a U.N. Basic Support Program of the sort we have outlined might be. Let us summarize: International support for national nutrition programs in low-income countries might initially be in the order of $1 billion per year, some part of which could be in the form of physical supplies of food.[39] About $2–3 billion over 5 years or ½ billion per year is needed for disease control efforts and another ½ billion for topping-up a disaster emergency fund. This $2 billion per year (less the supplies of food) would, according to our proposal, be derived from some form of international tax. Then let us say that the assessment for basic support grants might run

---

[38]Roger Hansen, *Beyond the North-South Stalemate,* op. cit., pp. 262–265.

[39]The World Bank estimated that about $1.5 billion would be required to cover the cost of meeting the 2 percent shortfall in cereals needed to meet the calorie deficiency of all undernourished people. But that does not include any of the costs of the administration of food programs. For a discussion of the difficulties in estimating costs of programs to meet immediate needs for food, see the annex to the Reutlinger study cited in note 12, above.

in the region, initially, of $1.5 billion, bringing the total of the assistance to be provided by the new UNBSP to around $3.5 billion (in 1980 dollars), plus additional food aid commitments that the Basic Support Program would handle.

Clearly, that figure falls far short of what would be needed to "put a floor" under global poverty. It is, however, about a half billion more than the credit allocated by the soft-loan window of the World Bank (IDA) in fiscal year 1979. And, a $3.5 billion program that provided for a large degree of automaticity in the distribution of funds and raised rather more than half the total by some form of global tax would represent a significant advance toward the realization of a global responsibility for the basic well-being of mankind. But the taking of such a large step requires some heroic assumptions: that member countries of the United Nations can come to agreement on some rather fundamental innovations in the methods of granting assistance and that developed and developing countries can agree on the governance of a program that not only departs in significant ways from traditional aid practices but also commands a not insignificant amount of resources.

The UNBSP, following the pattern of the main agencies it would be superseding, would be an organ of the central United Nations organization—not an autonomous Specialized Agency. Like UNICEF, it would have its own governing body, executive director, and staff. Taking UNICEF as a model, the governing body might be a 30-nation representative board, 10 members of the board elected each year for a three-year term by ECOSOC. Though not formally stipulated, the United States, the Soviet Union, France, and the United Kingdom are always represented on the UNICEF board, the remaining member nations providing a balance between "contributing" and "receiving" countries and among geographical regions. Often, regional blocs in effect decide which nations from within a region are elected, but, when the countries in a regional bloc cannot agree, it is the full membership of ECOSOC that determines the country composition of the UNICEF board. In general, this seems an appropriate model for the governing body of the new agency, but because the resources and role of the UNBSP would be substantially larger than those of UNICEF, decisions on the composition of the governing body would doubtless need to form part of the negotiation constituting the new agency. A balanced board would be essential but there is no reason why any country should always be represented. As we suggested, the Chairman of the U.N. Commission on Human Rights might also sit on the board and so too the President of the World Bank.

Under the governing board, there might be a number of standing committees concerned with various elements of the program. One such committee that it would seem particularly important to establish would be a food aid policy review committee, which would assume the oversight functions now performed by the Committee on Food Aid Policies and Programs of the World Food Program. That is, it would oversee the provision of all food aid administered by the UNBSP, it would regularly review bilateral food aid programs, and it would promote coordination between the two, continuing to work to improve food aid policy guidelines.

Perhaps it would also be desirable to establish a consultative committee of those private voluntary organizations that provide emergency and other international assistance to basic-needs-oriented programs. Such organizations include Oxfam, Catholic Relief Services, and CARE. Some of these programs, Oxfam being the notable exception, have been criticized in the recent past for well-intentioned but inappropriately designed assistance efforts. To establish a consultative committee, drawn from these organizations and from a representative group of recipient countries and chaired by the executive director of the UNBSP, might serve to make humanitarian, non-governmental aid more effective, might help to coordinate the activities of the voluntary organizations with the enhanced intergovernmental effort to meet essential needs, and might help to foster the development of non-governmental service organizations in developing countries.

* * *

To summarize: a new United Nations Basic Support Program would be formed out of a merger of UNICEF, the World Food Program, and UNDRO. It would take over the functions of the United Nations Fund for Population Activities and assume part of the financing and coordination of the technical assistance work done by the United Nations Development Program. The new agency would be sharply focused on the problems of those in extreme need. It would give help in emergencies, provide grants on a matching basis to poor countries prepared to undertake programs providing certain specified basic goods and services to the poorest groups in their societies, and it would organize and oversee the carrying out of a few internationally accepted "global tasks," ideally, in the 1980s, a major attack on starvation and acute malnutrition and the eradication of certain diseases. These "global tasks" would be financed in a new way by some form of global tax. So, too, would disaster relief. The basic support grants would be financed by assessments on all members of the United Nations using a formula based on capacity to pay.

All the activities of the UNBSP would entail reciprocal sets of obligations and responsibilities. Resources would be made available for certain agreed purposes, and they would be used for these clearly defined specific purposes. A program that met the criteria for support would be financed almost automatically, but this "automaticity" would be matched by adequate provision of information, the acceptance of audit procedures, and recognition that programs would be cut if abused.

Perhaps some will object that this narrowly defined basic support program is too limited a concept. Others may fear it will produce a kind of "welfare dependence" on a global scale. If it were to stand alone, the first objection would be valid; and, perhaps, if undertaken on a far more massive scale than here proposed, the second might be cause for concern. Except for a limited emergency relief function, there really ought to be nothing permanent about a global basic support program. But something along the lines we have described above seems an appropriate global response to the problem of "absolute" poverty in the decade or so ahead. It would relieve misery, but it would not provide the kind of assistance needed to ensure a permanent escape from mass poverty—that is a function of the process of development. To assist that process, not only are other forms of resource transfers needed, so, too, are changes in the institutional arrangements governing trade, investment, and the management of money.

FIVE

Trade and Production

UNRESOLVED ISSUES AND NEW PROBLEMS

The sudden, sharp increase in energy prices, turmoil in the money markets, high levels of unemployment, the little-understood phenomenon of stagflation, and a general expectation that economic recovery, when it came, would not mean a return to the high growth rates experienced by the old industrial countries in the fifties and sixties formed the backdrop for the most elaborate and ambitious set of multilateral trade negotiations (MTN) yet attempted. Judged against that background, the "Tokyo Round" (or the MTN) must be counted a success. But if the results are tested against the needs of the next decade or so, the judgment must be a rather more qualified one, for the negotiations failed to settle, and in some cases failed even to touch, some of the most troublesome questions that confront, or will soon confront, the international community in the fields of trade and of production.[1]

[1] It is far from clear how many countries will, in the end, subscribe to the agreements reached. Representatives of only 23 of the 99 countries that participated in the negotiations signed the procès-verbal in April, 1979, which marked the end of the major part of the negotiations. Of the LDCs, only the representative of Argentina signed at that time. The rest postponed the decision whether or not to recommend the agreements to their governments for approval until negotiations on the unsettled points, such as safeguards, had been concluded. Much dissatisfaction with the outcome of the MTN was voiced by the LDCs at the UNCTAD V session in Manila, which took place immediately after the formal conclusion of the MTN.

Not all the inadequacies of the MTN can be ascribed to the unpropitious economic climate in which they were held. Confusion, uncertainty, and deep differences of view existed about the objectives being sought, about the norms that should underlie international rule-making, and about the institutional arrangements needed to assist government to pursue these objectives and to encourage compliance with agreed rules and procedures. Even after five years of arduous negotiations, wide differences of view still exist. And this lack of consensus, among the old industrialized countries as well as between them and the LDCs, casts doubt on the claims which have been made that, as a result of the agreements reached in the MTN, the GATT has been modernized and made responsive to the needs of the next decade.

A fairer judgment might be that the negotiations helped brake the retreat into protectionism that was everywhere apparent during the mid-1970s, produced some useful further reductions in tariffs so that by the end of the eighties few of the tariffs of the old industrial countries will be important barriers to trade, and began—but only began—the difficult process of rule-making (both procedural and substantive) for controlling a number of non-tariff barriers, most importantly subsidies and government procurement procedures. The negotiations also sought to bring under better multilateral surveillance the resort by governments to safeguard action, and also tried to make the dispute-settlement machinery of the GATT more effective. As the negotiations ended, pessimists predicted that the new codes would remain largely dead letters, and that the net effect of the long debates over safeguards would not be to strengthen GATT control but to give governments greater freedom in restricting unwanted imports.[2] It is to be hoped that they will be proved wrong. Only time will tell whether the agreements reached on these matters will result in any appreciable change in government actions.[3]

[2]As of the summer of 1980, no agreement had been reached on the safeguards issue.

[3]This is not the place for a detailed assessment of the particular strengths, weaknesses, achievements, and failures of the Tokyo Round. For a balanced

Despite the fact that the results fell short of the needs, the immediate tasks are to consolidate the progress that was made in the negotiations and to breathe life into the new codes. But the process of thinking through the kinds of arrangements that should be sought at the global level must be a continuing one, not one that ends with the winding-up of the negotiations. For even on optimistic assumptions, the problems of the next decade have been broached, not solved, by the MTN. Before appreciable further progress can be made, a broader consensus than today exists must be found on two interrelated clusters of issues: the first is the cluster of issues having to do with the need to find ways to incorporate the LDCs more fully into a global trading system which they accept as both responsive to their needs and requiring certain obligations on their part; the second is the cluster of problems associated with the process of structural change and of moving to new patterns of international trade and production. Disagreements on these issues were posing difficulties well before the recent multilateral trade negotiations. They constantly bedeviled the negotiations, and they were left unsettled by the negotiations. Cutting across both sets of issues and adding to the difficulties of finding solutions are several developments which complicate the handling of almost all problems considered in this book: the increased demands being placed on governments; the increased involvement of governments—even those of the most "free market" economies—in economic decision-making; the growing reality of a closed economic system with feed-back effects; and the fact that political and social structures do not, in most cases, coincide with the economic dimensions of problems because few countries come close to being optimum economic areas.[4]

---

appraisal, see Robert E. Baldwin, *The Multilateral Trade Negotiations: Towards Greater Liberalization?* American Enterprise Institute: Washington, 1979.

[4]For a discussion of optimum economic areas, see Richard N. Cooper, "Worldwide vs. Regional Integration: Is There an Optimum Size of the Integrated Area?" in Fritz Machlup (ed.), *Economic Integration World-Wide, Regional, Sectoral,* Macmillan: London, 1976.

The Less Developed Countries

"Trade not aid" first became a popular slogan in the latter days of the Marshall Plan when the European countries, with their industries largely rebuilt after the devastation of the war, found tariffs and other restrictions hampering their exports to the United States. In the 1960s, it reappeared as a slogan of the Group of 77. In some respects, it is a misleading slogan, for most of the developing countries need both. The poorest developing countries require continuing assistance in the form of grants, and most of the rest need large amounts of credit on favorable terms for as far into the future as it is profitable to look. But reliable access to the markets of the rich is, without question, a central need of the developing countries, whether they be producers of raw materials, of competitive manufactured goods, or of food and agricultural products—not only tropical products, like coffee and cocoa, but also sugar and processed meat that compete with production in the rich countries.

The strong emphasis that many LDCs gave for a time to policies of import substitution as the high road to development has almost everywhere now been somewhat modified. Today, much stress is laid on the need for international arrangements which would enable the developing countries to exploit their comparative advantage in the production of many raw materials and of manufactures with high inputs of relatively unskilled labor and which would result in a "better" or "fairer" international division of labor. Less is heard today about the desirability of "decoupling" or "delinking." Even the more extreme developing-country advocates of a policy of collective self-reliance would probably admit that "delinking" and cutting their economies off from world markets was, in economic terms, a second-best policy, albeit one which accords with their rather bleak views of the inherent tendency of the strong to take advantage of the weak.[5]

The importance of trade and the gains the developing coun-

---

[5]For a discussion of LDC views and an appraisal of the costs and benefits of "delinking," see the essay by Carlos F. Diaz-Alejandro, in *Rich and Poor Nations in the World Economy*, by Albert Fishlow et al., McGraw-Hill, for the Council on Foreign Relations/1980s Project: New York, 1978.

tries could anticipate from better access to world markets have been convincingly demonstrated by numerous recent studies. What the World Bank now calls the "middle-income developing countries" and the OECD calls the "newly industrializing countries" (NICs) have the most to gain from lower tariffs and better access, particularly for manufactured products, although many of the poorest developing countries would gain substantially from a relaxation of the restrictions on imports of textiles and clothing, from the elimination of tariffs on processed raw materials, and also from more stable prices of raw materials.[6]

Within the developed countries, little disagreement exists with the general principle that developing countries must not merely be allowed, but frequently positively helped, to sell in world markets if they are to pay for essential imports and to generate the savings needed for investment. But practice lags well behind, and controversy and difficulties arise when efforts are made to translate the widely accepted principles of fair prices, equal access, and reliable markets into specific policies. Moreover, much of the LDC pressure during the last decade or so has been directed less to obtaining fair or equal treatment and rather more to securing various kinds of special treatment. Sometimes the argument has been that more advantageous arrangements were required to offset market dominance by established industries in the rich countries or to compensate for weaknesses in the developing countries, that is, a kind of generalized "infant industry" argument. Sometimes the argument has been that special treatment was "owed" the LDCs as compensation for patterns of dependency in trade and production that were often the legacy of the colonial era. Sometimes the argument has been the purely pragmatic one that special trade advantages or higher prices of various kinds are often easier for governments to provide than are substantial grants.

Pressure from the LDCs for better treatment for their exports

[6]For some general orders of magnitude, see the *World Development Report, 1978*, published in August, 1978, by the IBRD, and the essay by Albert Fishlow in *Rich and Poor Nations in the World Economy*, op. cit. See also Robert McNamara's *Address* to the United Nations Conference on Trade and Development, Manila, May 10, 1979.

has centered partly on issues connected with trade in commodities, partly on the nature of the rules governing trade generally. It is worth looking briefly at the state of the debate in each of these two main areas, the arrangements that have recently been reached in each of these areas, and the problems that now seem likely to be uppermost during the next decade or so.

Commodities

For many years the commodities debate was the lightning rod for a host of LDC grievances and, in particular, for claims that both the rules of the international economic system and the way the system operated were biased against them. For a time, much emphasis was placed on the terms-of-trade argument, that is, the contention that the raw materials which made up the bulk of the LDC exports were constantly becoming cheaper than the manufactured goods they needed to import. The terms-of-trade argument lost much of its force with the steep rise in the prices of many raw materials in the early seventies and with the publication of a study on the terms of trade, specifically commissioned by the UNCTAD, which, essentially, returned a verdict of "not proven."[7] But the argument that markets for raw materials were distorted and prices kept artificially low by arrangements inherited from the colonial past, by weaknesses in bargaining power inherent in periphery-center relationships, by the operations of multinational enterprises, or by other forces continued with unabated fervor. In the case of many LDCs, excessive dependence on a few raw material exports was undeniable. So, too, was the hardship caused by wildly fluctuating prices, and so was the fact that the roots of overreliance on a few exports frequently lay in the colonial past. But strong specific cases tended to be generalized beyond the facts. Many of the remedies proposed by the LDCs were designed not simply, or in some cases not even primarily, to deal with the widely acknowledged problems of fluctuating prices and excessive dependence, but rather to secure a greater transfer of real resources from the rich countries to the

[7]UNCTAD, Expert Group on Indexation, "Summary of Main Conclusions," Geneva, 1975. (Mimeographed.)

poor countries. And, too often, there was little regard for the disadvantages that introducing fresh distortions into the market might entail. For a time, there was hope on the part of some producers and fear on the part of some consumers that the example of the OPEC would be widely followed. In a few cases (e.g., bauxite), prices were pushed up by producer cooperation, but the scope for producer cartels was extremely limited, and both the hopes and the fears were fairly short-lived.

There are real problems for both sides in the commodities debate. Markets are imperfect. Prices fluctuate too widely. Overdependence is indisputable. Uncertainties about access to needed supplies and unacceptable conditions on investment required to ensure adequate global production of certain raw materials are also real problems.[8] But neither side in the commodities debate has conducted itself as sensibly as it might have done. For too long there was too much emotion, too much suspicion, too much clinging to doctrine, too little dispassionate examination of the facts, and too little willingness to separate the many different issues that tended to be bundled together.

Although far too long was spent in shadow-boxing, the main lines of a compromise on what had come to be the central issue in the debate—the establishment of a Common Fund—finally emerged. And, in the spring of 1980, agreement was reached on the objectives, financial structure, and organization of the Common Fund. It will have two quite different kinds of financing function. In the first place, it will contribute to the financing of buffer-stock arrangements where international commodity agreements designed to stabilize prices through buffer-stock arrangements can be negotiated. In the second place, it will have a "second account" or "window" which will help finance other kinds of measures designed to improve the production and marketing of commodities of particular interest to the LDCs and which will also help promote diversification schemes and the de-

---

[8]For a useful discussion of commodity problems, see the study by Rachel McCulloch and José Pinera, "Alternative Commodity Trade Regimes," in Ruth W. Arad et al., *Sharing Global Resources,* McGraw-Hill, for the Council on Foreign Relations/1980s Project: New York, 1979.

velopment of processing industries. According to the draft articles of agreement, the Fund, once established, will be brought into the United Nations as a new specialized agency.

With the establishment of the Fund, some of the steam and acrimony should go out of the debate. However, the compromises that have been made do not reflect a real meeting of minds, and it seems clear that there will be a continuing struggle between the LDCs which want to expand the scope and mandate of the Fund and the industrialized countries which want to confine it quite narrowly to the financing of stocking arrangements and to a rather limited range of "second window" activities.

The LDCs, strongly encouraged by the UNCTAD Secretariat, have looked to the establishment of the Common Fund as the way to meet far more of the wide array of problems they have identified as "commodity problems" than the Fund will, in fact, be able to do much about. The Fund's establishment and a new willingness on the part of the industrialized countries to examine stabilization arrangements with a more open mind may result in the negotiation of a few more commodity stabilization agreements.[9] The number of commodities for which stabilization agreements are practicable, however, is quite limited. Moreover, many "commodity problems," although real problems, are not truly "commodity" problems but aspects of wider and more general issues. Some, as we indicated, are actually part of the larger question of development but became identified as commodity problems because of the overdependence of a few countries on a few commodities. Others are really aspects of broader trading problems: difficulties arising from tariff structures that bear unevenly on raw materials or products at an early stage of processing; difficulties arising from arrangements (formal or informal) that limit access to markets; and difficulties arising from the domination of markets by established producers or multinational concerns in ways which mean that small or un-

---

[9]Four international commodity agreements, of various types, are now in existence: cocoa, rubber, sugar, and tin. An agreement on tea seems probable. However, negotiations on a new wheat agreement have broken down, and both the cocoa and the sugar agreements are in difficulties.

skilled producers need special help to compete. Many of these issues are important, and ones that are now not satisfactorily dealt with by today's trading rules. But it is in changes in the general trade regime, not in special commodity arrangements, that the remedies lie.[10]

Trade Rules

For many years, the LDCs have argued that the central trading rules of the international economic system, as embodied principally in the GATT, were designed to meet the needs of the rich, industrial countries and were biased against developing countries. It is, of course, true that the GATT was mainly drafted by the advanced industrialized countries to serve their own needs. Although a number of developing countries, in particular India, and some Latin American countries (e.g., Brazil, Chile, Cuba), took an active part in the postwar negotiations on international trade arrangements, many of today's LDCs were not yet independent states and played no part in the negotiations. The countries most interested in trade rules and carrying the most weight in the negotiations were, inevitably, those countries with the highest level of trade. And the need that was uppermost in the minds of those who drafted the postwar rules was to guard against a recurrence of the beggar-my-neighbor policies pursued

[10]The original charter for an International Trade Organization contained a chapter on commodity agreements which was not included in the GATT. This omission has been much criticized by the LDCs over the years. Whether or not the controversies over commodities that have characterized the past decade would have been much different had that chapter been retained is doubtful. For, although inclusion of the chapter was an explicit recognition of the fact that the production and trade arrangements in primary commodities posed special problems that might at times call for special commodity arrangements, the tone of the article strongly reflected the U.S. views of the time. These were extremely skeptical of the wisdom of commodity agreements, and the articles laid down conditions for safeguarding the interests of consumers, for encouraging rapid adaptation on the part of producers, and for limiting the life of any agreements. See Clair Wilcox, *A Charter for World Trade,* The Macmillan Company: New York, 1949. For an account of the on-again, off-again discussion of commodity arrangements within the GATT, see John H. Jackson, *World Trade and the Law of the GATT,* Bobbs-Merrill: New York, 1969.

by the industrialized countries during much of the interwar period.

At the time it was drafted, the GATT was assumed to be a temporary arrangement which would soon be superseded by the more far-reaching Charter for an International Trade Organization administered by a new specialized agency, the ITO. The commercial policy section of the proposed charter was substantially reproduced in the GATT, although a few special provisions secured by the developing countries during the Havana negotiations on the charter were not included in the GATT.[11] Moreover, and of more importance, many of the chapters of the charter that dealt with issues of concern to the developing countries, such as those on commodities, foreign investment, and restrictive business practices, disappeared when the ITO was sunk by the U.S. Congress. Instead of a comprehensive organization, and one in

---

[11]The relationship between the GATT and the Havana Charter for an International Trade Organization is a somewhat complicated one. The GATT was, essentially, a framework for the first postwar multilateral tariff negotiations which took place in Geneva in 1947 before the negotiations on the charter were concluded in March 1948. The trade rules in the GATT were based on *Proposals* negotiated between the United States and the United Kingdom during the war. These *Proposals* also formed the basis of the commercial policy section of the suggested charter which was put forward by the United States and served as the basis for successive rounds of negotiations on the ITO. At the Havana Conference (which came after the first round of tariff negotiations), the LDCs were in a majority. Very few of them, by contrast, took part in the first round of tariff negotiations at which the GATT rule-system was, in effect, accepted. Many of the proposals put forward by the LDCs at the Havana Conference (some of which were accepted, some of which were rejected) foreshadowed demands that reappeared later on in the context of the NIEO. Among the relatively few *commercial policy* provisions included in the charter but not reproduced in the GATT was Article XV which permitted discriminatory preferences among developing countries. See Robert E. Hudec, *The GATT Legal System and World Trade Diplomacy*, Praeger: New York, 1975, p. 49. A similar article was, however, added to the GATT in 1965. For useful accounts of the early negotiations on the charter and on the GATT, see Karin Koch, *International Trade Policy and the GATT, 1947–1967*, Almquist and Wiksell: Stockholm, 1969; and William A. Brown, Jr., *The United States and the Restoration of World Trade*, The Brookings Institution: Washington, 1950.

which agreement to rather strict commercial policy provisions had been balanced by somewhat less strict but nevertheless normatively important undertakings in other fields, all that remained was that part which had, from the start, been of most interest to the United States, Canada, and the highly industrialized countries in Western Europe and which these countries had done the most to shape.

How differently things would have turned out had the ITO been established is one of those "what would have happened if" questions that can never be answered. The fact that the GATT was only one part of a larger conception was later to play its part in the LDC view that the GATT was an inadequate instrument and unresponsive to their needs.

At the time the GATT was drafted, little real examination had been made anywhere of the nature of the links between trade arrangements and development, and charges of inadequacy and unresponsiveness are hard to refute. But the assertion that the GATT rules are biased against the developing countries is rather less well-founded. One of the most detailed studies that has been made of the charge of bias in the GATT concluded, in effect, that most of the bias stems not from the rules but from the ways in which the rules have been evaded and the way requests for exceptions and safeguard actions have been handled, or, too frequently, not handled.[12] In addition, the LDCs claim, and many impartial analysts share their view, that any system that puts its faith essentially in the market and in free trade will have a systematic bias in the distribution of benefits, favoring the powerful industrial exporters of the center and disadvantaging the weak producers of raw materials at the periphery.[13]

Because of the weaknesses and the biases they have seen in

[12]See Jackson, op. cit., pp. 663–671. Part of his argument is that disputes have been settled essentially by diplomatic negotiations rather than by legal processes, and this inevitably favors those with more bargaining power.

[13]For discussions of this thesis, see the essay by Albert Fishlow in the 1980s Project book, *Rich and Poor Nations in the World Economy*, and Harry G. Johnson, *Economic Policies Toward Less Developed Countries*, Allen and Unwin: London, 1967.

the GATT, the LDCs have, right from the beginning, sought special arrangements of two main kinds. They have pressed, in the first place, for release from the two central commitments of the GATT, that is, the general rule of non-discrimination and the principle of reciprocity, and, in the second place, for preferential treatment of various kinds. Much has been done to respond to these demands. From the start, the "infant industry" argument for protection was accepted, and, ever since the early sixties, the LDCs have received the benefits of most-favored-nation (m-f-n) tariff reductions without being required to offer reciprocal concessions. Preferential arrangements among the LDCs have been permitted despite the provisions of Articles I and XXIV, which, theoretically at least, require that any special tariff-cutting arrangement among subgroups of GATT members must take the form of a free trade area or customs union. And a waiver was also agreed upon to "legalize" one of the main achievements of the UNCTAD, namely, the adoption by the European Community, the United States, Canada, Japan, and a few other industrial countries of a general system of special preferences (GSP) for the developing countries.

During the Tokyo Round, the LDCs, strongly led by Brazil, sought to gain firmer recognition of the legitimacy of these "special and differential" forms of treatment and to extend their scope. As a result, not only were special provisions for the LDCs incorporated in the codes on subsidies and government procurement, but a general "enabling clause" was also adopted which recognized tariff and non-tariff preferential treatment in favor of LDCs as a permanent legal feature of the world trading system, not, as it had been previously, an exceptional arrangement permitted by virtue of a waiver.[14]

Somewhat ironically, this more explicit acceptance of the right to "special and differential" treatment has coincided with a growing realization that the LDCs were not particularly far-sighted in putting quite so much emphasis on obtaining special treatment. Not only have the results been disappointing, but the approach has had some positive disadvantages, and such bar-

[14]See GATT, *Press Release,* 1234, April 12, 1979.

gaining power as the LDCs possess might better have been used to obtain firmer guarantees of access. The results of the GSP have been quite limited either because many "sensitive" items—that is, products like textiles and shoes which the LDCs were most interested in but which competed directly with domestic production in the industrialized countries—have been excluded from the lists of goods accorded preferential treatment or because the amounts let in at preferential rates have been subject to quantitative limits. In many lines, the LDCs do not need preferences for their goods to be competitive. What matters far more are the reactions of the industrialized countries when LDC products are too successful in penetrating markets—the textile agreements, voluntary export controls, and "orderly marketing arrangements." Moreover, emphasis on obtaining and preserving preferential tariff margins has tended to make the LDCs less interested than they might otherwise have been in the lowering of the m-f-n rates on their principal products, again something which in the long term is of more importance to them.[15]

Similarly, although the fact that the LDCs have received tariff concessions without having had to make reciprocal reductions in their own tariffs has undoubtedly been of advantage to them, there have been some drawbacks as well. One of the disadvantages has been that, given the nature of tariff bargaining, the tariffs that have been lowered the most have frequently not been the ones in which the LDCs were most interested. This has fed their feeling that the "system" is biased against them.[16] Because most developing countries tend to buy all the imports that their availability of foreign exchange permits, the advanced industrialized countries probably have lost very little, if anything, by waiving the reciprocity requirement, as Harry Johnson pointed out long ago.[17] The result has been rather to make the LDCs less

[15]William R. Cline et al., *Trade Negotiations in the Tokyo Round: A Quantitative Assessment*, The Brookings Institution: Washington, 1978.

[16]Apart from the fact that tariff negotiations have inevitably tended to center on those tariffs where there were bargains to be made, it is true, and has been widely recognized, that the structure of tariffs has tended to be biased against the processing of raw materials in the country of origin.

[17]Johnson, op. cit. The same point was also made by Cline, op. cit.

effective participants in the negotiating process. Another disadvantage has been that many of the LDCs have maintained levels of protection that are far higher and less selective than they should be in their own economic interest, with the result that costs are inflated, inefficiencies protected, and the production of unessential luxury goods stimulated. It has also made it more difficult for other LDCs to sell to them, thus running counter to the general LDC goal of more "collective self-reliance."

Clearly, a case exists for special rules to apply to the trade of developing countries, but the past practice of the LDCs claiming and the developed countries eventually agreeing to wholesale exceptions from the rules of the GATT has not been in the long-term interest of either group. The question of the rules that should apply to LDC trade—both to trade between them and developed countries and to their trade with one another—needs to be addressed directly. It is in everyone's interest that the LDCs should be brought progressively into the central system of trade rules, undertaking obligations to greater freedom of trade as their development proceeds. But if the LDCs are to accept such obligations, the system must be one they feel is responsive to their needs. That is not the situation today, and, during the MTN, attempts to obtain LDC agreement to various forms of "graduation" in return for the explicit acceptance of the legitimacy of their claims to special and differential treatment came to very little.[18]

The Decline in the GATT's Effectiveness

It was the widespread recognition that the authority of the GATT had eroded and that countries everywhere were turning

---

[18]The following very general statement was adopted as part of the "Framework" report, but it is in such general terms and, as of the time of writing, has been endorsed by so few LDCs that it seems unlikely to have much force: "Less-developed contracting parties expect that their capacity to make contributions or negotiated concessions or take mutually agreed action under the provisions and procedures of the General Agreement would improve with the progressive development of their economies and improvement in their trade situation, and they would accordingly expect to participate more fully in the framework of rights and obligations under the General Agreement." MTN/FR/W/20/Rev.2.

to new forms of protection as they faced the new problems of the seventies that lay behind the decision in 1973 to undertake the Tokyo Round. And it was fear of the consequences of a break-down and the prospect of a return to the trade wars and economic anarchy of the thirties that led the key countries to make enough concessions to one another so that the negotiations could finally be brought to a reasonably successful conclusion six years later.

In the fifties and early sixties, the GATT had been a remarkably successful and very cost-effective international organization. But by the end of the sixties, its decline was well under way. GATT rules increasingly tended to be applied only in the easy cases. When an industry was in serious trouble, the remedy was sought outside that framework. No international judgment was brought to bear, and no international appraisal was made of the actions taken to safeguard an industry to see whether they bore disproportionately on outsiders or whether they accorded with the larger purpose of moving toward a distribution of international production that responded either to comparative advantage (efficiency) or to what might be called global welfare requirements (equity). Too often, only national interests were considered, and, frequently, these interests were calculated too narrowly and in too short a time perspective.

Sometimes the remedies employed should have come within the purview of the GATT, but countries were unwilling to have their actions subjected to the tests and conditions of the Agreement.[19] At other times, the remedies took the form of subsidies, tax concessions, privileged forms of government procurement, and other similar devices for which no adequate rules or codes of conduct existed.

[19]The main safeguard provision in the GATT is Article XIX which, inter alia, provides that any action to control imports must be taken on a non-discriminatory basis. This article was one of the main points of contention in the MTN. The European Community, in particular, argued that only if the article could be applied selectively to the country or countries whose exports were causing the problem would it be possible to bring the resort to safeguard action under effective international surveillance. The LDCs resisted selective application and were only prepared to contemplate it under stricter international controls than the Community was prepared to accept.

The decline in strict adherence to the rules of the GATT and the widespread resort to non-tariff measures of various kinds had many causes. The spectacular success of the Japanese in capturing markets in the other industrialized countries originally prompted many of the new forms of protectionism. The formation of the European Common Market and the subsequent snowballing of preferential trading arrangements removed much trade from the purview of the GATT and contributed to the decline in its authority. The severe recession, "stagflation," and high levels of unemployment that characterized the industrialized world in the mid-1970s further strained an already weakened system. In those years, although a massive retreat to protectionism was avoided through the collective exercise of good sense, many measures were taken to restrict imports and to promote exports in attempts to safeguard employment and to find, once again, the magic recipe of export-led growth.

The decline in the effectiveness of the GATT as a rule-making and rule-enforcing institution reflected, at bottom, the growing dissensus among its members about the objectives the system should foster. The "old GATT" had been remarkably successful because, for a decade or so, the commercial policy guidance it provided was consistent with the goals of its major members, and the "philosophy" behind the GATT, which had evolved during a series of wartime discussions and postwar negotiations, was still very much a part of the intellectual formation of the officials who did most of the negotiating with one another within the GATT. There was a strong element of continuity between those who had written the rules and those who were then charged with negotiating within that framework. Words acquired special meanings; compliance with rules meant observing the spirit of the rule, not simply its legal form; and those responsible for GATT affairs within governments frequently found it both easier and more comfortable to deal with their counterparts from other governments than with those representing other interests within their own government. The "old GATT" was a club, and, as in any club, there was far less loyalty to its conventions—written and unwritten—when its membership was trebled, particularly as the new members had not shared in the writing of the rules.[20]

The rise and fall of international organizations owes far more to personalities and to the chemistry at work in that amalgam of key governmental representatives and international officials that at any one time effectively constitutes "the organization" than most analyses would acknowledge. But the decline in the effectiveness of the GATT that was so apparent by the end of the sixties was not simply the result of the far different interplay of personalities and the expansion of the membership to include many new countries with new concerns and different attitudes. It reflected as well a very widespread feeling that the rules did not adequately respond to the situations that were posing the most acute problems to governments, including those which wrote the rules of the old regime.[21]

Despite their lack of enthusiasm for the GATT, a strict en-

[20]On the club-like atmosphere of the "old GATT," see Hudec, op. cit. The consensus on which the GATT approach to trade problems rested was probably never as complete as those who now look back with affection and nostalgia to the days of the "old GATT" tend to believe. Right from the start, there were governments (e.g., the French) which felt that the rules placed too much reliance on the market and tended to reflect a belief in freedom of trade as an end in itself and to pay insufficient attention to the need for a government to take measures to advance or protect the welfare of its people. And right from the start, there had been criticism from the LDCs that the GATT paid too little attention to their needs. But, partly because the early stages of trade liberalization were reasonably painless and partly because the rapid expansion of trade brought visible benefits all around, the criticisms were muted, and the system worked.

[21]The reluctance to resort to the dispute-settlement procedure provided by the GATT (Article XXIII) and the widespread avoidance of recourse to the formal procedures for invoking safeguard measures (Article XIX) and the adoption, instead, of measures such as "voluntary" export controls to limit imports were in large measure the result of this growing view that strict enforcement of the rules was not the right answer to many problems. For details, see Hudec, op. cit., and Gerard and Victoria Curzon, "The Management of Trade Relations in the GATT," in Andrew Shonfield and others, *International Economic Relations of the Western World, 1959–1971*, vol. I, Oxford University Press, for the Royal Institute of International Affairs: London, 1976.

forcement of its rules and the extension of GATT control to hitherto unregulated forms of protection would have been in the interest of the LDCs. But by the time the MTN was under way it was clear that the industrial countries themselves faced too many difficulties to make strengthening the GATT in these ways an easy task. Moreover, it was clear that the traditional, rather legalistic approach of the GATT and the focus on trade rules were likely to be an inadequate response not only to the needs of the LDCs but also to the most serious trade-related problems confronting the industrialized countries.

Structural Change

Much has been written about the new mercantilism and the rising tide of protectionism in the industrialized countries, and the daily press contains constant evidence of the multiplicity of devices by which governments today affect trade patterns.[22]

Trade-restricting measures other than tariffs and quotas became far more conspicuous as the tariffs of the industrialized countries were reduced to low levels in successive rounds of GATT negotiations and their quotas on trade largely eliminated; and the recent increased resort to protection has mostly taken the form of non-tariff measures. However, even had more protection from tariffs and quotas been available, and even had the expansion of the sixties continued, many of the measures that today hamper trade would be in force and creating problems, for the purpose behind them is often not merely, or even mainly, to protect the domestic producer from foreign competition but to induce him to do something that is socially desirable or believed to serve some broad national interest. Government contracts enable the aerospace industry to maintain high levels of research and development, special tax incentives encourage industries to locate in areas of high unemployment, and subsidies hasten the

[22]See, inter alia, Richard Blackhurst, Nicolas Marian, and Jan Tumlir, *Trade Liberalization, Protectionism, and Interdependence,* GATT Studies in International Trade, No. 5: Geneva, November, 1977; and Bahram Nowzad, *The Rise in Protectionism,* Pamphlet Series, No. 24, International Monetary Fund: Washington, 1978.

shift to less polluting forms of production. Because they are so central to the achievement of a government's domestic purpose of providing for the welfare and security of its own people, because their effect on trade or on the international location of industry is not infrequently an unintended by-product of the action, and because the protective effect is far more difficult to quantify than in the case of a tariff or a quota, trade-restricting and trade-distorting measures of these kinds are difficult to deal with internationally, and particularly hard to deal with by precise rules and automatic formulas. Sometimes the protective effect is fairly easily identified, and the traditional GATT approach of outlawing some kinds of measures, bargaining away others, and permitting compensatory action to offset others can be applied. But often it is difficult to isolate the element of protection. Frequently, even when the protective effect can be isolated, this approach misses much of the problem. For what is important is not simply the immediate damage done to the trade prospects of another country, it is the longer-term pattern of production that is being fostered or resisted.

Major efforts were made in the MTN to bring subsidies under better control: the Code on Subsidies and Countervailing Duties that was eventually agreed upon by most of the developed countries, and a few others, reflects the difficulties of trying to write precise rules or to agree on categories of domestic subsidies that should be presumptively outlawed. Instead, it places great reliance on consultative and dispute-settlement arrangements, procedures which can be set in motion whenever a signatory "has reason to believe that any subsidy is being granted or maintained by another signatory and that such subsidy either causes injury to its domestic industry, nullification or impairment of benefits accruing to it under the General Agreement, or serious prejudice to its interest . . . ."[23]

The prevalence of non-tariff measures of many kinds is, some-

---

[23]See Article 12 of the Agreement on the Interpretation and Application of Articles VI, XVI, and XXIII of the General Agreement on Tariffs and Trade. The new Code goes rather further in seeking to define and to outlaw *export* subsidies than it does in the case of domestic subsidies.

what paradoxically, both evidence of the process of encouraging and accommodating to the pressures for structural change and shifts in established patterns of production and also evidence of strong resistance to those pressures. It seems safe to predict that concern with structural change will be a dominant political issue during the next decade and that we face a long period of intellectual uncertainty and political controversy—nationally and internationally—about the kinds of change that would be desirable and about the methods that can best be used to promote, restrain, or accommodate to change.

"Structural growth policy" is the term used by Lincoln Gordon in a study done for the 1980s Project, and "industrial policy" is the term used by William Diebold in another Project book to cover much the same complex of non-cyclical, non-macroeconomic measures that are taken by governments to affect in more or less lasting ways the composition and location of economic activities.[24] Both authors see governments, even those of the most market-oriented countries, as already deeply involved in policy measures which sometimes deliberately, sometimes inadvertently, affect the structure of national economies; both identify factors that are likely to increase rather than to diminish governmental concern with structural problems; both point to the substantial spill-over effects policies of this kind have on other countries. And both authors conclude—indeed it is a central thesis of their books—that trouble lies ahead unless this international dimension is recognized more clearly and dealt with by new kinds of collective action.

It is worth noting that the two authors have come to their similar conclusions by different routes: Lincoln Gordon, by reflect-

[24]Lincoln Gordon, *Growth Policies and the International Order*, McGraw-Hill, for the Council on Foreign Relations/1980s Project: New York, 1979; William Diebold, Jr., *Industrial Policy as an International Issue*, McGraw-Hill, for the Council on Foreign Relations/1980s Project: New York, 1980. We have drawn heavily on both books in this section, in particular on Diebold's (which is more narrowly focused) rather than on Gordon's book (which is concerned as well with other aspects of growth questions). The Diebold book covers in far greater depth and with much subtlety the trade-related issues we touch on very cursorily.

ing on problems of growth, William Diebold, on problems of trade. Reflections on many different issues—growth, trade, development, energy, population, the environment—have led many people to the conclusion that structural changes are required if today's and tomorrow's problems are to be met. Indeed, the emphasis on the structural nature of many problems is in some danger of becoming today's cliché and, worse, an excuse for inaction. Frequently, the emphasis is on the need for and difficulty of structural changes within a given economy. At other times—and particularly in the context of the North-South dialogue—the emphasis is on the need for shifts in the distribution of production on a global scale. Sometimes the emphasis is on the need for change on an intermediate scale: the continuing search by the European Community for common industrial policies is evidence both of the belief in the need for shifts in production patterns within the Community and of the difficulties governments have in accepting the consequences of such shifts. And, in a slightly different way, the growing OECD interest in the industrial policies adopted by its members reflects concern with the impact on the OECD countries, as a group, of action or inaction by any of its members, as well as concern that slowness in adjusting, or ill-considered forms of adjustment, will adversely affect the economic prospects of the particular member state.

Structural changes in national economies are, of course, constantly taking place. Change is necessary to growth, and, in turn, much change can usually be absorbed without great difficulty if economies are growing.[25] Much of the recent preoccupation with the need for and the problems of structural change has been a by-product of the recession of the mid-1970s and the widespread expectation that slower rates of growth are likely to remain the norm in the industrialized world. There are many reasons for the widespread expectation of slower growth, some related to shifts in the composition of production (e.g., away from manufacturing

---

[25]On the other hand, if economies are growing, inefficiencies are less serious than they are in periods of slow growth. Some of the OECD work suggests that the very prosperity of the fifties and sixties tended to obscure the need for structural change.

and toward services), some related to energy problems and environmental constraints, and probably rather more reasons related to new social attitudes and concerns.[26] How durable these factors will prove to be is a matter of dispute. But, for the present, the fact of several years of stagnation and the general expectation that today's slow growth will set the pattern for the future make governments more interventionist and more ready to take industrial policy measures—both of a stimulative and of a defensive kind—than they were in the more expansionist sixties.[27] There is more interest in trying to identify and to stimulate investment in new growth industries, but there is also more concern with shielding weak industries from competition, saving lame ducks, and taking measures of various kinds to deal with or to forestall threats of overcapacity.

Slow growth, high levels of unemployment, and the difficulties the industrial countries have been experiencing throughout the seventies in running their own highly interdependent economies simply by relying on the macroeconomic policies that

[26]See discussion in Chapter 2 of Gordon, op. cit.

[27]Definitions are a problem, and readers are urged to see the discussion in the Diebold book, op. cit., particularly Chapter 1, from which the following quotation is taken:

"The link between structural change and industrial policies is that the latter are primarily concerned with maintaining the structure or with changing it one way rather than another. Much of the time—probably most of the time—industrial policy measures are efforts to resist structural changes that would otherwise take place, as when a new and cheaper producer appears in the world to displace former suppliers. Sometimes the aim is to induce change, as when a country wishes to become more industrial and less agricultural or wants to produce technologically advanced products instead of those using lower skills. Sometimes the two are combined, as when a country seeks to develop new industries to replace those in which it is no longer competitive while protecting the latter against the full blasts of foreign competition until new jobs and alternative uses of other resources can be found.

Although the distinctions may not always be sharp and clear, it is helpful to think of industrial policies as divided into three categories.

Those that are *defensive* are mainly concerned with keeping in being some structural arrangement, such as domestic production of certain goods that would not survive international competition or a given pattern of employment. They often resist change by limiting imports or subsidizing domestic activities

served them so well for most of the post-war period have undoubtedly been the major reasons these countries have lately resorted so widely to measures designed to affect the process of structural change—and usually to help resist pressures for change or to slow its pace.

Home-grown problems compounded by the energy situation have accounted for the lion's share of the structural adjustment difficulties that the industrial countries have faced. But much attention has recently been focused on the pressures coming from outside the OECD and OPEC areas, in particular, from a handful of new industrial countries: Taiwan, Hong Kong, Singapore, South Korea, Brazil, Mexico. Various studies done by international organizations and in several Western European countries have demonstrated that, thus far, the closure of plants or displacement of workers in established industries by imports from these countries has been quite small and far less than that which occurs "naturally" as a consequence of technological change.[28] Nevertheless, partly because competition from new sources is always a politically easy scapegoat, partly because,

---

in one way or another. It is often not clear whether a defensive policy will be pursued for a long time because its purpose is a lasting one (such as national security) or is more likely to give way or erode when economic and political circumstances change (as happens in some cases of simple protectionism).

Adaptive policies facilitate structural change by helping to shift resources to new uses that do not require protection or subsidy or by increasing efficiency in existing lines of activity. Simply permitting market forces to work is an adaptive policy; so too is help to injured workers and communities if this makes the change politically and socially acceptable. Such a policy may have defensive elements, as when imports are slowed down during a transitional period, but its purpose is to dispense with these elements before too long.

The third type of industrial policy *initiates change* rather than simply responding to it. This is what governments do when they have programs of economic development for the country as a whole or certain parts of it and when they seek to become producers of goods or services not formerly made at home." Pp. 7–8.

[28]See, in particular, "The Impact of the Newly Industrializing Countries on Production and Trade in Manufactures," Report by the Secretary-General, OECD: Paris, 1979. The NICs covered by this study were the six listed above and Spain, Portugal, Greece, and Yugoslavia.

although the overall effects have thus far been minimal, the competition has borne on a few particularly vulnerable industries, and mainly because, whatever the past record may show, the problem is clearly one that will grow with time, the structural adjustments that competition from imports from these countries (and other developing countries in the years to come) are likely to entail has generally been seen throughout the industrial world as a major threat.

The protectionist response that has thus far been all too evident points to serious trouble, but it is right that attention should now focus on the structural consequences of the needs of the developing countries for markets. As one looks ahead, it is difficult to see how the developing countries are to industrialize (which in most cases they must do if living standards are to rise to satisfactory levels) unless structural changes in today's patterns of production do occur. Barring some unforeseen cataclysm, adjusting to the trade needs of the LDCs and learning to live with high-cost energy are likely to be *the* big structural adjustments of the next few decades.

If the new codes on non-tariff barriers agreed to in the MTN do in fact lead to more intergovernmental discussion and to a greater willingness to adjust policies when injury can be demonstrated, a useful start will have been made on a large and many-faceted problem. But even on a very optimistic estimate of what might be built on the new codes, the "GATT approach," with its focus on trade effects and its reliance on quasi-legal remedies, is unlikely to be adequate to deal with the central issues: how to identify and encourage the shifts in production patterns that need to take place in the next decade; how to minimize the costs of adjustment; and how to share the costs of adjustment and of non-adjustment. Permitting a countervailing duty to offset a subsidy may discourage the resort to a subsidy, and it can offset a distortion. But an approach that is essentially limited to freeing trade and making it fairer does not embrace a wide enough range of those policies that affect the location and character of industry to deal as adequately as will be necessary with problems of structural change.

The OECD has also dipped its toes in these deep and murky

waters. The approach it has taken goes further, in some ways, than does that of the GATT in that it has sought not simply to keep trade channels as open as possible but also to encourage its member countries to resist defensive industrial policies and to adopt what it calls "positive adjustment policies." Acting on a Secretariat initiative, the Council of the OECD adopted, in June, 1978, a far-reaching set of "orientations" to guide governments in responding to calls for help from industries finding themselves in difficulties.[29] During the following year, various OECD committees discussed the "orientations" and tried to refine and to agree upon the somewhat elusive concept of "positive adjustment." And in June, 1979, the Council, prodded once again by the Secretariat, reaffirmed the need for "positive adjustment" and agreed on a two-year program of work.[30]

Although the declarations adopted by the Council and the reports and statements by Secretary-General van Lennep and other OECD officials have stressed that "positive adjustment" was needed to promote and sustain faster economic growth in the member countries, neither the Secretariat nor the member countries have been unaware of the need to accommodate more imports from the LDCs. But the emphasis in the OECD context has been on resisting measures that would, over time, tend to slow growth in the member countries, not, primarily, on the wider and longer-term problem of how to adjust to new patterns of global production. A few of the NICs have been invited to become members of some of the OECD industry committees examining sectors like steel and ship-building that are in particular difficulties, at least partly because of new competition from the more advanced of the LDCs. But the initial response from the NICs has been a cautious refusal to become involved, perhaps because they see participation in only the industry commit-

[29]See OECD Press Communiqué A (78) 1978: Paris, June 15, 1978, particularly Annex II.

[30]See the Resolution of the OECD Council establishing a special program of work for the Organization on Positive Adjustment Policies, C(79)93 (Final), June 15, 1979, and *The Case for Positive Adjustment Policies,* A Compendium of OECD Documents, 1978/1979, OECD: Paris, June, 1979.

tees as a form of second-class citizenship in a "rich-man's club," perhaps because they are reluctant to break ranks so visibly with the other LDCs, perhaps because they expect little from the committees except pressure to restrain production.

Today, as we have said, the need for adjustment comes mainly from technological and social changes within the industrialized countries. For this reason, and because there is no good alternative, the OECD must for the present be the main forum for discussing structural adjustment problems. But the problems posed by the need to encourage and to adapt to changes in production patterns are global ones, and, over the longer term, there must be more adequate global machinery than today exists to deal with this range of problems.

Thus, in looking ahead for the next decade or so, the two biggest institutional requisites in the general area of trade policy are the need to incorporate the LDCs more fully into the global trading system and the need for more international concern with problems related to the process of structural change. The first means both that the trade of the LDCs should no longer be largely exempt from any rule-system and that the global rule-system should be adapted so that it is more responsive to their needs. The second means not only that domestic policies affecting the pace and character of structural change should be recognized as matters of international concern but also that more should be done, internationally, to identify areas in which change is desirable and to assist the process of adaptation to new patterns of production. Both problems together mean that in the future more attention must be paid not simply to rule-making designed to promote "freer" and "fairer" trade—although that will remain necessary—but also to the effects rules and policies have on the location of industry, that is, on the international division of labor.

Although the failure of today's arrangements to deal adequately with the linked problems of LDC trade and structural change is likely to pose the biggest problems, there are other important omissions or inadequacies in the present trade regime. One is the almost total lack of rules or procedural arrangements to deal with restrictions on services, despite the growing role of services in the international economy.[31] Another is the fact that that old perennial, agriculture, still remains a highly protected sector, having emerged almost unscathed from the recent MTN. Problems connected with trade between market economies and command economies also are likely to become more important if, as seems probable, trade and other forms of economic intercourse between the two systems continue to expand. They are, today, not adequately looked at anywhere. Finally, there is the organizational problem—the lack of any widely supported global body where discussions of trade policy take place on a continuing basis.

In the second part of this chapter, we put the case for a new Production and Trade Organization (PTO) to supersede both the GATT and the UNCTAD, and in the third section we indicate what such an institution might look like and the approach it might take to some of the problems that seem likely to trouble the 1980s. First, however, something must be said about direct foreign investment, for some of the issues involved in rule-making in this area are closely analogous to those in the trade field. Moreover, if, as we have argued, it is not simply trade rules but the whole range of policies affecting the international location of production that should be brought under more adequate global oversight, rules and policies affecting foreign investment are central to this concern.

Investment

Multinational enterprises were an early target of the LDCs who argued that they tended to distort and to exploit the economy of the host country for the benefit of the parent company and were frequently conduits of unwanted political influence, inappropriate technology, and alien social customs. Harsh constraints

---

[31]Although the OECD has encouraged some code-making among its members and the UNCTAD has concerned itself with shipping, the growing role of services and the extent to which more regulation of the national restraints placed on services is needed has not received the attention it deserves from either governments or independent analysts.

on investment and sudden and uncompensated expropriations were, in turn, sore points in the North-South relationship in the eyes of the rich countries. Extravagant abuses of power on both sides undoubtedly fueled the controversy.

Real problems are posed by foreign direct investment. It is not easy to define the conditions that should legitimately be attached by the host government, by the enterprise making the investment, and by the home government of that enterprise, both to the initial investment and to the subsequent operations of the subsidiary. Although disagreements over the scope and role of foreign investment in the LDCs have recently provided much of the pyrotechnics, difficulties arising from the conditions attached to direct foreign investment are a continuing—perhaps growing—source of strain in relationships among the industrialized countries. Not only are these countries the source of most investment, but about three-quarters of the total stock of direct foreign investment is in the developed market-economy countries.[32] Small wonder that it has become conventional to include direct foreign investment in all lists of problems urgently requiring more international attention, whether they be of primary concern to the industrialized countries or of wider global concern.

Since the end of World War II, the United States has been by far the largest source of direct foreign investment, and, for many years, the other industrialized countries, like the LDCs today, were ambivalent about the advantages of receiving investments. U.S. capital and technical skills were welcomed, but there were fears that too much European (or Canadian) industry would come under U.S. domination. Some of these fears remain, but they have abated as the other industrialized countries have, once again, become important sources of direct foreign investment

[32]The total value of the stock of direct investment abroad of developed market economies increased from $105 billion in 1967 to $158 billion in 1971 and to $259 billion in 1975. See *Transnational Corporations in World Development: A Re-examination,* U.N. Economic and Social Council, Commission on Transnational Corporations, E/C.10/38, 20 March 1978, table, p. 237.

and as foreign investment in the United States has grown in importance.[33]

Recently, the ambivalence about the advantages of direct foreign investment, which in the past has been characteristic of host countries, whether industrialized or developing, has become pronounced in the home countries, that is, in those countries from which most of the direct foreign investment comes. There are charges not only that jobs are being exported but that enterprises in the industrialized countries are exporting to the fastest growing LDCs the technology on which the industrialized countries depend to compete with these lower-wage economies in their own home markets as well as in third countries. There is much dispute and little consensus, even at the analytical level, about the effects of direct foreign investment on either the host or the home country. The verdict seems to be that few generalizations are possible beyond a general presumption that freedom for movement of capital, like freedom for other factors, tends to contribute to greater global efficiency of production, although the distribution of benefits as between home and host country and among groups within each country depends on the circumstances surrounding each case.[34] What no one disputes is that direct foreign investment has been growing rapidly and that the problems surrounding it are not now adequately dealt with, nationally or internationally.

In national terms, each government will have to decide for itself how it makes the trade-off between the competing desires for efficiency and autonomy that lie at the root of many of the differences of view about the benefits of foreign investment and how it weights the competing views of the different groups within its own society that tend to gain or lose from the process. Presumably, there are clearer benefits to some countries than

[33]In the mid-1970s, the United States was the second largest host country for foreign direct investment. Canada was the first. C. Fred Bergsten, Thomas Horst, and Theodore H. Moran, *American Multinationals and American Interests,* The Brookings Institution: Washington, 1978, p. 14.

[34]See ibid.; also William Diebold's discussion in Chapter 6 of *The United States and the Industrial World,* op. cit.

there are to others in welcoming foreign investment or in encouraging their own enterprises to invest abroad. But there is a general international interest as well which should increasingly put some limits on the choices made and should also affect how a country implements its choices.

This international interest is of several, rather different kinds. First, the fact that there are few rules governing the conditions that can be attached by both home and host governments means that foreign investment is a rich source of friction between states which it is clearly in the international interest to reduce. Second, the policies followed toward foreign investment, by both home and host governments, affect both the amount and the direction of investment. There is a broad international interest in seeing that there is adequate investment in the aggregate and also that savings are channelled into the most productive sectors because both are crucial to an adequate level of overall growth in the global economy. There are, as well, international interests in seeing that there is adequate investment in certain processes (such as in the extraction of oil and of certain hard minerals) and in certain places (such as in countries where development plans are critically dependent on some given level of foreign investment). There is, too, a general international interest in the way national policies on foreign investment affect the location of production and in how such policies encourage or hinder the process of structural change briefly discussed in the preceding section.

Off and on for many years, it has been suggested that there should be a "GATT for Investment," that is, a code or codes governing the conditions that might be attached to foreign investment and a rule-system designed, like the commercial policy provisions of the GATT, to reduce frictions among states and to make investment, like trade, more "efficient" and more responsive to market forces by removing barriers and proscribing practices that introduce distortions or discriminations in investment flows.[35] Because direct foreign investment is, almost by defini-

---

[35]One of the earliest suggestions was that by Paul M. Goldberg and Charles P. Kindleberger, "Toward a GATT for Investment: A Proposal for Supervision

tion, done mainly by multinational enterprises, the discussion over the kinds of rules that might be desirable to control government actions in this field has frequently become entangled with the discussion of rules that should govern the operation of multinationals, and then, by a natural extension, with rules governing business practices generally.

Three broad classes of problem would seem to call for more rule-making, or at least for broader understandings among governments than exist today. First, one range of problems arises from overlapping or concurrent jurisdictions. Not infrequently, a subsidiary company, although subject to the laws of the host government, is not totally free from legal restraints imposed (either directly or through the parent company) by the home government of the parent. For example, the U.S. government, to the annoyance of foreign governments, has claimed the right to extend to foreign subsidiaries of American parents U.S. anti-trust legislation and controls on exports of goods restricted on security grounds. Second—and the issue that today attracts the most concern, at least on the part of American analysts—are the problems arising from the lack of any widely accepted rules about the inducements and the restraints that it is legitimate for home and for host governments to offer or to impose on foreign investment. Finally, there is a wide array of problems having to do with the practices of enterprises: multinationals can frustrate national plans and escape from various kinds of governmental control by the way they keep their books, exchange goods among their subsidiaries, shift production, and make their investments. And all enterprises, multinational or not, which possess a significant degree of market power may operate in ways that distort markets, undermine national policies, or undercut international agreements on trade and investment. The lack of much in the way of agreement on the standards that should apply

---

of the International Corporation," in *Law and Policy in International Business*, vol. II, no. 2, Summer, 1970, pp. 295–323. More recently, Marina von N. Whitman included a somewhat similar proposal in a brief but remarkably comprehensive review of economic policies requiring more international action. See her *Sustaining the International Economic System: Issues for U.S. Policy*, Essays in International Finance, No. 121: Princeton, N.J., June, 1977.

to state-trading enterprises is logically a part of this third array of problems.

More willingness on the part of home governments to regard subsidiaries as the nationals of host governments and to accept the implications of national treatment, and also acceptance of the corollary (that the host governments treat subsidiaries as nationals and not impose special restraints on them), would go a long way toward meeting the problems arising under the first heading, as Raymond Vernon, among others, has emphasized.[36] Questions of this sort have traditionally been the subject of bilateral negotiations between governments, although recently they have been discussed as well within the OECD. With the rapid growth in international production, these problems are likely to require some rule-making on a broader global basis.

The problems in the second category are more difficult to handle. It is hard to define, let alone to negotiate, what measures should be deemed "excessive" inducements for and "excessive" restraints on investment. Moreover, it is probably not logical (and it would clearly not be negotiable) to have the same standards apply to all countries, regardless of their state of development. By analogy with the long-accepted infant industry arguments, there are strong arguments for being more lenient toward tax advantages offered by an LDC to a foreign investor than those offered by a developed country. But what about "performance criteria"? Should, for example, an LDC be permitted to insist that an investor accept restrictions on capital repatriation that would not be permitted in the case of a developed country? Intergovernmental agreements on procedural arrangements and on substantive rules will not be easy to reach, but, clearly, there is here a long agenda for international action which, although it may start in the comparatively narrow focus of the OECD, must soon become lodged in a more broadly based organization.[37]

[36]See, for example, Raymond Vernon, "The Multinationals: No Strings Attached," in *Foreign Policy*, no. 33, Winter, 1978–1979.

[37]The most comprehensive recent study of the problems raised by direct foreign investment and the problems requiring more international surveillance and rule-making is that by C. Fred Bergsten et al., op. cit.

As one looks ahead, there will be a growing need for multilateral discussions in all three areas: overlapping jurisdictions, incentives and restraints, and business practices. Some of what is needed now takes place, rather slowly, in the OECD; and part of what is needed takes place, even more slowly, in various U.N. groups, like the Commission on Transnational Corporations. If, as we suggest below, it should become possible to establish a new Production and Trade Organization to supersede both the GATT and the UNCTAD, it would be logical to bring these efforts together under the aegis of the new institution and also to broaden their work. As in the case of trade policy, so in the case of investment policy, part of the problem (but only part) lies in removing restrictions and outlawing practices that restrict or distort markets. Another part of the problem lies in the need to bring more positive judgments to bear on the decisions that are made about the kinds of actions that should be encouraged if production patterns are to reflect changes in comparative advantage and to meet the needs of an evolving global economy. Today, such encouragement can only be of an advisory and facilitating character: we do not know enough to do more than that. But even that calls for some new institutional arrangements in the trade and production field and also for far closer working relationships among the three key institutions to which we should look for the better management of the international economy—the reformed Bank family, a new PTO, and a somewhat modernized IMF—for all three affect investment patterns.

THE NEED FOR A NEW APPROACH

In looking ahead, we see some strong reasons for questioning whether the international arrangements and the kind of rulemaking we have known in the past and which contributed so significantly to the manifold expansion of world trade will be adequate to deal with what promise to be the most troublesome problems in the future. We believe that the structure of rules and procedures that has governed trade relations since World War II stands in need of more fundamental rethinking and more drastic remodeling than it received during the recent Tokyo Round of multilateral trade negotiations.

A continuing process of rule-making and codification of behavior is necessary to the growth of order in international life. And more is needed in trade policy, as well as in other areas. But, as we indicated, many of the trade-related problems that can be foreseen involve questions extending well beyond the policy areas now covered by the GATT, raising issues that in today's world are not likely to be adequately handled by a further evolution of the GATT with its primary reliance on market forces to induce and accommodate to change and with its strong emphasis on rule-making and its quasi-legal approach.

A few years ago—before the recent wave of protectionism created a very cold climate for further trade liberalization but after much side-stepping of Article XIX and the sweeping exceptions made for free-trade areas, customs unions, and LDCs had highlighted some of the weaknesses in the GATT—the Atlantic Council put forward a proposal for reform called *GATT Plus*.[38] In brief, this was a plan for a supplementary agreement among the industrialized, market-economy countries of the GATT which would commit them to a new code comprising, in most instances, tighter versions of the main GATT trade rules, some further measures of trade liberalization, and a stronger system of administration based on weighted voting. The existing GATT undertakings would have continued in force, applying to trade between the members of the Code and the other GATT members as well as among the members of the GATT not joining the Code. In most instances where the Code rules differed from those in the GATT, Code members would be applying more stringent rules among themselves.[39] Additional measures of trade liberalization agreed upon among the members of the new

---

[38]Atlantic Council of the United States, *GATT Plus—A Proposal for Trade Reform,* Praeger: New York, 1976. The main drafters of this report (which was widely circulated in 1975) had been closely involved with the GATT from its inception.

[39]As Hudec has pointed out, *GATT Plus* would have meant a strengthening in the rules as compared to the way they were in fact being applied, but, in

Code would have been extended to all the members of the GATT wherever that is required by the most-favored-nation clause. Since the industrialized, market-economy countries which were assumed to be the subscribers to the new Code are, in effect, the only full members of the GATT (the rest making extensive use of special arrangements), the plan was a way of reforming and updating the GATT without having to amend the General Agreement, which, given the composition of the GATT, was deemed to be impossible.[40]

Judged in terms of the original objectives of the GATT and the weaknesses that had been revealed in the two and one-half decades it had been in operation, the *GATT Plus* proposal was a sophisticated and tightly drafted plan, an ingenious way around many problems. But some of the premises that underlay it have proved to be false, and it failed to deal with some of the problems that now seem likely to be important in the next decade or so. In consequence, it did not attract as much support as its drafters had hoped for and which, in less troubled times, might reasonably have been anticipated. As the MTN made abundantly clear, the advanced industrialized countries are not today prepared for the tighter rules contemplated by the proposal nor for the further steps toward free trade, particularly if that means (as it would under the *GATT Plus* proposal) extending these benefits, without safeguards and without reciprocity, to the new industrialized countries. The plan did not respond to the widely felt need for new ways of dealing with problems having to do with the process of structural change. And it did little to overcome one of the major weaknesses in the GATT: the failure to involve the "intermediate" or new industrial countries like Brazil, Mexico, South Korea, Taiwan in the rule-making process in

---

some instances, the changes were weaker than would have been the case had the 1947 GATT rules been strictly interpreted and strictly applied. See Robert E. Hudec, *Adjudication of International Trade Disputes*, Thames Essay No. 16, Trade Policy Research Centre: London, 1978, p. 42.

[40]In 1979, GATT had 84 members, of which some 50 were LDCs. Most amendments to the GATT require a two-thirds majority, others require unanimity.

any far-reaching way. Indeed, in these respects, it largely ratified the existing unsatisfactory situation.[41]

The drafters of *GATT Plus* were undoubtedly correct in their judgment that the GATT could not be substantially improved by amendment. But if the entire system is replaced, conflicting interests can be balanced in new ways and new trade-offs become possible. If one is to think seriously of a reform of the international trading system—and it is the argument here that the time has come to do so—it would seem wiser to think more boldly and to try for reforms that do not simply improve on the existing system in its own terms but seek to grapple with some of the problems that now escape existing arrangements. In doing so, it is important not to slip back but to build on the very substantial progress that has been made during the last 35 years in freeing trade among the industrialized countries.

As we have suggested, many of the difficulties with the GATT in recent years have arisen from the breakdown in the consensus that lay behind the old GATT. That breakdown owed something to intrinsic weaknesses in the rules and in the relatively narrow approach of the GATT, rather more to the expansion of the GATT to include many new members with new preoccupations and new problems, and a great deal to the fact that the character of the international economic system had changed radically since the rules were written. The recent multilateral trade negotiations were in part the last (probably) in a series of negotiations to lower tariffs and in part a negotiation to revivify the GATT as a rule-making and rule-enforcing body by reestablishing a consensus and bringing some of the newer problems (mainly nontariff barriers of various kinds) within the purview of the organization.

The negotiations succeeded in lowering industrial-country tariffs: although the process will be quite a leisurely one, few tariffs

[41]In the commentary on the *GATT Plus* Code, the hope is expressed that as developing countries become able to do so they will accede to the Code, but there are no provisions designed to encourage them to do so or even to encourage them to move out of the exceptional status they now enjoy in the GATT. On the contrary, they are faced with the high hurdle of having to accept the new tighter provisions in toto. See *GATT Plus*, op. cit., p. 11.

of the industrialized countries should be important barriers to trade by the end of the eighties. But how much content will, in fact, be given to the potentially important new codes on standards, government procurement, and, particularly, subsidies remains to be seen. This will be the real test of whether or not a new consensus exists. For the present, the outlook is, at best, uncertain. Clearly, little was done to bridge the gulf between the advanced industrialized countries and the developing countries. And the signs are that even among the industrialized countries there is more consensus about what the problems are than about what should be done to solve them. It is doubtless carrying cynicism too far to say that to the extent a new consensus did emerge it was achieved by weakening the rules, but that verdict comes just a little too close to the truth for comfort.

Part of the problem of dissensus—both as between the developing countries and the old industrialized countries and as among the countries in the latter group—seems to us to stem from the fact that the focus of the GATT is still too narrow. The GATT is still primarily a rule-making and a rule-enforcing institution, well designed to deal with the kinds of problems that were uppermost in the fifties when the need was to remove obvious and fairly easily defined types of trade restrictions and to let markets function, but much less well adapted to deal with the problems of the eighties. In the decade ahead, it will still be necessary to identify and bargain away various types of measures that impede and distort the operation of the market. But, in addition, it will be necessary to discuss internationally the wide array of policies which governments use today to affect domestic production patterns, because most of them also affect indirectly, if not directly, the location of industry on a global basis. Incompatibilities in policies will breed international problems—they are already doing so. But although there is much room for discussion, there is little likelihood that much in the way of substantive rules can be written. Perhaps discussion will not bring the understanding and the willingness to modify policies that is needed where clear difficulties are caused for others. But without it, conflicting policies are inevitable. Moreover, many trade-related practices, like subsidies, that do seem susceptible to being brought under some system of surveillance, consultation, and even rule-making are unlikely to be dealt with satisfactorily unless they are placed in this broader context. It is precisely the ability to look at issues broadly that the GATT today appears to lack.

Many people will agree that there should be more concern with problems that today escape the GATT and that better ways must be found for dealing with the new group of rapidly industrializing LDCs and with structural problems. Shortcomings in the existing arrangements for these and other trade-related problems figure on almost everyone's short list of international economic problems for the next decade or two. But most people will argue that the right approach lies in seeking improvements in existing international organizations, not in creating new ones.[42] The GATT is not, of course, the only organization with functions that concern us here; both the UNCTAD and the OECD have played important roles. Although opinion will differ on the respective roles of the three institutions, most people will feel that with some not very drastic changes in focus and methods of work the three organizations together can provide the international machinery we need. Perhaps they can. But as some reasons exist for concluding that it would be better not to go that route, it seems worth putting the case for thinking, instead, in terms of a new institution that would supersede both the GATT and the UNCTAD, and take on some of the functions that otherwise might be lodged in the OECD.

Some of the reasons for thinking about a new institution arise from the difficulties of escaping from attitudes and limitations that now surround existing institutions. Others have to do with possibilities for new starts and for innovation in institution-building that might be opened up by a new approach, provided it were launched in the right way.

Ever since the first session of the UNCTAD in Geneva in 1964, the LDCs have wanted to see it develop into a new ITO, that is, into a fully fledged specialized agency with the range of

[42]See, for example, the book by Lincoln Gordon for the 1980s Project, op. cit.

functions originally proposed in the Havana Charter although, obviously, not with the same rules on commercial policy as were contained in that document and largely reproduced in the GATT. But the industrialized countries, with a few exceptions (e.g., the Netherlands and the Scandinavian countries), have consistently opposed proposals which would give greater independence or anything more than a hortatory role to the UNCTAD. By dint of persistence and an increasing use of their voting majorities, the LDCs have gradually succeeded in building up the staff and role of the UNCTAD. The industrialized countries, however, have held the line against any action which would give resolutions passed by the UNCTAD anything more than the recommendatory force carried by resolutions of the General Assembly and its subsidiary bodies.

In retrospect, it seems reasonably clear that opportunities were missed in the fifties and early sixties. Had the industrialized countries been less preoccupied with their own problems and more aware of the growing strength, cohesion, and deep sense of grievance of the LDCs, as well as of their own real long-term interests in bringing many of the LDCs more effectively within the central trading system, perhaps the GATT could have evolved into the new specialized agency the LDCs were pressing for and the formation of the UNCTAD made unnecessary. As it was, the review of the GATT that took place in the mid-50s did little to make the LDCs feel that their problems were being approached in ways commensurate with their needs. The GATT, as an organization, remained essentially the guardian of a code of commercial policy responsive primarily to the needs of First World countries. In the following years, various GATT committees were established to examine LDC trade problems, but it was not until 1966 that Part IV was added to the General Agreement. This not only formally accepted the principle that developed countries would not expect reciprocity from the LDCs but also took a far more positive approach generally to the whole question of LDC trade than had been characteristic of the GATT and provided for the establishment of a permanent Committee on Trade and Development. But by then it was too late, for the UNCTAD had been formed. And more or less inevitably it came to be regarded by its members and its secretariat alike as a special pleader and a pressure group on behalf of the LDCs, a unique and rather curious role for a U.N. body financed by assessment on all U.N. members.

Given the rather restricted approach being adopted by the GATT in those years and the widespread ignorance about the problems facing the LDCs, something like the UNCTAD was probably needed for a time, not only to focus attention on these problems but to help the LDCs to identify the interests they had in common and to make the bargaining process between the developed and the developing countries a rather more equal one. But the UNCTAD's chosen role as special pleader for the LDCs has tended to harden the division between the developed countries and the Group of 77 and to encourage group confrontations rather than common efforts to solve problems. In recent years, the secretariat of the UNCTAD has become well aware of the disadvantages and handicaps—such as the loss of a reputation for impartiality—that have stemmed from the fact that it is so clearly identified with promoting the interests of the LDCs, and it has sought to escape the past. But, given the history of the organization and the continuing unwillingness of the developed countries to see it become, in effect, a new ITO, there is no easy way out of the problems that stem from the organization's over-identification with one group of countries.

Although it is possible to envision a partnership between the GATT and the UNCTAD in which each would compensate for the weaknesses or limitations in the other, the record of the past offers few reasons to believe that a fruitful relationship between the two organizations could be developed.[43] There has been too much bad blood. Rather than seeking to complement one another and work together, each institution has resented and been constrained by the existence of the other. As a result, the weaknesses of each have been accentuated: the GATT has become more doctrinally "market oriented" and more legalistic in its

---

[43]The only significant cooperation has been their joint sponsorship of the International Trade Center, which provides technical assistance to LDCs on markets, export promotion, and other trade-related activities.

approach; the UNCTAD, more wedded to planning, propaganda, and special pleading than might well have been the case if only one of them had existed. Today, both organizations carry too much history and too much emotional freight for either one to become the nucleus of the new global trade and production organization that seems to be called for. Their record of animosity and rivalry suggests that it would be difficult, if not impossible, for them to overcome their past and agree to some new form of cooperation.[44]

Given the limitations of both the GATT and the UNCTAD, some people have seen an increasingly important role for the OECD, particularly in dealing with the complex of issues having to do with structural change, accommodation to the trade needs of the NICs, and foreign investment. In all these areas, the OECD is probably the best institution for making some progress in the short term. It is not as tied to a rule-making approach as is the GATT, and far more consensus among the OECD countries than exists today is a necessary precondition of progress on the global level. But it is difficult to see how the OECD can take adequate account of the views of non-member countries or can obtain the cooperation needed from them over the longer term unless quite a number of the NICs are added to its membership. As noted, certain NICs have been invited to participate as associates in the industry committees (e.g., steel, ship-building) concerned with particular sectoral problems. Some people will argue that one should go further and deliberately practice a policy of co-option, holding out the prospect of full membership in the "rich man's club" to the LDCs as they industrialize, provided they are willing to play by the rules that the OECD countries for the most part accept. The strongest argument for following this course of action rests on the case of Japan. The decision to include the Japanese in the OECD, although resisted by some of the Europeans at the time it was first advocated by the United States, was undoubtedly a prudent and far-sighted one. And some will make much the same kind of argument for the inclu-

---

[44]This is true not only of the international staffs but of those governments that are the key supporters of each organization.

sion today of Brazil, Mexico, South Korea, and perhaps a few other countries.

There are several difficulties with seeing the OECD develop along these lines. Carried to an extreme, this course of action would simply replicate the United Nations, but this is doubtless to set up a straw man. For many years, the number of countries added to the OECD could be kept to, say, a dozen or so at the outside. But the expansion of the OECD by some such number would, in fact, change the character of the OECD. The rationale for the OECD—that it is essentially composed of countries which have a uniquely high level of economic interdependence requiring collective management and which also share certain common political and security concerns—is already strained by the fact that its membership includes countries whose presence is accounted for more by history than by an objective assessment of today's reality.[45] Expansion to include the non-European NICs would strain this already tenuous rationale even further. More important, the OECD's ability to perform the useful function of promoting the closer harmonization of policies among a few highly interdependent countries would become even more difficult than it is today.[46] Moreover, the almost inevitable result of an expansion to include the NICs would be a decline in the effectiveness of global economic institutions, some further polarization and probably deterioration in relationships between the OECD countries and the rest of the LDCs, and a strengthening of the LDCs' belief that the rich countries were determined to maintain their dominance of the international economic system.

---

[45]For a fuller discussion, see Miriam Camps, *"First World" Relationships: The Role of the OECD*, Atlantic Institute for International Affairs, Council on Foreign Relations: New York, 1975.

[46]The OECD is already too big and too disparate to enable the kind of intimate discussions that are the prerequisite of close coordination of sensitive policies to take place in formally constituted committees. Increasingly, the most important discussions now take place in what are sometimes called "fireside meetings" (i.e., informal meetings of representatives from a few of the most important countries), which normally take place not at the OECD headquarters but at the homes of representatives to the Organization, to the annoyance of those countries that do not participate.

Apart from the difficulties that stand in the way of any one of the three organizations that now share the field (or the three in combination) evolving to meet the needs, the bolder step of forming a new organization to supersede the GATT and UNCTAD (and progressively to assume some functions that might otherwise, *faute de mieux,* fall to the OECD) promises a number of positive advantages. It is easier to see ways of reconciling the need to have as many states as possible accept some rights and duties with, on the one hand, special arrangements for developing countries and, on the other, freedom for sets of states to go further than the membership as a whole would be prepared to go in accepting obligations vis-à-vis one another. Closely related to this point, it is also rather easier to see how one might break out of the pattern that today hampers and limits the effective operation of all international institutions (namely, the desire of all states to participate in all committees, councils, etc.) and move to a new pattern which would combine more use of limited groups with arrangements that effectively protect the rights of those not represented. And it is certainly easier to see how various functional problems that need to be looked at more closely together can be addressed in that way. Centering the responsibility for an important cluster of activities within one institution and then establishing clearer lines of authority and closer working relationships between it and the Bank and the Fund would also open the way to a less cumbersome and a more fruitful coordination within the U.N. system generally.

Finally, if handled in the right way, the agreement to establish what would, in fact, be a "new ITO" would go a very long way toward meeting the argument of the LDCs that the modern world needs a new international economic order. Rather than the existing practice of meeting bit by bit and frequently in a grudging way the most legitimate arguments put forward by the Group of 77 (and not infrequently making dubious concessions on some of their less legitimate claims for the sake of harmony), the international community would be taking a bold new step, one which did entail a new distribution of costs and benefits and sought to reconcile in a new way the competing demands of efficiency, equity, order, and autonomy. In this context, it would be reasonable to anticipate LDC agreement to the progressive assumption of responsibilities and commitments to a freer and more orderly trading system.

The proposal being made here—that there might be enough advantages to thinking in terms of a new institution to supersede both the GATT and the UNCTAD to justify the heroic effort that would be required—does not mean that the slate should simply be wiped clean. There is much of value in both institutions that should be saved. In particular, most of the contractual commitments now enshrined in the GATT must be preserved if the very substantial progress made since the war in freeing trade and in eliminating unfair and unscrupulous trade practices is not to be lost.

In the process of moving toward an improved system for promoting fair and mutually beneficial trade and for encouraging the structural changes in the pattern of world production needed to promote global welfare, it is important to build on what exists. To scrap it and start again would risk losing more than one could hope to gain. But if the project is to succeed, it is also important to build on what exists in a way that does not carry the connotation that the advanced industrialized world is now simply seeking to incorporate the developing countries (and the command-economy countries) in *its* system, insisting that all countries play by the rules that the advanced countries have found to be congenial and responsive to their own needs.

To illustrate more specifically some of the advantages that might flow from adopting an ambitious approach to the reform of the global trading institutions and to indicate in more detail how some of today's most troublesome problems might be made somewhat easier to handle, the rest of this chapter is cast as a description of a possible new global organization, which we shall call, for convenience, the PTO (Production and Trade Organization). No attempt is made to give a blueprint for a new institution. Instead, the purpose is to suggest, in general terms, the tasks a new institution should address; the kinds of rules one might reasonably hope to have accepted globally and by certain subsystems; the arrangements that might be adopted when procedures are more appropriate (or more likely to be feasible) than substantive rules; and the way in which it might be possible to reconcile the need to have most states accept some rights and duties with, on the one hand, special arrangements for developing countries and, on the other, freedom for sets of states to go further in accepting obligations vis-à-vis one another. We also suggest ways of making a start on the problems connected with encouraging and adapting to needed structural change. In a few cases, we deal with problems that we did not discuss earlier because the issues, although important and ones that should be covered by a new institution, are either not of the same importance as those already discussed or are old problems, like agricultural protection, where the nature of the problem is well known.

Many of the suggestions put forward could, of course, be adopted in modified form if the best that can be achieved (or the best that governments can be persuaded to try to undertake) is a further evolutionary development of the existing institutions. (Readers who find discussions of organizational arrangements tedious are advised to skip to page 190.)

ELEMENTS OF A NEW PRODUCTION AND TRADE ORGANIZATION (PTO)

The PTO would be a new specialized agency paralleling the World Bank family and the IMF and with a similar formal relationship to the United Nations. It would have a very close working relationship with a somewhat restructured IBRD-IDA-IFC complex and with the Fund. It would supersede both GATT and UNCTAD although it would take over some functions from both organizations, and most of the contractual obligations entered into by governments within the framework of the GATT would remain in force.

This new specialized agency would deal with trade and industrial policy questions, defined broadly, and specifically including problems of structural change and questions having to do with the global distribution of production. Its mandate should also extend to certain service industries. It would have rule-making, surveillance, and consultative functions with respect to direct foreign investment and business practices. Commodity arrangements affecting conditions of trade, except for arrangements dealing with energy (both conventional and nuclear), would also come within its purview, as, of course, would trade-related aspects of agriculture.

The new specialized agency would be rather different from any of the existing specialized agencies in that the weight of the institution would initially at least (and probably for many years) be in an array of formally subordinate boards, groups, or committees whose memberships would vary according to the task and which would operate with considerable autonomy. Some of these subordinate bodies would be concerned with the operation of precise and legally binding codes. Others would be looser and less concerned with rule-making and enforcement and more concerned with promoting consultation and cooperation. Membership in the overall organization, or umbrella organization,[47] would be open to any state prepared to accept a few basic principles (which we discuss below).

The overall organization would be global and open-ended, that is, any country which accepted the general principles would be able to join at any time. The plenary body of the organization should normally act by consensus. Formally, it might act, at first, on a one-nation, one-vote basis, but if, over time, more substantive powers were transferred upward to the umbrella organization, the plenary body should adopt weighted voting, as in the Bank and the Fund. Initially, at least, the plenary body of the overall organization might meet biennially. Its main function would be to discuss trends and objectives within the substantive areas coming within the purview of the PTO. These discussions would be similar to the discussions at the annual meetings of the Bank and Fund, although on a different, but complementary, range of subjects.

[47]This term is used in a report by the American Society of International Law (ASIL), which advocates a new World Trade Organization having some of the features of the plan proposed here. See American Society of International Law, *Re-Making the System of World Trade: A Proposal for Institutional Reform,* Studies in Transnational Legal Policy, No. 12: Washington, 1976.

The subsidiary boards, groups, and committees would *not* be subject to the direction of the overall body, since their powers would derive directly from the obligations undertaken by the countries concerned in establishing these semi-autonomous boards, committees, and groups. However, all these subsidiary bodies would operate transparently, that is, although non-members of the group, board, or committee could not normally participate in these bodies, the Executive Director of the new agency would participate ex officio in all subsidiary bodies and would be responsible for keeping the membership of the overall organization informed on a regular basis of actions taken in all sub-groups. And, as we explain (pp. 169–174), a country would have certain rights of complaint if it suffered from action taken by a subgroup of which it was not a member.

Governing Principles

One of the reasons for now thinking about a new trade organization is the desirability of having at least a few trading rules that apply universally (or nearly universally) and of laying the basis for a process of further codification in which all countries feel they have a stake. At present, the trade of neither the command-economy countries nor the LDCs is effectively covered by the rules of the GATT. And it is clear that much the same reasons that have led some of those countries to refrain from joining the GATT and prompted most of them to seek special arrangements which effectively removed their trade from the major constraints of the GATT would render fruitless any attempt to make membership in the new organization conditional on the acceptance of any very elaborate code or set of obligations. But it is, perhaps, not wholly fanciful to think that agreement might be reached on something like the following set of principles as the qualifying commitments for membership in the umbrella organization:

1. Acceptance of the general principle that national actions in the fields covered by the organization may have damaging external consequences and that another member state which considers itself adversely affected has a right to have the situ-

ation reviewed according to agreed procedures.

2. Acceptance of the principle that like situations should receive like treatment.

3. Acceptance of the principle that what entitles a member to the benefits of the rules and the procedural arrangements in the subsidiary groups is its acceptance of those rules and procedural arrangements.

Each of these general principles contains rather more than may at first be apparent, and each raises a number of questions and problems that are worth discussion. The first principle is the most self-explanatory.[48] And it is, perhaps, the easiest to dismiss as impracticable on the grounds that it would open the door to an endless stream of complaints, or that it is so broad as to be meaningless, or that it would constitute widespread interference in domestic affairs which would be solidly opposed by the East European countries, by most of the LDCs, and, although probably in a more sophisticated fashion, by many of the advanced industrial countries as well. But before writing off some such general principle as meaningless, dangerous, or non-negotiable, it is worth looking at some of the arguments that might be made on the other side.

It is now a commonplace that traditional distinctions between foreign and domestic policy have lost much of their meaning. If one is really trying to think through the kind of trade and production organization that would make sense in the future, there is much to be said for having this erosion of any hard and fast dividing line explicitly recognized. In the second place, one of the central problems with all organizations, and one that has become steadily more acute, is the desire of too many countries to seek membership, frequently because they see no other way of having their interests protected. The way we here seek to resolve this familiar efficiency/participation dilemma is by combining universality (or near universality) in the overall organization with much more limited membership in the more operational, or

---

[48]It is also very similar to the main commitment proposed for the World Trade Organization in the ASIL report, op. cit.

code-making and code-enforcing subsidiary groups. Making these groups subordinate in a substantive sense to the overall organization would simply stultify them. Providing some means whereby non-participating countries can complain if they are injured need not do so, but, rather, might well pave the way for more acceptance of limited member subgroups than would otherwise be probable. Clearly, the acceptability of the principle would depend, in large measure, on what would happen if a country claimed injury. We discuss the handling of this type of complaint later, together with complaints arising from other commitments.

The second principle—that like situations should be treated in like ways—could be formulated differently and called a new principle of equal treatment. It is, of course, a modification of the principle of non-discrimination that has been one of the two main pillars of the GATT. Non-discrimination as a general principle has many advantages, not least as a protection for small countries with weak bargaining power. But there is no prospect whatsoever of the principle being widely honored, whereas the modified principle suggested here might be acceptable and would be better than no commitment or than a commitment widely honored in the breach. That is the present situation, from which many of the weaknesses in the GATT today stem. Wholly apart from the fact that the LDCs do not accept the principle as applicable to their own actions (although they claim others should abide by it), the use of Article XXIV to justify preferential trading arrangements falling far short of full customs unions or free trade areas and the circumvention of other rules of the GATT (by negotiating "voluntary" export controls and orderly marketing arrangements, like the multifiber agreement, formally within the framework of the GATT, or like the various arrangements for limiting steel imports) do violence to the principle. So, too, in a more legalistic sense, do the limited-member codes negotiated in the MTN.[49] Finally, of course, the insistence of the

---

[49]There is an inconsistency (to say the least) between the agreements reached in the MTN on codes accepted by only some members of the GATT and applicable only to those who subscribe to them and Article I of the GATT which enshrines the principle of non-discrimination.

European Community during the Tokyo Round that when Article XIX was invoked, safeguards could be applied to the country or countries causing the problem and not simply on a non-discriminatory basis raises doubts about whether it is legitimate to claim that non-discrimination is still a fundamental tenet of the GATT.

Some will argue that non-discrimination is so basic to trade policy that it should be one of the commitments in any universal trade organization, even though it might be clear to all that the principle would be widely abused. The argument is that non-discrimination sets a standard and a goal which is desirable, even if it is one that is seldom attained. If the overall organization were essentially a rule-making body, and if it were envisaged as the central repository of the progressive codification of trade law, this argument would have considerable force. But the conception advanced here is a rather different one. The overall organization, at least for many years to come, would not be primarily concerned with rule-making, which would instead be centered in limited-member sub-groups. Non-discrimination among fully participating members of particular codes should be the rule. As already indicated, a fundamental conception underlying the new organization is that there would be quite a number of quasi-autonomous committees or groups negotiating and implementing codes of conduct that would apply only to those accepting the code. Such a conception is fully compatible with a like-treatment rule, although technically out of harmony with an overriding commitment to non-discrimination.

The like-treatment principle, if widely accepted, should result in some of the most invidious forms of discrimination being better controlled than they are today. Such a principle would meet the LDC's demand that their entitlement to special and differential treatment be formally recognized. It would also open the way to a more differentiated treatment among the LDCs according to their degree of industrialization, thus moving away from the untenable position that Brazil and Chad should be treated in the same way. The command-economy countries would doubtless have an ambivalent reaction to a like-treatment principle. On the one hand, it would be easier for them to subscribe to than would a general principle of non-discrimination, since there would be no suggestion that they would be required to give other countries the same treatment they accord one another within the framework of the Comecon. But, on the other hand, East European countries have laid much emphasis on the importance of receiving most-favored-nation (m-f-n) treatment, and, although nothing in the adoption of a like-treatment principle would limit the right of a country to extend m-f-n treatment, it might well be seen as weakening their claims to be treated in that way.

It would be disingenuous to imply that a like-treatment rule would be easy to apply. Who is to define "like treatment"? And how finely are "like conditions" to be defined? No situation is wholly like any other. Obviously, a rule of reason would have to apply. And obviously, too, the interpretation given to the principle would be mainly determined, over time, by the common law practice of the accumulation of precedents, largely stemming from the operation of complaints procedures of various kinds (discussed on pp. 169–174).

It is perhaps not far-fetched to see the arrangement proposed here as strengthening rather than weakening the force of the principle of non-discrimination. The non-discrimination rule would be more strictly enforced within the subcodes than it is today within the GATT. The like-treatment rule, if applied universally, particularly when coupled with the various complaints arrangements foreseen for the new organization, would not only cover more countries and more practices than does today's rule, but it seems likely to provide as good, or better, protection for weak countries than does today's system.

The third principle is that what entitles a country to the benefits of the rules and procedures of the overall organization and, in particular, of the subgroups, is acceptance of those rules and procedures. In a sense, it is a modified version of the principle of reciprocity, the second main pillar of today's GATT. Acceptance of the third principle is important if, as is our purpose here, one is seeking a system that will gradually bring larger and larger areas of interstate conduct under international surveillance. As we explain below, acceptance of this principle would not mean that the benefits of a particular code could not be extended to countries which did not participate in it. It would, however, affect the nature of that extension; that is, because the extension would have no contractual basis, it could be withdrawn at any time.

In addition to the acceptance of these and perhaps one or two other general principles, membership in the new agency should carry with it obligations to make information available, to respond to requests in the course of investigations of complaints, and so forth. The wording of such provisions is important and likely to be troublesome. But again our concern here is not to present a detailed blueprint but to give a broad-brush picture of the central elements of a possible new institution.

Membership in the umbrella organization might also carry with it an obligation to subscribe to various non-controversial codes, rules, or conventions that are already widely accepted and pose no significant issues of policy. There are several commitments of this kind in the GATT, such as the provision on marks of origin (Article X), which should simply be taken over by the new umbrella institution. Similarly, in the field of services and, perhaps, investment, there may be a few principles that are so widely accepted that they might without much controversy be codified and made part of the basic instruments of the new agency. Initially, however, no attempt should be made to codify—on a near-universal basis—any principles that raise controversial issues of policy. Such an attempt would court trouble and replicate one of the central difficulties of the GATT—the attempt to apply *substantive rules* to situations that are not susceptible to control in this way—with the result that the rules have too often been disregarded or undermined. Over time, as some commitments which are first undertaken only by limited groups of countries become more widely acceptable, they might be transferred upward and become rules or codes of the umbrella organization. (As this happened, the distribution of powers between the umbrella organization and the subsidiary bodies would be altered and some organizational changes would become logical, such as weighted voting in the plenary body.)

Principal Subsidiary Bodies

The subsidiary bodies of the PTO could be of many different kinds, some with broad mandates, others with narrow, issue-specific tasks, some essentially concerned with rule-making and rule-enforcement, others acting simply as consultative groups. As we envisage things, five of these quasi-autonomous groups would be of special importance:

1. A Trade Policy Review Board, which would be roughly analogous to the Executive Boards of the Bank and the Fund.
2. A Tariff and Trade Code, which would be the *main* successor body to the GATT, although there would be other "successors" as well, e.g., to some of the code-related groups agreed to in the MTN.
3. An LDC Trade Committee.
4. An Advisory Council on the Structure of the Global Economy.
5. A Council on Direct Foreign Investment.[50]

We sketch below some ideas about how each of these five main groups might function. Once again, it is important to say that this is not a blueprint: variants on all these ideas are easy to imagine. The more specific we become, the easier it is to see new questions that must be answered and the more we open ourselves to charges of having neglected this or ignored that. But only by a kind of spurious specificity can we illustrate some of the concepts that would repay thought. Let us start by looking briefly at the Tariff and Trade Code, for until we have explained what might, and what might not, be covered by that group, it is difficult to describe the potentially more important Trade Policy Review Board.

---

[50]If the special arrangements for commodities were brought within the ambit of the PTO, the Commodities Board (see pp. 183–186) would be a sixth principal body.

Tariff and Trade Code

The Tariff and Trade Code would be the main successor body to the GATT. Tariff reductions made in previous GATT rounds, including, of course, the recent MTN, would be consolidated and taken over by the new Code. But the new Code would be a *GATT Minus,* rather than a *GATT Plus,* and it would be more limited in the trade practices it covered than is today's GATT.

The new Code would be essentially a pact on tariffs and quotas, although it might also include rules on certain types of subsidies and other non-tariff measures where the protectionist element is fairly easy to measure and where tight rules admitting of virtually no exceptions could be agreed upon. In addition to the main Tariff and Trade Code, there might be other codes and code-related groups with somewhat different memberships. These groups would take over from today's GATT the enforcement of any substantive rules—such as the antidumping code—that can be agreed upon among any significant number of countries. Some of the codes agreed to in the MTN would also seem to fall in this category. For the most part, however, measures which cannot be simply outlawed because they are too embedded in key domestic policies would be dealt with by other means. And the most important of the new codes, that on subsidies, should (if the concept being outlined here were to be followed) probably be superseded only in part by commitments in the main Tariff and Trade Code, or by another code-related group, and in part by discussions elsewhere in the new organization. Thus, in the new organization, in contrast to today's GATT, codes—both the main Tariff and Trade Code and any additional ones—should be confined to enforceable commitments. The large gray area of trade policy questions that cannot be reduced to clear rules or automatic formulas—even among the advanced industrialized countries—without giving rise to frequent requests for safeguards and exceptional treatment, or to widespread evasion of the rules, would be dealt with by other means.

Although they would be more limited in scope than in today's GATT, the basic commitments in the new Tariff and Trade Code should go somewhat further in respect to quotas and tariffs. They should commit the members to eliminate tariffs (or reduce them to some nominal level) within some period, say 10 years, and to forswear quantitative import restrictions except when authorized by the Trade Policy Review Board (see pp. 169–174) in the context of a special sectoral arrangement or an adjustment program, or by the IMF for balance-of-payments reasons. It would be reasonable for the countries participating in this major Code to go further and to forswear the imposition of *any* trade-restricting measures for balance-of-payments reasons unless recourse to the measures had been specifically authorized by the IMF.[51]

Tariffs, quotas, and some of the more straightforward non-tariff barriers among the advanced countries could, we contend, be eliminated entirely without undue hardship and with consequent gains in efficiency, provided three conditions are met.[52] The first is that there are other means available for handling temporary balance-of-payments problems; the second is that there are means for handling true structural problems, including, but not limited to, those that will arise from competition from LDC imports; and the third is that some reciprocity is obtained from the NICS.

So far as the first condition is concerned, import quotas, surcharges, or similar measures might, in exceptional circumstances, be authorized by the IMF for balance-of-payments reasons. But, because the members of the new Tariff and Trade Code would be, for the most part, the highly industrialized countries whose currencies are today floating (and can be expected either to float or to be easily revalued in the medium-

---

[51]For a somewhat similar proposal, see C. Fred Bergsten, "Reforming the GATT: The Use of Trade Measures for Balance-of-Payments Purposes," *Journal of International Economics,* no. 77, 1977, p. 118.

[52]The experience of the European Communities strongly suggests that tariff and quota-free trade among the industrialized countries would lead to an expansion of trade and more intra-industry specialization. See also the study by Lincoln Gordon, op. cit., which reaches much the same conclusion about the feasibility, and desirability, of tariff and quota-free trade among the industrialized countries.

term future), only in rather exceptional cases should there be a need to impose trade restrictions for pure balance-of-payments reasons.

As for the second condition, the use of quotas, tariffs, or other trade-restricting measures (see p. 173) might be authorized to meet "structural problems" by the Trade Policy Review Board, but only as part of an adjustment program. Today, "structural problems" frequently impel countries to have resort to the escape clauses in the GATT or, more often, to find ways around their commitments to freer trade. Under the arrangement being proposed here, the remedy would not normally lie in granting exceptions to commitments embodied in the codes unless these were directly tied to adjustment programs. Structural problems would, in short, be examined and dealt with directly— not, as today, providing the reasons for exceptions and evasions of the rules but largely escaping any collective examination and any collective view of the appropriate remedies.

So far as the third condition—reciprocity from the NICs—is concerned, there would be no going back on the tariff reductions already made in successive GATT negotiations, including the recently concluded Tokyo Round. But there would be no automatic extension without reciprocity to the other members of today's GATT (or, *a fortiori*, to members of the new PTO) of further measures of trade liberalization made among the full members of the Code. On the contrary, the NICs and the command-economy countries would not only have to give certain commitments on trade and tariff policy to gain the benefits of any further tariff reductions, but also, as part of the move to the new Production and Trade Organization, the NICs would become associate members of the Tariff and Trade Code and agree to make certain reductions in their existing levels of protection. For example, the NICs might, on the entry into force of the new arrangements, reduce their own tariffs by some flat percentage—say a third overall—with, probably, some freedom within the overall percentage to decide which tariffs to cut more and which less. A further 33 percent cut might be made not later than five years after the first reduction, with further cuts after another five years.[53] The NICs, like the full members of the Code, would generalize these cuts to the least developed members of PTO. They would undertake similar obligations to a progressive enlargement of quotas and to the progressive adoption of any other rules for the removal of trade barriers that were a part of the Code.[54] As a part of the new overall bargain, the NICs should also agree to make use of multiple exchange rates only when authorized to do so by the IMF.

The NICs, as associates of the Code, would receive the benefit of any further reductions the advanced countries made in their own tariffs and would gain the advantage of the new restraints on the use of quotas. These further measures of trade liberalization would be extended to the least developed of the LDCs without reciprocity. But if any NIC decided not to become an associate of the new Code, it would not automatically receive the benefits of further trade liberalization by the advanced countries or of the measures of trade liberalization undertaken by other NICs, although there should probably be no prohibition on any country generalizing a tariff reduction if it wished to do so.

So far as the rest of the LDCs are concerned, they too would accept a commitment to reduce tariffs and remove quotas as a part of the new overall bargain. Some automatic test would be agreed upon—probably GNP per capita despite all the drawbacks and difficulties with that as a measure of the stage of development. When it was met, other LDCs, like today's NICs,

---

[53]Very likely, by that time some of the NICs would have decided to remove the remaining tariffs and become full members of the Code.

[54]As suggested above, one of the reasons for keeping the new Tariff and Trade Code to easily identified, quantifiable trade restrictions is to improve enforcement. Another is to ease the problem of progressive application to the NICs. It is possible to think of ways of phasing obligations to liberalize quotas and reduce tariffs, but far more difficult to think of ways that rules about some of the gray area restrictions can be progressively adopted. Compare the experience of the European Community: firm timetables for tariffs and quotas could be adopted (and they were generally adhered to), but not for the elimination of various kinds of market distortions.

would have an obligation to cut their tariffs and to enlarge their quotas according to the agreed formula. There are, of course, many LDCs which, although well below the point at which this would become obligatory, should, nevertheless, be encouraged to reduce their tariffs, both in their own interest and in the interest of other LDCs. And it is important that LDC protectionism generally should be brought under international surveillance. But this would be a function not of the Tariff and Trade Code but of a separate LDC Trade Committee.

Would the LDCs and, in particular, the NICs agree? It is now widely recognized that the tariff rates of many of the developing countries are far higher than required to give needed protection to infant industries or for revenue purposes and that they simply push up costs and shelter inefficiency. In their own interest, many developing countries should lower tariffs and liberalize imports. This is particularly true of the NICs, countries, like Brazil and South Korea, that are industrializing rapidly. Yet unilateral reductions in tariffs, even where they are in a country's own interest, are peculiarly difficult to make. They should become a good deal easier to contemplate if undertaken as a part of a general restructuring of the trade system and a move to a totally new arrangement with a new distribution of costs and benefits—particularly as the replacement of the GATT by the PTO should be seen by the LDCs as meeting their frequent demands for a new ITO and, more generally, as taking a long step toward the establishment of an NIEO.

Perhaps the command-economy countries should also be eligible for associate membership in the Tariff and Trade Code. Most of the smaller East European countries have already made commitments of various kinds to expand trade as a qualification for membership in the GATT or in the context of the MTN. Some further similar commitments to trade expansion, analogous to the tariff cuts to be made by the NICs as a qualification for membership in the Code, might be required of them. But it might well be preferable to limit associate membership and the prospect of full membership in the new Code to those command-economy countries that have introduced enough change in their methods of domestic economic management so that they could in fact be treated in the same way as the NICs. Today, only Hungary would probably then be eligible.

Membership in the overall organization and in many of the other organs coming within its ambit would be open to the command-economy countries. Unless they can undertake the same obligations as other members of the Tariff and Trade Code, there are strong reasons for not stretching the mandate of that group to deal with intersystemic problems but for dealing with them elsewhere in the organization. Some problems would arise as a result of the complaints procedure and would be discussed within the Trade Policy Review Board. Others might be handled by a new special group on state-trading, a subject on which some rules already exist in the GATT but which could well be the focus of more attention in the PTO.[55]

Other Codes on Trade-Related Questions

In addition to this main Tariff and Trade Code, there would also, as already indicated, be a number of limited-member groups concerned essentially with code-making or code-enforcement on practices (e.g., state-trading) and subjects (e.g., services) that were not covered by the basic Trade and Tariff Code.[56] The general principles governing the formation of these code-drafting and code-enforcing groups would be that any country wishing to participate in the negotiation or operation of the code could do so, provided, of course, that the country belonged to the umbrella organization. If the membership in some cases proved to be identical with that of the Tariff and Trade Code, it might be sensible to amalgamate the code with that major Code. In other cases, the adhering states to a particular code would constitute a

[55]The existing GATT provisions on state-trading have remained largely unimplemented. State-trading is not, of course, limited to the command-economy countries but is resorted to, in different degrees, by most countries.

[56]As discussed further below, rule-making on direct foreign investment and business practices should come within the purview of a new Council on Direct Investment and Business Practices.

separate group.[57] Like the main Tariff and Trade Code, these code-related groups are envisioned as being mainly concerned with rule-making, and rule-enforcement, in rather well-defined areas. Problems that are not susceptible to being governed by clear and enforceable substantive rules would not be dealt with by code-related bodies but by other parts of the PTO structure. Many of them would come within the purview of the Trade Policy Review Board.

During the MTN, agreement was reached on a number of limited-member codes which would operate in a way very similar to that envisaged here. The principal difference, and it is potentially quite an important one, is that our code-related groups would operate within the general framework of, and subject to the basic principles and procedures of, the PTO.

An LDC Trade Committee

Just how much scope there is for an expansion of intra-LDC trade is a subject on which views differ. Those who favor a policy of collective self-reliance tend, not unnaturally, to set the estimates much higher than do those who argue that the LDCs' best bet for rapid development lies in incorporating themselves as quickly and as fully as possible in the international economy. Intra-LDC trade is still at a rather low level, although it has recently been increasing fairly rapidly.[58] Some of the emphasis now being given to the desirability of expanding intra-LDC trade responds—a little *too* conveniently—both to the LDC emphasis on collective self-reliance and to the concerns in the advanced countries with competition from low-priced imports from the LDCs. A strong case for expansion can be made on grounds of

[57]In some cases, the difficulties in defining and agreeing upon arrangements for the progressive incorporation of new participants would probably be reason enough for a separate code.

[58]Total intra-LDC trade increased from $8.9 billion in 1968, to $23.0 billion in 1973, to $71.4 billion in 1978—an eightfold increase over the 10-year period. As a percentage of the LDCs' total worldwide trade, however, intra-LDC trade rose only from 20 to 23 percent in the same period. Derived from Appendix Table H in GATT, *International Trade 1978/79:* Geneva, 1979.

efficiency. However, the potential for expansion is unlikely to be realized unless there are reductions—either on an m-f-n basis or preferentially among LDCs or groups of LDCs—of the extremely high tariffs (sometimes several hundred percent) that are now common in the LDC world. Under the existing GATT rules, the LDCs have the right to make tariff concessions to one another that are not generalized to other countries, but little progress in reducing very high rates has as yet been made even on an intra-LDC basis.

The formation of customs unions or free trade areas on a regional basis as a way to expand intra-LDC trade has been tried in various parts of the world. With a few exceptions, these plans have not amounted to much.[59] There would appear to be considerable potential for specialization among groups of LDCs when large investments in new production are to be made, for, normally, national markets are far too small. But even this kind of market-sharing has proved difficult, largely because of the priority all LDCs give to their own development and, in many cases, to a more or less autarchical form of industrial development.

It seems reasonably clear that any intra-LDC agreements on specialization in production, and on the tariff reductions that would be the logical accompaniment, are more likely to be made on a regional basis (or, perhaps, among a limited number of countries that have something other than geographic propinquity in common) than on an LDC-wide basis. It would, nevertheless, be desirable to have the Tariff and Trade Code, which, as just outlined, is mainly concerned with the rules governing the trade of the industrialized countries, paralleled by a body in which only the LDCs would be represented.[60] This committee would not be tied to a code but would discuss ways of expanding trade

[59]The Central American Common Market, although small in scale, has probably been the most successful. For a detailed study of the CACM and a rapid survey of other regional arrangements, see William R. Cline and Enrique Delgado, eds., *Economic Integration in Central America,* The Brookings Institution: Washington, 1978.

[60]A rather similar committee exists under the UNCTAD. See TD/RES/90(IV).

among the LDCs. In this context, it would keep under review LDC trade arrangements, both national trade restrictions and regional or other arrangements among groups of LDCs. Any proposed LDC preferential tariff arrangement, regional or otherwise, should normally be discussed in the LDC trade group and, probably, be subject to approval by the group.

Although the newly industrializing countries (NICs) would be associated with the Tariff and Trade Code, they should probably also participate as members in the LDC group until they became full members of the Code. This might help to allay doubts among the LDCs that the advanced countries were seeking to co-opt the strongest LDCs and thus to split and weaken the Group of 77. Moreover, the NICs might well become the most persuasive advocates of the adoption of more liberal trade policies by those LDCs which, although not yet ready for associate membership in the Code, could afford to reduce tariffs and to liberalize their trade in other ways. Discussion on an LDC-wide basis of trade policies and programs might also be helpful in discouraging the NICs from themselves investing too heavily in lines of production in which comparative advantage might soon shift to the poorer LDCs.

Until an LDC became eligible for associate membership in the Tariff and Trade Code, it would have no *obligation* to generalize tariff concessions it made to other LDCs, to the advanced industrialized countries, to the NICs, or to the command economies, although it should frequently be encouraged to do so.[61] But, consistent with the principle in the basic obligations of the PTO that like situations should be treated in a like way, any tariff reduction made by an LDC to another LDC should be generalized to the rest of the (non-NIC) LDCs, unless the reduction were part of a regional plan or some other special arrangement.

The LDC Committee, like other bodies within the PTO system, would operate under the general rule of transparency. Complaints could be brought to the Trade Policy Review Board

[61]To encourage LDCs to reduce tariffs generally, and not just vis-à-vis other LDCs, it might be agreed that such reductions could count as part of the reductions required for associate membership in the Code.

by any PTO member adversely affected by actions of the Committee. In this way, a measure of surveillance and control by others in the PTO would be exercised over intra-LDC trading arrangements, although the main scrutiny of intra-LDC trading arrangements would be by the LDCs themselves.

Trade Policy Review Board

The Trade Policy Review Board would be—potentially, at least—the most important organ within the PTO. Like the Executive Boards of the Bank and the Fund, it would be a standing body in continuous session, and the number of members would be limited, each member representing a group of states, save in the case of the largest states.[62] The Review Board would be the

---

[62]The analogy with the Executive Boards of the Bank and Fund is not an exact one. It will be remembered that, unlike the situation in most organizations, the weight in the proposed PTO would be, for many years to come, in the subordinate bodies rather than in the overall organization. This seems the right, indeed the only practicable, concept for an organization which is seeking to bring together under one "umbrella" a number of related functions, but ones in which the participants in the bodies concerned with particular functions vary with the function and with the willingness of countries to undertake specific obligations. It would, for example, be undesirable for the implementation of the Tariff and Trade Code and of other codes to be subject to direction from the overall body. Moreover, if a Commodities Board and a Council on Direct Foreign Investment were to be established, they too, like the groups tied to codes, would derive their authority from the obligations undertaken by their members, not by delegation from the umbrella organization. Thus, the Trade Policy Review Board is not, like the Executive Board of the Fund, the executive body for *all* functions coming within the purview of the new organization. Much of its authority would, indeed, derive from the basic trade obligations undertaken as a condition of membership, but it would also have other functions, mainly those having to do with the authorization and supervision of sectoral arrangements and special adjustment programs. These powers would not derive from the basic commitments but would need to be assigned to it in the constituent act. The PTO, unlike the Bank and the Fund, would have no independent source of funds. Partly for this reason, partly because its function is in large measure to discuss policy in areas where there are as yet no rules, the members of the Trade Policy Review Board would be paid by governments, although the welfare of the system as a whole should be a central part of their charge.

169

principal global trade *policy* body. And it would be the main place where trade procedures and policies not ready for, or susceptible to, codification but of concern to many countries—developing and developed, market economies and command economies—would be discussed. It would be the body that both authorized and kept under surveillance any special sectoral arrangements (e.g., for textiles, steel, etc.). And the review and settlement of many types of complaint would come under its aegis.

Since World War II, trade among the advanced industrialized countries has accounted for a very high proportion of total world trade, and no doubt it will continue to be of central importance in the future. Hence, there would be good arguments for putting the trade arrangements among these countries at the center of the global trading system and, while building other arrangements around them, for assuming that the practices and rules this core group can agree upon will tend to set the standard for the system as a whole. This was, essentially, the concept in the *GATT Plus* proposal, as well as the concept underlying the approach to trade and structural policy problems in Lincoln Gordon's book.

The concept underlying the proposal being put forward here is a little different. Although it seeks to reflect the realities of today's economic preponderance and not only to preserve but to extend freedom of trade and the discipline of rules among the industrialized countries, it deliberately looks forward to a world in which many of today's LDCs carry greater weight in the total system than they have in the past (or yet do). And it looks to a world in which there is a rather less pervasive assumption that the system which best suits the old industrial world is necessarily the prototype for the global system (although it may, indeed, prove to be). Thus, in the PTO, although the Tariff and Trade Code is of great importance, the main *trade policy* body would not be the governing council of that Code but the Trade Policy Review Board, which would be representative of the entire membership of PTO. Working out formulas for representation on the Board, agreeing on the composition of constituencies, and finding acceptable forms of weighted voting would not be easy, and the difficulties in so doing would be directly related to

170

the powers given to the Board by the basic agreement setting up the new organization. "Hard" and "soft" variants are conceivable. The proposal sketched here is a fairly "hard" one.

It will be recalled that one of the PTO's basic principles to which all member states would subscribe would be that actions taken for primarily domestic reasons which nevertheless had an adverse effect on other countries were of legitimate international concern. Moreover, all the committees, groups, etc., coming under the umbrella organization would operate transparently. Member states not belonging to a particular committee but nevertheless adversely affected by actions taken by that committee would have some right of recourse, although their rights would clearly be different in kind from those of states accepting the obligations of membership in a particular group. The complaints procedures envisaged for the new system would be the main way some substantive content could be given to these general principles. But also, and more importantly, the complaints procedures would be a way of identifying and seeking to handle problems that can only be satisfactorily resolved by dealing with the underlying difficulties. Many of today's most troublesome trade problems, in particular those arising from rapid shifts in comparative advantage and from domestic industrial policies, cannot yet (perhaps, ever) be dealt with by enforceable substantive rules. They have not been addressed directly by the GATT but have either given rise to requests for safeguards or have been kept out of the GATT entirely because the remedies afforded by the GATT were too limited or too stringent.

The complaints process envisaged here is central to one of the main purposes of the PTO, namely, the need to find a way to deal more directly with problems that cannot be controlled or cured by an essentially rule-making approach and, if approached mainly in that way, will continue to give rise to infringements, evasions, and widespread opting out. A start along this road was made in the MTN: the new subsidies code places heavy reliance on complaints procedures and injury tests. In the PTO, the complaints procedure process would be expanded and carried further. Moreover, except for complaints arising in the code-related groups, the process would not be a quasi-legal one of dispute settlement (as it has mainly been in the GATT), but a means of identifying problems which would then be handled in a wide variety of ways. The complaints would usually be based on claims of injury rather than of violation of an agreement. And the remedies, which would normally be found through processes of mediation and negotiation, would usually result in policy adjustments rather than in penalties or counteracting measures (like countervailing duties).

Perhaps something like the following arrangements might be envisaged. Member countries would be able to file complaints at any time with the Trade Policy Review Board. These would be examined, in the first instance, by the international staff. If the staff decided the complaint merited further consideration, it would assemble any additional material required and report the case to a panel coming under the Review Board.[63] Panels would consist of experts in the main fields covered by the review process. Balance, both geographic and among countries at different stages of development, should be roughly maintained in the composition of the panels, but members of panels should be experts, not instructed representatives of governments. In most cases, the panels would act as mediators and try to resolve the problems by making recommendations to the states or groups concerned, usually for modification of the practice giving rise to the complaint, occasionally for compensation or off-setting action. In cases where mediation procedures produced no result and where the panel was satisfied there was a substantial injury or that an important principle was involved, the panel would refer the question to the Review Board. In some instances, investigation by the panel might reveal the need for adjustments in policy that could not be made without undue hardship or without recourse to measures, such as quotas, normally prohibited by commitments undertaken within the framework of the PTO.

[63]Not only is some screening process necessary to prevent abuse, the provision for staff scrutiny, coupled with the obligation to supply material in support of claims, would tend to hold down the number of complaints. Contrary to past GATT experience, given the wide range of reasons which could be used to justify a complaint and the nature of the settlement procedures, the danger would be that the organization would be swamped by complaints.

And, in some cases, the investigations by the panel might point to the need for special, multilaterally negotiated, adjustment programs for particular sectors. Both these kinds of cases would be referred to the Trade Policy Review Board.

The process of reviewing complaints should tend, over time, to expand the list of trade practices subject to codification and, short of formal codification, to promote wider agreement on generally acceptable and unacceptable practices, enabling the Review Board to establish categories of conduct that were unlikely to be challenged and others which would provoke predictable countermeasures. In some instances, the formation of new code-related groups would be the probable result. Complaints arising from non-compliance or evasion of the rules of the Tariff and Trade Code or other code-related groups would, in contrast, normally be settled within the context of each code-related group by a quasi-legal dispute settlement process. However, if settlement of the problem giving rise to the complaint required certain types of action, such as the imposition of quotas, the problem would be referred to the Trade Policy Review Board.

It seems probable that in the future, as in the past, difficult adjustment problems will tend to center on a few particular industries and that special arrangements will be needed to facilitate a desirable process of structural change. In many instances, restrictions that moderate the pace of change will be a necessary part of this process. Neither the textile agreements negotiated within the context of the GATT nor the recent steel arrangements adopted by the Community and the United States provide good models: the first have been far too restrictive; the second were unilateral in character; and in neither case has it been clear just what kind of long-term adjustment was being sought. Future sectoral arrangements should be negotiated under the aegis of the Trade Policy Review Board and performance monitored by the Board, which, as we have said, would have the power to authorize in the context of such arrangements the temporary resort to quotas, subsidies, or other measures otherwise prohibited under the codes. Before special sectoral arrangements were negotiated, advice should normally be sought from another new body, the Advisory Council on the Structure of the Global Economy, and this Council might also at times propose that countries negotiate such arrangements.

Advisory Council on the Structure of the Global Economy

The Advisory Council is the most difficult of the new bodies to conceptualize because there is almost no experience upon which to draw. It seems safe to predict that in the decades ahead there will be, and should be, important changes in the global location of industry. There will be continuing pressures from the LDCs for deliberate shifts in patterns of production along the lines of the call in the Lima declaration for what seemed at the time to be a dramatic increase in manufacturing in the LDCs by the year 2000.[64] And there will be the actual pressure of increasing exports from the LDCs as they industrialize. There will be changes arising from technological innovation, from altered social demands, from high energy costs, and doubtless from other, as yet unforeseen, developments. And, not least, the inevitable increase in population in the developing world and the pressures this will put on the rich countries for more generous immigration policies will add force to the other arguments for seeking to encourage the shift of some manufacturing to those areas of the world that face impossibly high levels of unemployment.[65]

It is always difficult to disentangle cyclical phenomena from longer-term structural phenomena, and it is particularly difficult to do so at present when the signs of recovery from the most

[64]The Lima Plan of Action was adopted in March, 1975, at the Second General Conference of UNIDO. It recommended that the share of the LDCs in total world industrial production should be at least 25 percent by the year 2000. Although at the time this was widely regarded as an unrealistic target, today's trend suggests that something on this order may in fact be reached. See Lincoln Gordon, op. cit., Chapter 7.

[65]"In low income Asia, the labor force increased by about 125 million people between 1950 and 1975; between 1975 and 2000 . . . it is expected to increase by almost 250 million to approximately 630 million. While not so overwhelming, the projected increments in the labor force for the last quarter of the century in Sub-Saharan Africa (120 million) and Latin America and the Caribbean (100 million) are nevertheless daunting." IBRD, *World Development Report, 1979*, pp. 48–49.

severe recession since the thirties are still uncertain and uneven. Some of what today looks like over-capacity in the old established industries of the developed world could disappear quite rapidly. And some of the present preoccupation with "structural unemployment" in the industrialized countries will look quite different as the "baby bulge" works its way through the system. Clearly, the prescriptions for meeting short-term difficulties should be different from the prescriptions for meeting problems arising from the need to adapt to desirable but difficult, and undesirable but inevitable, long-term changes. The first is largely a matter of finding ways to avoid undue hardship until the situation reverses itself; this means using forms of short-term remedies that do not themselves become entrenched, thus creating new distortions. The second is partly a matter of finding ways of avoiding undue hardship but also of finding ways to encourage shifts out of one line of production into another. Not infrequently, it also involves encouraging shifts in patterns of behavior and in expectations. The task of deciding which situation falls into which category is by no means easy. The further task of identifying the new growth areas into which declining industries should be encouraged to shift resources is even more formidable. And the process of encouraging behavioral change is the most difficult of all.

In trying to identify those situations to which the right response is a shift in resources out of one line into another, or some large new investment of a kind not likely to show commercially attractive short-term returns, it seems reasonably clear that sole reliance cannot be placed either on market indicators or on planning. Markets are better at signaling short-term needs than long-term requirements, and they are notoriously bad at bringing forth the right response when the need is for investment to meet social ends or public needs. Planning leads to rigidities, timidity, and over-bureaucratization, and, in most countries, it has not been particularly successful in identifying growth points. Moreover, when planners make mistakes, they tend to be big mistakes not easily cancelled out by other actions. Most of the shortcomings in planning arise from attempts to plan in too much detail and to plan things that could better be left to the market.

Most of the shortcomings in reliance on the market stem from not feeding into the market process incentives that give appropriate weights to longer-term goals and non-economic objectives. The advantages of blending the two processes so that they reinforce one another are obvious enough. It is what all democratic governments do all the time, whether or not they have anything explicitly called a "plan" or even an industrial policy. No government has yet found the ideal mix, but all accept the need for giving some kinds of guidance to the market if desired social ends are to be attained.

A rather similar process now needs to take place on the global level. Thus, there needs to be more international study and discussion of the goals to be sought, both the socio-political and the more strictly economic goals. And more information needs to be provided to the markets. In some cases, more than just information about what ought to happen (or ought not to happen) will be necessary to encourage change. Sometimes subsidies or guarantees will be required to encourage investment, or trade policies may have to be adjusted, or manpower policies may have to be changed. To further this process of identifying areas where structural change is required and of suggesting how change might best be encouraged, something like the Advisory Council on the Structure of the Global Economy proposed here seems to be needed.

Perhaps inevitably there tends to be a presumption in the old established industrial countries that there is something "right" about the existing international distribution of production (or international division of labor) or, at least, that changes need to be justified, compensated for, and so forth. And there tends, perhaps just as inevitably, to be a presumption on the part of the newly industrializing countries that existing patterns of trade and production are biased against them and that change is not something that must be "paid for" in some way but is owed them as a matter of right or historical justice. It is important to try to reach a more widespread understanding of the efficiency benefits all can derive from structural change and also of the very real hardships that too rapid a shift can entail.

The discussion thus far has centered mainly on problems that come under the familiar rubric of international economic problems. That is to say, the focus has been on how to improve the international economic environment for all states, but the assumption has been that the nation-state is the central unit of analysis. The concept underlying the Advisory Council on the Structure of the Global Economy, as the name is meant to suggest, is different; the focus now shifts to the global economy as the unit of analysis.[66] Thus the concern of the Council would be less with how the national industrial policies of the member states can be modified so that they do not give rise to trade policies or investment policies that conflict and rather more with what might be called the development of the main lines of a global industrial policy and the implications of that policy for the adjustment of national policies. Although this shift in perspective should be noted, the distinction should not be overstated, for the consequence—in terms of international action—is less different than is the point from which the analysis starts.[67]

How might such an Advisory Council be organized and what, in general terms, might its role be? Organizationally, the Advisory Council should be a standing body like the Trade Policy Review Board, broadly representative of the PTO membership but with a limited number of members, each member representing a group of states, save in the case of a few, very large countries. The technical qualification of the members would be of great importance. But the success of the Council might well depend on its being able to draw on a highly qualified research team that would work as a more or less self-contained unit with far more independence than is customary for the staff of an inter-

---

[66]It is easy to overstate the distinction because a global welfare calculus as well as a national one underlies the process of trade liberalization.

[67]Structural changes at the national level, even if not induced by external factors, frequently have consequences for third countries and for the "structure" of the global economy, so that any discussion of structural change, whether it begins from the pressure of the LDCs for a larger proportion of the world's production and trade, or, e.g., from changes that result from shifts in values of a modern society, tends to deal with much the same range of international problems: how to "manage change" so that the costs and benefits are distributed in a way that all the affected countries consider to be fair.

national agency. It should have great freedom to interact with private and governmental research staffs and with business and labor groups throughout the world and the right to publish its findings without prior approval by governments. Policy advice to the Review Board, to other parts of the PTO, and to other parts of the U.N. system would, however, have to be approved by the Council. In other words, the staff would have the right to undertake studies on its own initiative and to publish its assessments without government endorsement. Opinions that were required as part of the decision-making process elsewhere in the system, however, would have to receive endorsement by the Council.[68] It would also be desirable for this special research unit to have funds it could use for subcontracting studies. In part, this would be a way to keep the unit from being too big, and in part, it would be a way to encourage such research to be done more widely and particularly in the LDCs. Needed reforms will only be made if understanding is widely diffused.

In discussing the proposed Trade Policy Review Board, we suggested that a number of sectoral adjustment programs might be negotiated under its aegis for industries such as steel, shipbuilding, textiles, and perhaps a few others that faced particularly difficult problems. These sectoral arrangements would be dealing piecemeal with what could well be called aspects of a global industrial policy, although the problem would, in many cases, first have become apparent in its international aspect through familiar concerns of trade policy, such as a country's wish to impose restrictions, or to slow down on an agreed rate of liberalization, or to subsidize an ailing industry.[69] To ensure that

---

[68] In a discussion of this kind, it is not useful to try to spell out details like the nature of rights and prerogatives of research staffs. But if an Advisory Council of the kind suggested here is to have its opinions carry weight, they must rest on analysis of the highest quality. There is always a tension between the need to ensure independent research and the need for official participation in the formulation of recommendations to which governments must subscribe. Perhaps a better way than that suggested above for squaring the circle can be found.

[69] See Diebold, op. cit., pp. 266–272, for a discussion of the two routes to industrial policy: via trade problems and directly.

adequate attention is given to the effect special arrangements for one sector have on other sectors and for guidance about the prospects for the affected sector, the Review Board should seek prior advice from the Advisory Council as a matter of course. The panels should also normally seek advice from the Council before recommending certain types of adjustment. And advisory opinions from the Council might well be sought by other parts of the U.N. system, and in particular by the Bank group and the regional banks.

One particular idea seems to be well worth exploring when considering the future evolution of the World Bank. In brief, if, as seems probable, adjustment to structural change is likely to be one of the major international economic problems in the eighties and beyond, it might be desirable for the IBRD to do more than it has in the past in helping to finance the process of adjustment.[70] Loans might be made to any country at *any* stage of development that was having difficulty financing adjustments (retraining workers, financing new capital investments, writing off old ones). Applications to the Bank for such loans might be made by countries and, possibly, also directly by firms without having to go through national governments. The Trade Policy Review Board, too, might sometimes recommend that financial assistance be given rather than authorizing, or in addition to authorizing, temporary restrictive arrangements. If the Bank were to administer some such program of "adjustment loans," it would be logical for it to seek advice from the Advisory Council as a matter of routine in the processing of the loans.

Six general propositions about adjustment assistance are today fairly widely held. First, if the trend toward freer trade is to continue, there must be more adequate national programs of adjustment assistance. Second, it is difficult, and probably mistaken, to limit access to national adjustment assistance to dislo-

---

[70]See the discussion of some somewhat similar ideas in Diebold, op. cit., Chapter 5. See also *Employment, Growth and Basic Needs*, Praeger, for the ILO and the Overseas Development Council: New York, 1977, p. 122, for another similar idea put forward by the ICFTU in Mexico City in October, 1975.

cations resulting only from imports. Third, the grant of exceptions to commitments to free trade should be tied more directly than they have been in the past to specific timetables of adjusting. Fourth, there are costs of not adjusting as well as costs of adjusting. Fifth, the costs of adjusting or of not adjusting should be shared among the countries affected. And, finally, one must look beyond the confines of the nation-state if one is seeking to distinguish "positive" or desirable adjustment from "negative" or purely defensive adjustment. Some of these propositions point to the need for more generous and flexible national programs of adjustment assistance. But most of them call for more action at the international level as well: to link the right to impose trade restrictions to timetables for adjustment; to spread the financial burden of adjustment where this is appropriate; and to ensure that adjustments are made with the fullest possible information on the consequences of adjustment and of non-adjustment.

Under the proposal sketched here, the Trade Policy Review Board would be directly concerned with linking exceptional trade restrictions to timetables for adjustment. The World Bank would, where necessary, help with the financial costs of adjustment. And the Advisory Council would have as its mandate the constant study and dissemination of information about changing patterns of production and investment, pointing out places where (viewed from a global perspective) resources seemed likely to be used inefficiently unless changes in policy were made.

Is there any reason to believe that an Advisory Council of the kind suggested, even if composed of people of the highest caliber and assisted by the highest-powered research staff imaginable, could arrive at enough consensus on the kinds of change that should be encouraged or discouraged to make its opinions of the slightest use? Would there have to be some prior agreement on the objectives that were being sought, such as the attainment of some level of industrial production in the LDCs reminiscent of the Lima resolution? Or, at least, must some agreement exist that the goal was to raise per capita incomes to some level by some date and that shifts in patterns of production would be evaluated against a set of guidelines of this kind? Merely to ask the questions is to conclude that nothing useful can be done. Either one runs the risk of so much dissensus that confusion would be more likely than useful guidance, or the Council would tend to become committed to some over-rigid global plan, an outcome which might well be worse than confusion. But these are counsels of despair, which, we believe, seriously underestimate the amount of consensus that can be detected, even today, when intelligent people are asked to focus not on the needs of particular countries but specifically on the needs of a well-functioning global economy. Perhaps the results would be disappointing. But simply injecting a view of the consequences of particular developments for the system as a whole—as a kind of benchmark against which bargains should be tested—into what is still, essentially, a process of international negotiation would seem to be well worth doing.

Agriculture

Agriculture presents many special problems, some of which call for changes in other institutions. But a few points should be made here. Those manufactured agricultural products which are now dealt with in much the same way as other manufactured products would continue to be dealt with in that way and would be covered by the Tariff and Trade Code and the other code-related groups described above. But agricultural protection generally should be brought under more effective international scrutiny and regulation than it is today.

Agriculture is a sectoral problem writ large. It would probably be desirable to have a special agricultural group coming under the Trade Policy Review Board, broader than but conceptually similar to the special sectoral groups envisaged for textiles, shipbuilding, etc. Since agriculture comprises so many separate groups of commodities and activities, each with its own special problems, many people will immediately argue that this would unbalance the whole arrangement and that there should be a special agriculture group at least on a par with the two major policy bodies we have thus far identified: the Trade Policy Review

Board and the Advisory Council.[71] Despite the superficial logic of this argument there are strong reasons for resisting it and, in the context of the PTO, for dealing with agricultural sectors in much the same way as with industrial sectors because agriculture, in relation to and in competition with other lines of activity, is a dimension of the problem that is too infrequently given enough attention either within states or internationally.

It is widely agreed that only by a willingness to discuss and to modify domestic agricultural support arrangements can progress be made in reducing agricultural protection. For many years, the developed countries have recognized this as the road that must be followed, but little progress has yet been made in the GATT, in the OECD, or in the European Community despite much discussion, negotiation, and acrimonious debate in all three places. The international interest in open markets, the consumers' interest in lower prices, and the general goal of a more efficient use of resources—both nationally and internationally—would best be served by acceptance of the principle, at least in the developed countries, that farmers should be supported by direct income payments rather than by high prices maintained above free market levels by variable levies, production controls, import quotas, and other similar arrangements. But as the European Community's experience with the Common Agricultural Policy has shown, there is no prospect of any such principle being acceptable to countries that still have more than a small percentage of their population on the land. It puts too large and too visible a load on the exchequer.

Perhaps, though, it might be possible for the main agricultural producers in the developed world to agree that some percentage of the total support given to farmers should be through direct income subvention rather than through measures designed to support incomes through higher prices and that this percentage should increase gradually over time. This might be coupled with

---

[71]During the MTN there was some discussion of setting up a general group on agricultural trade, but in the end advisory groups (Councils) on meat and dairy products were all that could be agreed to by a significant number of countries.

some form of the *montant de soutien* approach to bargaining down agricultural protection that was proposed by the Community in the Kennedy Round.[72] Doubtless there are other approaches to bargaining down restrictions that might usefully be explored in one (or more) sectoral groups concerned with the problems of protection among the principal producers of temperate zone agricultural products. The results of the bargaining might, in time, become codes. Other countries not party to the bargaining or to the eventual codes would, of course, have the usual rights of complaint if these bargains or codes adversely affected them.

Commodities Board

The line is a thin one between the kind of discussion, surveillance, and bargaining that might be carried on by one or more sectoral groups concerned with agriculture under the Trade Policy Review Board and the kind of surveillance that was discussed for certain commodity groups in the context of the UNCTAD negotiations on the Common Fund. And any special sectoral groups for agriculture might (like similar groups for other commodities that present special problems) come under a Commodities Board[73] rather than the Trade Policy Review Board.[74]

---

[72]In brief, the Community proposed that as a basis for bargaining on agricultural products one should calculate the margin of support (*montant de soutien*) or difference between the world price and the price paid national producers. The proposal in the Kennedy Round was simply that these amounts be bound for three years, but, obviously, they might later, like tariffs, be bargained down.

[73]If the bold step were taken of forming a new Production and Trade Organization to supersede the GATT and the UNCTAD, it would be logical (and desirable in the interests of better coordination) to bring much of the work envisaged for the Common Fund within the ambit of the PTO. But it would not be essential to do so. A separate Commodities Board or Council might simply be closely linked with the PTO but not formally become a part of the new structure.

[74]The Wheat Agreement should become a Cereals Agreement and be brought within PTO, presumably under general aegis of a Commodities Board.

183

The reason for having a separate Commodities Board is in part historical. Rightly or wrongly, commodities were singled out for particular attention by the UNCTAD, and, after many years of arduous negotiations, it has been agreed that the Common Fund for commodities should be established as a new specialized agency of the United Nations. To eliminate all "specialness" in the treatment of commodity problems would be to ask for too much in the interests of neatness and consistency. In any case, there are some positive reasons for suggesting that a Commodities Board should have a place in the new institution. Although many of the problems that have in the past been called commodity problems are aspects of other issues that should be dealt with elsewhere in the new organization, some questions, mainly having to do with the principles that should underlie any negotiations on specific commodity arrangements, do raise questions of a distinctive kind. And there are some issues, common to all commodity agreements, that might usefully be considered by such a Board.

Like the Trade Policy Review Board and the Advisory Council, the membership of the Commodities Board, although limited in number, should be representative of the entire membership of the PTO. It would have under it both any formal commodity arrangements (ICAs) that are negotiated and any less formal commodity study or surveillance groups that are found necessary. In these subordinate commodity groups, membership would be restricted to those countries participating in the agreement, or, in the case of less formal groups, those concerned either as principal producers or as principal consumers. Here, as elsewhere in the PTO, the rule of transparency and the right of complaint would apply.

The Commodities Board would be the review board for complaints arising from the operation of commodity agreements, and it would be the successor to the Committee on Commodities of the UNCTAD as the place where the need for new commodity agreements or less formal commodity arrangements were first explored. It would formally succeed the Common Fund and would administer the account designed to facilitate the operation of buffer stocks in the (rather limited) number of cases where this proves to be a desirable way to stabilize prices around the long-term trend.

It might also assist poor countries to finance nationally held stocks where this was agreed by the Board to be desirable (taking over that function from the IMF's buffer-stock facility). Although, as currently conceived, the Common Fund would also finance diversification schemes, the development of processing industries, and similar projects, it would be more consistent with our conception of the respective roles of the PTO and the Bank for these "second window" functions to be handled by the Bank.[75]

If the commodities work now centered in the UNCTAD and which can be expected to gravitate to the new Common Fund were *not* brought within the ambit of the PTO in this way but simply floated free, two problems would arise. First, there would be a considerable danger that too many trade-related aspects of commodity problems would escape from the discipline of the general trade rules, and this would run counter to one of the central purposes of the PTO which is to bring a higher proportion of world trade within a common rule system. The second problem is that it would be far harder to establish the links with the Advisory Council that would seem desirable.[76] Special commodity arrangements are not much different in concept from special arrangements covering particular industrial sectors, such as textiles and steel. The argument in both cases is that special

[75]In negotiating the "second window" or "second account," the LDCs, strongly supported by the UNCTAD Secretariat, argued that neither the World Bank nor the regional development banks took sufficient account of world market conditions when financing projects in individual countries. The broadening of the Bank's operations in the commodities field, by absorbing the development financing functions foreseen for the second window of the Common Fund, would be consistent with the general direction in which we think the Bank should move.

[76]Although the Advisory Council would not have direct power, its advice should be sought before any special agreements—for industrial sectors or for commodity groups—were negotiated, for it should be in a better position than any other group to set the prospects of a particular sector in the broader context, a process that not infrequently casts a somewhat different light on the problem.

factors make it undesirable simply to rely on the market and on free trade. And usually, in both cases, the problem is seen as one of over-supply of the market in the absence of some form of market management or production control.

Many aspects of what is today known as the commodities problem are, of course, aspects of trade policy generally: how to make markets work openly, fairly, and efficiently. Or they are aspects of questions having to do with structural adjustment and location of production discussed above in connection with the Advisory Council on the Structure of the Global Economy. If those parts of the PTO function efficiently, much of the heat should go out of the commodities debate, and the Commodities Board should tend to become less important.[77] Similarly, many of the commodity issues that have in the past been particularly contentious, especially those associated with extracting raw materials, are aspects of the set of interrelated issues having to do with the norms that should apply to and the rules that should govern direct foreign investment and are best considered in that context.

Council on Direct Foreign Investment and Business Practices

Some of the problems that have led people to argue for a "GATT for Investment" were touched on earlier when we discussed the weaknesses and gaps in the existing arrangements. Both the OECD and the United Nations have tried to find enough common ground to make the drafting of codes a productive exercise, but even the relatively homogeneous OECD group has, as yet, made only modest progress. Nevertheless, for the reasons already suggested, the main emphasis for the present should probably continue to be placed on discussions within the OECD. But rule-making at the global level also needs to be fostered. If the GATT and UNCTAD were replaced by a new PTO, it would be logical to establish a Council on Direct Foreign Investment and Business Practices as a principal body in the new organization

[77]In any case, it probably should not be a standing committee, in continuous session like the other principal bodies, but a Board that meets two or three times a year.

and for it to absorb much of the work in those areas now done elsewhere. Probably the Council should be constituted in much the same way as the Trade Policy Review Board, that is, the membership should be limited to some manageable number (20 to 30) and drawn from the full membership, with most countries grouped into constituencies and represented collectively by a single member. As on the trade side of the PTO, there could be any number of limited-member subgroups concerned with rule-making and rule-enforcement on various aspects of foreign investment: overlapping jurisdictions, rules for enticing investments, the conditions on investment that might be imposed by host governments, and the conduct of enterprises.

The Council's role, like that of the Trade Policy Review Board, would be to discuss issues that were not ripe for or susceptible to code-making and to try to expand the area of agreed practices, and to consider complaints that could not be settled by panels charged with investigating and mediating complaints. Since rule-making in this area is still far behind that on the trade side, there would be few cases calling for quasi-legal dispute-settlement arrangements. But the general rules of the PTO (with appropriate modifications) should apply to investment as to trade, that is, any country considering itself injured by the action of another should have a general right of complaint, like situations should be treated in like ways, and what would entitle a country to benefits of a particular code would be its acceptance of the obligations of that code. There would thus be plenty of scope for complaints, and, as with trade issues, these should first be examined by expert panels and solutions found at that level wherever possible, mainly by mediation. Intractable cases or those raising larger points of principle would be referred to the Council on Direct Investment.

* * *

This brief sketch of what a new Production and Trade Organization might look like has doubtless raised more questions than it has answered. To discuss in detail just what would be taken over from the existing GATT and what the precise content of new codes might be, to explore ways in which structural adjustments might be facilitated, and to do justice to issues, like direct foreign investment, that have simply been ticked off in this discussion would require several books.

For the next few years, the key governments will be preoccupied with implementing the agreements reached in the MTN and testing the limits of the new codes that were reached in that context. Decisions on what should come next must be based, in large measure, on the outcome of that process. But it is not too soon to begin the discussion of what more is likely to be needed. Even on optimistic assumptions about the way the new procedures agreed to during the MTN will be implemented, that leg of the tripod which is today represented by the GATT and UNCTAD seems likely to remain the weakest of the three and unlikely to be able to support for long the rule structure and the other forms of cooperative behavior on trade and production questions that are becoming increasingly necessary at the global level.

In the first part of this chapter and in the course of the discussion of what a PTO might look like, we have identified a number of gaps that should be filled and suggested various changes in existing ways of doing things. As we have tried to make plain, the discussion of the PTO is meant to be illustrative and suggestive; it does not purport to be an exhaustive or a definitive analysis of how the problems that need to be thought more about can best be handled.

It is very important to build on the substantial progress that has been made during the last three decades in freeing trade and subjecting national commercial policies to international surveillance and to a system of rules. Efforts at reform can all too easily be pretexts for backsliding. But, one way or another, steps need to be taken in the decade ahead to move beyond the essentially "first world" system of trade regulation that we have today to a more comprehensive, yet, at the same time sensibly differentiated system. The traditional processes of rule-making need to be expanded, both to cover more practices and to incorporate more countries. But it will also be necessary to bring under more multilateral surveillance and influence those aspects of national industrial policies which most strongly affect global patterns of trade and production. Here substantive rules are difficult to draft, and, in any case, that will frequently not be the right way to find the answers to many of the problems that are likely to arise. Structural changes within countries and the growth of the world economy are far too closely interrelated to say that the international community has no interest in these matters except insofar as they give rise to the kind of trade disputes with which we have some experience and for which we have some tested rules.

There are many variations on the ideas on institutional reform that have been sketched out. For example, although we see conceptual and practical advantages in keeping the major Tariff and Trade Code limited to those rules which the advanced industrial countries can accept without much qualification and without cumbersome safeguarding arrangements and for deliberately shifting the weight of trade *policy* discussions to a high-level restricted Board representative of all members of the PTO, a case can be made for a less radical shift, for keeping rather more of a rule-making function in a "GATT-minus" group and not seeking, at this stage at least, to make the Trade Policy Review Board as central an organ as we envision.

We prefer the bolder approach which makes a more radical break with the past, partly because we think the LDCs would be likely to be more prepared to participate constructively in an institution that would be such a clear and positive response to some of the more well-founded demands in the NIEO. Some people will argue that the LDCs are not yet ready for compromises which involve any acceptance of new responsibilities on their part, and that confusion in trade policy at the global level (with perhaps rather more order among the industrial countries maintained within the framework of the OECD) will prevail for a decade or two before the LDCs are ready for a trade and production organization that would compare in strength and in importance with the IMF in the monetary area. This seems to us unduly pessimistic: if it becomes the excuse for inaction, it may well become a self-fulfilling prophecy.

Other people will argue that the experience with the ITO should be taken to heart, that one of the reasons why it failed to secure the approval of the U.S. Senate was because it tried to do too much. There was something in it for everyone to be against. The PTO is, quite unashamedly, a modern version of the ITO. But times have changed, and much of what we are now suggesting be brought together under one umbrella is already being looked at somewhere in the system, although not usually very adequately. Moreover, today it is far more evident to far more people than it was 35 years ago that not only are economies interdependent but that issues, too, are interdependent. Action in any one area, if it is to bring the intended result, frequently requires action in a closely related area. We are not proposing the creation of a vast new international organization to add to an already over-rich array but, rather, the replacement of two not very satisfactory global-level organizations with one which might both be more efficient and command wider support. But it cannot be said too often that no institutional arrangements will be of much use unless governments are prepared to adopt policies to reverse the present slide toward protection and to encourage the process of an orderly adjustment to new patterns of global production.

POSTSCRIPT ON EAST-WEST TRADE

We have thus far had little to say about problems of East-West trade, not because they are unimportant but because, in themselves, they do not constitute strong reasons for thinking in terms of much change in the existing system. Unlike the problems posed by the virtual exclusion of the LDCs from today's rule-system and the need for more global concern with the process of structural adjustment, the problems posed by inter-systemic trade could probably be well enough dealt with, for the next decade or so, in the makeshift ways they have thus far been handled. Some aspects of this relationship, however, might be better handled if there were a new institution along the lines we have proposed. And little, if anything, would be lost by moving to the new system.

The substantial increase in trade and other forms of economic intercourse between the Soviet Union and other East European countries and the industrialized market economies of the West that has taken place during the sixties and seventies has led to mixed reactions on the part of Western analysts. Some have seen a danger that the state-controlled economies of the East would manipulate trade, credit arrangements, co-production, and "buy-back" agreements to the disadvantage of the Western countries. The latter, eager to expand their export trade, have thus far been reluctant to coordinate their actions with one another on such things as credit terms, and, in any case, have only limited control over the bargains struck by their enterprises with their counterparts in the controlled economies. Other analysts have argued that the expansion of economic relationships poses more problems for the command economies than for the market economies, and that the growing economic involvement of East European countries with the rest of the world not only places strains on their internal domestic systems but means that they have enough interest in the efficient functioning of the international economic system to make them less willing to take actions to disrupt it than their rhetoric about the collapse of the capitalist international economic order might suggest.[78]

Perhaps something more should be done to see that Western countries do not find themselves in credit wars with one another in their efforts to find markets in Eastern Europe, and there may be a case for rather more intra-OECD information sharing, given the far-reaching coordination that takes place within Comecon.[79] But our main concern here is with the future needs at the global

[78]Extreme proponents of each view are easy enough to find. For a moderate and balanced statement of the first view, see Raymond Vernon, "The Fragile Foundations of East-West Trade," *Foreign Affairs*, Summer, 1979; and of the second, see Caldwell's study in Lawrence T. Caldwell and William Diebold, Jr., *Soviet-American Relations in the 1980s: Superpower Politics and East-West Trade*, McGraw-Hill, for the Council on Foreign Relations/1980s Project: New York, 1980.

[79]The OECD holds some discussions on these questions, but it is unlikely to go very far, partly because of the reluctance of the European neutrals, probably more importantly because the major OECD countries are not yet convinced they have more to gain by cooperation than by competition in this area. Rather more coordination of economic policy vis-à-vis Eastern Europe than has in fact yet taken place would seem to be logical for the countries of the European Community.

level. And, unless there is a sharp deterioration in the political climate, it seems reasonably safe to predict that trade and other forms of economic intercourse between the socialist economies and the market economies, developed and developing, will continue to expand. If this is true, it would seem desirable—whether one subscribes broadly to the first or (as we incline to do) broadly to the second view about where the balance between advantage and danger is likely to be struck—to seek to bring these trade relationships under rather more international surveillance than is the case today and to provide for more multilateral discussion of problems posed by systemic differences. Moreover, where participation in substantive rules or in code-making is likely to be useful to all participants, there is every reason for helping it to take place.

Of course, sharp differences exist in the way economic relationships with the West and with the rest of the world generally are looked at by the smaller East European countries and by the Soviet Union. Not only are the smaller countries far more dependent economically on their links with other countries, particularly those with Western Europe, but they attach great political importance to these ties. Moreover, most of them have introduced enough changes into their systems of economic management to make it not too difficult to find ways to incorporate them in the GATT. Except for the German Democratic Republic, Bulgaria, and Albania, all the smaller East European countries are members of the GATT, and Bulgaria participated in the MTN, which was not limited to GATT members.

The relationship between the Soviet Union and the central trading system has evolved very differently. At the very start of the ITO negotiations, the United States put forward provisions intended to enable the Soviet Union and other state-trading countries to participate. But the Soviet Union took no part in the negotiations, and those sections of the U.S. proposal that had been drafted with the Soviet Union specifically in mind were dropped. All that remained were some provisions on state-trading which were mainly concerned with seeking to ensure that state-run enterprises within states that were generally market-oriented followed the same rules as did other enterprises and did not operate so that they undermined the commercial policy rules of the proposed Charter. When the first round of tariff negotiations was undertaken and commercial policy provisions similar to those being considered for the Charter adopted as the negotiating framework, the Soviet Union again showed no interest in participating. Nor during the years since this first meeting of the GATT has there been any Soviet interest in joining the GATT or in participating in multilateral negotiations, although obtaining m-f-n treatment from the United States and other countries has been a priority item for some years.

The Soviet Union is a member of the UNCTAD, which, of course, is an integral part of the central U.N. structure, and, from time to time, the Soviet Union has shown some interest in the establishment of a new world trade organization. But there has been little indication of just what the Soviet Union envisages as the role of a world trade organization, and one is left with the impression that support for it is simply a part of the general Russian preference for U.N. organizations, where the one-nation, one-vote principle is strongly entrenched. Possibly, too, this may be seen as a way to guard against the development of too much independence on the part of the smaller East European countries, which the Soviets might feel participation in the GATT could tend to encourage. Whatever the motivation, no specific plan has ever been put forward, nor have the Soviets given anything but routine support to various efforts made by the LDCs to turn the UNCTAD into a new ITO.

Although the General Agreement contains an article on state-trading (Article XVII), it, like the provisions in the ITO from which it was derived, is mainly concerned with seeing that state-run enterprises in market-oriented economies follow the same rules as other enterprises. Little has been done to give much content to this article, which is somewhat surprising because the amount of trade carried on by state-controlled enterprises in both the old industrialized states and the LDCs is very substantial and a rich source of non-tariff barriers. Probably rather more should be done to try to give content to this article in the future, perhaps through developing a more elaborate code built on the principles contained in the article. But a state-trading code built

193

on Article XVII would not, by itself, be adequate to handle the problems that seem likely to follow in the wake of any substantial expansion of East-West trade and related activities.

Problems of East-West trade were looked at in some detail by William Diebold in another study for the 1980s project.[80] As he pointed out, several different types of device can be used to bring about more participation by the Eastern European countries, including the Soviet Union, in a common system of rules and procedures. In the past, access commitments of various kinds have frequently been the counterpart for the tariff concessions granted by the market economies, and he suggested that a formula based partly on access commitments, partly on undertakings of equal treatment might well be used more generally and more multilaterally as one bridge between the two systems. As we have seen in our earlier discussion, and as Diebold points out in his study, two rather different processes now characterize the international approach to problems of trade policy. One process is concerned with refining rules to make a system based essentially on free market concepts fairer and freer. The other process is concerned with seeing that government interventions of various kinds do not shift the burden of adjustment onto others or do not create new problems in the course of solving old ones. Participation in the first process is even less easy for command economies than for many LDCs; participation in the second presents far fewer problems. In a world in which this second process seems likely to become more important, systemic differences tend to become, if not wholly irrelevant, at least far less important as hindrances to collective action.[81]

A somewhat similar picture emerges when one looks at the various types of industrial cooperation arrangements between Western firms and Eastern state-owned enterprises that are in-

[80]See Diebold's study in Caldwell and Diebold, op. cit.

[81]For the discussion from which this point was derived, see William Diebold, "The Soviet Union in the World Economy," a paper prepared for the Joint Economic Committee of the U.S. Congress and reproduced in John P. Hardt, ed., *Soviet Economy in a Time of Change*, Joint Committee Print, 96th Cong., 1st Sess., GPO: Washington, 1979, vol. 1, pp. 51–70.

creasingly characteristic of East-West relationships. As William Diebold, again, points out, these, too, provide ways of linking the two quite different systems by bypassing the market. Some of these interfirm agreements raise questions that are similar in kind to questions that arise from the transnational activities of multinationals generally. And where this is the case, there may be value in having at least some of the East European countries participating in any code-related groups that are discussing these issues. Rule-making on a global basis, to the extent it proves to be possible, should ease rather than intensify the difficulties Raymond Vernon foresees if deals of this kind proliferate and there is no coordination among the West European countries. It is unlikely to go far enough to run into the rather different problem that Diebold has drawn attention to, namely, that premature codification of rules governing interfirm arrangements might impede the desirable process of increasing differentiation among the countries of Eastern Europe.

In short, the main thrust of the analysis in William Diebold's 1980s Project study is one that tends, if not positively to support, at least to be congruent with the changes that we suggest might be made in the existing trade regime. His central argument—that it is feasible and desirable to incorporate the command economies in certain codes, such as those on standards, where there is nothing to be lost and much to be gained by the widest possible adherence to agreed rules, and yet at the same time important that the highly industrialized, highly interdependent market economies be free to go ahead without these countries where they would be at best passengers and at worst troublemakers— is easy to meet under our proposed system. Moreover, if, as seems probable, there is increasing concern with problems arising both from the shifts and the reluctance to see shifts in the patterns of global production, the command-economy countries will, at least in certain sectors, be producers who cannot rationally be left out of the discussion, for their production and their trade with the rest of the world will be too important to be treated as a residual. A recent analysis of today's GATT— looked at from the standpoint of the smaller countries of Eastern Europe—also suggests that our PTO might respond rather well to a number of the difficulties those countries encounter with the present system.[82]

Whether or not the Soviet Union would decide to join the umbrella organization is impossible to tell. Consistent with its views about the importance of keeping to a minimum any international concern with domestic policies, the Soviet Union would doubtless seek to weaken key elements in the new organization which derive essentially from the belief that more rather than less global concern with domestic policies is becoming essential, starting with the first basic principle we have proposed for the new PTO. These principles are too important to be sacrificed to obtain Russian agreement.[83]

[82]See M. M. Kostecki, *East-West Trade and the GATT System,* St. Martin's Press, New York, for the Trade Policy Research Centre: London, 1979. Kostecki is a Polish economist, now living in Canada.

[83]After this chapter was completed, and indeed after it had been informally published by the Council on Foreign Relations, the People's Republic of China began to show interest in joining the GATT. It seems likely that China will become a member before the book is published. Again, the arrangements suggested for our proposed PTO would seem to be rather better tailored to the special requirements of the Chinese system than is today's GATT.

SIX

The Management of Money and Coordination of Macroeconomic Policy

Perhaps surprisingly, in view of the frequency with which one hears that the Bretton Woods system has broken down and efforts to build a new system have failed, there is less need, in our view, to think about drastic organizational change in the monetary field than there is in the trade field. Bagehot's comment that "money does not manage itself" was made in the context of national policy, but it is accepted in the international context as well. And, in contrast to the uneasy GATT/UNCTAD partnership, the International Monetary Fund (IMF) would seem to be capable of evolving to provide the management at the global level that is needed and of becoming a strong second leg of the "tripod."

Turmoil in the foreign exchange markets, widespread inflation, unprecedentedly high interest rates, low growth, the skyrocketing price of gold—all these and other signs of economic disorder were all too apparent at the end of the seventies. They provided powerful evidence that the countries most responsible for the health of the economic system were bewildered by the economic problems they faced and unable to handle them effectively, either on a separate, national basis or collectively. For the most part, the difficulties besetting the system pointed to the need for better domestic management by national authorities, but they also underlined the need for more coordination of policy among the key countries and for strengthening, in various ways, the IMF's role at the center of the system.

In some ways, the IMF was a less important institution by the end of the seventies than it had been in the sixties. The abandonment of the par-value system had removed the key to the Fund's role at the center of the exchange-rate system, and the growth of Eurocurrency markets and the huge amounts of petrodollars had made it tempting for many LDCs to raise money in commercial markets—frequently at very short term and at very high rates of interest—thus escaping the strict conditions traditionally imposed by the Fund. The Fund seemed to some observers to be too detached from the "real" world and to be becoming increasingly irrelevant. The slow, deliberate, IMF-based effort to move in an orderly way from a system in which the dollar was the principal reserve asset to one in which the Special Drawing Right (SDR), or an improved "man-made" asset, played this role was being outpaced by an unplanned and disorderly shift to a multicurrency world. The private sector was running well ahead of official institutions in adapting itself to new needs and supplying the "public good" of recycling funds from surplus to deficit areas. And yet, when thinking about the institutions needed at the global level, we come back to a strengthened IMF as the essential centerpiece of the monetary system.

As in the trade area, so in the monetary area better ways should be found to combine the common rules and procedures that are required if there is to be order in the global system with special arrangements to meet special needs. The tension between the global character of many economic phenomena and the national character of the principal political units is most evident in the monetary sphere. And more far-reaching coordination of policy among the key countries is needed both to underpin the system and to make it more orderly. These countries must be ready to go further than most states need to do in organizing relationships with one another, and they must be permitted by other states to do so. At the same time there is a particular need to ensure that the key countries give more weight to longer-term and systemic concerns in national policy-making and in their collective decisions because the health of the system is largely determined by their actions. Institutional arrangements (both organizational forms and guiding principles) must not be static, they must respond to shifts in the distribution of economic power. And here, as elsewhere, when looking at the changes that might be made to improve the system, the distribution of costs and benefits, of powers and responsibilities should be seen not as a bargain on its own but as one part of the broader picture we are sketching. The balance struck in the Fund will, and should be, rather different from that in the World Bank.

In the very long term, the IMF should become a true global central bank: issuing and managing the world's common reserve asset, presumably an improved SDR; regulating the practices of financial institutions; promoting the harmonization of macroeconomic policies; perhaps providing countercyclical financing; and acting as the system's lender of last resort. There is no possibility of taking a quantum leap forward to that world in the decade of the eighties or, indeed, for the foreseeable future, for a true global bank presupposes a high level of political integration. But short- to medium-term reforms should lead in that direction, not away from it. The piecemeal reforms being made and the slow process of evolution that is under way lead, for the most part, in the right direction, although the trend line is a jagged one. Here, as elsewhere, the seventies have witnessed a swing away from collective action toward more national freedom of action.

At the end of the seventies there were fairly wide areas of disagreement about the lines along which it was desirable to move, both to deal with the urgent immediate problems and to improve the functioning of the system over the longer term. Some of the disagreements stemmed from disputes at the theoretical level, some from differences about the lessons to be drawn from the available empirical evidence, while others derived from the way different answers to apparently highly technical questions (e.g., asset settlement, guidelines for floating) affected national freedom of action or altered the distribution among countries of powers and benefits. Nevertheless, there were reasons for thinking that the evolutionary route (as well as being the only feasible one) could prove to be fruitful and not, as it threatened to be in the trade field, a prescription for organized backsliding. In the first place, the breakdown of the par-value system, coupled with the need to meet new crises (e.g., the massive supply of petrodollars) dealt a healthy blow to some shibboleths, made some new thinking inescapable, and led to hitherto "unthinkable" arrangements being tried. Second, the years spent in the early seventies discussing fundamental issues in an attempt to arrive at agreement on the essentials of an improved system were not spent wholly fruitlessly, despite what critics said. Finally, there is in the monetary field a large community of government officials and professional experts, national and international, who have now had wide experience both with crisis management and with the humdrum, day-to-day management of money. They have few illusions about the limits of national autonomy, and they are generally readier to think in systemic terms than are their counterparts in other areas.

It comes as a surprise to anyone who is reasonably familiar with the broad sweep of international relations, but only recently introduced to the mysteries of money management, to find that some of the least starry-eyed and most hard-headed economists not only believe that the IMF should gradually evolve into a global central bank—a central bankers' Central Bank—but also do not regard that outcome as a wildly improbable one.[1] They do not see, nor would they advocate, quantum jumps into such a new régime, but they are surprisingly willing to draw analogies —with appropriate modification—between the evolution of the modern banking system at the national level and a similar evolution on the world level. Moreover, as demonstrated most clearly by the decision taken a decade ago to create SDRs, governments have been prepared to take rather more explicit

[1]For example, Richard N. Cooper, Robert A. Mundell, and the late Harry G. Johnson. The term "global central bank" is frequently used rather loosely, and not all economists who use the term would define the functions such a bank would need to perform in precisely the same way. In particular, some economists would only use the term in the context of a fixed exchange-rate system. Others would use the term for a less far-reaching centralized system in which a "central bankers' central bank" would control the creation of international reserves but only "affect" not "control" national money creation. Moreover,

steps toward new forms of collective management with regard to money than they have yet shown themselves prepared to do in other fields.

It is worth pausing to ask why this should be so, for money lies very close to the bone of national sovereignty. A large part of the answer lies in the fact that money markets are more truly internationalized, or denationalized, than are other markets and that governments, whether they like it or not, have had to find forms of management that correspond with the factual situation. Moreover, an exchange rate is a shared instrument: it cannot be effectively "managed" by a single country. Another part of the answer may lie in the fact that for 20 years or so there was an international money system run by the dominant economic power, the United States, and most other countries' economic policies were highly constrained by external factors. As the distribution of economic power became more evenly spread, resistance to U.S. economic dominance and to a system run by the United States was inevitable. But except, perhaps, for the United States itself, there were few illusions that monetary policy could be exercised autonomously. Yet another part of the answer may lie in the fact that very few people really understood what was happening in the monetary field. While the old U.S.-run system was providing, and providing rather efficiently, the public good of a reasonably stable international money, very few political leaders—General de Gaulle being the outstanding exception—felt a need to make it clear to their people how little real freedom of action governments have in the conduct of monetary policy. Economic analysis may not have been de Gaulle's strongest suit, but he was clear that only by constraining the

---

economists would differ, as they do in the context of national policy, on whether or not a global central bank should attempt countercyclical financing. For one very general discussion of the attributes of a global central bank and an appraisal of the IMF's slow but steady progress toward that goal, see *Toward a World Central Bank?*, The Per Jacobsson Foundation, Lecture and Commentaries by William McChesney Martin, Karl Blessing, Alfredo Machado Gomez, Harry G. Johnson: Basle, September, 1970.

freedom of action of the United States could the "indepen-dence" he claimed for France be regained.[2]

A basic disagreement exists between the industrialized coun-tries and the LDCs over the extent to which the monetary sys-tem should be looked to as a resource-transfer mechanism.[3] As in the trade field, there is considerable LDC feeling that today's institutional arrangements respond to the needs of the rich coun-tries at the center of the system but not to the needs of the poor countries on the periphery. But many of the disagreements that today bedevil the continuing process of reform are not along North-South lines, nor do they arise from fundamental dis-agreements about the "public goods" an adequate international monetary system should provide. Rather, they stem from differ-ing views about *how* the necessary functions should be per-formed. Behind most of these differences of view are essentially political issues having to do with such questions as how much autonomy is to be permitted, who decides, who manages, who pays, and who benefits, although it is fair to add that differences

[2] I am grateful to Peter Kenen for pointing out that de Gaulle was more con-cerned with symmetry in determining how the system was run, i.e., curbing the power of the United States and expanding that of France, than he was in re-gaining autonomy in the sense of the ability to pursue his own monetary policy.

[3] The dominant industrialized-country view is summarized in a somewhat ex-aggerated form in the following quotation from Tom de Vries: "The developing countries maintain that a smooth-running monetary system is not an end in itself, but a means to promote growth. They have selected the wrong policy instrument to further their end, for unfortunately the monetary system cannot promote growth directly. An automobile cannot directly improve the spiritual or intellectual well-being of man, even though it can transport people to church, the concert hall, or the university. Similarly, a rational monetary sys-tem can only lead to a better functioning of the world economy with more opportunities for trade and aid, thus promoting growth indirectly." This makes the central point but overstates the position, as de Vries himself recognized, for he added a footnote: "This short and rather harsh paragraph cannot, of course, do justice to the question raised, for even if monetary reform cannot attack the heart of the development problem, there are many measures of a different or-der that the Fund can and in part indeed has taken." "Jamaica, or the Non-Re-form of the International Monetary System," *Foreign Affairs*, April, 1976, p. 600.

arise as well from genuine intellectual disagreements about how things really work in today's highly interconnected economic system.

Although at a high level of generality there is little disagreement that the IMF should be at the center of the system, what specifically is meant by being "at the center of the system" is subject to a wide variety of interpretations. Thus, although the United States has consistently argued for the primacy of the IMF, it is not difficult to discern beneath many of the positions it has taken on substantive issues a desire not only to preserve a high degree of freedom of action but also to retain a large measure of control over the future evolution of the system. We will say more about the role of the United States with regard to the problem of leadership. The point being made here is simply that although in one sense the United States has been exemplary in insisting on the primacy of the Fund, its insistence has been on the Fund's primacy in competition with other organizations which happen to be less subject to U.S. control. Its position has been more ambiguous when the point at issue involved accepting limits to its own freedom of action.[4] It has also frequently preferred informal consultations with a few key countries to the more formal procedures of the Fund.

In a different way, although the European countries also accept the general proposition that the Fund should be at the center of the system, the nature of the Fund's role and the "scope" of its primacy, will, as we later discuss, be directly affected by—and perhaps weakened by—the way the European Monetary System (EMS) evolves.

There is no dearth of academic analysis of possible alternative international monetary arrangements. Indeed, the formal analysis of the implications, both political and economic, of possible alternative monetary regimes has recently become something of

[4]On the general theme of U.S. dominance of the IMF and the American preference, for this reason, for having questions considered in that setting rather than in the more European-oriented Group of Ten or the OEEC/OECD, see Guillaume Guindey, *The International Monetary Tangle*, M. E. Sharpe, Inc.: White Plains, N.Y., 1977.

a growth industry.[5] We do not pretend to add anything new to that outpouring of analysis. Rather, our purpose is to suggest some factors that should be given weight in the choices to be made in the next few years and to indicate, in general terms, some of the changes we think should be made as part of a deliberate attempt to move to a more efficient and more equitable international economic order. Perhaps the clearest way of doing this is to sketch our own views of the role the IMF should play in the short- to medium-term future, suggesting some changes in existing arrangements and procedures and indicating how the relationship between the Fund and other institutions, whether formally constituted organizations like the OECD or the informal institution of Summitry, should evolve in the years ahead.

THE FUND AND THE MANAGEMENT OF THE INTERNATIONAL MONETARY SYSTEM

For most of the postwar period, the dominant role in the management of the international economy has been played by the United States. There are two main opposing views about the nature of its performance. Obviously, most opinions fall between these polar views, and just where on the spectrum they do fall tends to shift with the play of events. The first view is that,

[5]See Richard N. Cooper, "Prolegomena to the Choice of an International Monetary System," *International Organization,* vol. 29, no. 1, Winter, 1975, pp. 63–97; Benjamin J. Cohen, *Organizing the World's Money: The Political Economy of International Monetary Relations,* Basic Books: New York, 1977; Marina v. N. Whitman, "Coordination and Management of the International Economy: A Search for Organizing Principles," in her *Reflections on Interdependence: Issues for Economic Theory and U.S. Policy,* University of Pittsburgh Press: Pittsburgh, 1979; Edward L. Morse, "Political Choice and Alternative Monetary Regimes," in Fred Hirsch and others, *Alternatives to Monetary Disorder,* McGraw-Hill, for the Council on Foreign Relations/1980s Project: New York, 1977 (also Selected Bibliography, pp. 141–142); Harold van B. Cleveland, "Modes of International Economic Organization," and Charles P. Kindleberger, "Systems of International Economic Organization," both in David P. Calleo (ed.), *Money and the Coming World Order,* New York University Press for the Lehrman Institute: New York, 1976.

given its great economic weight and the unwillingness of all countries to endow the Fund, or any other international institution, with adequate powers, the United States became, inevitably, the leader and maintainer of the system, the crisis manager, and for much of the time the main source of the reserves required to support the manifold expansion of world trade which contributed so dramatically to world prosperity. Although it is accepted that this role brought some benefits to the United States, this view stresses that leadership also had heavy costs. True, the United States might not at all times have played its role in a wholly blameless way, but until the very end of the sixties, both in its sound management of its own economy and in its willingness to extend credits, run deficits, accept discrimination against itself, and provide massive foreign aid, the U.S. record was an outstandingly good one and the U.S. role as leader of the system an absolutely indispensable one. From this view, it is a short step to the conclusion that the system now requires a reassertion of U.S. leadership, although not everyone who holds this view of the past would subscribe to this prescription for the future.

The opposite view is that although the United States did, indeed, act in a far-sighted way in the immediate postwar period by providing generous Marshall Plan aid and in accepting discrimination against itself, it also has always taken steps to preserve the dominance of the dollar. Although there may be some costs connected with the task of supplying the world's principal transaction and reserve currency, these are, in this view, far outweighed by immense advantages that go far beyond the conventional benefits of seigniorage. Not only has the United States deliberately used its position to extend the reach of U.S. industry, it has also used its dominant role in the management of the world's money to support its foreign policy goals more generally, for example, by forcing other countries to hold dollars (rather than converting them into gold) and thus, in effect, requiring the dollar holders to contribute to the financing of policies they disapproved of, most notably the Vietnam war. From this position, it is a short step to the argument that the system must now rid itself of U.S. dominance. But those who incline to this view of U.S. dominance would differ among themselves on the way in which a more balanced system should be sought. Some believe that the route lies through greater reliance on gold as a reserve and more national control by all countries. Others think the route lies through measures which would make the SDR the central reserve asset and through a compulsory asset-settlement arrangement that would eliminate much of the special privilege now attaching to the dollar. Still others see the answer in a multicurrency reserve system.

It seems likely that the judgment of history will be that a record of rather unusually far-sighted statesmanship on the part of the United States in the early postwar period was later blemished by poor judgment and misuse of power. But regardless of one's views about the past, it is clear enough that with the diffusion of economic power and the politicization of monetary questions there can be no going back to the golden fifties. Moreover, although it has been fashionable since the abandonment of the Bretton Woods par-value system to point to the fact that the world is, in some ways, more firmly than ever on a dollar standard, it is a very different kind of dollar standard, with the United States much less securely in control, either of its own policies or of the system as a whole, than it was in the fifties and early sixties. Dollars may still be the principal vehicle currency and the principal reserve asset, but the system itself is different and so is the role of the United States when all the major currencies are floating, when many LDCs look to the Eurocurrency markets for credits rather than to official sources, when short-term capital moves in huge amounts in search of interest rate differentials or speculative gains on the exchange markets, complicating the management of domestic monetary policies and driving rates up and down in a way that sometimes bears little relation to underlying economic factors, and when new reserve centers are beginning to emerge.

Although it is neither probable nor desirable that there be a return to a U.S.-run system on the pattern of the 1950s, as the decade of the seventies closed it was a rather open question whether the greater stability and the prudential management that the system undoubtedly needs would come about by strengthening the process of collective management through the Fund and other institutions, or whether it would come about by something that might be more aptly described as a process of interbloc ad hoc-ery, or crisis management, with the United States, Germany, and, increasingly, Japan, in effect, playing the key roles. The system seemed to be moving toward the second pattern. In our view, it is desirable to move further in the direction of the first pattern, although realism suggests that aspects of the second will continue to be needed as well.

If the Fund is to play a larger role in the management of the system, the evolutionary process that is under way needs to gain momentum, and some changes need to be made in the tasks the Fund performs and in the way the Fund operates. Perhaps of most immediate importance, more should be done to strengthen the surveillance role of the Fund and to combine it with more coordination of macroeconomic policies (not just of exchange-rate policies) among the key countries and to bring this coordination within the context of the Fund. As we explain below, this means that ways must be found to involve those responsible for national policy formation more closely and continuously in the Fund's deliberations, and it also means that more use will need to be made of limited member groups within the general framework of the Fund. Further steps should be taken to improve the SDR and to diminish the reserve role of the dollar. Eventually, the SDR (or some similar unit) should become the central reserve asset of the system. But that is not a goal that is likely to be reached in the eighties during which the task will be to pursue in a balanced way a two-pronged approach to the reserve currency problem: on the one hand, the process of sharing the dollar's role with the D-mark (or the ECU) and the yen needs to be managed in an orderly way; but, on the other hand, efforts to improve the SDR and to make it a more important reserve asset should continue and not be sidetracked by today's preoccupation with the problems of adjusting to a period during which a multicurrency reserve system (whether desirable or otherwise) seems inevitable. Both prongs of this approach need to be fol-

lowed in ways that introduce more symmetry—of two kinds—
into the system: more symmetry between debtors and creditors
and more symmetry between reserve currency countries and
other countries. Perfect symmetry is a counsel of perfection, not
likely to be attained this side of Utopia, but a better balanced
system must be a constant quest.

An efficient international monetary system needs enough—
but not too much—liquidity, and reserves need to be in the right
place at the right time. And, above all, it needs a generous lender
of last resort. More needs to be done to strengthen the capacity
of the Fund in all these respects. But for many years to come,
the role of steerer, manager, and underwriter of the system will
continue to be one that is shared between the Fund and the governments of the key countries.

Analyses of the Fund tend to concentrate either on its role
vis-à-vis the key countries in the management of the international economy and, in that context, essentially on the exchange-rate regime and other aspects of the adjustment process,
or on its role as a lender to and source of "discipline" for member countries, particularly the developing countries. Our discussion roughly follows this conventional pattern in that we look at
these two main aspects of the Fund's role sequentially. But the
line is, of course, an artificial one, and not only because of the
nexus between the provision of credit and other forms of adjustment nor because some of the countries most in need of "discipline" are key countries. More profoundly, it is because the
health of the system as a whole depends, and will depend to an
increasing extent, on the health of all parts of the system and not
simply on that of a few key countries at the center. Or, to put the
same point another way, the health of the key countries on
which the system depends will increasingly be affected by
changes in the periphery.

THE EXCHANGE-RATE REGIME

Since the early sixties much analysis and much argument has
taken place about the advantages and disadvantages of the var-

ious possible exchange-rate regimes.[6] And, in the last few years, there has been much experimentation with the way-stations between the polar extremes of fixed and floating rates. It seems reasonably clear that the exchange-rate regime that will prevail for a considerable time, almost certainly for the decade and perhaps longer, will be a mixed one. The main ingredients of this mixed system will be: the principal currencies will float within limits vis-à-vis one another; smaller and weaker countries will tend to peg their currencies either to one of the major currencies or to the SDR, or to some other basket of currencies; the principal currencies will be the dollar, and either the D-mark (or possibly a composite European unit of account—the ECU—if the EMS succeeds in developing into something more than a slightly larger "snake"), and the yen. In such an exchange-rate regime, there will be a continuing need for intervention, not only by those countries that continue to peg their rates but also on the part of countries whose currencies are formally floating. Completely free floating, even among a few major currencies, is widely recognized not to be a realistic option in a world where capital markets are joined and modern democratic governments are held responsible by their electorates for providing ever-rising standards of living and low levels of unemployment. If intervention is to work, there must be consultation between central banks because each rate is, of course, the relationship between two currencies, and unless there is some understanding about the rate to be sought, countries may intervene at cross-purposes. Of more importance, the process of intervention also requires

[6]During 1969, the Executive Board of the IMF spent much time examining the implications of a number of exchange-rate regimes. Although there had been strong arguments from the academic community, in the United States in particular, urging the advantages of floating, the Report of the Executive Directors, which was circulated to the Governors in September, 1970, came down in favor of a continuation of the par-value system, perhaps because to have done anything else—given the state of the markets—would have put intolerable pressure on the dollar. Ironically, and indicative of the way the Fund has tended to trail rather than to anticipate events, a year later the United States disrupted the system in order to force other countries to accept a realignment of currencies.

wider multilateral supervision if there is to be confidence that it is not being abused to serve domestic needs at the expense of other countries or of the system as a whole. Confidence in the appropriateness of exchange rates necessarily involves judgments on the consistency of other policy targets. In consequence, since the breakdown of the par-value system, there has been much discussion about the rules that should be used to guide (and, in the view of some, to control) the intervention that is now widely felt to be desirable as well as inevitable.

After much discussion, the Fund's Executive Directors adopted, in June, 1974, some rather general *Guidelines for the Management of Floating Exchange Rates*.[7] These, in turn, were superseded by the decision on surveillance over exchange-rate policies adopted on April 29, 1977, and which became effective on April 1, 1978, the date of the entry into force of the Second Amendment to the Articles of Agreement, which, *inter alia,* marked the end of the par-value system and legalized the resort to floating. The 1977 decision (unlike the earlier *Guidelines* which applied only to the issuers of currencies that were floating) applies to all members of the Fund whatever their exchange-rate arrangements. Like the earlier *Guidelines,* the Principles adopted to guide the exchange-rate policies of member states were fairly general in character, the bulk of the Board's decision on surveillance being concerned with the nature of and procedures for Fund surveillance over these policies.[8]

SURVEILLANCE AS THE KEY TO ADJUSTMENT

The 1977 decision was a first step in trying to formulate with some precision the Fund's new role under Article IV of the

---

[7]For the text of the *Guidelines*, see IMF, *Annual Report, 1974,* pp. 112–116.

[8]For text, see IMF *Survey,* May 2, 1977. The section on Principles for the Guidance of Members' Exchange Rate Policies is as follows:

"A. A member shall avoid manipulating exchange rates or the international monetary system in order to prevent effective balance of payments adjustment or to gain an unfair competitive advantage over other members.

amended Articles. It was understood at the time it was adopted that the decision would be reviewed frequently and modified in the light of experience. No changes had been made in the Principles by the time this book was completed, but, in supplementary decisions, the Executive Directors had sought to strengthen the role of the Managing Director in the surveillance process. As of the end of 1979, the general arrangements for surveillance could be summarized as follows. The Fund conducts Article IV consultations annually with all member countries and these consultations—unlike the previous "voluntary" consultations with countries acting under Article VIII[9]—culminate in "conclusions" drawn by the Executive Board. In addition, periodic reviews of general exchange-rate developments are conducted by the Executive Board in the context of the discussion of the international adjustment process which is part of the general preparation of the semi-annual *World Economic Outlook*. Finally, and potentially of great importance to the evolution of the Fund, special discussions with a member country may be held at any time on the initiative of the Managing Director.

The original 1977 decision on surveillance provided that there had to be some evidence that the general principles were not

---

"B. A member should intervene in the exchange market if necessary to counter disorderly conditions which may be characterized *inter alia* by disruptive short-term movements in the exchange value of its currency.

"C. Members should take into account in their intervention policies the interests of other members, including those of the countries in whose currencies they intervene."

[9]Before the Second Amendment entered into force, the countries that were still operating under Article XIV were bound to consult with the Fund annually. The countries that had accepted the provisions of Article VIII were not, although a practice of voluntary consultation had, in fact, developed with most, although not all, of the "Article VIII countries." Article VIII prohibits the use of restrictions on payments or transfers for current international transactions, discriminatory currency arrangements, and multiple currency practices, except with the approval of the Fund. Article XIV releases a country from these commitments for a transitional period. On this and other aspects of the Second Amendment, see Joseph Gold, *The Second Amendment of the Fund's Articles of Agreement*, Pamphlet Series No. 25, IMF: Washington, 1978.

being observed before the Managing Director could begin the process of consultation. And various developments—such as a large-scale, protracted intervention in one direction in the foreign exchange market—were listed as the kind of occurrence which would suggest that a member was not abiding by the principles. But these requirements were relaxed in January, 1979, and the Managing Director was encouraged to initiate discussions whenever he considered that a "modification in a member's exchange arrangements or exchange rate policies or the behavior of the exchange rate of its currency may be important or may have important effects on other members. . . ."[10] The Managing Director is to raise the matter "informally and confidentially" in the first instance, then to enter into a more formal but still confidential consultation if he concludes on the basis of his informal discussions that a real problem exists, and, in this case, he is to report to the Executive Board on the result of the consultation.

It is clear from the new Article IV, from the Fund's decisions on surveillance, and from the amplifications that have been made by the Managing Director and others that surveillance, if it is to be an effective tool for the "management" of exchange rates, cannot be limited to the examination of exchange markets, exchange rates, and exchange arrangements. As Mr. de Larosiere put it:

It is not possible to understand or assess exchange rate developments without looking to the policies which create the underlying conditions; it is those policies which in the end determine the course of the balance of payments and the exchange rate.

I trust that we have learned that exchange rate stability—along with domestic price stability and sustained economic growth—can best be achieved through stable and compatible domestic policies adopted by all countries. Exchange market intervention alone cannot be counted upon to attain such stability, and exchange and trade restrictions are almost always undesirable, apart from generally being ineffective, as a means to exchange stability. I should also emphasize that a member which persists in inflating rapidly or in growing at a rate far below that of its potential output may not be fulfilling its obligations under Article

[10]Decision No. 6026-(79/13), reprinted in IMF, *Annual Report, 1979*, p. 136.

IV, even though it may not appear to be contributing to exchange market disturbances in some overt way.[11]

In the past when examining the appropriateness of a member's exchange rate, the Fund reviewed as well the member's general macroeconomic policies. But since the adoption of the Second Amendment the Fund's concern with the appropriateness of the whole range of macroeconomic policies has become much more explicit. Time and again, Fund documents and speeches by authoritative representatives of the Fund now emphasize that the way to promote stability of exchange rates is for member countries to pursue "orderly economic and financial conditions" and stress that the Fund must be concerned with policies that lie behind the exchange rate.[12] Earlier attempts to agree on statistical indicators and to define in detailed ways rules to govern intervention in exchange markets have been abandoned. "Surveillance," in the words of the Executive Board at the time it made its first formal review of the procedures in 1980, must be "judgmental."[13]

As well as placing greater emphasis on surveillance, and surveillance not just of exchange rates but of the policies that underlie them, the Fund has also begun to pay rather more attention to the consistency of policies across countries and to emphasize rather more than it once did the need for the coordination of macroeconomic policies among the key countries.

The need for more and better coordination of macroeconomic policies among the countries that carry the most weight in the international economic system is not specifically mentioned anywhere in the amended Articles. Nevertheless, it is the direction in which some of the discussion of the content to be breathed

[11]Managing Director's address in Chicago, Illinois, Nov. 14, 1978, IMF *Survey*, Nov. 20, 1978.

[12]See, *inter alia*, text of the Second Amendment, Article IV; Fund decision, cited; speech of Managing Director, cited; Joseph Gold, op. cit. The same theme is emphasized in speeches by high U.S. Treasury officials. See, for example, Under-Secretary of the Treasury Solomon's speech at the Royal Institute of International Affairs, London, January 12, 1979 (text released to press on delivery), and Mr. Solomon's address before the Alpbach European Forum, Alpbach, Austria, August 27, 1979, International Communications Agency, *Press Release*, August 28, 1979.

[13]IMF, *Annual Report, 1980*, p. 58.

into the process of "surveillance" points. For example, Anthony Solomon, then Under-Secretary of the U.S. Treasury, speaking in London in January, 1979, clearly identified the current inadequacy of policy coordination as the basic problem confronting the international monetary system.[14] And he went on to link this problem with the new "surveillance" role given to the IMF:

The basic problem facing the system is recognized clearly in the new IMF provisions on surveillance, which stress that the attainment of exchange market stability depends on [the] development of underlying economic and financial stability in member countries. These provisions equip the IMF with major potential to address the problems of policy coordination with a view to achieving a more sustainable pattern of payments positions among its member nations and a more smoothly functioning international monetary system.[15]

It is clear enough that surveillance by the Fund is beginning to be seen not simply as a way of guarding against abuse of intervention in exchange markets (that is, intervention designed to gain "unfair" advantages or to export domestic problems) and of promoting order in exchange markets, but also as a means of ensuring that the macroeconomic policies of the main countries not only do not conflict but reinforce one another and positively contribute to an international economic system that is open, orderly, and conducive to noninflationary growth.

The dilemma identified by Richard Cooper more than a decade ago is truer than ever today, despite the floating of key currencies. Interdependence and full national autonomy are incompatible. Countries cannot have the fruits of open economies and high levels of interdependence without far-reaching coordination

[14]"As I see it, the basic problem is . . . how to coordinate better the economic performance of the major countries, to reduce inflation rates and inflation differentials, and to manage domestic growth rates so as to bring about a better balance in global economic relations." *Press Release* issued on January 12, 1979, at time of lecture.

[15]*Press Release*, cited above.

of domestic policies.[16] The prescription in Article IV of the Second Amendment was essentially one of loosening the connecting links a little by floating rates and of tightening coordination a little by means of improved surveillance. But the evidence is mounting that "loosening" links through floating rates is a more limited option than it was once thought by some to be. Moreover, the immediate results of exchange-rate changes are frequently perverse and the longer-run effects not as clear and predictable as traditional economic theory would suggest. If, as seems the safe prediction—and the right prescription—the outlook is for an indefinite period of *managed* floating by the key countries, there will need to be consistency in the policy targets pursued by the key countries and, generally, closer coordination of their macroeconomic policies. But does this mean that the Fund should be the central locus of such policy coordination, or is some sharing out of the task of policy coordination both feasible and desirable? And how should whatever part of this task that should rest with the Fund be handled?

Before examining this question further, it is desirable to look at another aspect of the Fund's role—the management of liquidity—for here, too, closer policy coordination among the key countries, within the context of the Fund, has a part to play.

LIQUIDITY

The international reserve or liquidity tasks that an efficient international monetary system must perform, and that should be performed in the future with more certainty and with more even-handedness (as between reserve currency countries and other countries and as between creditor and debtor countries) than has been the case in the past, are, broadly speaking, of three kinds: to ensure that there is enough liquidity in the system as a whole;

[16]Richard N. Cooper, *The Economics of Interdependence: Economic Policy in the Atlantic Community*, McGraw-Hill, for the Council on Foreign Relations: New York, 1968.

to see that there is not too much liquidity in the system as a whole; and to see that reserves are distributed among countries in such a way that they facilitate noninflationary growth and an orderly expansion of world trade.

The IMF can do more about the first and third of these tasks than about the second, although, over time, its power to ensure not only an adequate supply of international money but also to regulate that supply in much the same way as a national central bank regulates the domestic money supply is clearly necessary if the IMF is gradually to assume more of the functions of a global central bank. Today, the important suppliers of international reserves are: the U.S. monetary authorities and, to a lesser extent, the monetary authorities of other countries whose currencies are held as reserves by third countries (the Federal Republic of Germany, the United Kingdom, France, and Japan); the IMF, by virtue of its power to create SDRs; and the Eurocurrency markets, by means of the extensive deposits and borrowing in these markets by LDC governments. The monetization of gold by some central banks also still plays some part in the creation of internationally usable reserves.

The decision empowering the IMF to create a man-made asset, the SDR,[17] means there is no fundamental reason why the world should again be short of reserves, as it has been from time to time in the past when the rate of mining of new gold effectively determined the level of international reserves, or as there were fears it might be in the mid-1960s when the United States was, for a time, running a surplus on current account which, had it continued, might have so reduced the supply of dollars as to create problems for other countries. In the future, Fund members may well have differences of view about the need for new issuances of SDRs. Therefore one cannot be sure the supply of reserves will, in fact, always be large enough, but the means exist to create enough reserves, provided the need is widely recognized. Today, it takes an affirmative vote of 85 percent to create

[17]The Governors of the IMF approved the decision to create SDRs in May, 1968. The necessary ratifications were concluded about a year later.

216

new SDRs. This, in effect, gives a veto both to the United States and to the European Community, provided the member countries vote as a bloc. As we discuss later in this chapter, it would be desirable to strengthen the role of the Fund by having somewhat lower majorities for a number of purposes when the Executive Board or the Governors are acting on a proposal from the Managing Director. This would, in principle, be desirable in the case of creating and cancelling SDRs, for (as already recognized by the requirement that the Managing Director must make proposals on these issues) it is the Fund staff that should have the needs of the system as a whole as its primary concern.

The member governments of the IMF have frequently reiterated their intention of making the SDR *the* principal reserve asset.[18] By the end of the seventies, a fairly steady increase in the supply of SDRs seemed probable, and the process of trying to make the SDR a more attractive reserve asset was slowly under way.[19] The potentially important step of establishing some kind of substitution account through which dollars and other reserve currencies could be converted into SDR-denominated assets— which had seemed an unlikely development when it was first proposed—was under active consideration. So, too, were ways to make these new SDR-denominated assets more attractive to hold than the SDR itself had proved to be; in particular, there was some prospect that the new asset might in time be usable not just for certain types of official transactions among governments

---

[18]Most explicitly in Section 7 of Article VIII of the Amended Articles: "Each member undertakes to collaborate with the Fund and with other members in order to ensure that the policies of the member with respect to reserve assets shall be consistent with the objectives of promoting better international surveillance of international liquidity and making the special drawing right the principal reserve asset in the international monetary system." IMF, *Articles of Agreement:* Washington, 1978.

[19]New issues of SDR were agreed upon in 1978, and the interest rate was increased. In 1979, decisions were taken authorizing the use of SDRs in swaps and forward operations among member countries. In 1980, the list of holders of SDRs was extended, the currency basket on which the valuation of the SDR is based was simplified, and the interest rate was increased again.

but privately as well.[20] But it is hard to believe that even if all the steps now under consideration are taken, the SDR (or a similar asset) will become in, say, the next decade, the only significant reserve asset, or even the most important one.

Today, SDRs are a minor component of total reserves. And the likely prospect for the decade ahead is for the D-mark (or possibly the ECU, discussed further below) and, probably, the Japanese yen increasingly to be used as reserve currencies and for these two to share with the dollar the major part of the stock of international reserves. The reserve roles of the French franc and the pound sterling will probably continue to decline. Although the SDR may become somewhat more important, it seems bound to remain far less important than the dollar, the D-mark, and the yen. The future of gold is somewhat uncertain. For a time in the seventies, demonetization seemed well under way, but a proportion of the reserves of the EMS are held in gold, and the commitment entered into by the Group of Ten in 1975 not to fix an official price for gold or to deal in it officially has lapsed. The recent extreme volatility in the price of gold has probably decreased rather than increased its attraction as a reserve for the major central banks, although the high price may well have enhanced its attractions for the central banks of some small countries. The Eurocurrency markets also remain available to governments, and when pressure on reserves becomes acute, they are likely to be used. Governments and banks are not likely to forget the tricks they learned in the sixties and the seventies, and if the demand for money is strong enough, ways to create it are likely to be found. In short, the IMF now has, in the SDR, the means of providing enough liquidity to the system, but

---

[20]See the cautious statements on this point in the article on the substitution account by Walter O. Habermeier (the Treasurer of the Fund) in the IMF *Survey,* February 4, 1980. Many experts (though not all) argue that if the SDR (or some variant, is ever to become the central reserve asset of the system, it will have to become a marketable instrument. There are technical reasons (having to do with the desire to avoid having to amend the Articles of Agreement) for using what is described as a "new SDR-denominated asset" rather than the SDR in the new account.

a shortage of *overall* liquidity seems unlikely to be much of a problem.

Views differ about the inflationary dangers of too much liquidity in the system, about the importance of trying to get better control over the growth of international money, and about the role of the IMF in the process. If governments were really prepared to see the SDR become the major reserve asset, there are various ways—analogous to the reserve-ratio arrangements used by national banking systems—which might help the Fund gain some control over the growth of international money. Indeed, one such proposal was put forward by Mr. Witteveen, the former Managing Director of the Fund, in a speech in Frankfurt in 1975 and reiterated later in an interview shortly after his resignation as Managing Director of the Fund. His proposal was "for an arrangement whereby SDRs would have to be used in a certain proportion with other reserve assets in settling international balances. In that way, they could really become the *principal* reserve asset without necessarily having to be the *largest* one. One could then, by determining internationally the amount of SDRs issued, have a great influence on the total amount of international liquidity."[21] Mr. Witteveen acknowledged that the world was not yet ready for such a large step forward, but he felt the idea was a good one and "something for the future . . . ."

Clearly, if the IMF is to evolve in the direction of a global central bank, some such arrangement will one day have to be accepted. But the Witteveen proposal contains difficulties that will have to be overcome before it, or any similar scheme, is likely to be adopted. Perhaps the main one is that, to be effective, a reserve-ratio scheme needs to be accompanied by a compulsory asset-settlement arrangement, otherwise a reserve-currency country like the United States can undermine the scheme. And if compulsory asset settlement is to be acceptable, there must be more international agreement than there is today on exchange rates, otherwise the United States (or any other reserve-

---

[21]The text of the interview is to be found in *Finance and Development*, IMF/IBRD, Washington, Sept. 1978, pp. 6–9. Emphasis in the original.

currency country) could find itself having to convert balances of its currency that were acquired defending exchange rates which were contrary to its own interests and to which it had not agreed.[22] Moreover, a reserve-ratio scheme relating only to official reserves would probably not be adequate unless accompanied by more control over Eurocurrency and other markets than seems likely to be feasible, or, perhaps, desirable.[23]

Controlling the upper limit on reserves is likely to be a far more difficult problem than ensuring an adequate stock of money, and it is hard to see either any automatic formula or any form of supranational control which would be acceptable in the

[22]For this and other critiques of the Witteveen proposal, see the paper by Kenen and the comments by Williamson and Whitman in Robert A. Mundell and Jacques T. Polak (eds.), *The New International Monetary System,* Columbia University Press: New York, 1977. Although agreement on a substitution account may be reached in the near future, it will be a voluntary scheme, not one calling for compulsory asset settlement.

[23]In his Per Jacobsson Foundation Lecture in September, 1970 (already cited), William McChesney Martin outlined the essential steps needed to turn the IMF into a World Central Bank and gave his appraisal of the progress being made in that direction. In discussing the role of the SDR, he said: "Perhaps we can view the IMF not merely as a creator of one type of international reserve asset but also as a regulator of the total volume of reserves." His line of reasoning was that the Fund would take into account other forms of reserve creation in deciding how many SDRs to create. This would be a very weak form of regulation, as he would have been the first to recognize. Later in the speech, he referred to the need for more supervision in the Eurocurrency and Eurobond markets, as indeed did Mr. Witteveen in the interview cited above. Harry Johnson in a comment on Mr. Martin's lecture, while agreeing with the main thrust of his speech about the desirability of the IMF assuming more of the attributes of a global central bank, questioned the desirability of closer supervision of the markets: "It is one of the temptations of central bankers to believe that they know better than the market does what sorts of credit instruments are creditworthy and what are not, and to believe that without their help private competition must inevitably result in financial disaster. I don't believe that. I believe the Euro-dollar market and the Euro-bond market instead are developments which reflect the weaknesses of central banking, particularly in Europe, and I do not really see that anybody has the intelligence or the ability to do better than that market does." P. 48.

near- to medium-term future, because any real control necessarily implies greater international control over national monetary policy than is today foreseeable.[24] The only feasible short- to medium-term restraint on excessive reserve creation by governments is self-restraint. Self-restraint, like better exchange-rate management, could be enhanced by improved policy consultation and coordination among the key countries.

Consideration of the problems posed by the Eurocurrency and other uncontrolled markets leads to a similar conclusion. For the last decade or so, there has been much debate about the structure, magnitude, and consequences of the Eurocurrency and similar markets. Views have shifted from concern to complacency and back again. Although direct control over such markets seems unlikely to be either feasible or, perhaps, desirable, there is fairly widespread agreement on the need for closer monitoring of the markets. As in the case of the impetus to global inflation given by too generous national money creation, so the inflationary consequences of credit expansion in these markets result essentially from the action or inaction on the part of a handful of countries whose currencies are widely used. In this case, the reluctance of some of these countries to seek more formal measures of control stems partly from a belief that efforts at control might simply drive the banks to indulge in even more opaque arrangements, centered in less easily monitored places than London, and partly from the fact that the markets have proved highly useful—perhaps literally indispensable—in recycling petrodollars and in extending badly needed credit to the LDCs. More can and doubtless will be done to monitor the markets, and the Bank for International Settlements (BIS), which

[24]Unless the United States and other important countries which today rely on monetary policy as an important tool of domestic management shift to greater reliance on fiscal measures, it is difficult to see how, even in the long run, the kind of multilateral management of international money that is needed if the IMF is to evolve into a global central bank can come about. See Cooper, last few pages of "Prolegomena," and Polak and Mundell, op. cit., p. 241.

watches the markets closely and has committees examining the possible forms of control, would seem to be the right international institution for the performance of this task.[25] But any real control over the expansion of credit will come about, if it comes at all, through the action and attitudes of the national central banks of those countries whose currencies form the bulk of the deposits.[26] Thus, indirectly if not directly, the rate of credit creation in these "uncontrolled" markets is likely to be considerably affected by the extent of policy coordination among the key countries.

In short, better procedures for coordination of policies among the key countries have a part to play in ensuring the appropriate amount of overall liquidity in the system as a whole as well as being central to the guidance of exchange rates and to the orderly functioning of a multicurrency reserve system. An efficient international monetary system should, of course, ensure not only that there is neither too little nor too much liquidity in the system as a whole, but also that the right kind of reserves are in the right place at the right time. Later in the chapter we look at the Fund's role as lender. First we pursue a little further some of the institutional implications of the need for closer coordination of policies among the key countries.

[25]The BIS dates back to the early thirties and is one of the very few international organizations to have survived the war. Its most active postwar phase was probably in the fifties and early sixties, first as agent for the EPU (European Payments Union) and later as the place where—at least in the corridors, if not in the more formal meetings—the groundwork was laid for the inter-central-bank swaps which, during the late fifties and early sixties, were widely resorted to as the major defense against speculators, first in defense of sterling, later in defense of the dollar. It is conceivable that if attitudes toward the BIS had been different at the end of the war it might have evolved as a rival to the Fund. The United States was for a time rather hostile to the BIS, and the Bretton Woods conference recommended that it should be liquidated, a recommendation that was, of course, never acted upon.

[26]In October, 1979, the United States Federal Reserve took action which, in effect, required U.S. banks to hold reserves against their Eurocurrency deposits. See IMF, *Survey,* October 15, 1979.

THE INSTITUTIONAL PICTURE: SURVEILLANCE AND COORDINATION

Today, the key industrial countries discuss their macroeconomic policies in several forums. The first in the field, and in some ways still the most important, is the OECD. There were many motives behind the decision, taken in 1960–1961, to replace the OEEC by the OECD, but high among them was the realization that the postwar period was ending and that the United States and Western European economies were becoming increasingly interdependent. The economic preponderance of the United States was still unchallenged, but its balance of payments was in deficit, foreign dollar holdings exceeded U.S. gold reserves, and the U.S. economy was no longer felt to be largely immune to external factors. The extent to which the economies of the highly industrialized countries were becoming interconnected was, as yet, only dimly realized; so, too, was the fact that Japan would soon take its place among this group of countries. Although it was clear that changes were taking place, many people in the Western European governments were rather dismayed that the United States was urging not simply that the purpose of the organization be reformulated and Canada and the United States be included but that Japan should also soon be admitted to membership.

Throughout the sixties, the Economic Policy Committee of the OECD, and particularly its Working Party Three (WP-3), was the focal point for discussions of a broad range of questions having to do with the balance of payments, although monetary questions tended to be discussed not within the OECD framework but in the Group of Ten (G-10). This Group drew its membership from much the same countries as WP-3, but it was loosely linked to the IMF, had no secretariat, and, perhaps partly for that reason, was the venue preferred by Treasury officials.

The Group of Ten had its origin in an agreement known as the General Arrangements to Borrow (GAB), negotiated in 1961. This was, in effect, an arrangement for mobilizing short-term credits from members of the group for the benefit of other members of the group because it was clear that the resources of the Fund were not adequate to meet simultaneously substantial drawings by several major countries. At the time the Arrangements were negotiated, there was strong French opposition (and also some opposition from other Common Market countries) to a substantial increase in the resources of the Fund, but the United States, and to a lesser extent the United Kingdom, was opposed to the continental European view that the new facility should be housed within the OECD. The compromise, found after much hard bargaining, provided for special credit commitments which were formally made to the Fund by the Group of Ten countries, but these credits were to be kept separate from the Fund's general account and were to be drawn on only by other G-10 members with the agreement of the Group. The Ministers of Finance of the member countries participated in the Group of Ten (there was also a Deputies-level group). During the period in which it was most active (roughly the 1960s), it served as the principal forum for the discussion of monetary questions.[27]

The Managing Director (or the Economic Counsellor) of the Fund participated in meetings of the Group of Ten, but, inevitably, there was considerable tension between the Group of Ten and the Executive Board of the Fund. This tension became particularly acute during the mid-1960s when the Group of Ten discussed at length various measures that might be taken to expand world liquidity. The discussions within the G-10 were long and heated, mainly because of the sharp differences of view between France and the United States, differences that owed much to the

[27]The members of the Group of Ten are: the United States, the United Kingdom, France, the Federal Republic of Germany, Canada, Belgium, the Netherlands, Italy, Japan, Sweden, and as an eleventh member, Switzerland, despite the fact that Switzerland is not a member of the IMF. In the case of Germany and Sweden, the participants in the G-10 are from the central banks, not the Finance Ministries. For further details on the G-10, see Guindey, op. cit.; Fred Hirsch, *Money International*, rev. ed., Pelican Books: Harmondsworth, 1969; and Brian Tew, *The Evolution of the International Monetary System, 1945–1977*, Hutchinson: London, 1977.

French desire to limit U.S. domination of the system and something to genuine disagreements about the economic merits of making gold, the dollar, or some new reserve unit the principal reserve asset. Much of the intergovernmental discussion and negotiation which led, in the end, to the decision to create the SDR took place in the G-10. And some of the G-10 countries, France in particular, would doubtless have preferred that the new reserve asset should have been created and managed by that group in much the same way as the GAB has been. But the final stages of the negotiations were, quite rightly in our view, moved to the Fund.[28]

The G-10 again played a prominent role in the renegotiation of new par values in late 1971 (the Smithsonian agreement) after the United States had, in August, abruptly stopped the convertibility of dollars into gold and taken other measures designed to force agreement on a realignment of currencies. But the G-10's heyday was over. In July, 1972, the IMF decided to establish a Committee of Twenty to examine measures for the reform of the international monetary system, the Committee to be composed on roughly the same constitutency basis as the Executive Board. For the next few years, the C-20 and, more particularly, its committee of deputies was the center of the reform debate.[29]

[28]The Managing Director of the Fund at the time, a Frenchman, P. P. Schweitzer, took a very strong stand against the French government on this issue. The creation of the SDR was formally approved by the IMF in 1968. For details, see *Official History*.

[29]The decision to set up the C-20, rather than letting the G-10 pursue the issue as most of the member countries of that group would have preferred, was partly the result of irritation on the part of John Connally, Secretary of the U.S. Treasury, with the Europeans, who, he felt, were not doing enough to assist the dollar. This made him more receptive than he might otherwise have been to the strong pressure from other members of the Fund (and the Managing Director) to base the reform negotiations squarely within the Fund. Because of the "political" character of the Committee's work, the need to involve people from capitals, and the difficulty of asking the Fund to reform itself, it was obviously desirable to charge a new committee, not the Executive Board, with the task. It was also decided, although this was perhaps less clearly necessary, that the Committee should have its own bureau rather than using the Fund staff.

Although the Committee of Twenty cleared much useful ground, the deteriorating economic climate and the abandonment of the par-value system by the key countries made it an unpropitious time to carry out the original plan and seek a definitive reform of the Fund. Accordingly, the Committee turned its efforts to the immediate changes needed to legitimate and to bring under some kind of discipline the de facto system of floating. These efforts culminated in the Second Amendment to the Articles of Agreement. The Committee of Twenty was succeeded by the so-called Interim Committee (also of twenty and drawn from the same constituencies), which was to provide the "political" element many had felt missing from the Fund, until a new Council provided for in the Second Amendment was established. However, in 1974, when the oil crisis and the ensuing deep recession made closer cooperation among the key governments imperative, it was not the C-20, nor the G-10, nor WP-3 that became the important center but, for a time, what was inevitably called the G-5. This was an inner group of the Finance Ministers of the five most important G-10 countries (the United States, Germany, Japan, the United Kingdom, and France, sometimes also joined by Italy) that met more or less secretly, mostly at various French chateaux. The G-5 still meets occasionally, and there is much consultation on the telephone among the five Finance Ministers or their deputies. But, beginning with the Rambouillet meeting in November, 1975, the center of the stage for the next several years was preempted by Summitry.

Between the Rambouillet meeting and the end of 1979, five fully fledged economic summits were held, each rather more organized than the one before, with officially designated "preparers" meeting between the later summit meetings to discuss the agenda and to monitor the follow-up.[30] The first summit was

[30]The dates and locations of the economic summits were as follows: November 15–17, 1975, Rambouillet; June 27–28, 1976, Puerto Rico; May 7–8, 1977, Downing Street, London; July 16–17, 1978, Bonn; June 28–29, 1979, Japan. In addition, there was a kind of mini-summit in Guadeloupe in January, 1979. This was called by the French President, Giscard D'Estaing, and was on a much more limited basis than previous summits. In this instance, the head of government was to be accompanied by a single advisor only, and although economic

attended by the heads of government of the United States, Germany, Japan, the United Kingdom, France, and Italy, accompanied by their Foreign and Finance Ministers. The Canadians attended the second and subsequent summit meetings. And, starting with the third summit, in response to strong pressure from the smaller countries of the European Community, the President of the Council of the Community and the President of the Commission, Roy Jenkins, attended the meetings for the discussion of those matters that fell within the competence of the Community. The discussions at the summit have ranged widely over all the important economic questions and some non-economic subjects (e.g., the supply of nuclear equipment to non-nuclear countries, highjacking), but the main purpose of the meetings has been to try to work out an overall economic strategy that would once again set the industrial world on the path of steady, non-inflationary growth. Whether or not Summitry has come to stay, it was, as the decade of the eighties began, an institution in the sense that that word is used in this book. How it should fit into the scheme of things is a central issue for the future.

Although there is today widespread intellectual acceptance of the need for a great deal of surveillance, consultation, and harmonization of the macroeconomic policies of the leading industrial states, no very clear agreement exists about what states need to be included in the process; or about which institutions should bear the primary weight in the process; or about how far into traditional domestic policies it is now necessary for international action to reach; or about how far national actions should today, in fact, be disciplined by international rules; or about the effectiveness of national and international measures in achieving desired results.

Ad hoc-ery is today the dominant pattern. And many will argue that this is as it should be because it makes for flexibility and

---

matters were reviewed, the focus of discussion was less on those topics and more on a general appraisal of the political scene, with considerable emphasis on the emergence of China and on the remaining issues in SALT II. A sixth economic summit was held in Venice on June 22–23, 1980.

that is what is needed most in a rapidly changing world. Perhaps so, but ad hoc-ery unrelated to some picture of the main lines of evolution that should be encouraged over the long term can set patterns that foreclose options it would be desirable to keep open. With a little forethought, it should be possible to combine the virtues of ad hoc-ery with desirable long-term institutional reform.

Today, Summitry, the OECD, and the IMF all have important roles to play in the coordination of macroeconomic policy, but, over time, we think the weight should shift so that a more dominant role is played by the IMF than is the case today. If this is to happen, changes will be needed in the way issues are considered by the Fund, and very likely in its structure as well. The relationship of the European Monetary System to the IMF also becomes important in this context: views about the desirable future of the IMF inevitably affect how one sees the role of the EMS, and vice versa.

One of the reasons economic summitry appears to have taken on a quasi-permanent form is that there is no place within modern, industrialized countries short of the head of government where decisions can be reached on all the important interlocking economic policies that, taken together, broadly determine the rate of growth and general health of an economy and also its impact on third countries and on the wider international economic system. A U.S. energy policy that was widely judged to be inadequate weakened the dollar, and poor labor relations undermined external confidence in the pound. Policies for energy, manpower, trade, competition, structural change, and many other subjects normally handled domestically by separate departments or ministries—all today are to some degree matters of international concern. Awareness of the need to look at a broad array of domestic policies, recognition of the political sensitivity of doing so in any international forum, and the fact that today the exceptional density of interconnectedness is still characteristic of only a handful of economically important countries made limited-membership, economic summits almost inevitable in a period in which these countries were experiencing some combination of inflation, slow growth, and high unemployment.

Summitry in situations of crisis is clearly desirable (and is in the wider global interest), even though it will almost always be resented by some, at least, of those who are excluded.

But Summitry, although it may at times be indispensable, has its own limitations. Summits tend to be preoccupied with problems of the moment, not to mention their greater concern with resolving policy differences among the participants than with trying to arrive at a common view of the longer-term needs of the system as a whole. Economic summitry is unlikely to become the keystone of the international economic system unless it is underpinned by some continuing institutional arrangement, either a streamlined OECD or a new organization which would, in effect, render the OECD superfluous. It is tempting to argue that, with the decline in the preponderance of the United States, "institutionalized summitry" is the way to give the economic system the steering and leadership it needs. In a world where there was a clearly defined hierarchy of states, with a small group of reasonably homogeneous "top powers" which was either powerful enough and determined enough to impose its will or so widely revered and respected that it commanded obedience, one could imagine such a system working with reasonable efficiency. But, today, we live in a kind of twilight zone between a world in which economic power, defined in terms of power to affect the system as a whole, is still highly concentrated in a handful of countries and a world in which economic power seems likely to be far more widely distributed. Moreover, both the determination of the top group to impose its will and the once widespread respect and confidence of others in the leadership of the top group have declined in recent years. Although both are probably waning rather more quickly than is their real power, the trend toward a less hierarchical system seems clear.

Perhaps for a time, Summitry, strengthened by more preparation and follow-up in the OECD than now takes place, will, in effect, prove to be the uneasy surrogate for a dominant power. For reasons explored at some length elsewhere,[31] the OECD,

[31]See Miriam Camps, *"First World" Relationships: The Role of the OECD,* op. cit.

229

although not ideal either in its membership or in its mode of operation, is the best available existing institution to underpin Summitry and to provide the continuing review and frequent intergovernmental discussion of the full range of macroeconomic policies that is needed today among the old industrialized states of Western Europe and North America and the new industrial giant, Japan.

Improvisations are necessary to live with today's political realities. But Summitry underpinned by the OECD should be a temporary expedient, not a lasting solution. It is our contention that, in the longer term, more of the much-needed continuing consultation and harmonization of policy among the advanced industrial countries should take place within the context of a few, key global institutions. The IMF is one of these key institutions, and its role in the process of surveillance, consultation, and coordination of policy needs to be considered with this longer-term objective in mind.

Strengthening the Fund's role would have some drawbacks, and it may be useful to begin by looking at some of the more obvious disadvantages to having the IMF become more deeply involved in the examination, and harmonization, of the macroeconomic policies of the group of countries whose policies will largely determine whether there is to be order in exchange markets and whether the "public good" of an adequate supply of stable international money is to be provided to the system as a whole. In the first place, there is an unresolved tension in concept that has existed right from the start of the Fund between those who have seen its role as essentially that of a strict disciplinarian and a bulwark against inflation and those who have seen its main purpose as that of contributing to growth and full employment.[32] Related to this fundamental disagreement, which will inevitably continue to bedevil efforts to give greater content to Fund surveillance, there is undoubtedly some incompatibility between arguing, on the one hand, that progress should be made toward the very long-term objective of the Fund's developing

[32]See postscript by Richard N. Cooper in Fred Hirsch, *Money International,* op. cit.

into a global central bank and managing the global money supply in ways analogous to those of a national central bank, and, at the same time, arguing that it should get more deeply into the highly politicized realm of overseer and harmonizer of a broad range of macroeconomic policies.

There are good reasons, as all nations recognize, although with varying degrees of fervor and success, for insulating the creation of money from the political process. But no country is prepared to give its central bank complete autonomy, and the trend today is toward more rather than less use of monetary policy as an instrument of domestic demand management. If the IMF were really to function as a global central bank, some of today's dilemmas would not arise, for ex hypothesi countries would have accepted enough "supranational" control of the creation of reserves and of the process of adjustment to limit some of the divergence in policies and in performance that now causes problems. We are very far from that goal today, in some respects even farther than we were in the late sixties. And, in the long progress toward it, there is no way to avoid some "politicization" of the Fund. In fact, the process of politicization is not as much in conflict with progress toward the eventual goal as it may at first appear to be. Giving an institution like the Fund real control over the supply of international reserves and the means to play the key role of lender of last resort is a highly political act, one that could only come about after a long period of experience with policy surveillance and coordination.[33]

It is clear enough that the surveillance plus harmonization role which we suggest the Fund should now undertake could not be

---

[33]Compare the history of the efforts to create a European monetary union. The European Community may become an economic and monetary union one day. If so, at some point there will have to be a step that represents a break with the past and a quantum jump into a new system. But efforts to take that quantum jump without more cooperation, coordination, and harmonization of policies than has thus far occurred have always failed. As indicated above (see footnote 1, pp. 200–201) one can envisage a "global" central bank without a fixed exchange rate system. But even the loosest form of "global central bank" implies enough supranational control to make far more convergence of policies among the key countries an essential precondition.

carried on by the Executive Board nor simply by the staff of the Fund consulting with governments. It must be a multilateral process participated in by those who carry policy responsibilities in the governments of the key countries. It is also clear enough that the kind of surveillance and coordination that is needed for the management of key exchange rates and of *overall* liquidity is not a process in which many countries need to be involved. The important countries today are those which have taken part in the economic summits.

A central argument in this book is that more of the weight of "management" in key areas must, in the future, gradually shift from the formal, and the informal and ad hoc, arrangements of the rich countries to a few strong and efficiently organized global institutions. But, if this is to happen, provision must be made within these institutions for chambers, tiers, or inner groups, so that limited groups of countries that need to do so—both in their own interest and, frequently, in the interest of the wider system as well—can go further among themselves than it is possible or necessary to do on a global basis in coordinating policies, accepting more stringent rules, etc., provided always that these additional measures are not in conflict with the basic charter of the organization, in this case, the Articles of Agreement.

Those countries that do not participate in these "inner groups" will be in a far better position to influence these discussions if the "inner groups" meet within the framework of a global institution than they will be if their unwillingness to see this happen means (as it is almost certain to do) that the "inner group" simply meets elsewhere. The staff of the Fund, like the staff of the proposed Production and Trade Organization discussed in the previous chapter, must act as "keeper of the global conscience." To do so, it must participate in all meetings of any limited-member groups and be in a position to see that both the interests of other countries and broad systemic considerations are taken fully into account. The staff must also act as a transmission belt—both ways—between any limited-member groups and bodies, like the Executive Board, which represent the full membership and bear the general responsibility for the governance of the institution.

If some such inner group mainly concerned with this surveillance plus coordination-of-policy function were to be established, it should probably be, technically, a committee of the Interim Committee or, better, the Council that was foreseen in the Second Amendment as the successor to the Interim Committee, although there are some difficulties with this procedure. The group must include representatives of all those countries whose rates (and the policies underlying those rates) have to be considered together. The constituency principle, which is the basis of the composition of the Executive Board, of the present Interim Committee, and of the proposed Council, is not appropriate in this case. Moreover, the level of representation in this group (hereafter called for illustrative purposes the Special Surveillance Committee) should presumably be similar to that on the Interim Committee/Council rather than that on the Executive Board.[34] Although the Second Amendment envisages the new surveillance functions as coming within the purview of the Council, it is difficult to see how the kind of intimate multilateral consultation on all the closely interrelated aspects of policy that affect the exchange rate could really occur in any body except one composed only of representatives of those countries whose rates must be examined together.[35] The language of the Second

[34]As explained above (see p. 226), although a new decision-taking Council composed of policy-level members (e.g., Central Bank Governors, Finance Ministers) was provided for in the Second Amendment, it has not yet been established. An 85 percent majority of the total voting power is required to establish the Council. Meanwhile, much the same role as that envisaged for the Council is being played by the Interim Committee. It is composed of members of similar rank and, like the Council, has roughly the same pattern of country representation as does the Executive Board. The Council would have more power to take decisions than does the Interim Committee, and it would be desirable to establish it.

[35]Section 2(a) of Schedule D (which provides for the establishment of the Council) reads as follows: "The Council shall supervise the management and adaptation of the international monetary system, including the continuing operation of the adjustment process and developments in global liquidity, and in this connection shall review developments in the transfer of real resources to the developing countries." If surveillance were entrusted to a special Surveillance Group established by the Council, the Managing Director would, of course, need to perform the same kind of two-way transmission-belt role between the Surveillance Group and the Council as he would do between the Surveillance Group and the Executive Board.

Amendment would seem to permit the Council to establish Committees, and there would seem to be no insuperable impediment to its vesting this multilateral surveillance function in a Special Surveillance Committee, even though it is somewhat at variance with the rest of the structure of the Fund.[36]

Over time, as a result of further experience with floating rates, the Special Surveillance Committee might find itself able to agree on rather more precise rules or guidelines to govern the process of intervention than has yet been possible. It might possibly adopt some version of the target-rate or target-zone schemes that have been proposed by various experts.[37] But given today's economic difficulties and the uncertainties about the consequences of exchange-rate changes, and also the difficulties that beset democratic governments trying to manage open and highly interdependent economies while also satisfying a wide array of welfare demands, it seems clear that there will be great reluctance to accept the "supranationalism" or the restrictiveness of hard and fast substantive rules.[38]

The role of the Managing Director of the Fund in this new surveillance and consultation process would be crucial: not only, as we have said, should the Managing Director be specifically mandated to see that the discussions in the Special Surveillance Committee never lose sight of the larger needs of the system as a whole, but there must also be more acceptance of his right—and duty—to push the big countries to modify their poli-

---

[36]See Schedule D, section 5(a) and Article XII, section 2(j).

[37]See, for example, John Williamson, *The Failure of World Monetary Reform, 1971–1974,* New York University Press: New York, 1977, and Benjamin J. Cohen, *Organizing the World's Money,* op. cit.

[38]There is a parallel to be drawn with trade. So long as border controls (tariffs, quotas) were the main obstruction to the free flow of trade, it was not too difficult to write rules providing for their reduction or elimination. Now, as the main impediments become subsidies and other similar measures whose effect on trade, although important, is frequently of secondary concern to the government granting the subsidy, it becomes almost impossible to write hard and fast rules permitting some subsidies while outlawing others. The most that frequently can be done is to agree on procedures for more consultation.

cies than has been traditional, or deemed expedient, thus far in the Fund's history. Under the original Articles of Agreement, the Managing Director had no power to propose an exchange-rate change, and removal of this limitation was one of the measures included in the Outline of Reform. In the regime of managed floating, the role of the Managing Director should be a far more active one than the large countries have been prepared to see him play in the past. He should have a view about the appropriateness both of the rate structures and of the government policies that lie behind those structures, and he should set forth this view as the starting point for the discussion in our proposed new Special Surveillance Committee.

Under the amended Articles of the Fund, all member countries are subject to surveillance, not, as previously, only those countries making conditional drawings on the Fund or still operating under Article XIV. If the Fund's role in this process becomes a strong one, this should help correct what seems to many LDCs to be a bias in the Fund, that is, a difference in the stringency of the treatment meted out to developing countries and to the most highly developed countries. The Fund staff would still not have the same control over the policies of those rich countries that do not need Fund support as it has through its power to lay down conditions for stand-by arrangements. And, in the future as in the past, the poorer countries will be the main clients of the Fund. But the advanced countries are peculiarly sensitive to the criticisms that a review procedure of this kind could bring to bear, particularly as the main findings would inevitably leak and the markets could be counted on to bring the pressures that are likely to be denied to an international staff.

If something like this Special Surveillance Committee were formed and worked as we have suggested, it would, over time, tend to diminish the importance of the OECD. For the reasons already discussed, this is what ought to happen, and it is not a development that should be resisted. Conversely, if, because of opposition on the part of the LDCs or for other reasons, effective surveillance, consultation, and policy harmonization among the key countries do not develop within the framework of the Fund, the OECD should continue to be used. In any case, there should be no premature axing of the Economic Policy Committee (EPC) and WP-3 in anticipation of an outcome that is uncertain. However, if something like the suggested Special Surveillance Committee were established and did become the central place for macroeconomic policy surveillance and coordination, the problem of adapting the membership of the group to include new countries as they become important members of the inner network would present fewer problems than will be the case if the function remains in the OECD. Moreover, since the Surveillance Committee would be a new creation of the IMF Council—it should not be simply the G-10—it should be possible to limit membership to those few countries that are really necessary.[39]

THE FUND AND THE EMS

Just as the content given to the Fund's new surveillance role vis-à-vis the key countries will affect and be affected by the OECD's formal and informal arrangements for multilateral surveillance, so also there will be a two-way interaction between measures taken to bring about greater exchange-rate discipline and policy coordination within the European Community and the evolution of the Fund.

During the sixties, far-reaching plans for economic and monetary union on a Community basis were launched and largely shelved. The economic performance of the principal countries of the Community was too divergent to make progress possible without a larger transfer of resources from the rich countries of the Community (the Federal Republic in particular) than they were ready to provide and without more external control over the management of their domestic economies than the weaker

---

[39]The OECD has managed to keep the WP-3 more or less restricted to the key countries, but this is not true of the EPC which includes the full membership. In order to get around the membership problem, use has been made of what is known in OECD jargon as the "bureau technique," that is, informal meetings, frequently over dinner, of the Chairman of the Committee and representatives of the key countries.

countries (the United Kingdom, France, and Italy) were prepared to accept. An ambitious attempt to maintain the exchange rates of the Community countries within a narrower band than that permitted by the IMF rules then operative soon shrank into the so-called "snake," an arrangement dominated by the mark and participated in by only those countries whose economies were already very closely linked with the German economy.[40] However, although the ambitious efforts to form a monetary union came to little, there was a steady increase in the process of consultation among the members of the Community throughout the sixties and seventies, and, in some cases, it was the European Community that came first to the rescue when member countries were in need of substantial financial support.

In the mid-seventies, the Commission of the Communities returned to the charge and urged, once again, that the member countries renew their efforts to establish a system of closer monetary cooperation and narrow margins for exchange rates.[41] In 1978, agreement in principle was reached on a plan for a European Monetary System which was introduced in March, 1979, by all the Community countries except the United Kingdom.[42] In brief, the EMS: limits the fluctuation of European currencies vis-à-vis one another; enables them to float as a group against the dollar and the yen; provides for intra-European interventions in European currencies; and strengthens the role of the ECU so that it is not only a unit of account but also the numeraire of the

[40]The Benelux countries and Denmark, and, for a time, Norway and Sweden. Sweden left the "snake" in August, 1977, and Norway in December, 1978. Neither one has joined the EMS although the arrangement is open to them to join despite the fact that they are not members of the Community.

[41]See the speech by the President of the Commission, Roy Jenkins, in Florence, Italy, in September 1977. He would have been very unlikely to have made this proposal without some indication of German support. And the main lines of the eventual plan were largely worked out by German and French experts rather than the Commission. See Tom de Vries, *On the Meaning and Future of the European Monetary System*, Essays in International Finance, Princeton University: Princeton, N.J., forthcoming.

[42]The United Kingdom's position as of mid-1980 is one of partial participation. It has, technically, joined the EMS but does not participate in the exchange-rate mechanism that lies at the heart of the scheme.

new system for stabilizing rates. The ECU is also used for settlement among members of the system. For that purpose, an initial supply of ECUs has been created against a deposit of 20 percent of the members' reserve holdings of both gold and dollars. Substantial five-year loans are available for the less prosperous members of the Community in addition to unlimited but very short-term credits which are available as part of the intra-European settlement process. The European Council also agreed that two years after the entry into force of the EMS, an EMF (European Monetary Fund) would be established that would put the system on a firmer institutional basis and enhance the role of the ECU as a reserve asset. (Just what further steps will, in fact, be taken remains unclear; in any case, the timetable seems likely to slip, for no substantial decisions are anticipated before the French elections in 1981). The hope of some of the promoters of the plan is that the new European Currency Unit will develop as a parallel currency, interchangeable as an exchange unit with the main European currencies and sharing a reserve-currency role with the dollar, and that, in the very long term, the ECU will supplant national currencies as the basic monetary unit of a real union.[43]

Some diminution of the role of the IMF is inevitable if the EMS flourishes because certain questions will become internal to the Community in much the same way as the creation of the customs union removed certain intracommunity trade questions from the purview of the GATT. In itself, this is not a cause for much concern: the real question is whether or not the global monetary system will be strengthened or weakened by the establishment and further development of the EMS. Views differ. Some of the difference depends on whether one shares the long-held and strongly argued views of Professor Triffin that the surest road to the eventual development of a freer and more stable system of world trade and payments lies through regional mone-

[43]For further details, see Commission of the European Communities, *European Economy*, no. 3, July, 1979; de Vries, op. cit.; and Robert Triffin, *Gold and the Dollar Crisis: Yesterday and Tomorrow*, Essays in International Finance, No. 132, December 1978, Princeton University, Princeton, N.J.

tary integration, most particularly although not exclusively in Europe, or whether, as the U.S. Treasury has frequently been inclined to argue, one thinks such action will weaken efforts to improve the world monetary system and that the advantages of greater regional integration will be bought at the expense of third countries.[44] Another part of the argument derives from differences of view about the stability and desirability of a multi-reserve currency system. Political preferences clearly underlie many of the arguments: those who fear that the ECU will turn out to be a rival to the dollar argue the disadvantages; those who hope it will, the advantages. Nor is the argument uncolored by the differences in view about the advantages and disadvantages that accrue to a country running a reserve currency. There are differences of view as well about the extent to which the experiments with the ECU will accelerate or diminish interest in improving the SDR and taking the steps required to make it *the* central reserve asset.

We do not propose to become enmeshed in these arguments. Only time will provide the answers. What can be said is that the larger the amount of short- and medium-term credit available to help the weaker countries in the context of the EMS, the more the Community rather than the IMF will be the first recourse for European countries needing balance-of-payments support. As many people interested in the development of the Fund today fear, this may mean that the Fund will come to look more and more like an institution that imposes conditions mainly on poor countries, many of the rich in effect escaping its strictures by being able to help one another on less exacting terms. If the EMS prospers, there is no way of avoiding this problem, although perhaps the formation of the Special Surveillance Group suggested above would help somewhat by putting the Fund in a stronger position to comment on the broad range of macroeconomic policies pursued by the key industrial countries. But the Fund's ability to play a more important role in the surveillance

---

[44]The view of the U.S. Treasury on this issue recently seems to have changed somewhat. See Under-Secretary of the Treasury Solomon's speech on August 27, 1979, in Alpbach, Austria, already cited.

plus coordination process will also, of course, be affected by the development of an EMS, for even closer coordination of policies will have to take place among the member countries of the EMS if that system is to prosper. And this will inevitably complicate discussion in the broader IMF and OECD contexts.

This is simply another variant of a problem that the European Community has always posed for third countries. So long as the European Community is something between an international organization and a true union, its relationship with third countries and the nature of its participation in broader intergovernmental groups is bound to be troublesome. In some cases, it can and must act as a unit, and in other cases, it cannot and should not try to do so. A Special Surveillance Group within the Fund of the kind proposed above might act either as a catalyst, impelling more prior policy coordination among the members of the Community in order to permit the Community countries to follow a common line in the broader consultations, or it might weaken their impulse to do so. Which way things go will depend, ultimately, on the strength of the drive toward unity among the Europeans. That is as it should be. If the drive toward unity is not strong enough to survive the competition of a Special Surveillance Group encouraging policy harmonization within the Fund, there is no point in trying to spoon-feed it by weakening the cooperation within the Fund. But, conversely, if the EMS takes off and there is a promising effort to create a European monetary zone with a higher degree of policy coordination internally than is possible, or probably necessary, on the broader, developed-country basis, the IMF group should adjust its procedures to encourage the European process rather than seeking to frustrate it.

THE FUND'S ROLE AS LENDER

Thus far we have been mainly concerned with the problems of "managing" exchange rates, promoting policy harmonization among the key countries, and ensuring an appropriate amount of overall liquidity in the system as a whole. The discussion has, therefore, focused on the Fund's role vis-à-vis the countries that carry the most weight in the system. In this section we look at the distribution of liquidity, that is, at the Fund's role in organizing and supervising drawings on (technically, purchases from) the Fund to meet balance-of-payments problems. In this context it is the Fund's relationship with the LDCs that is of more importance.

There are several rather different aspects to the Fund's function of providing balance-of-payments support to enable a country to "correct maladjustments" without "resorting to measures destructive of national or international prosperity."[45] In the first place there is the classic function of providing Fund resources to tide countries over short-term, clearly reversible, balance-of-payments difficulties, the reserves being sold back to the Fund when the situation reverses itself. So long as the need is a modest one and the drawings are within what is called the reserve tranche[46] and the first credit tranche (25 percent of a country's quota), the process is largely automatic and no problems arise. But, more often than not, a country needs to make larger drawings, and these must be specifically authorized by the Fund. Normally, the Fund negotiates a stand-by arrangement with the country concerned. This, in effect, authorizes a country to make drawings, in installments, up to some stipulated amount (usually closely related to the size of the country's quota) on condition that it undertakes a program of adjustment designed to bring its payments back into balance. As a guide to compliance, "performance criteria" of an objective, if rather mechanical, character are usually set out; and, if these are not being met, a country's right to complete its drawings may be terminated before all the installments have been drawn. Sometimes the need for even very large drawings arises from the kind of balance-of-payments problem that is clearly temporary or from economic mismanagement that can be corrected within a short period. But sometimes

[45]Article I, IMF, *Articles of Agreement.*
[46]The reserve tranche was formerly called the gold tranche. If, because of drawings made by other countries, the Fund's holding of a member's currency is less than its quota, the difference is called the reserve tranche.

241

(and particularly in the case of developing countries) the difficulties are more deep-seated and require adjustments that are not easily or quickly made by countries with fragile political and social structures working on thin economic margins. Sometimes the difficulties arise from factors that are beyond a country's control, such as the steep increase in the cost of oil or the failure of an essential crop. Sometimes the difficulty is really of a quite different kind and the country concerned should at its stage of development be running a deficit on its balance-of-payments beyond that which it can finance.

So far as the advanced countries are concerned, improved surveillance, coupled with "managed" floating, should reduce the need for massive short-term balance-of-payments assistance. But because problems are too often allowed to become crises before they are corrected, the need will not disappear entirely. Close relationships among the Treasuries and Central Banks of the key countries make ad hoc arrangements, such as the swaps negotiated in the sixties, easier, swifter, and less painful than recourse to the procedures provided in the Fund. But, if the Fund is to play the role it should play at the center of the system, the powerful countries should discuss their problems and negotiate their special assistance deals within the context of the Fund, not outside it. Ad hoc arrangements negotiated among a few key countries not only feed the feeling of the LDCs that "the system" is biased against them, they are also subject, if not to outright abuse, at least to the weaknesses that arise from the reluctance of any small club to discipline its own members. Members of such groups typically resist disciplining each other for the very good reason that each knows it may be the next to need help and that it will then want help as freely and unconditionally as possible. The Golden Rule becomes a prescription not for self-discipline but for permitting others to follow doubtful policies so that they will permit you to do the same.

The Fund, at least in the person of the Managing Director, was not wholly uninformed of the arrangements being made by the United States to support the dollar in late 1978, and he was doubtless in contact with the Secretary of the Treasury on an informal basis for some time before action was eventually taken.

But only by an extraordinary stretch of the imagination could the Managing Director be said to have been at the center of things. The Fund will only become the instrument that many official U.S. statements appear to envisage for it if U.S. practice lives up to its rhetoric. Part of the problem, but only part, lies in the structure of the Fund. Establishment of the Council, and even more of something like the limited-member Special Surveillance Committee suggested above, should encourage the kind of consultations that ought to take place far more often than they now do. The willingness of the key governments to have their own problems discussed within the framework of the Fund will be the critical factor determining the importance of the Fund.

The advanced countries have been reluctant to draw on the Fund until all else has failed, partly because they feel they have a closer understanding of their own problems than does the Fund staff and the Executive Board, partly because they suspect the medicine that might accompany purchases from the Fund would not be the corrective they wanted to apply, partly because recourse to the Fund is taken as a sign of domestic mismanagement, and partly because the conditions imposed by the Fund tend to make visible to domestic electorates the reality of the loss of autonomy in monetary matters.

Much the same reasons have also made the LDCs reluctant to go to the Fund. But they have not had the option of the kind of ad hoc arrangements that the rich countries could make among themselves, and they were more frequently compelled to swallow the Fund's deflationary medicine. During the seventies, however, the huge surpluses of the OPEC countries flooded the commercial markets and gave some, at least, of the LDCs an alternative which they were quick to exploit. The result was a vast accumulation of commercial debt on the part of many LDCs and a decline in the use of the Fund. By the end of the decade, the commercial banks had become concerned at the extent of the debt they had piled up, and they had begun urging the LDCs to seek Fund assistance as a way of obtaining some discipline over the debtors.

Many aspects of the Fund's lending practices to the LDCs were strongly criticized during the seventies: the rigid and simplistic character of the Fund's performance criteria; the bias toward deflation in its recommendations; its apparent insensitivity to the political constraints that limited the actions governments could take and its apparent lack of concern with the political consequences of the programs of economic reform that it imposed; the shortness of the time periods allowed for adjustments; the fact that the advice given a country by the Fund was not always consistent with the advice it was receiving simultaneously from the Bank; the fact that advice to an individual country was too seldom set in the context of the advice being given to other countries; the narrow definition of the purposes for which drawings were permitted; and, above all, the inadequate amounts of money available to the LDCs. Finally, in September, 1979, the Group of Twenty-four[47] adopted an "Outline for a Program of Action on International Monetary Reform" that brought together in an organized and comprehensive way the many complaints made both by the LDCs themselves and also by impartial outside observers about the Fund's lending policies. Much of this analysis and many of the G-24's recommendations for improvement were later repeated and endorsed by the Brandt Commission Report, and became the basis for the very strong pressure for reform of the IMF, which characterized the special session of the General Assembly in the late summer of 1980.

The Fund was undoubtedly slow to recognize its own shortcomings and to respond to valid criticisms. But by the end of the seventies a number of new facilities had been established which helped lengthen the period for which funds were available (thus easing somewhat the adjustment problems), increased the amounts which countries with small quotas could draw from the Fund, and removed some of the stigma that had been attached to going to the Fund by permitting drawings to meet exceptional problems that arose not from internal mismanagement but from factors beyond the control of a country, such as crop failures or

---

[47]The Group of Twenty-four is roughly parallel to the G-10. It is composed of Finance Ministers from the LDCs, eight from each region: Africa, Asia, Latin America.

a steep rise in oil prices.[48] The combination of well-orchestrated pressures, the visible decline in the LDCs' use of the Fund, despite their acute and growing balance-of-payments problems, and increasing doubts about the ability of the commercial banks to handle the recycling of OPEC surpluses as successfully in the eighties as they had done in the mid-seventies was producing

[48]For a useful description and analysis of the Fund's special facilities, see Joseph Gold, *Financial Assistance by the International Monetary Fund: Law and Practice*, Pamphlet Series, No. 27, IMF: Washington, D.C., 1979. Briefly, the Fund's special facilities are as follows: The *Compensatory Financing Facility* (CFF) was first introduced in 1963 and substantially liberalized in 1966, in 1975, and again in 1979. This facility was originally established to help countries that were highly dependent on exports of primary products when they experienced balance-of-payments difficulties because of instability in world commodity markets or because of crop failures. Although initially countries were permitted to draw only 25 percent of quotas, since August 1979 they have been permitted to draw up to 100 percent of quotas, and shortfalls arising from declines in tourism and workers' remittances now also entitle a country to draw on the facility. The *Extended Fund Facility* (EFF) was established in 1974 and liberalized in 1979. This facility was designed to meet the contention that some balance-of-payments problems arose from structural maladjustments that could not be corrected in the short time covered by the normal stand-by arrangements. Purchases under the EFF can be phased over three years and repurchases (repayments) spread over ten years. Rather larger drawings than are available under normal credit tranche drawings can also be made. The *Supplementary Financing Facility* (SFF), sometimes also called the Witteveen facility, was established in 1977 to provide additional financing for countries whose quotas were very small in comparison with their needs. The Fund also has a *Buffer Stock Facility* that can be drawn on to assist poor countries in making payments to (or fulfilling other conditions of participation in) buffer stock arrangements, and a *Trust Fund* which has, in the past, extended loans to some of the poorest of the LDCs from the proceeds of the Fund's sales of gold. New loans from the Trust Fund will not be made after 1980, but it seems probable that repayments on the loans (which will begin in the summer of 1982) will be used for the benefit of the poorest LDCs (i.e., those countries which were eligible for Trust Fund loans) most probably to lower the interest paid by these countries when drawings are made under the SFF and perhaps also the EFF. The possibility of the Fund's either establishing a new facility or further expanding the CFF to help countries, particularly low-income countries, finance unexpectedly heavy food import bills arising either from crop failures or from sharp rises in the cost of food imports was also under consideration in 1980.

results. And by the time of the Annual Meeting of the Board of Governors in October, 1980, there were numerous signs that the Fund staff and the Executive Board had been re-examining the Fund's role as lender to the LDCs in a more open-minded and more profound way than had hitherto appeared to be the case. The striking increase in LDC purchases from (drawings on) the Fund, which became apparent during the first six months of 1980, bore witness not only to the worsening plight of many of the oil-importing LDCs (and to the fact that commercial markets were overloaded with debt) but also to the familiar phenomenon of criticism reaching a crescendo just after the process of change has begun.[49]

Are the changes that have recently been made adequate, and is the more open-minded approach that seemed to characterize the Fund's examination of the criticisms that have been made likely to endure? Part of the problem in the past has stemmed from the "mind-set" of the Fund (i.e., of the staff and Executive Board), part from the fact that the old industrial countries dominate the Fund and they have been both slow to recognize the validity of many of the points made by the LDCs and unwilling to make any changes that would diminish, in any substantial way, their control over the Fund, and part from the fact that LDC pressures in the past have often been highly indiscriminate, and their valid claims frequently intermingled with ones the Fund has been right to resist.

The Fund's staff has a great deal of autonomy in the advice it gives to countries needing stand-by arrangements or having recourse to the various special facilities administered by the IMF. It is desirable that the staff should continue to be in a strong position, but perhaps its advice would be more acceptable if there were more opportunity for the countries affected to have their views listened to by a political organ of the Fund. Today, the Executive Board has to approve all loans formally, and, in the process of so doing, it frequently expresses views—in rather general terms—about the conditions that have been laid down by the staff. In order to safeguard the authority of the staff, the

[49]See IMF, *Survey,* July 21, 1980.

Executive Board does not normally alter the conditions. The Board's discussions undoubtedly affect the way the Fund staff handles future cases, but this may be rather too indirect and too leisurely a way to take corrective action. Moreover, by its very composition, the Executive Board is frequently not in a position to have the intimate knowledge of the country concerned that would enable it to act as an effective counterweight to the members of the Fund's staff who have been in close contact with the country concerned and are usually, in technical terms, very well informed. And, like the staff, the Executive Board attaches high importance to its disciplinary role.

The establishment of the Council would be one way—and probably the most desirable way—of injecting more "political" concerns into the judgments made by the Fund. Rather ironically, the Executive Directors from the LDCs have been among the strongest opponents of the establishment of the Council, fearing, probably rightly, some erosion of their own authority if the Council were to be established.

Perhaps a more serious concern is that the establishment of the Council would limit the authority of the Managing Director. There is undoubtedly a trade-off to be made: a larger role for the Fund against somewhat more political control by member countries. But, as we have indicated in the discussion of the Fund's surveillance/consultation role, it seems to us unlikely that the role of the Fund in that context can be strengthened appreciably unless there is more contact on a continuous basis with policy officials: much the same line of reasoning applies to the Fund's relationship with the LDCs.

There are dangers in overpoliticizing the Fund, but today the dangers lie in the opposite direction. The Executive Directors and the staff tend to be too remote from the political process. Like any staff of a large organization, the Fund staff, and the Executive Board as well, tends to become rigid in its views. And in part because it enjoys more real power than the staff of most international organizations, the Fund staff is in more danger of having too "orthodox" a view, of lagging rather than leading informed opinion. Because the Fund staff and the Executive Board want to be listened to, they tend to be super-cautious and to play safe: it is better to make no errors than to take chances.

One way of introducing more flexibility into the Fund would be to have more fixed-term appointments. At present, only the Managing Director and the Deputy Managing Director have limited terms (five-year renewable terms). Perhaps the same arrangement should apply to a few other key staff members. Almost certainly, the Fund would profit by having more "inning and outing"; in particular, a system providing for some rotation between the Fund staff and national governments would seem to offer the advantage of injecting a more systemic view into thinking at the level of national governments and more political sensitivity into the Fund.[50] This might be one way, too, of bringing more people from the LDCs into the Fund. It is important to keep qualifications for Fund staff very high and to resist any suggestion that the Fund should adopt a quota system, such as prevails in the United Nations. It is also important that competent people remain in responsible positions in LDC governments and not be lured away to the frequently more lucrative IMF positions. Making it easier for potential high-flyers in national administrations to spend some time at the Fund as an essential part of their experience would seem likely to pay dividends all round.[51]

Establishing the Council and injecting some new blood into the staff of the Fund would help make it more aware of the problems of those countries which seem bound to be its main clients in the future. But both symbolically and operationally the change in governance that is most needed if the Fund is to command widespread support is some re-weighting of votes in the Executive Board and the Board of Governors to reflect the shifts in economic power and to give more adequate recognition to the fact that those who are dependent on a system as well as those who have the ability to affect it are entitled to a "voice" in its

---

[50]The Fund (i.e., the Managing Director), not national governments, would have to control the process because it is important to maintain and protect the international character of the staff of the IMF.

[51]The Fund is now (in 1980) investigating possible term appointments designed to do just this.

governance. Over the years, the "voice" of the LDCs has been substantially increased, but the United States can still effectively veto many issues, and the voting power of some of the other old industrialized nations (e.g., the United Kingdom) is larger and that of some of the LDCs smaller than indicated by their current weight in the world economy. Moreover, in recent years, the trend in the Fund has been to increase the number of decisions that require high majorities (frequently 85 percent of the votes), a trend which, although it ensures that a measure enjoys a very large degree of support, also makes it easier for countries with large quotas to block action.[52] The Fund, like other effective international organizations, prides itself on the fact that many decisions are reached without recourse to voting. But voting formulas are far from irrelevant, and, frequently, it is the threat of a vote that makes agreement, or compromise, possible. It might be a desirable innovation in the Fund, and one which would both strengthen the position of the Managing Director in a useful way and be a controlled way around the blocking power of the high-quota countries, if certain kinds of decisions required somewhat lower majorities when formally proposed or endorsed by the Managing Director.[53] As suggested above, there would seem to be a case for lowering the majority required for the allocation or cancellation of SDRs (decisions taken by the Governors on a proposal from the Managing Director, concurred in by the Executive Board) since the Managing Director represents the global interest and the questions at issue are the adequacy of global liquidity and the composition of reserves.

More also needs to be done to adjust quotas. Today, a country's quota in the Fund serves a number of purposes that are logically distinct: the quota determines or importantly affects (1)

[52]See Joseph Gold, *Voting Majorities in the Fund: Effects of Second Amendment of the Articles*, IMF Pamphlet Series, No. 20: Washington, D.C., 1977.

[53]This is analogous to the arrangement in the Treaty of Rome which provides for smaller majorities when the Council is acting on a proposal from the Commission than when it is not. In the context of the Community, this provision was seen as a safeguard for the small countries, as well as a recognition of the special role of the Commission in promoting a Community rather than a national viewpoint.

the member's basic subscription to the Fund; (2) its drawing rights on the Fund; (3) its share of SDR allocations; and (4) its voting powers in the Fund. The fact that quotas serve so many different purposes complicates immensely both the increases in quotas that should be made to keep pace with the expansion of trade and the adjustment of quotas to the shifts in need and in relative power among member countries. The formula for the calculation of quotas is a complicated one, and it is tortuously revised from time to time. Another revision will probably take place in the context of the eighth general review of quotas in 1981. But no single formula could be devised which would take fully into account the rather different factors that should be considered if quotas are to serve so many disparate purposes. Already some of the links with quotas are being stretched and modified in various ways. Thus, for certain drawings from the Witteveen facility (the SFF) there is no mandatory link with quotas. Perhaps of even greater potential importance as a precedent, the Fund, in the spring and summer of 1980, authorized drawings by Turkey and Guyana that were far larger in relation to quota than any previously permitted.[54] More can be done and should be done to see that the link with quotas is attenuated, and that quotas increase almost automatically with the increase in trade (over the years the trend has, in fact, been the reverse); and the original IMF members must be more willing than they have been in the past to see adjustments made to reflect shifts in economic power.

Eventually, if the Fund is to play the role it should play at the center of the monetary system, the Articles of Agreement will have to be amended and the links between quotas, drawings, and governance altered or abandoned. But it is difficult to see this becoming practical politics until most member countries are readier to see much more power devolved onto the Managing Director and his staff than is the case today. Power can and

---

[54]For Turkey, a stand-by was approved, enabling it to purchase an amount equivalent to 625 percent of its quota over a three-year period. See IMF *Survey*, June 25, 1980. In the case of Guyana the amount approved was 400 percent of its quota over a three-year period. See IMF *Survey*, August 4, 1980.

should be shared more fairly, but as radical a shift as many of the LDCs would like to see would boomerang; the consequence would almost certainly be less willingness on the part of countries like the United States which, whatever the basis of calculation, will continue to have very large quotas to see the Fund's resources increase as regularly as they should. Thus, until the LDCs and the advanced countries alike are willing to see more power vested in the Managing Director, that is, in a "neutral arbiter" at the center of the system, it is safe to predict that "governance" will remain an issue.

Perhaps the magnitude of the recycling problems confronting the system as the eighties opened will push the Fund to raise money directly in the market, as the Articles of Agreement permit it to do. In our view, this would be a desirable step for the Fund to take, not only as a way of increasing the resources of the Fund and enabling it to play a more active role in recycling the OPEC surpluses, but also as a way of moving the Fund closer to the markets, which is something that should happen if the Fund is to play a strong role at the center of the monetary system.

Much of the LDC dissatisfaction with the Fund stems essentially from the fact that the flow of resources to the LDCs has not been adequate and the Fund has been expected to meet needs that should be met in other ways. Criticisms of this kind are essentially criticisms of the international economic system as a whole, of the policies of the rich countries, and of the nexus—or, rather, the lack of an adequate nexus—between the Bank and the Fund.[55]

---

[55] A Development Committee (technically the Joint Ministerial Committee of the Boards of Governors of the Bank and Fund on the Transfer of Real Resources to Developing Countries) was established in 1974, in part to try to prevent conflicting advice from the Bank and Fund and to identify needs which were not being adequately handled by either agency. For a variety of reasons, the Committee has proved to be of rather limited usefulness. Part of the problem undoubtedly stems from the fact that it was set up as a more or less costless gesture to the LDCs, without any very clear understanding about its role, and neither the Bank nor the Fund has been particularly cooperative or receptive to its advice. Rather than giving it strong support, they have sought to clip its wings and to reduce its independence.

Until very recently there was a gray area between the short-term stabilization and adjustment assistance provided by the IMF and the long-term, mainly project financing provided by the Bank.[56] The stretching-out of Fund loans and new loans by the Bank to help finance structural adjustment have gone some way to meet the needs that have tended to fall between stools. But the continuing pressures on the Fund to lengthen even further the time period for repayment of drawings and to permit drawings for many reasons not connected with temporary balance-of-payments problems raise important questions about the relative roles of the Bank and the Fund. As discussed in more detail in the next chapter, what many developing countries need most is long-term credit permitting them to pursue sound policies of "debt-led" growth. This type of financing should come primarily from commercial markets, supplemented in some instances by Bank loans. In some cases there may be a need for some Fund financing as well. To review long-term programs in which both institutions are involved and to deal with closely related aspects of the debt problem, it might be useful to establish a Joint Standing Committee drawn from the Bank's and the Fund's Executive Boards. Such a Joint Committee would create the functional link between the Bank and the Fund that is now lacking and would promote better coordination on problems that have in the past tended either to fall between the two institutions or sometimes to be handled in part by each, but not always in ways that were complementary or mutually reinforcing. "Debt management," not simply more credit on longer terms, is a part of the problem, and the Joint Committee might be a logical place in the international system for discussion of how debt relief can best be handled, that is, seeing whether some general rules and principles can be agreed upon and providing a place where individual cases can be examined in detail.

Closer cooperation between the Bank and the Fund, larger and more frequently adjusted quotas, more political sensitivity, and more recognition than there has been in the past that there are some situations in which deficits should be financed for an

[56]See, for example, IBRD, *World Development Report,* 1979, p. 32.

appreciable period rather than eliminated at the cost of deflation and hardship are the main changes that should be sought in the Fund's relations with the developing countries in the next decade. But most of the biggest problems of the LDCs are ones that do not come directly within the ambit of the Fund, a point that was rightly, if rather surprisingly, made in a recent UNCTAD report:

> At a more fundamental level the IMF's institutional mandate is too restrictive to deal in a satisfactory manner with the multiple sources of payments problems. These problems can no longer be treated as largely monetary in character. They are inextricably linked with, and must be treated in conjunction with, the question of long-term capital flows, trade policies, development, and national objectives with regard to employment, which are often in conflict with one another. When the situation is seen in this light, it becomes clear that it is unreasonable to expect an institution that has no influence over decisions in these interrelated areas to realize in practice the objectives of collective management of the world economy.[57]

So it is. The IMF can, and should, only play a partial role, and efforts to load onto the IMF functions that should be performed elsewhere in the system should be resisted. But, by building up the first leg of the tripod, the PTO, and by organizing better relationships among the three key institutions—the Bank Group, the IMF, and the PTO—the task of "collective management" could, we believe, be handled in a more satisfactory way than heretofore, although the problems that must be dealt with will be difficult, complicated, and, perhaps, insoluble.

---

[57]See pp. 11–12 of TD/233, March 8, 1979, a report by the UNCTAD secretariat on International Monetary Issues prepared for UNCTAD V at Manila. It might also be noted that one of the conclusions reached in the report is that the failure to establish the ITO left a vacuum which has been a critical weakness in the system.

SEVEN

International Resource Transfers

The creation and expansion over the last three decades of a system of international resource transfers represents a major development in international economic cooperation. Developing countries now receive many kinds of external financing from a wide variety of official sources: other governments; the international financial institutions, particularly the World Bank, but also the regional banks and the IMF; a number of U.N. agencies; the European Community and other regional institutions; and the OPEC Special Fund. During the 1970s, the importance of private capital flows relative to official resource transfers increased—dramatically for a number of the higher-income developing countries. This increase in private lending to developing countries was part of the sea-change of international economics in the seventies. Still, official resource transfers—on concessional terms for today's low-income developing countries and on non-concessional terms for the higher-income developing countries—remain, and will remain for the foreseeable future, a key factor in prospects for global economic growth and a major issue in economic relations among states.

Several issues have become familiar elements in the continuing debate on how to improve official resource transfers. The main issues have to do with the amounts, terms and predictability of official development assistance; with the criteria for making choices about the countries and the activities to be given priority in the allocation of resources; and with coordination among today's many multilateral and bilateral programs. All these issues demand more attention if resource transfers in the 1980s are to match development needs. So, too, will some new problems having to do with the growing diversity of financing needs. As we commented earlier, the increasing differentiation among states is rendering obsolete the sharp dichotomy between North and South, between rich and poor, making it more useful to see the universe of states as a continuum or spectrum rather than a collection of discrete groups divided by hard and fast lines. Clusters of states remain, some very rich, some very poor, some highly developed, some just started down that road. But, increasingly, one is aware that the demarcation between groups is fuzzy and that there is great diversity even within groups.

In thinking about reforms needed in the system of official transfers, we should put particular emphasis in the 1980s on instituting something like the U.N. Basic Support Program, discussed in Chapter 4, on increasing the amounts and broadening the types of financial assistance provided by the multilateral development banks, on giving recipient countries a greater voice both in development institutions and in the organization of their own assistance programs, on streamlining today's international resource-transfer system, which has grown haphazardly and become far too cumbersome, and on improving coordination with other parts of the system, and primarily between the World Bank and the IMF.

In recent years, there has been much reassessment of, and some change in, theories about strategies for development. These reappraisals and revisions cover a wide range of issues. After almost a quarter-century of disagreement and debate, fairly broad agreement is now beginning to emerge on the benefits to be gained from following a more export-oriented and less protectionist trade and industrial development stategy. As said in Chapter 5, despite these signs of a changing attitude, many LDCs still have very high levels of protection. If the more "pro-trade" view is, in fact, translated into practice, it should contribute to sounder patterns of industrialization. But shifts in trade and industrial policy in developing countries may also tend to increase, at least initially, their needs for balance-of-payments financing.[1]

Views on the role of industrialization have also undergone change. Rapid industrialization continues to be seen as central to the process of development. But it is recognized today, perhaps more than ever before, that to have the desired results, industrialization needs to be part of a broad process of structural transformation, leading not only to aggregate increases but also to widely distributed improvements in real income and employment opportunities. It is also now generally recognized that to "grow first and redistribute later" is likely to be more difficult than early theories of economic development assumed.[2] Problems remain of reconciling policies to accelerate growth with policies to promote a broad distribution of the benefits of growth, but in few countries is sole reliance being placed on a "trickle down" strategy of development.

For many LDCs—especially today's slow-growing, low-in-

[1]As noted by Donald B. Keesing in "Trade Policy for Developing Countries," World Bank Staff Working Paper No. 353, August, 1979, p. 1: " . . . among international and development economists strongly concerned with trade policy questions, one now finds considerable convergence of views on what trade policy regimes should ideally be like and which changes would constitute improvements in any particular case. . . .Unlike the situation twenty years ago, recently there has been very little intellectually argued opposition to the dominant view on these matters, even from people who stand apart from the mainstream of economics and view its findings with suspicion." See also the series of country studies directed by Anne O. Krueger and Jagdish N. Bhagwati and the summary volume by Krueger, *Foreign Trade Regimes and Economic Development: Liberalization Attempts and Consequences*, Balinger: Cambridge, 1978, for an analysis of the external payments difficulties that developing countries have encountered in making adjustments in their trade policies.

[2]See Morawetz, op. cit.; also, the various studies on income distribution and development, including, most importantly, Hollis Chenery et al., *Redistribution with Growth*, Oxford University Press: New York, 1974; Hans W. Singer et al., *Employment, Incomes and Equality: A Strategy for Increasing Productive Employment in Kenya*, ILO: Geneva, 1972; and Charles R. Frank, Jr., and Richard C. Webb (eds.), *Income Distribution and Growth in the Less-Developed Countries*, Brookings Institution; Washington, 1977.

come countries—the key to more rapid and broad-based development is now seen to lie in a much increased emphasis on policies designed to stimulate improvements in agricultural productivity and to promote employment in rural areas. With population increases in many areas running ahead of food and agriculture growth rates, increased investment in the agricultural sector and rural areas has become a critical factor both in ensuring a more adequate supply of food and in broadening the distribution of rising income levels and thus providing opportunities for expanding domestic markets.[3]

Events of the past decade have also altered fundamentally many of the global conditions under which national development plans must be pursued. At the outset of the seventies, it was widely assumed that high rates of economic growth in the developed countries would continue and that with some (substantial) improvements in aid, trade, and technology transfers this growth in "the North" would have a positive effect in "the South." In fact, the early 1970s saw a large increase in resource transfers to LDCs, a remarkable rise in export growth rates of some middle-income LDCs, and, for some, the achievement, on a sustained basis, of quite rapid growth. But inflation, recession, and high unemployment in the developed countries, together with the sharp hike in oil prices and slowed growth in trade, damped growth prospects in the developing world, particularly in the lower-income LDCs. With the changing world economic conditions, there has been a steep rise in the current-account deficits of most non-oil-producing LDCs, and the external payments positions of a number of countries have become seriously strained.[4]

---

[3]As explained by W. A. Lewis: "The principal cause of the poverty of the developing countries, and their poor factoral terms of trade is that half their labor force (more or less) produces food at very low productivity levels. This limits the domestic market for manufactures and services, keeps the propensity to import too high, reduces taxable capacity and savings, and provides goods and services for export on unfavorable terms." W. A. Lewis, *The Evolution of the International Economic Order*, Princeton University Press: Princeton, N.J., 1978, p. 76.

[4]The current account deficit on the balance of payments of the oil-importing

The dramatic increase in oil prices in the mid-1970s did not have as destabilizing an effect on the developing world as a whole (though individual countries were severely hit) as was feared at the time. This was so partly because there was rapid recycling of OPEC "petrodollar" surpluses through commercial banks and the international financial institutions and an expansion in the aid programs of the oil-exporting states; partly because of increases in commodity export prices; and partly because several years of good weather eased somewhat the difficulties created for the poorest oil-importing countries (notably India). By the end of the seventies, however, the much altered "economics of energy" had become a major new factor affecting LDCs both directly—through enormous increases in their oil import bills—and indirectly through the impact of the rising cost of energy on the health of the global economy.

Different groups of developing countries have fared rather differently over the course of the turbulent 1970s. And, consequently, they enter the 1980s with very disparate development prospects and development financing needs. At one end of the spectrum are the poor and populous countries of South Asia and the least developed countries of middle Africa—some 40 or so countries with a total population of nearly 1.5 billion people. As we saw in Chapter 4, most of these nations have extremely low

---

LDCs (as measured in 1979 prices) rose from $11.5 billion in 1973 to $52.9 billion in 1979, and it is expected to exceed $60 billion in 1980. As pointed out in 1979 by the IMF: "The nature of the actual and projected increases in the combined current account deficit of the non-oil developing countries from 1977 to 1979 gives as much cause for concern as their size. Of the $22 billion rise . . . some $16 billion would be attributable to deterioration of the terms of trade of these countries, whose export prices did not keep pace with prices of their imports in 1978 and are expected to lag again in 1979, while about $6 billion would probably reflect increased net payments of interest and other forms of investment income. . . .The prominence of interest charges and deterioration of the terms of trade in the rise of the deficit of the non-oil less developed countries since 1977 is a cause for concern, since these factors have been absorbing borrowed funds without increasing the real flow of external resources for development." International Monetary Fund, *Annual Report, 1979,* IMF: Washington, 1979, p. 23.

per capita incomes and, particularly in Africa, continue to experience slow, if not stagnating, economic growth. In many of these countries, the basic economic and institutional infrastructure remains little developed. Many, though not all, are more heavily dependent on food imports than they were 10 to 20 years ago. And, having been hit hard by the economic "shocks" of the seventies, many are now confronted with even weaker external payment positions than at the outset of the 1970s.

For the low-income countries access to sources of external financing other than official development assistance on concessional terms is extremely limited. They can little afford to borrow from private capital markets, nor do their economies offer much that attracts private direct investment (except where there are fuel or mineral resources). It is of serious concern to them, therefore, that the total flow of official development assistance (ODA) has increased rather slowly in the 1970s.[5] Moreover, despite a growing consensus among developed and developing countries alike that concessional resource transfers should go mainly to the poorest countries—whose access to other forms of financial flows is limited and whose economic and social development is lagging seriously—in practice, less than half of all bilateral ODA and less than two-thirds of the total (bilateral and multilateral flows) goes to the low-income LDCs.[6]

At the other end of the "development" spectrum are countries that have achieved, or seem likely to achieve in the decade of the eighties, moderate standards of living and significant advances in industrial development. Their economies are now among the most dynamic in the world. Their exports are growing

[5]During the 1970s, ODA from member countries of the Development Assistance Committee increased in real terms at an annual average rate of some 3 to 4 percent, roughly keeping pace with growth of GNP. This growth amounted to an increase of about $6.7 billion (in 1977 dollars) in DAC-ODA flows between 1970 and 1979. ODA from all sources (DAC, non-DAC OECD countries, OPEC, and CMEA) grew at a more rapid pace (roughly 4.5 percent) than DAC aid flows, due to the very rapid rise in OPEC aid. In total, there was an increase in ODA from approximately $15.1 billion to $21.8 billion (in 1977 dollars).

[6]For a further breakdown, see the Annual Reports of the OECD, Development Assistance Committee.

at unprecedentedly high rates. And they have gained much improved access to the vast resources of the private capital markets. About four-fifths of the external financing of all middle-income countries is now met by loans at market terms, with private sources accounting for over 85 percent of this lending.[7] Still, most of these middle-income countries face problems of acute poverty and imbalances in development in sectors or in regions of their economies. As they seek to industrialize and grow, they must deal with massive problems posed by rapid and highly concentrated urbanization—including the need to expand quickly urban public services and the need to strengthen economic links between urban industrial growth and rural-agricultural development.

A few of these countries, including Mexico, Brazil, and South Korea, began borrowing fairly large sums on private capital markets before the first oil price increases and the onset of the global recession in the early 1970s. They then chose, to the extent they were able, to "ride out" the recession of the 1970s by borrowing even more heavily. And other upper-middle-income LDCs that had previously used private markets only occasionally (or for relatively small sums) followed suit. Available liquidity created by huge petrodollar deposits and reduced business activity in the West made it good business for the commercial banks to extend, and even to solicit, major new loans in those developing countries which seemed most likely to achieve continuing growth in both GNP and export earnings. According to the banks and to official estimates, private sector lending to the more advanced developing countries is not a temporary phenomenon. Private banks will continue to be a major source of financing for these countries. And the number of LDCs that will be borrowing from private banks will continue to grow.

[7]*World Development Report, 1979,* Oxford University Press, for the World Bank: New York, p. 8. According to this report, developing countries' outstanding debt doubled in 1969–1973; and their medium- and long-term debt outstanding and disbursed increased at 21 percent a year (in current prices) between 1973 and 1977. Medium- and long-term debt outstanding totaled $258 billion at the end of 1977. Of this, the middle-income countries accounted for $211 billion. In addition, developing countries had outstanding short-term obligations of $50 to $60 billion and IMF credits of about $8 billion (p. 29).

However, many analysts argue that commercial bank lending to LDCs cannot continue to grow at the same rapid pace in the 1980s as was achieved in the 1970s. Nor can large borrowers sustain rates of growth attained in the late 1960s and 1970s unless some new actions are undertaken internationally to ensure a steady flow of external capital. Several different aspects of the recent and rapid rise of LDC borrowing cause concern.

Having borrowed heavily in the late 1960s and 1970s, many middle-income countries now require a large, continuing flow of external resources merely to amortize and service past debts. While the debt of the middle-income countries as a group is not high by historical standards and does not exceed reasonable levels, given the growth potential of this group of countries,[8] the continuing supply of private credit to even the most highly regarded developing countries is not entirely within their control. It has been to a considerable degree a reflection of economic conditions within the industrialized world. Those economic conditions—especially sluggish investment demand—have been responsible in part for the increased availability of credit to LDCs, but they have also led to a shrinking of markets which threatens both the high export growth rates of LDCs and the future debt-servicing capacity of LDC borrowers.

In addition, the rapid rise in private financing has had a serious effect on the structure of LDC debt. That is, with the increase in commercial lending, developing countries must now cope with shorter maturities and somewhat higher interest rates than when the bulk of their external financing was from official sources. None of the borrowers will be able to repay its debt any time soon—but that is not the cause of concern. (No one would expect the U.S. government or General Motors, for example, to pay off its debt, and creditors would not be interested in having them do so.) The critical issue is whether LDCs can continue to service their mounting debts, roll-over the principal on existing debt, and also arrange for additional financing.

[8]Helen Hughes, "Debt and Development: The Role of Foreign Capital in Economic Growth," *World Development,* volume 7, no. 2 (February 1979), pp. 95–112.

Most countries which have borrowed heavily in recent years have used their improved access to private credit to adjust to higher oil prices and the changing patterns of world economic growth. But mounting LDC deficits and the shortened maturity structures of LDC debt are a source of uncertainty with respect to future flows of capital. Sudden changes in export earnings or import expenditures, and fluctuations in the flow of investment funds can always cause disruptions in the debt-servicing capacity of individual countries—even in those countries that pursue sound debt strategies. Moreover, no matter how good their financial management, LDCs can do little to protect themselves against a situation in which new problem borrowers like Peru, Zaire, or Turkey affect the borrowing climate for other developing countries.

An optimistic assessment of the debt and development-financing situation facing LDCs must assume that there will be continued new lending. But even in the absence of ripple effects from other Perus, doubts have been raised about the future rate of growth of commercial lending to the developing world. U.S. banks became less active in developing countries at the end of the 1970s, in part because of the inadequacy of spreads on syndicated Eurocurrency credits. It also now appears that the capital ratios of big lending banks have been deteriorating.[9] And there has been growing concern, expressed both by banks and bank regulatory authorities, over the relatively high degree of concentration in the loan portfolios of the commercial banks that have been the leaders in extending credit to the fast-growing LDCs.[10] Indeed, by the late 1970s, bank spokesmen were expressing con-

[9]After improving from a low of 3.7 percent in 1974 to 4.3 percent in 1976, the ratio of equity capital to total assets of the nine U.S. banks most active in international business declined to 3.9 percent by mid-1979. *Journal of Commerce*, January 25, 1980.

[10]In the mid-1970s, three-fourths of the total claims on developing countries were held by 10 U.S. banks. By 1977–1978, non-U.S. banks (notably German and Japanese) began expanding their lending to LDCs at a faster rate than U.S. banks were. This diversification among lenders is a trend that much enhances the outlook for stable growth of private lending to developing countries. But there are constraints of various sorts on the future growth of these comparatively new lenders as well as constraints on the lending U.S. banks.

cern that exposure limits were being approached in some countries. And, as many leading banks point out, a prominent role in influencing adjustment policies in developing countries is a job that private commercial banks are ill-suited to perform.[11] Nor are the LDCs best served by such heavy dependence on short-term money.

THE CHANGES NEEDED IN DEVELOPMENT FINANCING

The gravest problem, and the one likely to be most difficult to meet, is the need of low-income countries for substantial increases in concessional assistance. Though there is no wholly satisfactory way of determining just how much concessional assistance is "required," several things seem clear. For some time to come, the amount of capital assistance that the 40-odd low-income countries can productively use will be increasing as their rates of economic growth and levels of industrialization rise. Moreover, more aid to these countries in the short-to-medium term may mean that less aid is required in the long run.

The Committee for Development Planning of the United Nations, in making its recommendations for a "New International Development Strategy" for the 1980s and beyond, has proposed that the goal of doubling the per capita income of low-income countries by the year 2000 be made the keystone of the international development effort for the rest of the century. This would mean, according to the Committee, achieving a per capita growth rate of 3.5 percent and a total growth rate for these countries on the order of 6 percent (about 1.5 percentage points above current forecasts).[12] It has been estimated that such a step-up in the economic performance of the low-income coun-

[11]See, for example, Morgan Guaranty Trust Company of New York, *World Financial Markets,* January, 1977; and the series of papers and comments in Stephen H. Goodman (ed.), *Financing and Risk in Developing Countries,* Proceedings of a Symposium on Developing Countries' Debt, Sponsored by the Export-Import Bank of the United States, August, 1977. Mimeograph.

[12]United Nations, Committee for Development Planning, "Report on the Fifteenth Session," E/1979/37, United Nations: New York, 1979.

tries would call for an increase in annual investment of roughly $20 to $30 billion in real terms over a 20-year period. The amount of investment capital needed would increase over that time period, but, after a rather quick and sizable increase in official external financing during the decade of the 1980s, the share of external official financing in the total should be able to be scaled down.

To increase substantially official development assistance at a time when governments are under domestic pressure to cut back taxes and hold down government spending is, obviously, difficult. Yet even a doubling of ODA to today's low-income countries—the order of magnitude of an increase likely to be needed to make a significant impact on their development prospects—would be equivalent to something less than one-quarter of one percent of the combined GNP of OECD donors.[13] In other words, the increase needed, while large in comparison to current ODA flows to low-income countries, is small in absolute terms.

It will be said by some that the absorptive capacity of these countries is too limited to justify such a large rise. As is often pointed out, a large backlog of undisbursed aid funds regularly exists.[14] However, in countries where capital constraints are so clearly pervasive, undisbursed aid flows may be more indicative of problems in the way assistance is provided than of the adequacy of current resource-transfer levels.

[13]In 1978, total ODA flows to low-income countries from all sources were $12.5 billion. This amounted to something less than two-thirds of all ODA transfers. For a discussion of the proposal to establish a separate ODA target for low-income countries that would aim at a doubling of aid for that category, see Development Assistance Committee, *Development Co-operation, 1979 Review,* OECD: Paris, 1979, pp. 39–48.

[14]A study done in 1978 calculated that undisbursed balances on all loan commitments to the governments of 84 developing countries stood at $52.9 billion at the beginning of 1976. The undisbursed funds of the IBRD as of the end of June, 1977, totaled $15.3 billion—an amount equal to more than 5½ years of disbursements at that year's rate of expenditure. Undisbursed "soft loans" from the World Bank amounted to another $4.3 billion, the equivalent of about four years' expenditure. Jacob J. Kaplan, *International Aid Coordination: Needs and Machinery,* American Society of International Law: Washington, 1978.

Today, "project financing"—that is, assistance to cover the foreign exchange costs of a specific productive enterprise or undertaking—is the principal form of official resource transfers (both those made on concessional and those made on non-concessional terms). In the late 1960s and through the 1970s, resource transfer agencies made changes in the orientation of their project-lending programs which expanded considerably the scope of development financing. Those aspects of development generally referred to as "social development" (including, for example, education and housing) and both rural development and the agricultural sector began receiving considerably more attention.[15] Furthermore, in an effort to extend the reach of development assistance to the once forgotten 40 percent of the population of the developing world, development agencies changed somewhat their "style" of project lending. As a result, more assistance now goes to small-scale, labor-intensive projects. But, there are still restrictions and biases in donor policies that limit the effectiveness of project financing and that limit, in effect, the capacity of the least developed countries to absorb official development assistance. Greater efforts to simplify, harmonize, and liberalize the myriad of national "foreign assistance" procedural regulations would improve the situation. The need for this kind of change is widely recognized, and some, but not enough, improvement has been made. In fact, the shift in orientation to more and smaller assistance projects aimed at reaching the very poor has exacerbated problems in administering project financing.

More integration of technical assistance and project financing might be another way to improve the situation. Here, again, some progress has been made, particularly by increasing the

[15]It might be noted, for example, that while, a decade ago, 55 percent of World Bank lending was devoted to large-scale, capital-intensive infrastructural development, by 1977 this proportion had dropped to 30 percent. Lending for rural development increased from a negligible amount to more than 20 percent of total lending in the same period. And lending for agricultural development rose from less than 10 percent to more than 30 percent. Mahbub ul Haq, "Changing Emphasis of the Bank's Lending Policies," *Finance and Development,* vol. 15, no. 2, June, 1978, pp. 12–14.

amount of technical assistance that is covered by the multilateral development financing institutions in project loans. But, improvement in project financing is not enough. If the external financing needs of low-income countries are to be met more adequately in the years ahead, there needs also to be a significant increase in long-term "non-project" lending on concessional terms—that is, assistance that finances a variety of imports (e.g., repair and maintenance supplies, capital goods, technical expertise, fertilizer, etc.) required for an economy as a whole rather than items destined for specific project sites.

The multilateral development banks (particularly the World Bank) already provide some long-term non-project loans—including sector loans, program loans, and "structural adjustment" loans. Each of these requires a word of description. A sector loan is, basically, financing for a package of projects in one sector of a country's economy with some additional "planning money." A program loan, simply put, is long-term balance-of-payments financing. Though provided more frequently in the 1960s, before aid bureaucracies had taken on a life of their own, program lending now tends to be used to support governments' efforts to remedy the consequences of a temporary crisis, such as a civil war or natural disaster, an unanticipated export shortfall, or a sudden and substantial deterioration in terms of trade. The World Bank's new structural adjustment loan (introduced in the spring of 1980)—which it will offer on "soft" terms to low-income countries and on "hard" terms to higher-income borrowers—is, in essence, conditional long-term balance-of-payments financing to promote changes in economic policies and programs. To receive a "structural adjustment" loan a country must anticipate or have experienced a serious deterioration in its balance of payments due to factors which are not likely to be reversed easily or quickly. Secondly, the government must undertake to formulate a program of structural adjustment that would improve the country's payments position over time and on a sustainable basis.

While the multilateral development banks have increased their sector lending over the last 10 years, and the World Bank is likely to expand its new program of structural adjustment lending if experience proves it a success, we would argue that the low-income countries, with only limited access to commercial bank borrowing, also need more program lending on a continuing basis, unrelated to emergencies.

There are many reasons why more program lending has not been made available over the years. For one thing, it is widely believed to be harder to administer program loans than project loans. It is, for example, more difficult to establish criteria to ensure that program loans will be used productively. It is also more difficult to ensure that program loans will be "self-financing" or generate means of repayment. And, it is more difficult to monitor and evaluate the effectiveness of program loans.

Some of the advantages that would be obtained through more program lending can be achieved in other ways. For example, one of the arguments made in support of program loans is that they are faster because they do not require the allocation of budgetary resources from the recipient to cover the internal costs of a development project, and recipients frequently face difficulties mobilizing these counterpart funds. A willingness on the part of donors to cover local-cost financing can, of course, meet this problem, and, in some cases, this has been done. Nonetheless, in the years ahead there are several reasons for increasing the amount of program lending to low-income LDCs that do not have access to private credit. More long-term program lending on concessional terms is probably a better way of providing general balance-of-payment support for the poorest and least developed countries throughout a decade in which it is anticipated that their payments positions will be under particular strain than is continuing to invent new IMF facilities to cover these needs. And a mix of project and program financing, provided on a more coordinated and regular basis than heretofore, would make it easier for aid-receiving countries to use the assistance they receive in ways that meet their particular needs.

For the middle-income LDCs, quite different kinds of international financial assistance are needed. The recent increase in private lending to these LDCs has not eliminated the need to improve the capacity of international financial institutions to provide assistance, but it has changed the type of assistance that is now required. For many of these countries, there is need for considerable readjustment in the balance between short- and long-term borrowing. For many—those that have the least certain access to private capital, those that have borrowed heavily in recent years but can little afford much more borrowing on commercial terms, and those that continue to need external financing for a variety of developmental activities not suitable for commercial lending—there is a continuing need for official long-term development financing largely on non-concessional terms (with variations in interest rates consistent with the ability of countries to assume debt).

One of the ways to help meet the need for more long-term financing is to increase the flow of regular loans from the multilateral development banks (the World Bank and the regional banks), loans which are typically repayable over 15 to 20 years and carry interest rates close to those of the commercial market. Agreements reached at the end of the 1970s to increase the capital base of the World Bank and the regional banks are an essential first step. But additional steps will also be needed to increase further the lending of the multilateral banks. A range of options for expanding non-concessional lending is now under consideration by an intergovernmental task force of member countries of the World Bank and IMF (as we discuss on pp. 297–302).[16] In addition, it should be possible to do more non-concessional project lending on a co-financing basis—involving private lenders along with the multilateral banks—thereby increasing the amount of available capital for development. Although the co-financing involving public and private lenders has thus far involved primarily the major private lenders and established LDC borrowers, it is potentially a means of promoting a diversification of private

---

[16]The Task Force on Non-Concessional Flows was established in 1979 by the Joint Ministerial Committee of the Boards of Governors of the Bank and the Fund on the Transfer of Real Resources to Developing Countries (referred to as the "Development Committee"). Its task is to examine the various proposals made to encourage capital flows on non-concessional terms to developing countries. The Task Force's recommendations will be reported to the Development Committee and, in turn, to the Executive Boards of both the Bank and the Fund.

lending to LDCs, bringing more private lenders into contact with an increasing number of creditworthy LDCs in arrangements involving the multilateral banks in the identification, appraisal, and joint financing of viable projects. Improvements in relations between host countries and direct foreign investors—which, as we suggested in Chapter 5, might usefully be the subject of more rule-making—would also help accelerate capital formation in the middle-income LDCs.

It is, however, not more of the same, so much as more and varied official financing that middle-income LDCs will require in the decade ahead. Three additional types of international financial assistance—all of which have been much discussed in recent years—would seem particularly important. First, some countries need relatively long-term balance-of-payments financing to support sound programs of "debt-led" growth. As indicated in the preceding chapter, this need might be met either by expanding IMF lending and lengthening the period over which it remains available or by new forms of Bank assistance. The World Bank's new program of structural assistance loans is clearly designed to help meet this need. But as we suggested earlier (and discuss further, pp. 300–302) in many cases what would be desirable would be a combination of Fund, Bank, and private financing.

Second, the middle-income countries that have embarked on strategies of debt-led growth may frequently need assistance in debt management. Debt relief operations have been handled in past years by informal arrangements among creditor countries. Developing countries complain that the ad hoc nature of the "creditor club" operations results in unequal treatment of countries and ignores long-term development needs of debtor developing countries. Therefore, they would like to see a more formal international debt commission. Creditor countries, for their part, resist the establishment of formal arrangements because they do not want debt relief to be considered a form of aid or a standard practice.

In recent debt negotiations, creditors have required debtor countries to adopt stabilization programs supported by the IMF through stand-by or extended financing agreements. Also, staffs of both the World Bank and the IMF have been invited to attend meetings as observers and are increasingly asked to supply technical information and advice on debt situations. Their participation as technical advisers could, we believe, be usefully increased, and, were both debtor and creditor countries willing to be guided by their advice, more use perhaps could be made of Bank and Fund resources in debt negotiations.[17]

Third, it would be desirable for efforts to be made internationally to stimulate the development of a market for long-term bonds issued by developing countries. While developing countries have succeeded in gaining significant access to commercial bank lending on a short- to medium-term basis, they have not yet gained the same degree of access to the private bond markets that make capital available on longer terms.[18] In many ways, to promote the development of LDC bond-marketing capabilities would be the most direct means not only of accelerating development financing but also of improving the recycling of surplus capital. Regulations imposed on bond transactions tend to favor established borrowers and make markets inaccessible to the inexperienced. Multilateral development institutions would seem to have a role to play in this area by providing technical assistance, guarantees, and, perhaps, by acting as underwriters.

It is also now apparent that new and different international financing will be required in the years ahead to ensure an adequate supply on a global scale of certain critical resources when, for various reasons, it is not possible to rely on market forces to provide the investment capital required. Today's concern focuses on food and energy, and to a somewhat lesser extent on non-fuel mineral resources.

In the last decade, an increasing number of developing countries have shifted from being food exporters to food importers. Increased income and a growing population have in many of

---

[17]Since the mid-fifties multilateral debt renegotiations have led to 44 reschedulings, involving 14 countries. Review of this history leads to the conclusion that the relatively short-term focus of the creditor club negotiations has necessitated, all too frequently, further rescheduling.

[18]In the period of the rapid rise of commercial bank lending to LDCs in the 1970s, borrowings from the private bond market rose only from $1 billion to $3.1 billion, three countries accounting for 60 percent of the financing received.

these countries significantly outpaced growth in food production. The result has been both a sizable drain on the foreign exchange earnings, particularly of the poorest countries of Asia and Africa, and an increase in the number of hungry and malnourished poor.

Although the world does not now face an immediate food crisis of the sort experienced in the early 1970s, current trends suggest that developing countries could need to import as much as 145 million tons of food by 1990 (80 million of which would be needed by the poor countries of Asia and Africa). It is not likely that such massive food imports of the low-income, food-deficient countries could be financed by their export earnings and additional food aid or that major grain producers could supply the amounts needed. Rather, the situation calls for increased investment in food production in developing countries and for international measures to ensure adequate food supply worldwide in the event of major crop shortfalls.

The impact of global food shortages would, obviously, be most strongly felt by food-deficit, low-income countries, but the inflationary impact of higher food prices would be felt by all. Moreover, the plight of the hungry and malnourished is something an increasingly interdependent international community simply cannot ignore.

In the field of energy, many developing countries need assistance to finance programs to reduce their dependence on foreign oil, and the world is in need of the development everywhere of conventional and new sources of energy. In minerals, although the threat of absolute shortage is not imminent, new investments in LDCs have slowed in recent years. Financing new production in both areas, it can be said, is thus required, not just to assist national development but to help meet the "needs of the global economy." The bulk of resources for the exploitation of these natural resources will continue to come from private sources, but there remains a need for additional international assistance in technical training as well as to ensure an adequate flow of financial resources at the various stages of energy and minerals exploitation. And, because of the scale of financing that is now involved in the successful exploitation of these natural resources, new forms of financial cooperation are called for.

Now, or in the future, there may be other "global" activities that require international financial cooperation, ensuring adequate water resource management, for example, and preventing serious erosion of the earth's productive land or further degradation of the natural environment. There is also the possibility, as mentioned in Chapter 5, that, as one looks ahead, there should be some role for international resource transfers to support national efforts—in a Britain as well as a Bangladesh or a Brazil—to accommodate or to facilitate structural change in the international division of labor where that financing would contribute to a more efficient use of resources on a global scale.

In sum, the international resource transfers that are required in the years ahead vary widely and call for some radical new approaches. The needs of the low-income countries can still only be met by large transfers on concessional terms, including more program lending. The needs of the more advanced LDCs call for different responses. And there are new needs, ranging from increased investment in food and energy production to financing to facilitate structural change, that pertain to the health of the global economy.

STREAMLINING THE RESOURCE-TRANSFER SYSTEM

One way to meet needs for more program lending, for financing resources development, and for other needs as they emerge is to create new funds, agencies, and programs. That has been the route followed since the 1960s. And, as a result, there is now a vast array of resource-transfer institutions.

In addition to the roughly 30 bilateral aid programs[19] which continue to provide over half of today's concessional ODA, there are four major multilateral development banks, a complex

---

[19]This includes programs of varying sizes of 17 OECD donor countries, 8 OPEC donors, the Soviet Union, and others.

web of U.N. assistance programs, and numerous other regional, subregional, and multilateral undertakings. By far the largest multilateral development financing institution is the World Bank Group, comprised of three legally separate institutions: the International Bank for Reconstruction and Development (IBRD), the International Development Association (IDA), and the International Finance Corporation (IFC).

The IBRD, established in 1946 at the same time as the IMF, makes loans on near-market terms to developing countries (primarily middle-income countries) to finance a wide variety of investment projects, capital infrastructure, and, since the mid-1970s, projects aimed at meeting the needs of the very poor. Each loan is made to a government or guaranteed by the government. The Bank, which is owned by its 134 member countries, has a capital base subscribed by those countries, and it finances its lending operations primarily by borrowing in world capital markets. (An increasing amount of the Bank's resources also comes from retained earnings and repayments on its loans.) IBRD lending amounted to $7 billion in 1979.

The other two components of the World Bank Group were established after the IBRD—the IFC in 1956 and IDA in 1960—in order to broaden the capacity of the Bank to assist underdeveloped countries. Today, IDA lends on highly concessional terms to about 50 countries with an annual per capita income of $625 or less (in 1978 dollars), and the IFC makes direct loans (without government guarantees) or takes an equity position in, mainly, private sector enterprises in developing countries. Although both IDA and the IFC are legally separate institutions, they share a president with the IBRD. And IDA "exists only as an elaborate fiction."[20] That is, although it is funded separately from the IBRD (by periodic voluntary contributions from member countries), IDA "soft" loans are managed by the same staff and approved by the same board of Executive Directors.[21] IDA

[20]Mason and Asher, op. cit.

[21]Some countries are members of the Bank but not members of IDA, and, as explained below, the distribution of votes among member countries is calculated differently in IDA and the IBRD—but the same 20 officials serve as Executive Directors of the IBRD and IDA as well as the IFC.

credits in 1979 were $2.6 billion. Loans and investments by the IFC in that same year amounted to $354 million. Together, the IBRD and IDA account now for about half of all official development financing.

The other three multilateral development banks—the regional banks—are financed in the same way as the World Bank, and they provide hard and soft loans on much the same terms and for much the same purposes as the World Bank. Like the World Bank, most of their loans are in the form of project financing. But there are some differences among them and between them and the World Bank—differences that reflect the politics and economics of the respective regions and their relations with extraregional donors. None have the equivalent of the IFC.

The Inter-American Development Bank (IDB), established in 1959, increased its commitments rapidly in the decade of the 1960s and through the 1970s. From the start, it defined its development role somewhat differently from that of the IBRD, preceding the Bank in making loans for "social development." But differences in emphasis have narrowed over time, and the World Bank and the Inter-American Bank now lend for essentially the same wide variety of purposes. In 1979, the IDB committed slightly over $2 billion in loans from ordinary capital and $696 million in "soft" loans from its fund for special operations.

The Asian Development Bank, which began operations in 1969, has also expanded rapidly. By 1979, its loans totaled $985 million, some $402 million of that total being concessional lending. The African Development Bank, which began lending in 1967, was for a time unique among the multilateral development banks in that its membership was drawn entirely from countries in the region. Consequently, its capital base and lending program has remained far smaller than those of the other regional banks (total loans committed between 1973 and the end of the decade amounted to just under $500 million). But in May, 1979, the Bank agreed to admit members from outside the region and, at the same time, to increase the Bank's capital from $1 billion to $5.2 billion.

Although the World Bank Group and the regional development banks are the most important multilateral sources of development financing, numerous other multilateral agencies are also important in providing technical assistance and in supplementing the capital flows of the development banks. Within the United Nations system, the three basic types of organizations that play a role in development assistance are the specialized agencies, the regional commissions, and the specialized funds which have increased markedly in number since the mid-1960s. One of the most important funds today is the United Nations Development Program, which provides technical assistance and preinvestment financing for projects in developing countries administered by the U.N.'s specialized agencies. Established in 1965 as a result of a merger of the Expanded Program for Technical Assistance and the Special Fund, the UNDP is the central resource-allocating and coordinating agency for the bulk of voluntarily funded United Nations technical assistance. However, in recent years, several of the specialized agencies have sought to build up technical assistance funds under their own control.

Other special funds within the U.N. system—including UNICEF, UNFPA, the World Food Program, and the newly established International Fund for Agricultural Development—conduct some of their own operations and channel some of their resources through the specialized agencies or the development banks. The regional Economic Commissions for West Asia (ECWA), for Latin America (ECLA), and for Africa (ECA), as well as parts of the U.N. Secretariat, undertake research and provide advice and technical expertise in scientific, educational, and economic fields.

Outside the U.N. system, there are other development banks and financial assistance agencies that are, for the most part, regionally oriented. These include: the development assistance institutions of the European Community (the European Investment Bank and the European Development Fund); the Caribbean Development Bank; the Andean Development Corporation; and the newer oil-exporters institutions, such as the Arab Fund for Economic and Social Development, the Arab Bank for Economic Development in Africa and the OPEC Special Fund.

276

As the "development system" has grown, various efforts have been made to coordinate both bilateral and multilateral development assistance programs. Formal agreements and informal arrangements have been established between multilateral agencies. Development projects are often jointly financed by two or more international agencies or by a multilateral and bilateral donor. And, for some 25 countries that receive ODA from a number of different donors, there are now aid consortia or consultative groups, often "led" by the World Bank. These groups, which periodically bring together a recipient government and its major donors, were designed to promote coordination and avoid duplication among separate bilateral and multilateral assistance efforts in countries and, also, to foster a constructive "dialogue" between donors and recipients. But, in fact, most aid-coordination groups have not worked as well as had been hoped. As one long-time observer of the aid process has noted: "The Consultative Group mechanism, originally intended for a serious annual review of aid and policy packages, has increasingly turned into rather stylized occasions for the obligatory mutual exchange of compliments," and it has also tended to "focus on the quantitative rather than the qualitative aspects of development."[22]

Donors, particularly the large ones, have demonstrated little willingness to work closely together within recipient countries. Each tends instead to pursue, independently, its own preferred program of lending. And recipients, for their part, prefer not to have to deal with a "cartel" of donors but, rather, to "bargain" with each. As a result, heavy demands are made on the developing world's scarcest resource—skilled manpower. And no institution plays the role of "residual" lender.

Had the World Bank Group developed differently—had it become a more nearly universal organization, with a more balanced distribution of power between donors and recipients—there might now be somewhat fewer separate funds, agencies,

[22]Gustav Ranis, "Foreign Aid: Euthanasia or Reform?" *Worldview* (forthcoming). See also Kaplan, op. cit.

and programs and fewer problems arising for lack of coordination. But there would still be, in all likelihood, numerous bilateral aid programs and funding agencies composed of clusters of donors. Some amount of "pluralism" in lending institutions is inevitable and, indeed, desirable. A wholly centralized system would probably not be as responsive to divergent needs, capabilities, and preferences as one in which there are "options."

Nevertheless, it is the argument of this chapter that the time has come to stop the proliferation of resource-transfer institutions at the global level. Instead of continuing to create new institutions as new needs arise and then concocting ways of coordinating the resulting elaborate array, we think it better to undertake the harder task of consolidating and reforming existing institutions. We discussed some of the steps that we think should be considered in Chapter 4. As far as other resource-transfer arrangements are concerned, the main needs, we believe, are for *both* reform of the World Bank Group and a strengthening of its central role, bringing under its aegis a number of the existing multilateral funds and more of the concessional aid that is now handled bilaterally, at the same time broadening the range of the Bank's concessional and non-concessional financing activities.

Not everything should, of course, be done at the global level. Some activities by their very nature belong primarily at the regional level. The LDCs have argued for some form of multilateral export credit financing to stimulate, in particular, increased trade with one another. This might usefully be done by the regional banks, since the bulk of intra-LDC trade is intra-regional. And, as we discuss below, it would seem desirable to strengthen the regional development banks relative to the World Bank for some other purposes. In addition, some resource transfers can most effectively come from other parts of the United Nations system—not only from our proposed UNBSP but also, in some cases, from the specialized agencies. But the World Bank Group should play the key long-term financing role at the global level. The sine qua non of an expanded role for the World Bank is, however, reform in its structure of governance.

THE ISSUE OF POLITICAL CONTROL

In one way or another, the issue of political control—or influence in decision-making—is at the heart of the dispute over shaping, or reshaping, the institutions that will support and define the international economic order in the years ahead. For reasons we have already discussed, we think it is right, indeed necessary, that in different issue areas different groupings of states (and sometimes non-state actors) exercise different degrees of influence or control in the making of decisions or the management of relationships.

In the resource-transfer area, there are really three dimensions to the issue of political control: how the amount of official capital that is transferred from richer to poorer states is determined; where, as between a resource-transfer agency and a recipient country, responsibility lies for determining how resources transferred are to be used; and how the formal governance of resource-transfer institutions is organized, that is, how decision-making power is distributed.

Today's system is characterized largely by donor control or donor discretion in each of these three regards. The amounts of concessional assistance are strictly a matter for decision by donor countries. The target set (in discussions within the United Nations on an International Development Strategy for the 1970s), which called for each donor country to increase its aid to a level of 0.7 percent of its GNP, was not accepted at the time by the largest donor country (the United States) nor has it come close to being matched by the world's strongest economies.[23]

---

[23] A few donors—particularly Sweden, Norway, the Netherlands, and Denmark—increased their aid levels substantially in the 1970s and, consequently, the level of ODA now provided by each of these countries exceeds the 0.7 percent target. In addition, the ODA contributions of OPEC donor countries amount to more than 2.0 percent of their combined GNP. But the three countries with the largest gross national products in the "OECD World"—the United States, Germany, and Japan—fall far below the target. U.S. aid as a ratio of GNP fell to a low point of 0.19 percent in 1979. And, although both Germany and Japan have increased their share of total ODA flows since the

Patterns have been set over the years that affect how much a country is likely to contribute annually to one or another international agency. But, in fact, the provision of official development assistance is voluntary and subject to continuing debate and fluctuating support year after year in donor country legislatures.

In the case of the bulk of multilateral transfers, that is, the hard loans provided by the multilateral development banks (MDBs), the situation is more complex. How big the capital base of a development bank is, and, therefore, how large its borrowing and lending potential, is determined by the bank's member countries. More specifically, countries own shares in the development banks, the basic distribution of those shares having been determined when each bank was established. Countries subscribe capital to a bank in accordance with the distribution of shares and take joint decisions about how large the amount of subscribed capital should be. But the capital contribution of each member country mainly takes the form of "callable capital," that is, it represents a commitment of funds to back up the borrowing and lending of the bank, but it is not primarily the capital that is used to finance lending operations. For the most part, operating capital derives from the bank's borrowing on private capital markets and from some countries' central banks. Thus member countries—with varying degrees of influence based largely on their shares of subscribed capital—determine the scale of the banks' lending potentials. But the international capital markets affect not only the amount, they also affect the terms on which non-concessional loans are made, lending being related to the costs of borrowing. And because of a bank's concern to maintain access to capital on favorable terms, the private markets, as well as donor country policies, act as a kind of disciplinary force on lending policies and practices.

1960s, the increase in their volume of aid has not matched the rise in their GNP, and, therefore, their ratios of aid to GNP have also declined over the past decade. It is largely the record of these three large economies that caused the overall ODA to GNP ratio of the group of OECD donors to remain at 0.34 percent of their combined GNP in 1979—the lowest level since the start of the U.S. bilateral aid program.

It is also the case that, in today's system, donor countries exercise or attempt to exercise a considerable degree of leverage over how development assistance is used within recipient countries. Development, it has repeatedly been said, is principally a domestic problem to be dealt with through the application of domestic resources and domestic policy choices. Meaningful goals and objectives can only be set on a country-by-country basis. Yet foreign donors insist that they "have a legitimate interest in maximizing the effectiveness of their aid,"[24] and they argue that they must design their development assistance programs in ways that give them assurances that assistance will be used "effectively" if they are to satisfy their own publics and thus have resources to transfer. The result, over the years, has been the development of rather elaborate aid programming procedures (at least in major donor countries) and the introduction of "aid criteria" designed to promote what, in the view of donor countries, are "sound" development policies. Donor aid policies include not only broad statements of objectives but also an indication of the sectors within developing countries that should receive priority in the allocation of resource transfers. The extension of loans is often conditional upon recipients making changes in their economic policies which the donor agencies believe will assist development efforts. In this way, leverage may be exerted to get recipients *inter alia* to change pricing policies that do not adequately compensate farmers and therefore work against attempts to increase agricultural production. Or, donors will seek to influence aspects of a recipient's macroeconomic policy, including its exchange-rate policies, interest-rate policies, or sectoral-investment emphasis. In other words, "aid leverage"—which involves the use of both carrots and sticks—is exercised in ways that go far beyond assessments by donor agencies of the cost-effectiveness of individual projects.

Much of the effort on the part of donors to establish criteria and to develop rather elaborate aid programming and review

[24]United States, Department of Treasury, Office of Assistant Secretary for International Affairs, "Shaping U.S. Participation in the International Financial Institutions," February, 1978. (Mimeograph.)

procedures has been motivated by the desire to get away from piecemeal assistance and to move to a more comprehensive and more helpful program of support. But the result has too often been criteria that are more attuned to the donors' own interests or preferences than to the recipients' needs.

Not surprisingly, the attempt by donors to influence basic policy choices of recipient countries has met with increasing resentment. Recipients are troubled not only by the degree of interference but also by the ponderousness and long delays of aid-programming procedures and by the tendency of donors to shift priorities with each new "discovery" of "the key" to development.

A decade ago, the response to the complaints of aid-receiving countries that official resource transfer programs were too "interventionist" was to urge that more assistance be channelled through multilateral agencies. Multilateral institutions, it was believed, could avoid the political antagonisms and conflicts that result from performance criteria imposed by national donors. And less-developed countries could be expected to be more receptive to advice from multilateral institutions than to advice that was often felt to be politically motivated. However, as developing countries have argued with increasing force, the multilateral agencies that handle the bulk of international resource transfers are themselves largely controlled by a few donor countries.

The LDCs have, therefore, not only called for new financing facilities in which they would exercise a large voice but also for "greater automaticity" in the transfer of resources. That is, LDCs have argued for far less "conditioning" by donor agencies of resource flows, and they have argued for new ways of mobilizing resources for development, such as a tax on deep sea-bed mining, that would not be dependent on periodic decisions by national governments.

An international resource-transfer system that would operate wholly automatically, both in the sense of raising funds by non-appropriated means and distributing them on a formula basis, is clearly beyond the bounds of feasibility. As we said in Chapter 4, we propose that a small step in this direction be taken in our Basic Support Program. More generally, it should be possible to move from today's highly discretionary system to one that would provide for more "continuous, assured, and predictable" resource transfers, as the LDCs have urged; one that would give recipients a greater voice in the resource transfer institutions; and one that would set the resource-transfer process more firmly on a basis of mutually agreed criteria and standards.

There is no way to avoid normative choices and the articulation of goals in the process of transferring resources. But there is also no reason to think that donor countries have a monopoly of wisdom on development policy issues. What is needed, as was emphasized over a decade ago, is to move, on the one hand, "toward vesting more responsibility in the less developed countries themselves for programming their development, deciding on their priorities, and putting priorities into effect"; while, on the other hand, "vesting more responsibility in international bodies . . . for developing standards and criteria, receiving and appraising country programs, and arranging for agreed requirements to be met."[25] As multilateral aid has grown in importance relative to bilateral aid, the system of official resource transfers has come closer to this ideal. But further changes are needed in the way aid is programmed and in the distribution of decision-making power in resource-transfer institutions if the process of setting criteria for allocating and monitoring the transfer of official resources is to be made more legitimate in the eyes of recipient countries. Of major importance, we think, is that change be made in the procedures and the decision-making structures of the World Bank Group—change that is consistent with the continuing central role in the resource transfer system that the Bank should play.

REFORMING THE WORLD BANK GROUP

For many years, the World Bank Group has been criticized for being too much under the control of a few donor countries, for being too project-oriented, and for being too headquarters-domi-

[25]Robert E. Asher, *Development Assistance in the Seventies*, The Brookings Institution: Washington, 1970, p. 23.

nated. If the Bank is to command the widespread support that is needed for it to act as the central international resource-transfer institution in the decades ahead, it will have to become a substantially different institution.

The reforms we see as essential are not as extensive as those entailed in replacing the Bank by a World Development Authority.[26] As we indicated earlier, we would have the problems of developing countries addressed functionally within our "tripod" of economic institutions, not taken out and dealt with together by a new agency. Thus, while there would be an expansion in the World Bank's capacity to provide necessary long-term resource transfers, short-term, balance-of-payments financing for LDCs, as for other countries, would continue to be handled through the IMF, and LDC trade problems would be dealt with in the proposed PTO. Not only does this seem to us administratively cleaner, it is more in accord with our basic view that the North-South dichotomy is becoming obsolete and that the emerging reality is that of a continuum.

Also, instead of supplementing the Bank by a World Development Fund to do mainly program financing, we should have the Bank itself move in that direction.[27]

The changes that we consider necessary in the operations of the Bank are not ones that have much to do with the basic structure of the Bank. Rather they involve broadening the kinds of assistance provided by the World Bank Group, altering its way of dealing with client countries, strengthening its ties with other international economic institutions—particularly the IMF and the proposed PTO—and making changes in the governance of the Bank. Various changes made as the seventies ended and the eighties began—including the introduction of "structural adjustment" lending, energy, financing, and participation of the People's Republic of China (PRC)—have moved the Bank in the right direction. But further reforms are still needed.

[26]Mahbub ul Haq, *The Poverty Curtain: Choices for the Third World,* Columbia University Press: New York, 1976.

[27]The Report of the Brandt Commission, which contains the recommendation for consideration of a new Fund, became available as this book was being edited.

To begin with, we should have more of the assistance that is now provided bilaterally and some of what is now provided from sources elsewhere in the United Nations system handled by the World Bank (IDA).

We have noted the dangers in making the Bank too dominant and the resource-transfer system too monolithic, and some people argue that bilateral assistance programs are often more flexible and innovative than multilateral programs in general and World Bank programs in particular. Nonetheless, we think the present resource-transfer system would be strengthened by bringing more of today's concessional assistance under the administration of the multilateral development banks and by having the World Bank assume, as part of an improved aid-programming process, the role of "residual" lender. Channelling more ODA through multilateral institutions is probably the best way to ensure that resources for development go to countries that need them most.[28] Furthermore, both "multilateralizing" more of today's concessional assistance and consolidating some of the multilateral funds and programs would reduce the burden on the LDCs of having to comply with a myriad of different agencies' policies.

A third, and perhaps most important reason for consolidating and "streamlining" the system is to facilitate a shift in the way aid is given, making it easier to move to a system in which more of the responsibility for program planning rests with the recipient and resources are transferred rather more routinely than at present, once basic criteria and procedures have been agreed upon.

Some of today's international development programs might usefully be transferred to the World Bank (or, in some cases, to the regional banks) and integrated with existing lending operations. In some cases, the Bank might simply assume the financing of an existing program. In other cases, existing funds might

[28]As noted above, less than half of today's bilateral assistance goes to the poorest countries. Under the World Bank, soft loans are limited to countries with average annual per capita incomes of less than $625 (in 1978 dollars), and those loans are concentrated on countries at or below the $300 level. In 1979, 87 percent of the soft loans—or "credits"—committed by IDA went to countries with a GNP per capita of $360 or less.

be made subsidiary facilities administered by the Bank. Three changes in existing arrangements seem particularly desirable (although more streamlining might usefully occur). Each one involves a somewhat different type of merger with the World Bank.

First, the World Bank (and the regional banks as well) should take over the preinvestment work and much of the technical assistance financing now done by the UNDP (excluding the technical assistance which would come under the Basic Support Program proposed in Chapter 4). There are several reasons for suggesting this change: one has to do with the importance of integrating capital and technical assistance; another, with the inefficiencies in the way the UNDP operates; and a third, with the nature of technical assistance itself. The long-standing separation in the administration of multilateral capital and technical assistance stems from the rather narrow interpretation that was originally given to the "development financing" role of the World Bank—a definition that stressed large-scale, foreign-exchange-intensive development of infrastructure and productive enterprises. However, as the development function of the Bank has been redefined, and as experience has shown the importance of providing technical assistance together with capital assistance, the World Bank and the regional development banks have been steadily increasing their financing of technical assistance.

Moreover, the use by the UNDP of other international organizations as "executing agents" for its technical assistance programs has made the supply of such assistance both costly and ponderously slow.[29] In recognition of the inefficiencies and delays caused by UNDP financing being channeled through the specialized agencies, the UNDP has, for its part, begun to work di-

---

[29]"The executing agents charge their own percentage for administrative and infrastructure costs ranging from 14 to 21 percent. If one were to add the infrastructure costs incurred by the donor agency, the executing agency, and, finally, the recipient agency, the amount left for actual technical assistance comes down to a very small percentage of the total." Jyoti Shanhar Singh, *A New International Economic Order: Toward Fair Redistribution of the World's Resources,* Praeger: New York, 1977, p. 92.

rectly through independent contractors. Simultaneously, the specialized agencies have sought to build up technical assistance funds under their own administrative control. This may, in fact, prove to be more cost-effective, but it clearly undermines the principal rationale for the UNDP which has been to centralize and coordinate U.N. technical assistance activities. Moreover, what recipient countries now want—and can efficiently handle—is to be given the funds and to be free to choose for themselves the outside experts or the executing agencies (in cases where that kind of help is needed), and also to be free to use external assistance to develop more technical expertise within their own societies.

The process of preinvestment financing, that is, the financing of feasibility studies for capital investment projects, could also usefully be changed. Too often, no capital investment follows a UNDP-financed preinvestment study unless one of the development banks serves as the administrator of the preinvestment grant. And, in some cases, where the World Bank does finance a project that has had a feasibility study done by some other agency (with UNDP-supplied funds), the Bank does a second project appraisal of its own. In our view, it would be more efficient to have the preinvestment financing, as well as much of the technical assistance, handled directly by the multilateral banks. This does not mean that the banks would do all the follow-up investment. But they are probably better able than the UNDP to help developing countries link up with other sources of investment capital, including private sector investors.

In making this shift, we would be effecting three changes in the way the bulk of multilateral technical assistance is provided to LDCs. First, some countries (the upper-income LDCs) would cease to be eligible for technical assistance on concessional terms. Second, the technical assistance previously provided by the UNDP in the form of a grant would be available from the Bank on a soft-loan basis. Although there is not much real difference between a grant and a soft loan from the World Bank, it has been argued that technical assistance is accepted "all too casually" and that consumers of technical assistance should become more "product conscious." Putting technical assistance on a soft-loan basis might contribute to this change in attitude.[30] Finally, technical assistance loans provided by the World Bank, as in the case of other Bank loans, would be made directly to governments. They would not, as in the case of most UNDP grants, be handled through U.N. specialized agencies. And this would mean that recipient governments would gain the greater responsibility *they* seek for "hiring" technical expertise. In many cases, the assistance of a specialized agency might be requested by a recipient country, but there would be no presumption that a technical assistance loan would be used in a way that would involve one or another of the specialized agencies.[31]

As a second step in streamlining the development assistance system, the World Bank should assume the financing function of the proposed "second window" of the Common Fund. That is, the Bank should do more of the kind of financing—for the development of raw-material-processing industries, for improvement of marketing capabilities, and for diversification of commodity production—that the "second window" is to be set up to do, some on a soft- and some on a hard-loan basis. (And, as we indicated in Chapter 5, the Common Fund as a buffer-stock-financing facility should be brought within the ambit of the proposed PTO.)

[30]Asher, op. cit., pp. 129–132.

[31]The effect of this change would really be to eliminate the need for the UNDP. Some technical assistance funding should continue to flow through the specialized agencies. However, in our view, most of the technical assistance should come from the Banks, and the specialized agencies should serve as a resource base from which to draw information and expertise. In addition, each specialized agency should have its own small technical assistance budget to be used for a variety of purposes, including: to provide information on technical assistance services and available alternative technologies, to provide funds for research and development in technology appropriate to the development needs of LDCs, and to support R & D or experimental projects involving a number of countries. Two conferences held at the end of the 1970s—one on technological cooperation among developing countries and one on science and technology for development—expand rather than narrow the future role of the UNDP. It is our view that this represents a move in the wrong direction. Instead, we would have more technical cooperation organized along sectoral or functional lines and more technical assistance provided through the development banks.

The establishment of a "second window" account under the Common Fund was, in large part, a matter of political expediency. That is, the "second window" was designed to ensure that the Common Fund proposal would be supported by the large number of LDCs which could not expect to benefit directly from the operations of international commodity agreements. In addition, LDCs, supported by reports of the UNCTAD secretariat, argued that existing international financial institutions were not providing enough "commodity development" assistance.[32]

Today's development-financing institutions are not able to provide the financing that is needed in the commodities field, because their lending operations are too "country oriented." That is, the multilateral banks finance projects which will be productive investments for the borrowing countries, but they do not take adequate account of the secondary effects upon other countries, nor do they finance cooperative commodity research and development projects involving more than one country.

More lending for this sort of activity was recommended by the Bank's management in a report to the Executive Directors in 1973, but not much movement in this direction has yet occurred. And, to date, the Bank has done little to finance a range of activities that have to do with market promotion or that would involve making loans to commodity organizations rather than to individual countries. Yet, typically, the activities envisaged for the

[32] An analysis of 1977 World Bank lending done by the UNCTAD commodities division indicated that, of a total of $7.1 billion in loan commitments made that year, only $837 million were for the key commodities that have been the focus of UNCTAD's Integrated Commodity Program. Most of the loans were aimed at expanding production. Less than a third went into the development of commodity-processing industries, and not all of those projects were export oriented. There was virtually no market promotion activity and no projects that involved joint activities among a group of commodity-producer nations, which LDCs have viewed as important in improving their manufacturing power. See, United Nations Conference on Trade and Development, Commodities Division, "Measures Other Than Stocking: Activities of Existing Institutions and the Role of the Common Fund," Internal Secretariat Paper, ACP/cc, 1978; see also UNCTAD, Report of the Secretariat, "Marketing and Distribution of Primary Commodities: Areas for Further International Cooperation," TD/229/ Supp. 3, March 8, 1979.

"second window" are ones that belong to a development-financing institution, not to a market-stabilizing mechanism. (Indeed, the two major "commodity development" issues—promotion of improved marketing capabilities and development of processing industries—would seem to be particularly appropriate concerns of the International Finance Corporation which can make loans to enterprises without the backing of government guarantees.) And, to separate "commodity development" from a country's overall development program risks distorting its path of development.

A third step that we think should be taken to consolidate and improve the resource-transfer system is to bring the International Fund for Agricultural Development under the administration of the Bank. But, in this case, instead of merging its resources into the Bank, we would make IFAD a subsidiary body.[33] The reason for retaining a separate pool of concessional assistance for agricultural development is to help ensure that sufficient resources are made available in the years ahead to meet the critical objectives for which the Fund was established, that is, to increase food production, particularly by small farmers and in the poorest food-deficit countries, and to see that, in the process of promoting agricultural development, nutritional levels of the poor improve.

The World Bank and IFAD now operate on the basis of a formal Agreement according to which the Bank will appraise projects exclusively financed by the Fund and may administer IFAD loans to these projects. It may also engage in co-financing with IFAD as well as exchange information. By making IFAD a subsidiary of the Bank we would be going rather further in integrating the management of IFAD's resources with other operations of the Bank. That is, while IFAD would continue to have its own Governing Council and Executive Board, the President and staff of the Bank would become responsible for conducting the operations of the Fund. Loans made by the Bank with resources from the Fund would be subject to review by the Fund's own Board, not the Executive Directors of the Bank. And deci-

[33]For details on the composition of IFAD, see Chapter 3, footnote 3.

sions about the size of the lending program and terms of financing would also be the responsibility of the Executive Board of IFAD.

In making this transfer of the agriculture fund to the Bank, we would be seeking to avoid two otherwise probable developments: the expansion over time of an independent IFAD loan operations staff that would duplicate existing World Bank staff with expertise in the food and agriculture sector, and distortions in development-assistance programs that would result from looking at the needs of one sector, in this case clearly a critical sector, independently from a country's economic development as a whole. But, other than transferring responsibility for the administration of IFAD resources to the management of the Bank, few changes in the operations of IFAD seem to be needed. That is, objectives, criteria, and terms of lending all seem to be essentially right.

Some might argue that these (and other similar) steps would produce a resource-transfer system that would be even less flexible and less responsive to the diversity of LDC financing needs than today's system is. And, they might argue, the effect of merging programs into the World Bank would increase recipient countries' dependence on a financing institution that is already too dominant. If the steps so far described were all the changes that were to occur, this would be a legitimate concern. However, in addition to consolidating some development assistance programs, we would make other changes which should counteract any negative effects of streamlining the system.

PROGRAMMING CONCESSIONAL AID FLOWS

Most low-income countries will continue for some time to receive concessional aid from a number of bilateral and multilateral donors. And, therefore, the question remains of how to "program" resource transfers to reduce wasteful duplication and maximize the effectiveness of the available assistance. In our view, the World Bank should do more than it has in the past to improve aid-programming and coordination efforts. The objectives should be to vest more responsibility in the LDCs (even the least developed countries) for the design of their own externally assisted programs and projects and to provide for better coordination of external assistance to those countries that receive sizable amounts of concessional aid from a number of different donors.

A decade or so ago, a rather grand country-programming scheme might have seemed the right prescription—one that would have brought a recipient and its principal donors together regularly to discuss a coordinated "development assistance plan" and to negotiate specific multiyear aid commitments to be made in support of the plan. Although that kind of elaborate aid planning might still lead to the most effective programming and coordination of aid flows, few countries are likely to be receptive to consortia of donors passing judgment on their overall development programs. Moreover, few donors are likely to be willing to commit themselves to the kind of multiyear aid pledges that such a scheme would demand.

Effective coordination among donors and with recipients has occurred most often in the past when only one or two major issues or activities have been addressed at a time. A regular process of coordinated country programming has proved difficult. The more sharply focused and more coordinated efforts have usually occurred only in response to crisis or near-crisis situations, in the case of a potential default, for example, or famine or other natural disaster. On a more regular basis, donors, both bilateral and multilateral, have been "reluctant to dilute control over decisions about the allocation and use of funds at their disposal. Much of this reluctance results from the felt needs and interests of their constituencies, but it also reflects bureaucratic resistance to yield authority."[34]

Yet some country-programming process—less formalized and less highly structured—would seem desirable. The essential ingredients of a more workable and more effective process are the following: (1) improved "aid programming" at the country level by the aid recipient; (2) a central role for the World Bank in

[34]Kaplan, op. cit., p. 23.

facilitating the "aid programming" process at the country level; and (3) on a continuing basis and at the global level, a discussion among donors and recipients of the general principles, the objectives, and the procedures that should guide the transfer of concessional resources. The emphasis, in other words, should be on improving a recipient's capacity to plan how best to use and itself to coordinate external assistance. And the World Bank should help a country become its own programmer and coordinator, as well as continuing to be a major donor.

Not only should the World Bank provide technical assistance to countries that requested help in designing programs and projects, it might also "certify" on the request of a recipient and a donor that a country's programs could be accomplished in the context of its overall development plans and policies. Small or "new" donor countries which do not have the capacity to evaluate a recipient's overall program might find this particularly helpful. Also, we would have the Bank, as donor, be more ready than it has been in the past to "fill gaps" or "facilitate" the implementation of recipients' programs—in particular, by providing concessional program loans on a more regular basis.

The need for more program lending, and, indeed, the need for program lending of different kinds and on different terms, has been discussed. Currently, program lending is permissible under the charters of the World Bank institutions (the IDA and IBRD) only in "special circumstances."[35] Some of the arguments that have been made in the past against increasing this form of assistance from the Bank have to do with fears that program lending would have a detrimental effect on the Bank's ability to maintain a good credit rating in the markets that now accept World Bank bonds. But this is not an issue in the case of IDA program lending.

The more difficult problem is that of establishing criteria for program lending to the poorest and least developed countries that would both be acceptable in the eyes of recipients and give

[35]International Bank for Reconstruction and Development, Articles of Agreement, Article 3, Section 4(vii); and the International Development Association, Articles of Agreement, Article V, section 1(b).

donors some assurance that such assistance would be used productively. There is really no easy way to get around the "conditionality" issue if more of this kind of "quick disbursing" assistance is to be provided.

Donors are not willing to make all loans to low-income countries wholly on a program-lending basis. But, it ought to be possible to move beyond the current, very restricted use of program lending and come to some agreement on the more regular use of program lending. For this, the member countries of the Bank would have to agree on general criteria for regular program lending; recipient governments would have to accept thorough scrutiny by the Bank of their economic development policies; and the Bank would have to lift its current ceiling on program loans and coordinate more fully with other donors. Program loans would thus become a kind of facilitative financing—or the lubrication needed to make other, more specific, undertakings more likely to succeed.

The kind of "facilitative" role that we would have the World Bank play in the provision of concessional aid to low-income countries would represent a considerable departure from its current mode of operation. Not only would we be having the World Bank do more concessional program lending, but also we would define the Bank's lending role as that of "residual" lender, thereby drawing the Bank into a closer working relationship with other donors than it has been willing to accept in the past. At the same time, we would clearly be enhancing the role of the Bank in aid planning and coordinating. This might be more acceptable to recipients and donors alike if there were regular high-level exchanges of view on resource-transfer policies and procedures that would, in a general sense, provide guidance not only to recipients and to national donors but also to the Bank as donor and as "advisor." (We return to this point below, pp. 316–318.)

THE ROLE OF THE REGIONAL DEVELOPMENT BANKS

The main function of both the World Bank Group and the regional development banks is now, and should remain for some time, the same: to provide financing for a broad range of projects to countries that cannot obtain needed capital or technical assistance on manageable terms from other sources. But, along with the changes in the operations of the World Bank that we are suggesting, we would also envisage an expanded role for the regional banks relative to the World Bank, particularly in project lending.

During the 1970s, the World Bank sharply increased its hard- and soft-lending activities. By the end of the decade, it provided roughly four-fifths of all hard loans from multilateral development banks and two-thirds of total MDB soft loans. In addition, the World Bank assumed an ever-increasing role in the sphere of development research and policy analysis. This growth in World Bank activities has been accompanied by what some see as an "abdication of innovative thinking elsewhere" and an "absence of any division of labor" in the development assistance field among the many bilateral and multilateral donors.[36] It would seem desirable to strengthen the technical and analytical capacity of the regional banks as well as to increase their hard- and soft-lending activities, both in absolute terms and relative to that done by the World Bank.

Several arguments are made against shifting too much of the project-financing function to the regional banks. There is a need to see development in a global context, that is, to take account of economic developments occurring outside a country or region because these developments frequently impinge on the success of individual country efforts. There is the problem, already evident, of domination by regional powers. And there is some question whether the regional banks can raise capital as effectively as the World Bank. None of these difficulties seems to us insurmountable. The Asian and the Inter-American Banks are already

---

[36]These concerns and the concomitant recommendation to bolster the research and technical capacities as well as the lending levels of the regional banks were expressed to us by Gustav Ranis. Each of the regional banks has a small research and planning unit, and each now follows a rather cautious and traditional approach to LDC lending. Even the IDB, which was once considered too "soft" and too heavily oriented toward social development projects, now emphasizes "hard" infrastructural projects.

well-established borrowers. No region is clearly dominated by one or a few states, and the extraregional members of the banks should help to see that the interests of smaller powers are fairly met. And it ought to be precisely the function of the World Bank to maintain a global perspective on investment flows and financing patterns, filling gaps and warning of the build-up of excessive capacities. An important positive feature—and perhaps most true of the IDB—is that they tend to be rather less donor-dominated than is the IBRD.

Overall, the advantages of depending increasingly on the regional banks for official project financing would seem to outweigh the potential problems. Centering everything in the World Bank would be a mistake, and more use of regional banks seems preferable to "regionalizing" the World Bank, as is frequently suggested. Although the diversity that is now evident among LDCs is not mainly diversity arising from regional differences, there are regional differences. And economic ties, especially trade ties, have tended to grow faster within than between regions. For that reason, as mentioned above, it might make sense for the regional banks, in addition to assuming a proportionally larger share of the project-financing function, to provide trade financing through regional export-credit-guarantee facilities. Also, some large-scale development activities (e.g., transportation, communication, water projects) might be usefully organized on a regional or subregional basis. And there is technological cooperation that could usefully be occurring within a regional context.

The World Bank could help strengthen the regional banks, both by lending capital and lending expertise; but the regional banks should not simply follow the path of the World Bank. Rather, they should develop certain perspectives, orientations, and expertise of their own. And the World Bank, as the central global resource-transfer institution, should now begin to perform a number of different functions and to provide new kinds of financial assistance. This means that, in addition to playing a larger role—both the lead and the residual role—in the overall organization of official development assistance, the Bank should also broaden its range of non-concessional lending.

BROADENING THE RANGE OF WORLD BANK NON-CONCESSIONAL LENDING

In the course of the next decade or so, many countries that now receive financing from the World Bank only on concessional terms will be receiving a mix of financial assistance, that is, some loans on concessional terms and some on non-concessional terms. And there will be countries whose economic position so improves that they can both use effectively and afford more financing on non-concessional terms than they can today. Still other countries, indeed, some of today's largest World Bank borrowers (e.g., Brazil), are rapidly becoming less dependent on investment capital from the multilateral banks. This has raised the issue of "graduation"—a poor word but a significant concept for arrangements guiding resource transfers as well as international trading rules. Under present World Bank policy, a country whose average annual per capita income reaches $625 is "graduated" from IDA to the IBRD, that is, it ceases to be eligible for IDA loans. (At an earlier stage, countries may receive a mix of hard and soft loans, the "blend" depending on a country's ability to service the debt assumed.) Then, according to current policy, when a country's per capita income reaches $2,000, it is phased out of Bank "hard-loan" operations over a period of five years. For various reasons—most of which have to do with the changing conditions of the world economy—this may prove to be too early a point at which to phase a country out of the Bank (although it is desirable to concentrate lending on countries without access to substantial amounts of private capital). As an intermediate step in the process of "graduation," the Bank ought to offer a different kind of financial assistance.

The broadening in the 1970s of World Bank co-financing with the private sector marked the beginnings of the kind of change that ought to be occurring. Private sector co-financing, which involves the World Bank with a private lender in the financing of a capital investment project in a developing country, not only increases the total resource flow, it also establishes a relationship between the borrowing country and the private lending institution. For the more advanced developing countries, there are at least two further changes in Bank operations that should be made: the Bank should assume a more active role in assisting "credit worthy" countries to gain access to the international bond markets that provide investment capital on relatively long terms; and the Bank, acting in conjunction with the IMF, should take the lead in medium-term adjustment financing.

Each of the multilateral development banks is empowered in its charter to guarantee, in whole or in part, bond issues of member countries. These guarantee powers have not been invoked by any of the multilateral development banks on a regular basis since the World Bank terminated such activity in the mid-1950s.[37] Since then, other forms of cooperative financing arrangements between the multilateral banks and private lenders have evolved: first, through the selling of participations in World Bank loans, without guarantees, and since 1975, through the more direct co-financing of project loans. One of the reasons the guarantee powers have not been used again is that the charters of the multilateral development banks require that the institutions consider the provision of guarantees as being equivalent to

[37]Indeed, the original expectation was that the World Bank would mainly guarantee the obligations of borrowing countries floated in international capital. But "it quickly became evident that if the Bank were to establish its credit, then it was much better for it to issue its own obligations." Michael L. Hoffman, "The Challenges of the 1970s and the Present Institutional Structure," in Lewis and Kapur, op. cit., p. 13. See also the more recent article by Jessica P. Einhorn, "Cooperation between Public and Private Lenders to the Third World," *The World Economy,* vol. 2, no. 2, May, 1979. As Einhorn explains: "In 1949 . . . the Bank loaned $16 million to Belgium, having already arranged for the whole loan to be taken up by private institutions with the Bank's guarantee. Thus, the Bank's role was not to provide capital; it was simply to give the Belgians a guarantee. As the World Bank entered the bond market on its own, management preferred to restrict the use of the Bank's name on private securities and the practice was ended altogether in 1955.

"In 1954, again on behalf of Belgium, the Bank inaugurated a new form of cooperation with private investors by engaging in joint financing with the investment market. The Bank took a $20 million share and the later maturities of a $50 million bond transaction. Over the next six years, the Bank engaged in fifteen such joint operations, benefiting among others, South Africa and Japan. The program ended in 1960 as these borrowers graduated from the Bank and came to rely on the private marketplace." Pp. 236–237.

direct lending for purposes of determining the Bank's total amount of outstanding loans. That is, guarantees must be counted in full as potential claims on the banks' capital (which cannot exceed the total amount of banks' capitalization). Because the immediate cost to the borrower is likely to be somewhat higher than the cost of borrowing directly from the development bank, clients have generally preferred to take direct loans. Nevertheless, the advantage for "threshold" countries over the long term of establishing a borrowing capacity in the private bond markets might outweigh the disadvantages of the higher cost. That is, although the costs of funds obtained from the private markets with guarantees from a multilateral facility would, in general, be higher than that associated with a direct loan from a multilateral development institution, the use of this guarantee arrangement should pave the way for more regular borrowing from the private institutions by upper-income LDCs in the future. The bond guarantee action would, in that way, have a kind of multiplier effect on the financing available to the more advanced LDCs.[38] However, it would probably be of only limited benefit to debtor countries for the Bank to make much greater use of its guarantee authority until agreement has been reached to ease the requirement that guarantees be counted as a loan in calculating the Bank's lending-to-capital ratio and to alter the "gearing ratio" itself. And these changes, as we discuss below, would require an amendment to the Bank's Articles of Agreement.

A second change that we would make was touched on briefly at the end of Chapter 6. In recent years both the Bank and the Fund have taken steps to help countries finance balance-of-payments deficits that cannot and should not be corrected in the short term. The Fund in December, 1979, extended from 8 to 10 years the repayment period permitted under its Extended Fund Facility. And as we discussed above (p. 267), in the spring of 1980

---

[38]The World Bank might also provide technical assistance to help LDCs secure better information about the operations of private capital markets, and might act as the promoter of LDC borrowers, sponsoring the issuance of a bond and perhaps acting as an underwriter.

the Bank made its first "structural adjustment"—or conditional long-term balance-of-payments—loan. With each step, the two institutions moved to close the gap that had existed between the Fund short-term balance-of-payments financing and Bank long-term capital investment.[39]

Both institutions recognize that structural adjustment financing can be looked at either as extended balance-of-payments support or as medium-term program lending and that frequently countries receiving structural adjustment loans will, almost by definition, also be drawing from the Fund. In such situations, close cooperation between the two institutions will be needed, and doubtless there will be more consultation about individual countries than has frequently been the case in the past. As suggested in Chapter 6, it might be desirable to give this collaboration a firm institutional underpinning by establishing a Joint Standing Committee drawn from the Executive Boards of the two institutions.

The principal function of this Joint Standing Committee would be to review proposals for financing made by the staffs of both institutions before formal approval by either Executive Board in cases where countries sought extended adjustment assistance from both the Fund and the Bank. Actual decisions on Fund financing and Bank lending would continue to be made by the Boards of the two institutions, but the review by the Joint Committee would ensure coordination between the programs of the two institutions.

It would be desirable, further, to encourage private commercial banks to participate in the financing of World Bank struc-

---

[39] A UNDP/UNCTAD study on adjustment assistance, undertaken in the late 1970s, recommended that to deal with this problem either governments agree to establish on a permanent basis the Supplementary Financing Facility or that a new medium-term facility be established within the IMF. UNDP/UNCTAD Project INT/75/015 "The Balance of Payments Adjustment Process in Developing Countries: Report to the Group of Twenty-Four," United Nations: New York, January, 1979. Extension of the repayment period of the IMF's Extended Fund Facility and the provision of structural adjustment loans by the Bank are alternative solutions to the problem addressed by the UNDP/UNCTAD study.

tural adjustment loans. Since the mid-1970s investment projects have been co-financed by the World Bank (and the Inter-American Bank) and private banks, but there has not, as yet, been co-financing of non-project loans.[40] Improved coordination between the Bank and the Fund might encourage commercial banks to participate in "deficit financing packages"—consisting of World Bank structural adjustment loans; some shorter-term IMF financing, if appropriate; and, whenever possible, private funds. In this way, the bulk of medium-term adjustment financing would tend to come not from the IMF but from the Bank and from the private sector in the form of conditional, co-financed program loans.

As suggested in Chapter 6, the Joint Standing Committee might also serve as an advisory body on debt renegotiations, thus supplanting the informal "creditor clubs" that are now favored by the developed countries and providing an alternative to the independent Debt Commission that has been proposed by the LDCs. The role of the Joint Committee in this second function would be to hear the case of a debtor country and then "sponsor" an appropriate response. Since in most cases the debt-relief response would require actions by an array of creditors (often both public and private), the Joint Standing Committee would mainly be a facilitating body. On the basis of information it received from the Bank and Fund staffs—including technical information on a country's position, estimates of external capital requirements, and assessments of the impact of alternative debt relief solutions—it might recommend Bank and Fund financing in cooperation with other creditors. This could, perhaps, include the renegotiations or rescheduling of outstanding World Bank loans;[41] but the debt relief, rescheduling, or reorganization would mostly involve the financial arrangements

---

[40]Co-financing of IBRD-assisted and IDA-assisted projects amounted to $6,521 million in 1979/80, an increase of 101 percent over the previous year. The advantages of co-financed program lending are discussed in Einhorn, op. cit.

[41]It should be noted that the Bank stands staunchly unwilling to do this, yet it cannot be much of a leader if it remains unwilling to take the kind of action it recommends to other creditors.

of private institutions and national governments with a debtor country. While the debt "crises" would be looked at on a case-by-case basis, the build-up of "case law" over time ought to make the development of certain guidelines and criteria possible.

OTHER GLOBAL FINANCING FUNCTIONS

As the seventies ended and the eighties began, the World Bank had begun to respond to certain financing needs that really extend beyond what has traditionally been thought of as the development financing function. Both the expansion of the Bank's lending program for the exploration and development of energy and non-fuel minerals and its lending program for structural adjustment mark the beginning of an evolution toward a global financing function. Having begun with reconstruction as its primary concern, the Bank then moved on to development; it is now moving to "restructuring" and to more concern with global resource needs. As the Bank moves in this direction—over time—the critical unit of analysis becomes less the national economy and more the global economy. This is, we believe, a desirable trend.

The decision by the member governments of the World Bank in 1977 to begin a lending program to finance oil and natural gas production and to expand lending for coal and non-fuel minerals was based on recognition of the urgent need of developing countries to exploit their indigenous sources of energy, the considerable underdeveloped potential in many parts of the developing world in the production of natural resources, and the importance of stimulating new capital investments to prevent shortages in supplies worldwide of critical non-fuel minerals. In 1979, a second decision was made to expand further the program for petroleum development, including, for the first time, financing for exploration.

A study done for the Bank estimated that by 1985 oil-importing developing countries might have an oil deficit of some 4.35 million barrels a day and that the yearly costs of covering this deficit might total as much as $38.3 billion—up from $14.3 billion in 1975. At the same time, however, the survey commissioned by the Bank indicated that 23 developing countries (14 of which were not yet petroleum producers) had prospects of finding "high" or "very high" quantities of petroleum while another 15 (13 of which were not yet petroleum producers) had prospects of finding "fair" quantities—enough, at least, to affect their import needs.[42] It is also believed that there is a far greater potential for coal production in the developing world—far greater than is being realized. And, although medium-term market prospects for non-fuel minerals are not now sufficiently promising to ensure the financial and economic viability of many new mining projects, it is generally recognized that the tendency in recent years for mining companies to concentrate on "safe countries" in the developing world is not in the long-run interest of either developed or developing countries. Given even a moderate rate of economic growth from now to the end of the century, demand for energy and non-fuel minerals will require much development of new resources. And to a considerable extent, the richest and most efficiently accessible ore bodies now lie in the developing world. Most member governments of the World Bank agree that the Bank has a role to play in years ahead in assisting countries to gain greater knowledge of their resource endowments and greater technical expertise and that it has a "catalytic" role in the minerals field as well as in the energy resources field in stimulating production, partly by promoting mutually acceptable investment arrangements between host countries and foreign private investors.

Given the magnitude of the capital investment required for both fuel and non-fuel minerals development and the importance of the technical knowledge that the private oil and mining companies have, it is clear that much of the investment in natural resources development will need to continue to come from the private sector. But World Bank financing can play a useful role in encouraging adequate flows of investment capital by providing assistance to mineral-rich developing countries at all stages

[42]World Bank, *Annual Report 1979*, op. cit., pp. 18–22.

of the resource development process, from national energy and minerals development planning to surveying, discovery, and production. Particularly costly, and particularly critical, is the investment capital needed at the exploration stage. To encourage a greater flow of private funds for this, the Bank agreed in the late 1970s to help finance a host country's share of the cost of a program undertaken in partnership with a foreign oil company (and similarly in the case of a minerals project). Also, where national oil companies are technically and financially able to undertake exploration on their own, the Bank will be willing to assist.

As currently planned, the Bank's energy program will rise to $1.5 billion a year by the end of 1983. It will provide technical assistance to developing countries in the design of national energy plans. It will lend for research and development in the use of traditional (non-commercial) fuels (which now account for over 80 percent of the energy used in the rural areas of poor countries). It will finance a range of preinvestment work, including basic geophysical data collection, as well as financing for the high-cost, high-risk phase of exploratory drilling for oil in a few instances. And it will provide up to 20 percent of the cost of some production facilities. In the minerals field, the Bank plans to provide similar assistance, although not at the high-risk phase of exploration (which is met by the Revolving Fund, on which, see below).

Clearly, on the scale of financing now planned, the Bank (like the regional development banks) is limited in what it can do— even assuming that the major part of its role in the energy and minerals field is a catalytic one, providing a kind of "presence" that should encourage stable and mutually acceptable arrangements between resource-rich LDCs and private foreign investors.

For this reason, as the eighties opened, serious consideration was being given by member countries to the establishment of a World Bank affiliate to finance energy development. In our view, the facility should be established and should provide risk capital for exploration as well as financing for the other phases of energy resources development, and it should also probably finance exploration and development of non-fuel minerals as well.

The establishment of a new energy and minerals fund would effectively eliminate the need for the Revolving Fund for Natural Resources Exploration, now managed by the UNDP. The Revolving Fund is distinguished from other international financing programs in that borrowers assume an obligation to "replenish" the Fund when production results from Fund-financed explorations. That is, the Fund is entitled to a repayment of 2 percent of the gross value of a successful mining operation for a period of 15 years from the start of commercial output. However, if no commercially viable development results from explorations financed by the Fund, borrowers pay nothing back to the Fund. In other words, the Fund takes the risk.

Currently, the $24 million Revolving Fund finances only the exploration of hard minerals. It does not cover exploration for oil and natural gas because the costs are too great. A recent study prepared by a group of experts for the United Nations proposed that a separate oil exploration facility be established and administered by the World Bank and that the Revolving Fund be somewhat revised and its resource base enlarged.[43] More desirable, we think, would be the establishment of a single, larger, new fund affiliated with the World Bank that would lend for both petroleum and minerals exploration.

Developing countries have, to date, been reluctant to accept the "replenishment obligation." Indeed, the resources of the Revolving Fund are not now being fully used. However, it seems to us that this arrangement as a way of contributing to an adequate flow of risk capital is correct, in principle. Perhaps it would be possible to devise somewhat more flexible repayment procedures, but as long as there is reason for some "international presence" in mobilizing financing in the high-cost exploration phase of energy and minerals exploitation, some form of

---

[43]United Nations, General Assembly, Report of the Secretary-General, "Multilateral Development Assistance for the Exploration of Natural Resources," A/33/256, October 16, 1978.

repayment that makes the financing mechanism self-sustaining over time would seem appropriate.

It also seems to us that it would be desirable for the World Bank Group to do more than it has in the past to help finance shifts in global production patterns and to facilitate processes of adjustment to industrial change. For this purpose, the World Bank ought perhaps to make loans to *any* country at *any* stage of development that encountered difficulties in financing adjustments.

Fostering development and promoting structural change are clearly overlapping objectives. Development is really nothing less than the structural transformation of an entire society and its economy. Moreover, development policies, plans, and priorities have to be adjusted constantly to cope with changes taking place in the international economy if more difficult problems of adjustment down the road are to be avoided (as the Bank's new program of structural adjustment lending acknowledges). But, in turn, the rapid rate of growth of some LDCs and their new export potential is one of the structural changes in the world economy to which the advanced countries must adjust. As discussed in Chapter 5, what the OECD calls "positive" adjustments will be needed in the developed world not only to enable the less developed countries to achieve acceptable rates of growth and development but also to promote the more efficient use of resources that is needed if there is to be continuing improvement in the standard and quality of life world-wide.

For the most part the kind of international cooperation required to facilitate structural changes in advanced countries is likely to be more a matter of information-sharing and rule-making, as we said in Chapter 5, than of providing financial resources. Market forces will tend to take care of most of the adjustment required; and the countries themselves will normally be able to mobilize sufficient financial resources to guide or to supplement market processes. Yet, the pressures for structural change in the global economy in the decade ahead may turn out to be more extensive than can be accommodated, even by some of today's developed countries.

In his speech at UNCTAD V in May, 1979, the President of the World Bank recommended that the World Bank help finance trade-policy reforms in developing countries.[44] Paraphrasing what McNamara said: Some developing countries have pursued policies that have discriminated against their own expansion of exports. They need now to carry out structural adjustments favoring their export sectors. And additional international assistance ought to be provided to those countries that undertake such adjustments to promote exports in line with their long-term comparative advantage. Movement toward a more open trade policy on the part of the upper-income LDCs in particular would not only be in their own interest, it also would likely benefit lower-income, less-advanced countries which would gain improved access to traditional and new (LDC) markets as comparative advantage in some areas of manufacturing shifts from the upper- to the lower-income LDCs, just as it has recently shifted from the established industrial countries to the newly industrializing countries.

The Bank's new program of structural adjustment lending is responsive to this problem (and to the need of developing countries to make other adjustments as a result of changed external economic conditions). We are, in effect, carrying this idea a step further and suggesting that, in the future, there may be a few situations in which financial assistance from the Bank (appropriately coordinated with our proposed PTO) might be given to enable (or induce) a developed country to make difficult adjustments that will be needed if an open trading system is to be maintained.

In expanding and diversifying the role of the World Bank Group in the various ways proposed—enhancing the Bank's concessional aid program, increasing long-term concessional program lending and collaborating with the Fund on medium-term adjustment financing, reverting to the use of guarantee powers (to back issues of LDC bonds or to back government incentives for adjustment processes), expanding the financing of critical resources development, and, perhaps, in the years ahead, expanding further the concept of adjustment loans—one

[44]Robert S. McNamara, Address to the Fifth United Nations Conference on Trade and Development, Nairobi, May, 1979, World Bank, 1979.

would be moving toward a kind of "global investment bank" that would be more responsive to the needs (some of which can now be seen quite clearly, others only dimly) for investment flows and international financial cooperation that will prevail through the 1980s and beyond.

PARTICIPATION AND GOVERNANCE

These changes in the operations of the World Bank Group, together with continuing build-up of the lending capacities of the regional banks, should improve the capacity of the international economic system to meet the increasingly diverse needs for financing in ways that are in the mutual interest of both developed and developing countries. But few developing countries are likely to be willing to see the World Bank strengthened as the central global resource-transfer institution unless some changes are made in the decision-making power in the Bank.

Although the Bank's membership has increased substantially over the past two decades, the First World still largely controls the activities of the Bank, most of the Second World remains outside the Bank, and the Bank's major clients have too little effective voice. Under these circumstances, LDCs are hardly likely to agree to the streamlining of development assistance and to the enhanced role for the Bank in coordinating development assistance that we have suggested. Rather, as long as the Bank remains heavily donor-controlled—indeed, American-dominated—developing countries are likely to continue to argue in favor of filling "financing gaps" by creating new institutions in which they can have a greater voice instead of modifying existing institutions to meet changing needs. And there will be problems in bringing funds (such as IFAD) that have a more nearly universal membership under the administration of the Bank, as well as problems in expanding the role of the Bank in areas (such as energy, mineral, commodity development) where the participation of non-member countries is desirable.

Like the International Monetary Fund, the Bank is governed—on a day-to-day basis—by a Board of Executive Directors, each Director representing a country or, in most cases, a constituency of member countries. Formally, the Directors set Bank policy and must approve each loan that the Bank makes. Also, as in the Fund, the Board's formal decision-making power is based on a system of weighted voting, reflecting, largely, the economic position of the member countries at the time the Bank was established (although some adjustments have been made) and the cumulative contributions they have made to the World Bank's resource base. In earlier chapters, we have argued that weighted voting should continue in the major global economic institutions with operational functions but that the distribution of weights should give fair representation to those affected by, as well as those who can affect, the activities of those institutions. Applying this principle to the World Bank would mean some adjustments in the allocation of votes on the Executive Boards of the IBRD, IDA, and IFC and on the Board of Governors.

The formal distribution of votes is, however, only one aspect of the "governance issue." In practice, few Executive Board decisions are taken by vote, and, to a large extent, the Bank is not only management-run, but management-led. That is, most decisions about changes in the direction of Bank policy come at the initiative of the Bank's President and his staff, and the "style" of Bank operations is largely determined by the management. Therefore, in considering changes that should be made to give developing countries a more appropriate voice in the Bank, it is necessary to look at the management side as well as the executive side of the Bank.

For reasons of history, the United States has played a dominant role in the management of the Bank (in addition to controlling close to one-quarter of the IBRD/IDA/IFC votes). This American predominance in the Bank's management has become an anachronism and, to some extent, a liability. The American commitment to the IBRD has been important politically and financially, contributing to the establishment of the Bank's creditworthiness as a financial intermediary between borrowers and the private capital market. And U.S. support has, over the years, been essential to the build-up of IDA. When the United States provided roughly 40 percent of the resources pledged to

IDA, and when Bank bonds were marketed solely in the United States, the case for having an American as President of the Bank was a strong one. But, in recent years (1978 and 1979), most Bank borrowing was undertaken in other markets. And other countries now play significant roles in development financing through contributions of official development capital and through the activities of their private lending institutions.

The time would seem to have come, therefore, to break the tradition of an American president. And, the United States probably ought also to agree to reduce—through attrition—its presence at all levels in the Bank's management, especially at the level of the senior staff.

Over the past 10 years, there has been an increase in staff drawn from developing countries, but the LDCs remain underrepresented in the upper echelons of management. The last thing in the world that it would make sense to do would be to destroy the Bank by imposing on it the kind of member-country personnel quota system that now cripples the United Nations. Nonetheless, there ought to be more LDC nationals in senior positions. The desirability of these changes has been recognized for some time. They have become more important with the passage of time, and they are necessary if the Bank is to play the role we envisage for it.

It would also be desirable—again, this is not a new suggestion—that there be more rotation of staff between the Bank and national government services, not only to increase the two-way learning process but also to reduce the institutional bias that any large organization soon acquires and to improve the ability of client countries to affect the manner in which the Bank carries out its activities.

Because the Executive Board of the Bank rarely rejects policy recommendations or loan applications put to it by the management and rarely takes decisions by vote, an increase in LDC participation on the management side of the Bank may have more real significance in "righting the balance" of power than a change in the distribution of votes on the Board. Indeed, what would probably be most important is to make changes in the programming of assistance and in the modes of financial intermediation, such as those discussed above, that place more responsibility in the hands of recipient countries for setting their own priorities and implementing their own development programs. Nonetheless, changes in the composition and in the practices of the management will not diminish the political significance of the distribution of voting power which today vests the formal decision-making power firmly in the hands of a few major donor countries. The Board has the power ultimately to determine the size, scope, and direction of Bank lending operations, and the views (even when there are no votes) of the Executive Directors—and especially of those representing major donor countries—are carefully taken into account in the day-to-day operations of the management. Disparities in influence cannot be wholly avoided so long as there are real disparities in economic power. But today's wide disparity in country influence on policy-making in the Bank should be reduced, and the position of some individual countries altered.

There are today 21 Executive Directors on the Boards of the IBRD and IDA. As stipulated in the Articles of Agreement, five are appointed by and represent the five member countries owning the largest number of shares. The rest are elected by constituencies of member countries which they represent. Originally, this meant that the United States, the United Kingdom, France, China, and India were represented by appointed directors. In 1965, Germany replaced China (Taiwan), and, in the 1970s, Japan was added and India dropped from this group of five. The number of other elected Executive Directors has been increased at various times as the membership of the Bank has expanded. Most recently, in mid-1980, one new Executive Director's seat was added to accommodate the People's Republic of China.[45] But although the Board has grown in size there has been little real change in the ratio of votes of developed and developing countries on the Board.

Votes are distributed slightly differently in the case of IDA

[45]Following a decision of the Board of Governors that the PRC represents China in the Bank and its affiliates, it was agreed that China would "elect" its own Executive Director, forming, in effect, a constituency of one.

and the IBRD/IFC, but, in general, each member country has a base number of votes (250 in the case of IBRD/IFC, and 500 in the case of IDA) plus one additional vote for each unit of its share of financing, that is, for each share of stock held in the IBRD and for each $5,000 of its initial subscription to IDA. Given this arrangement, the United States controls (as of 1979) 21.48 percent of the votes in the IBRD and 20.58 percent in IDA. The advanced industrial countries, taken as a group, control over 60 percent of the votes of each institution.

There is much discussion today of giving a greater voice to oil-exporting countries commensurate with their growing contributions to development financing. But giving more voice to new donors does not go to the heart of the issue, which is the need to increase the voice of recipient countries. We think there is a case for changing the way votes are weighted so that there is somewhat less emphasis placed on a country's contribution to the overall resources of the institution and somewhat more emphasis placed on a country's dependence on the institution. There are various ways this could be done. The simplest and most straightforward way—suggested nearly a decade ago— would be to increase each member country's number of base votes, say, by one per one million people in its population.[46] Although this would not be a wholly accurate way of achieving a better balance between developed and developing, or donor and recipient countries, it seems to us that some variant of this proposal (involving perhaps a somewhat more complex formula that would put a reasonable limit on the advantages that this arrangement would afford very populous countries like India and, particularly, China) would be a reasonably good way of moving into better balance.[47]

This change coupled with larger capital contributions by some

[46]See Escott Reid, *Strengthening the World Bank,* Adlai Stevenson Institute: Chicago, 1973; and the introductory essay in Lewis and Kapur, op. cit.

[47]For example, base votes might be increased by one per 1 million up to some number of million, and, beyond that, additional votes would be calculated on the basis of progressively larger population figures—5 million, 10 million, 25 million, and up.

oil-exporting developing states could reduce the developed countries' shares to close to 50 percent (and deny the United States the veto its more than 20 percent of the votes ensures). As discussed further in the next section, there is some risk that this shift in the relative voting power of developed countries would lead traditional donors to reduce their contributions to the Bank or that the Bank bonds would become less attractive to the market and, as a result, the Bank would have less money to lend. There are other, more gradual, changes that would result in a less dramatic redistribution of voting power: for example, votes might be weighted differently for different kinds of decisions—perhaps giving borrowers considerably more say than they have now in decisions regarding Bank lending policies and practices but retaining control for creditor countries in decisions concerning the capitalization of the Bank and regulations governing its borrowing. In principle, we prefer the simpler and more radical change.

It would also be desirable for the World Bank, as the main international lending institution, to become more universal. This means, primarily, expanding the Bank's membership to include more of the Second World countries. Some of the changes we have suggested would transfer to the Bank some programs in which the Soviet Union and other centrally planned economies have played a role (e.g., some UNDP functions). And the changes would expand the Bank's role in some areas in which it would seem desirable to secure the cooperation of the Soviet Union and other non-member countries. One way to make the decision to join easier for some of the smaller Eastern European countries might be to drop the requirement that members of the Bank must be members of the Fund. But, it seems unlikely that the Soviet Union would be prepared to accept the full obligations of a "donor" member country. Perhaps, therefore, it would be worth considering the establishment of some form of associate membership for the Soviet Union and any other country that was a member of a fund administered by the Bank even though not a Bank member. One aspect of that "associate membership" would be participation in a development assistance review committee, which we discuss below.

WORLD BANK RESOURCES

Obviously, there is a connection between the degree of change that can be made quickly in the lending policy and in the distribution of power in the Bank, on the one hand, and the availability of capital, on the other. As we have explained, the Bank depends on both government subscriptions and money raised on the private capital markets to provide the resources it lends to LDCs. Although, in our view, too much weight is now given in Bank policy-making to major donor countries (in terms of their positions in both the management and executive side of the Bank), the impact of change on the Bank's dependence on private capital cannot be ignored. How much change will be tolerated without hurting the Bank's ability to borrow? If one looks at the more than three decades of World Bank history, it is clear that considerable change has taken place. The constraint posed by the Bank's dependence on the market seems likely to be more on the speed with which changes can be made than on the nature of the financing functions member countries would be prepared to accept.

In 1979, the Executive Directors of the Bank agreed to recommend to the Board of Governors that the Bank's authorized capital stock be increased by an amount equivalent to $40 billion. The increase, roughly a doubling of the Bank's current authorized capital stock, will enable Bank lending to continue to grow, in real terms, by about 5 percent a year through the mid-1980s. Once this general capital increase has been completed, the issue of how to expand further the lending capacity of the Bank should be addressed.

Among the various options currently under consideration is one that would change the requirement on the ratio of loans to subscribed capital from 1:1 to 2:1.[48] To make this change in the

---

[48]As Charles Frank has pointed out to us, the European Investment Bank and the Nordic Investment Bank both have the authority to extend loans equal to 2.5 times their total capital. Commercial banks typically operate at a ratio of

"gearing ratio" would require amending the Bank's Articles of Agreement. Another method of increasing Bank lending without requiring new capital contributions would be to change the "rule" (in the Bank's Articles of Agreement) that each World Bank guarantee be counted as a loan for purposes of calculating the "gearing ratio." Such a change might either exclude guarantees from the calculation of the gearing ratio or establish two separate ratios—one for loans, which involve an actual outlay of funds, and another, higher ratio for guarantees.[49] There are still other ways of expanding the lending capacity of the World Bank. The important issue is not the gearing ratio, per se, but rather how to expand the flow of financial resources in a way that is compatible with both a diversification in the range of World Bank activities and an increase in LDC influence in the operations of the Bank.

Finally, there is the issue of IDA resources. On an annual basis, the IBRD transfers one-half of its earned profit to IDA. With the growth in the Bank's lending, the size of this resource transfer will increase. But this will not meet the need for more concessional transfers. (In 1979, the Bank transferred approximately $100 million to IDA.) LDCs have been right to emphasize the need for continuous, assured, predictable resource transfers. The current way of financing IDA by rounds of voluntary member-country pledges every three years is not a satisfactory way of ensuring that. Indeed, the 1970s have been marked by a serious faltering of commitment on the part of IDA's largest contributor, the United States.

---

something more like 20:1. It may also be worth noting that in the 1940s, when the IBRD was under negotiation, there was talk of establishing a lending ceiling of two to three times total capital. Now that the Bank is a "proven" institution, this issue should be reconsidered. See Edward Mason and Robert E. Asher, *The World Bank Since Bretton Woods,* Brookings Institution: Washington, 1973, Chapter II.

[49]The Export-Import Bank of the United States currently makes this kind of distinction, by permitting up to 75 percent of its liabilities under guarantees and insurance to be excluded from its aggregate lending, insurance, and loan limit.

Today, IDA financing is the great weakness of the World Bank system. If firm agreement could be reached on the demonetization of gold, there would be strong arguments for selling the remaining two-thirds of IMF gold and transferring the windfall profits to IDA to be used for long-term concessional development financing. But no such agreement seems probable.

The thrust of the argument in this chapter, and indeed in the book, points to the logic of putting IDA financing on an assessed rather than a voluntary basis. Ideally, all countries which had a per capita income above some minimum level should agree to provide IDA annually with resources based on a percentage of their GNP per capita. That percentage would not be a flat 0.7 percent; rather, there would be an increasing ratio of aid to GNP per capita so that the richer the country, the higher the ratio. This would mean, among other things, that as today's middle-income developing countries moved into higher income brackets in the decades ahead, they would be contributing more to IDA than they have in the past. It is not very likely that governments will be prepared to agree, in the 1980s, to this prescription, but nonetheless it seems to us to be the right one and efforts should be made to move in this direction.

DEVELOPMENT ASSISTANCE REVIEW COMMITTEE

Underlying this discussion of World Bank reform is the view that there will continue to be a variety of needs for official resource transfers (indeed, an increasingly diverse variety) which it will be in the interest of countries to meet through collective efforts. Today, there is no place where the full array of needs is adequately reviewed and discussed on a regular basis (although there are a number of different forums in which pieces of the problem are discussed).

The annual meetings of the Boards of Governors of the IMF and World Bank Group are occasions for broad-ranging discussions but not for in-depth review and long-term planning. The Executive Board of the Bank discusses broad policy issues, but it is responsible for the running of the Bank and addresses issues primarily in terms of Bank activities, not issues that go beyond that. Outside the Bank framework, the Development Assistance Committee of the OECD holds regular reviews and appraisals of the OECD donor-country policies and procedures. But these are discussions by a "club" of donors. Recipients do not participate. Nor do OPEC and other aid-giving countries take part, which means that DAC reviews now cover a smaller percentage of total aid transfers than they once did.

UNCTAD has recently done some good studies of international financial issues, but it was not set up to deal with development-financing problems, and the attempt by its secretariat to carve out an expanding role for the agency in this field adds to the bureaucratic and political confusion that already hampers the development assistance effort. Within the central United Nations, the Committee on Development Planning, established in 1961 to follow the progress of the first United Nations Development Decade, continues to function as a review and advisory body. But the Committee is an expert group, and its deliberations are not a substitute for the kind of high-level, continuing discussion that ought to go on between donor and recipient governments concerning criteria, objectives, gaps, and ways of improving the flow and use of resources.

The joint IMF/Bank Development Committee, established in 1974, was an experiment along these lines. But it was designed mainly to deflect pressures for other, more radical changes in the Fund and the Bank, and it is composed of finance ministers rather than heads of development assistance agencies and planning ministers. Partly for this reason, it has too limited a view of its role to carry on the broad, regular multilateral review of resource-transfer policies and practices that is needed.

To perform this role, it would be desirable to establish a Development Assistance Review Committee of the World Bank.[50]

---

[50]Variations on this theme have appeared over the years. Some recommendations have called for a permanent, independent group of experts to monitor obligations undertaken by governments, appraise progress in the development

This Review Committee would be a limited-member group composed of high-level government officials. All members of the Review Committee would represent groups or constituencies of countries. And some constituencies would include countries that were not members of the Bank inasmuch as all countries that participated in funds administered by the Bank should be represented.

Because of the nature of its activity, it might be desirable for the Review Committee to be somewhat larger than the Executive Board of the Bank, and it might also be desirable for the constituencies of the Review Committee to be composed in a somewhat different way. That is, rather than having committee members that mainly represent groups of countries within geographical regions or subregions, it might be useful to try to give representation to "categories" of countries defined according to their economic capabilities and needs. For example, constituencies might be composed of groups such as low-income resource-poor countries, less-developed resource-rich countries, middle-income LDCs, LDC donors, and advanced country donors. The membership of the Committee should not be static but frequently reviewed.

The Review Committee, which might meet several times a year, would have research support from the Bank's staff, not a large separate secretariat, but it should also make use of exper-

---

field, and identify problems in need of attention. See, for example, the proposal for a World Development Council in Asher, op. cit., pp. 95–97. Others have called instead for a standing intergovernmental group. In a 1979 report prepared by the UNCTAD Secretariat, for example, a proposal was made for deliberations within "an international forum," the purpose of which would be "to carry out regular reviews of developments in the financing area with a view to assessing the linkages among the various financial components, their impact on the level and structure of world trade and production and their consistency with the internationally agreed objectives of development . . . [and] to recommend international measures designed to ensure that the components of the financial system, when taken together, function in a manner that is consistent with the requirements of internationally agreed objectives regarding world trade and development." United Nations Conference on Trade and Development, Report by the UNCTAD Secretariat, "Towards an Effective System of International Financial Cooperation," TD/235, Manila, April 23, 1979, p. 12.

tise in other parts of the U.N. system, particularly the IMF and the proposed PTO.

In essence, this committee would be a policy review group. It would discuss a broad range of issues relating to the transfer of real resources, including the development assistance policies and procedures of donor countries, assistance and lending criteria of both bilateral and multilateral programs, appropriate performance criteria, and the goals and priorities that should guide the distribution of official long-term resource transfers and official policies affecting long-term private transfers. Assuming that the committee did not become simply another forum for rhetorical exchanges, there would cease to be a need for OECD's Development Assistance Committee: the Review Committee of the Bank would be a multilateralized DAC. And, over time, one can envisage the new committee moving beyond today's familiar discussion of resource transfers for development to a broader discussion of the adequacy of resource allocations and the distribution of investment on a global basis.

* * *

To recapitulate: Structural changes in the world economy, a growing diversity among developing countries, and changing patterns of international capital flows are altering in various ways the nature of the resource transfers that are needed at the global level.

To respond adequately to the increasingly diverse financing problems, it will be necessary in the decade ahead not only to increase the volume of international resource transfers between richer and poorer states but also to make substantial innovations in the resource-transfer process.

While some improvements are still needed in the process of project financing, the major reforms needed in the years ahead are ones that broaden the range of international financial assistance beyond the traditional focus on project financing to include more non-project lending of various kinds and measures to enhance more certain access for LDCs to private capital on manageable terms. Rather than continue the current trend of creating new agencies to meet new needs, it would be desirable to try, instead, to streamline the present system and to reform old institutions to fit changing financial needs. It would also be desirable to try to define the rights and obligations of states as participants in the resource-transfer institutions in a way that fairly reflects relative needs and capabilities. This means that, in general, there ought to be better balance between donors and recipients in the distribution of power in resource-transfer institutions. It also means that the allocation of resources should be governed to a far greater extent than today by internationally agreed-upon criteria that take account both of relative need and of the commitment of a country to development, not to mention the need for a closer correspondence between a country's economic well-being and its contribution of official resources, that is, the richer the country, the higher the percentage of GNP it should contribute.

The key to many of the needed improvements lies, we believe, in reforming the governance and broadening the range of activities of the World Bank Group.

The principal changes that are needed in the operations of the World Bank are not ones that have much to do with the structure of World Bank Group institutions. Rather, they are changes that expand the role of the world's central resource-transfer institution, that alter its way of dealing with "clients," that give less-developed member countries a greater voice in making World Bank policy, and that strengthen Bank ties with other international economic institutions.

Through the 1980s, the core activity of the World Bank and the regional development banks should remain much the same: to provide financing for a wide range of development projects. But, as the lending capacity of the regional banks is increased, much of today's project financing ought to be provided by them, and the World Bank should, increasingly, be carrying out a number of different functions.

The World Bank should do more to help the least developed countries with their own development programming, and, as part of that effort, the Bank should provide an increasing amount of its concessional "credits" in the form of program loans and should become more of a gap-filler and residual lender.

For the more advanced, structural adjustment lending should

probably become more dominant. And, for countries in need of extended IMF assistance as well as structural adjustment loans, coordination between Bank and Fund financing ought to be enhanced, and perhaps given an institutional form by establishing a Joint Standing Committee drawn from the two institutions' Executive Boards.

In addition, the role of the World Bank in relation to the more advanced developing countries should shift from direct project and sector lending (except for essential large-scale investment projects that ought typically to be co-financed) toward the somewhat more "aloof" activity of providing financial guarantees.

Finally, the World Bank should be concerned increasingly with the financing needs of "the global economy." Entry into energy and mineral resources development moves the Bank in this direction. And, in the years ahead, the Bank should do more to help finance structural change, providing loans to any country faced with serious problems in adapting to changes in the world economy.

If the World Bank Group is to play the principal long-term financing role in the years ahead, it should become a less donor-controlled, a less American-dominated, and a more universal institution. To this end, the presidency of the Bank should cease to be an American prerogative. The distribution of votes on the Executive Boards of the IBRD/IDA/IFC should be altered to give "client countries" more voice. And, a new Development Assistance Review Committee should be established to provide the kind of continuing high-level discussion of resource-transfer needs and practices that the management of change in a global economy requires.

EIGHT

Concluding Comments

Most of this book has been concerned with problems and prescriptions, both substantive and organizational, in the main areas covered by our tripod of global level institutions: a new Production and Trade Organization, a reformed IMF, and a reformed World Bank Group. A little has also been said about some of the central United Nations bodies, both in the discussion of our proposed Basic Support Program and in the context of other chapters. Several important issues—food, energy, population—have been touched on in a number of places, but the threads need to be pulled together. And a few words need to be said about the role we see for the over-arching U.N. institutions, the General Assembly and the ECOSOC.

Any study of the most essential institutional needs at the global level should, of course, have included an appraisal of the arrangements foreseen in the Law of the Sea negotiations. But what should or should not happen next in this area is something we have deliberately left aside, for a decade of negotiations is coming to an end as we write. Clearly, the outcome will fall short of the kind of regime for the oceans that would be consistent with our general views of the way events should be encouraged to move. The extension of national jurisdictions and the shrinking of the area that might, in time, have become a true "global commons" was not a surprising outcome in a period when nationalism has been on the rise everywhere. But it is unfortunate that the opportunity to have made a bold break with the past—

which for a brief period at the start of the negotiations seemed possible—was not taken.[1]

FOOD

Dramatic shortfalls in cereal supplies in the early 1970s drew global attention to world food problems and gave rise to a flurry of international activity, culminating in the World Food Conference held in Rome in the fall of 1974. This was one of a series of U.N. Conferences on global problems (environment, population, habitat), and, in some ways, it was the most successful. It was well-prepared, and the resolutions correctly identified the central issues and, for the most part, spelled out sensible approaches to the problems that were identified: (1) the need to increase food production, particularly in the food-deficit developing countries; (2) the need to enhance world food security, in part through the establishment of an international network of nationally held reserves; (3) the need to undertake special measures to eliminate starvation and chronic malnutrition on a global scale; and (4) the need to bring food and agriculture more centrally into international trade negotiations.[2] In the years following the Conference, the World Food Council has given sharper definition to the actions that need to be taken at the national and international level in these main areas and has added some new targets to those accepted in 1974.

But few of the goals set by the World Food Conference have been met. Contributions to an International Emergency Food Reserve—to meet emergency food needs—fall short of the internationally agreed target of 500,000 tons. The Food Aid Con-

[1]For an appraisal of some of the problems that seem likely to remain unresolved, see Ann L. Hollick, "An Oceans Regime for the 1980s," in Ruth W. Arad and Uzi B. Arad et al., *Sharing Global Resources*, McGraw-Hill, for the Council on Foreign Relations/1980s Project: New York, 1979.

[2]The "Programme of Action" agreed to at the conclusion of the Conference, including the "Universal Declaration on the Eradication of Hunger and Malnutrition," and the 22 resolutions can be found in the Report of the World Food Conference, E/CONF, 65/20, United Nations: New York, 1975.

vention (FAC)—an international agreement to guarantee a minimum flow of cereal food aid regardless of market conditions—has been cut loose from the International Wheat Agreement and FAC pledges have increased from 4.2 million metric tons in 1971 to 7.6 million in 1980; but that is substantially below the 10 million ton target set by the World Food Conference. The amount of development assistance going to the LDCs to help them attain the 4 percent growth rate in their food production (which the Conference accepted as a reasonable goal) falls short of what is needed.[3] The much discussed world grain reserve and the International Wheat Agreement (of which it is a part) reached an impasse in 1979 because of failure to agree on stock size, accumulation and release prices, and special provisions for developing countries. The trade regime for agricultural products remains a highly protectionist one, despite minor improvements made during the MTN. And, as we noted in Chapter 4, the FAO estimates that at least 450 million people suffer acute hunger or malnutrition, despite the fact that the world's population could be adequately fed if supplies were differently distributed among countries and as between its use for human food and animal feed.

Over the years, institutional arrangements for food and agriculture at the international level, like their counterparts at the national level, have tended to proliferate with too little concern for how they relate to the system as a whole, or even, at times, to one another. According to one estimate, there are now 89 intergovernmental organizations in the food-agriculture and nutrition fields.[4] No amount of improvement in institutional ar-

---

[3]The World Food Council has urged that development assistance (particularly to a group of countries designated "food-priority countries") be increased to $8.3 billion, of which $6.5 billion would be, ideally, on concessional terms in order to help the LDCs attain a 4 percent growth rate in food production. This amount is about double the present level of external assistance. It would have to be matched by substantial domestic investments if the target growth rate in food production is to be approached.

[4]U.S. Senate, Select Committee on Nutrition and Health Needs, "The United States, FAO and World Food Policies: U.S. Relations with an International Food Organization," 94th Cong., 2d Sess., Washington, 1976.

rangements will solve the problem of malnutrition, eliminate excessive protectionism, ensure adequate production, provide security in supplies, and moderate violent swings in prices of certain key commodities. But a more sensible institutional pattern would help, and in the preceding chapters we have suggested some changes in that direction. We have proposed that food-aid programs, both emergency and continuing programs, be brought under our proposed U.N. Basic Support Program and that the elimination of starvation and acute malnutrition be accepted as a special "task of the system." We have also suggested (see Chapter 7) that the IFAD become a subsidiary of a somewhat restructured World Bank.

As we were finishing this book, there seemed little prospect that negotiations would soon be resumed on a new International Wheat Agreement designed both to stabilize prices and to provide greater security through the operation of a reserve-holding scheme. Both objectives are important and should be pursued, and the agreement should be expanded, in time, to cover coarse grains and rice. Meanwhile, the United States could usefully establish a food-security reserve on its own, having suddenly become embarrassed by 17 million tons of grain originally destined for the Soviet Union.[5] Other food-aid donors should join the United States in establishing nationally held reserves to backstop their commitments of food aid. The World Bank should be encouraged to carry through on its plans to assist with the development of food storage and distribution capacities in developing countries. And food-deficit developing countries should be helped to achieve higher levels of food self-sufficiency even though full self-sufficiency is clearly not an economically rational or desirable achievement for all. Each of these measures would contribute to greater world food security, but the total package does not do away with the need for an international grain agreement to stabilize the market and make food consumers more secure.

[5]Grain exports (over and above an annual figure of 8 million tons covered by a 1975 agreement) to the Soviet Union were embargoed after the Soviet Union invaded Afghanistan. Some of the grain may find other markets, but a substantial amount is likely to be purchased by the government in any case.

The establishment of the World Food Council as a continuing organization was, in part, a vote of no confidence in the FAO, in part an indication of weakness at the center of the United Nations system, notably in ECOSOC, and in part an example of the all too frequent tendency of governments to seek to solve problems by creating organizations rather than by making the changes in policy that lie at the root of the difficulty. It was desirable to take steps to ensure that the important undertakings accepted at Rome were implemented, but because much of the problem of ensuring action required that the tasks identified as urgent by the Conference were looked at in a broader context than had been the rule and were given a higher priority on national agenda, the follow-up body should not have been composed mainly of ministers of agriculture or their representatives. This simply recreated the FAO Council on a slightly different basis and in a different venue.[6]

In time, that part of the World Food Council's mandate which consists in monitoring the world food situation and identifying gaps in technical knowledge should revert to the FAO where it logically belongs, and that part of the mandate which consists essentially in a general oversight of the extent to which commitments accepted at the Rome Conference are being lived up to should be assumed by a strengthened ECOSOC, as we discuss below.

ENERGY

As with the world's food problem, so with its energy problem: the critical need is for changes in national policies on the part of both the producing and the consuming countries. In energy, as in

---

[6]The only substantial difference in membership is that the Russians are members of the WFC but not FAO. The usual reason given for the fact that the Russians are not members of the FAO (though they work with FAO on projects through the UNDP and exchange some technical information) is that they are unwilling to supply all the factual information required of member governments. By belonging to the WFC, they have a voice in policy formation but escape the obligations of membership in the FAO.

food, many of the obstacles to sensible policies are "political" in the most parochial sense of that term. But, as in the case of food, there are also aspects of the problem that cannot be handled by national actions alone. And, with energy, there is an even more highly politicized atmosphere at the global level which severely limits the kinds of international action that it is reasonable to contemplate during the next decade or so. Moreover, there is far more uncertainty about almost all the basic data on which energy decisions for the future now have to be made, and there is a far more complicated interrelationship among the various aspects of the energy problem: price, security of supplies, adequacy of supplies, research into and development of alternatives to oil, and the security, financial, economic, environmental, and other consequences of the choices that are made.

Although estimates of the figures vary, there is virtually no disagreement among the many studies made in the last five years that there will be a critical dependence on oil throughout the 1980s and 1990s, that the path to the eventual replacement of oil by other sources of energy is fraught with hazards; and that even if this passage is negotiated with much more skill than has yet been displayed, there will still be severe problems of adjustment to the abrupt income transfers that have taken place (and may continue to take place), to supply interrruptions and overall stringency, and to the size and discontinuous character of increases in energy prices.

In contrast to the situation in food and agriculture, which has suffered from an embarrassment of riches in institutional terms, there was little intergovernmental cooperation in the energy field—apart from OPEC—before the prevailing assumptions about the availability of abundant cheap energy were abruptly shattered in 1973–1974.[7] In the aftermath of the OAPEC em-

[7]The main institutions that did exist (the International Atomic Energy Agency (IAEA), Euratom, and the OECD's nuclear energy agency) were concerned specifically with the development and protection against diversion of nuclear energy. The European Community has special responsibilities for coal, arising from the Treaty of Paris, as well as for nuclear energy, arising from the Treaty of Rome; but repeated attempts to develop a more comprehensive energy policy have met with little success.

bargo and the price increases at the turn of the year (1973–1974) the OECD countries, with the exception of France (which resisted the move partly on the ground that it would antagonize the oil producers, partly because it favored a "European" initiative, partly out of pique at the clumsiness with which the United States pushed for action), established the International Energy Agency, loosely linked with the OECD. One of the first actions taken by the IEA was the negotiation of an emergency stand-by, oil-sharing agreement (which has, as yet, never been tested and is felt by many people to be too complicated to be likely to be workable). In addition, the IMF established a special oil facility in June, 1974, to meet acute balance-of-payments problems attributable to the increased cost of oil imports.[8] In the summer of 1974, both the OECD and IMF adopted trade pledges committing members not to attempt to shift the oil burden onto others by adopting import restrictions. And, as we indicated in Chapter 7, by the summer of 1980 members of the World Bank had begun seriously to consider the establishment of an energy affiliate to finance exploration and development in developing countries.

Over the years, the IEA has shed some of the confrontational overtones that accompanied its birth and has done some useful work in promoting greater "transparency" of the international oil market and in encouraging conservation and the reduction of imports. But it has had only limited success in encouraging cooperation rather than competition among the principal industrialized country oil importers. Instead, the efforts to seek privileged positions (U.S.-Saudi Arabia, U.S.-Mexico, the Europe-Arab dialogue) have intensified. In contrast, the decision at the Summit in the summer of 1979 to set limits on imports was an encouraging, if belated, development.

Cooperation among the principal consumers to avoid competitive scrambles for oil resources and the mindless bidding-up of

[8]There have been two IMF oil facilities: the first was established in June, 1974, and the second in April, 1975. Both have now lapsed and no further purchases can be made under either facility. The U.S. attempt to establish a somewhat similar fund (the so-called "safety-net," loosely linked, like the IEA, with the OECD) failed to be approved by the U.S. Congress.

329

prices, together with emergency stand-by sharing schemes, are obviously important and a precondition for effective negotiations with oil producers. The meetings at the Summit and within the OECD-IEA complex clearly have a role to play in promoting better cooperation among the main consuming countries and in encouraging the adoption of national policies designed to conserve energy and to stimulate the development of alternatives to oil. The need to deal more effectively with the economic consequences of the changed energy picture, that is, with such things as the severe impact of higher prices on the balance of payments of many countries, the maldistribution of liquidity, the deflationary effects on world demand of unspent OPEC earnings, the inflationary effects in most countries of higher prices, the longer-term impact of high energy prices on the structure of industry, strengthens the arguments for many of the kinds of changes in the IMF, World Bank Group, and trade institutions that we discussed in earlier chapters. The question nevertheless remains whether additional action is required at the global level, focused either specifically on oil or on energy more broadly.

In many ways oil would seem an obvious, almost a classic, candidate for a commodity agreement—not, of course, a buffer-stock, price-stabilization agreement to smooth out variations in price around the trend, but a broader kind of agreement designed to reduce the havoc in the oil market and to make the adjustment to higher energy prices a more manageable one. The essential features of an oil agreement would presumably be understandings concerning: (1) the rate of increase in price; (2) the rate of oil production; (3) supply schedules; (4) consumption controls; and (5) some guarantees for the oil producers to ensure them, through indexation or otherwise, against the erosion of the value of their oil. It would also be desirable to offer them investment opportunities which would be continuing sources of income in the post-oil era and, as part of a general agreement, to make special price arrangements for the poorest LDCs.[9]

---

[9]Some of the essential ingredients in an oil agreement were analyzed in Øystein Noreng, *Oil Politics in the 1980s: Patterns of International Cooperation*, McGraw-Hill, for the Council on Foreign Relations/1980s Project: New York, 1978.

For a number of well-known reasons, negotiations between consumers and producers got off on the wrong foot, the possibilities of an oil agreement have never really been explored, and any efforts to discuss oil prices and supplies apart from the broader agenda of North-South issues have been seen as attempts to deprive the Group of 77 of its most powerful weapon.

Throughout the 1980s there will, however, be need for discussions between the principal producers and consumers of oil about how to bring about more orderly market conditions. And it is important for political as well as economic reasons to try to curb the splintering of the market and the proliferation of special deals. Perhaps the best solution for the immediate future would be to have a U.N.-sponsored oil "study group," ideally a committee of limited size, the members to be drawn on a constituency basis from four groups of countries (although not in equal numbers from each group): the OPEC countries, the non-OPEC oil producers, the industrial-country oil importers, and the developing-country oil importers.[10] The study group's mandate would not be to negotiate a formal commodity agreement, although it might well be specifically asked to explore the possibilities. But there are oil-related issues that need examination and discussion, whether or not something in the way of a more formal understanding ever materializes: in particular, there is a need for a better understanding of, and more consensus on, demand and supply projections and on market trends.

In looking at the array of international economic institutions needed at the global level for the 1980s and beyond, the question arises whether there should be a specialized agency for energy, comparable in conception (although not to today's reality) to the FAO. Our tentative judgment is that to create such an agency would be a mistake. Over the longer term, the most critical energy problems requiring some form of global management are likely to be connected with nuclear energy problems, and these should remain within a strengthened IAEA. In addition, an oil

---

[10]For an analysis of the growing importance of the LDCs as importers, see Joy Dunkerly, William Ramsay, Lincoln Gordon, and Elizabeth Ceceleski, *Managing the Energy Transition in Developing Countries,* Resources for the Future: Washington, forthcoming.

331

agreement—in some ways parallel to a cereals agreement in that security of supplies, not simply more orderly pricing, should be a major purpose of any agreement—would be desirable and should not be written off but, rather, fully explored. As discussed in Chapter 7, the necessary intensive exploration and development of alternative energy resources should be encouraged by loans from the World Bank. And where additional international financing or other measures are needed to facilitate adjustment to the economic consequences of the changed energy situation, the response should come from one or another element of the strengthened tripod.

There are, however, technical problems, related in particular to energy conservation and the development of new sources of energy, which would normally form a large part of the mandate of a specialized agency for energy, analogous to the FAO. The right answer here would seem to be not a purely intergovernmental agency but rather a mixed governmental-nongovernmental agency parallel in some respects to the CGIAR (Consultative Group on International Agricultural Research). It might well be funded partly by voluntary subscriptions from governments, partly by the World Bank, and partly by the energy industry. It would serve both as a clearinghouse for research and, like the CGIAR, sponsor and support research and training programs, mainly in the less technologically advanced countries.

There remains, as there does with food, the problem of national policies: how energy questions are to be given the priority they should have on national agenda, and how public opinion can be aroused to support appropriate and often painful national programs. Mostly, again, this must be the task of national governments, not of international institutions.

POPULATION

A host of problems is connected with the inevitable increase in population that will occur even on the most optimistic assumptions possible about when the world's inhabitants will simply reproduce themselves.[11] Barring a major catastrophe, the eventual stabilization of the total population will be a function of changed attitudes, economic and social development, and the easy availability of family-planning information and devices. Their importance in reducing birth rates is probably in that order, although obviously all three are interdependent and none by itself would suffice. Global bargains involving any very rigorous conditioning of economic assistance on the adoption of family-planning measures, although frequently recommended, are more likely to result in starving children than in fewer children. However, any program of direct support for any basic service can be used to help promote family planning. By bringing all of today's basic support programs (UNICEF, WFP, UNFPA, and UNDRO) within a single U.N. agency, with a stronger mandate and a larger and more reliable resource base, it should be easier to ensure that family-planning assistance is routinely supplied as part of other basic services. But population control is mainly an aspect of social and economic development, and the consequences of uncontrolled growth are among the strongest arguments—in prudential terms—for adequate resource transfers from rich countries to poor countries.

The increases in population that we know are inevitable will make almost all problems—social, political and economic— more difficult to handle. The very steep increases in population foreseen for some of today's already most overcrowded regions threaten to overwhelm efforts to raise the living standards of some of the poorest people in the world. And there will be immense pressures for migration, particularly, as we are already seeing, where densely populated poor areas are adjacent to, or have historic ties with, relatively rich, relatively empty countries—Mexico and the United States, the Mediterranean and Northern Europe, Southeast Asia and Australia. There will be a nexus with some of the structural problems discussed in Chapter 5. Clearly, one of the pressures making for shifts in the pattern of

[11]See Georges Tapinos and Phyllis T. Piotrow, *Six Billion People: Demographic Dilemmas and World Politics,* McGraw-Hill, for the Council on Foreign Relations/1980s Project: New York, 1978.

global production will be the very high levels of unemployment in some developing countries, and the trade-off between importing people and exporting industries is likely to become one that the old industrial countries will increasingly confront. Migration policies are bound to become very important and highly contentious issues. Rule-making in this area will be needed, but it will not be easy. Increased mobility of people across frontiers and increased demands on governments for job security and social welfare benefits push in opposite directions. There will be strong temptations to make deals between pairs of countries "importing" and "exporting" people and for "threatened" countries to agree among themselves on ways to restrict or, at best, to "share the burden" of immigration. Some special understandings between pairs or among groups of countries may be desirable. But discussion and some rule-making at the global level will also be necessary. For unless there are broader discussions and understandings about what constitute acceptable arrangements, weak countries will be at a disadvantage, and, in some cases, problems are likely to be solved by simply shifting them onto others. The analogy with the problem of adjustment to sharp shifts in comparative advantage is a close one. But freer movement of people raises far more difficult problems than does freer movement of goods and capital. So, too, will the elaboration of "fair" rules. We do not pretend to have the answer to what the governing norms should be. It is tempting to see here a role for the ILO, but much would have to change before rule-making in this area is likely to be feasible (even in the highly elastic and optimistic way we have been using the concept of feasibility).

THE U.N. FRAMEWORK

At a high level of generality, the United Nations General Assembly plays a global goal-setting and coordinating role, and it sets the general policy framework in the sense that it reflects and helps mold global views.

In an ideal world, the General Assembly would be constructed differently, so that peoples as well as states were represented. And voting strength would be based on a fairer and more sensible principle than one nation, one vote. But one of the constraints it is as well to accept for the time-frame of this book is that any substantial amendment of the U.N. Charter is not a practical possibility. The General Assembly will remain an indispensable part of the international system, a world forum, albeit an imperfect one, the one place where, in a very general way, all problems can be looked at, the views of all countries voiced, and, at times, some consensus reached on what new tasks are urgent and where priorities need rearranging. As events at the Sixth and Seventh Special Sessions made plain, resolutions adopted by overwhelming majorities can have an effect on the actions of the minority, even though such resolutions may have no power to compel action.

Recent years have seen both an excessive proliferation of intergovernmental bodies of all kinds and attempts to strengthen the General Assembly and the ECOSOC in an effort to give greater direction and cohesion to the system as a whole. In part, this second, centralizing and unifying effort has been a response to the excesses of the first, decentralizing and proliferating trend. But to some extent both the creation of new intergovernmental bodies and the pressure to upgrade the General Assembly and the ECOSOC have been driven by the LDC demands for a system more responsive to their needs and, somewhat paradoxically, by the desire of the developed countries to contain these LDC pressures and demands. Thus, new organizations or new funds have sometimes been set up in response to LDC demands (e.g., UNIDO and the U.N. Capital Fund), while at other times new organizations have been set up in an effort to find a way around the cumbersomeness of existing institutions and the automatic majorities of the LDCs in those organizations. The short-lived CIEC (Conference on International Economic Cooperation), which met for a time in Paris, was such an attempt. Similarly, some of the recent interest in restructuring the United Nations has come from a desire to prune down, to consolidate, to improve efficiency, and to save money, and some of it has come from the desire on the part of the LDCs to build up and to give greater authority to those organizations in which the one nation, one vote rule is still unchallenged. Frequently, of course, the motives have been mixed on all sides.

Wholly apart from the interest of the LDCs in seeking a system that gives them a greater say in the setting of the rules, goals, and other guidelines of the international system, more coordination and somewhat greater centralization is needed in the total system. In a world in which one is becoming constantly more aware of the interconnectedness among issue-areas—how action in almost any functional field depends on supporting action in some other field—other arguments for rather more centralization are reinforced.

Under the U.N. Charter, the "Organization" has the right, and indeed the obligation, to "make recommendations for the coordination of the policies and activities of the specialized agencies" (Art. 58), and it was clearly envisaged that the ECOSOC would take an active part in coordinating the economic work of the total U.N. system, under the general authority of the General Assembly. Over the years, there has been much criticism from all sides of ECOSOC's failure to play the role foreseen for it by the Charter or, for that matter, to play any role with much success. Proposals for revitalizing the Council and strengthening its capacity to formulate policies and to ensure their implementation throughout the U.N. system were included in a Report prepared by a Group of Experts in 1975. Some greatly watered-down suggestions to this end were finally endorsed by the General Assembly in a resolution on restructuring adopted in January, 1978.[12]

---

[12]The Experts' Report was a rather forthright document, but few of its recommendations found their way into the final resolution. See *A New United Nations Structure for Global Economic Cooperation,* Report of the Group of Experts on the Structure of the United Nations System, United Nations: New York, 1975. An official Ad Hoc Committee spent two years reviewing this report and hearing other evidence on the needs of the system, and it was a resolution proposed by this committee which was finally adopted by the General Assembly, A/RES/32/197, Jan. 9, 1978. About the only tangible result of

Efforts to turn the ECOSOC into a central organ for policy formulation and coordination on a system-wide basis, although they have been made from time to time over the years, seem unlikely to succeed. Not only do attempts to upgrade the role of ECOSOC run into the unwillingness of the specialized agencies to look to ECOSOC for guidance and coordination, but there is no widespread consensus among governments that ECOSOC should, in fact, be a strong body capable of giving the international economic system the kind of coordination and leadership envisioned by the Charter. Nor would that seem to be the right role for ECOSOC to seek to play. Suggesting ways of pooling efforts or of taking mutually reinforcing actions when problems cut across the jurisdictions of a number of organizations cannot be done by a Council of government representatives with no functional responsibilities meeting a few times a year as "coordinators," however talented and dedicated these representatives may be. That kind of coordination can only be accomplished by the people who are actually responsible for different activities meeting together and working together. And it is, of course, a multilayered process, involving international staffs, government officials, and ministers. Our answer to the need for more of that kind of coordination is to restructure and to refocus the work of the key agencies (our tripod) that carry the weight of the operational needs of the global system, and then to improve the day-to-day cooperation among them.

An appropriate role for ECOSOC is not easy to define. Given the right kind of substantive staff support, and provided governments sent highly qualified representatives to it, the Council could play a far more useful role than it has in the past as a kind of "global watch" group, scanning the international horizon for

---

the whole exercise was the creation of a new top-level position, that of a Director General for Development and International Economic Cooperation, to rank in the U.N. hierarchy directly after the Secretary General. The new Director General was charged with the almost impossible task of ensuring "leadership" and "coordination" for the system as a whole within the context of a General Assembly resolution which made it very clear that no real change in the autonomy of the specialized agencies or in the quasi-independence of the multitude of other U.N. organizations was to be expected.

new problems and providing a forum for a wide-ranging exchange of views on issues that are important but in danger of being overlooked, or issues that although critical are still too controversial for settlement but do need an airing. It could also serve as a useful place to follow up decisions reached in global conferences where no specialized agency or other body seemed appropriate. The decision—which was part of the General Assembly resolution on restructuring—to have ECOSOC hold shorter, more frequent, subject-oriented sessions was a move in the right direction. But little, if anything, has come of it.

The interest the LDCs had at one time in revitalizing ECOSOC had shifted by the end of the seventies to the General Assembly, and, in particular, to the Committee of the Whole, which was established by the General Assembly (at the insistence of the LDCs) in December, 1977, to monitor progress on the array of demands comprehended by the NIEO. The Committee was also to prepare for a new round of "global negotiations," which the LDCs hoped would be launched in the fall of 1980 at the time of the General Assembly's special session on development.[13]

Any serious attempt to restructure the international economic system is likely to be composed of ingredients which, like the suggestions in this book, cannot be brought together in one overall negotiation. Some of the things that need to be done amount to governments being willing to approach new problems, and sometimes old problems, in new ways. Very frequently, what is most needed is a more long-sighted evaluation of where countries' real interests lie. Existing institutions do need to be changed and new tasks do need to be undertaken, but the timing of the changes varies enormously. In some cases, the improvements that are called for are already in train; in other cases, the groundwork has yet to begin. It is, therefore, difficult to see a body like the Committee of the Whole, or indeed the General Assembly, undertaking or overseeing, except in the most general way, most of the negotiations that are now needed.

A continuing process of stock-taking of where we are and

[13]The special session ended in deadlock.

where we should be going is something that the international system probably does need. But that is not best done by special sessions of the General Assembly, nor is it best done by taking some list of past demands—any group's list of past demands—and assessing progress in terms of whether or not they have been met. The world did not stop evolving in 1974 at the end of the Sixth Special Session. Few problems remain the same, and some of the answers which then seemed appropriate to the Group of 77 many of those countries would no longer advocate. The kind of continuing stock-taking that would be useful—given a constantly changing, dynamic system—would not be easy to do. But it is the task we should like to see the ECOSOC perform. An ECOSOC capable of carrying out this function would have to be composed of high-caliber representatives, capable of thinking not simply in national but in systemic terms, and it would need to be serviced by a talented and reflective staff. But sophisticated, continuing evaluation of systemic needs—not coordination, not negotiation, not the kind of economic analysis that is far better done by the Bank and the Fund, and not today's routine approval of routine reports—would be a useful role for the right kind of ECOSOC to play.

HOW "UNIVERSAL" IS "GLOBAL"?

The central theme in this book is that the changing nature of economic interrelationships means that in the decade ahead there will be a need for more global-level "rule-making" and more global-level "management," and, accordingly, institutional arrangements in certain key areas should be reformed so that they are more widely accepted and more responsive to these needs. But when we use the word "global," or, indeed, when we talk about national governments giving greater weight to "global welfare" and to "systemic" effects, do we mean "universal" (that is, are we really including *all* states) or is our concept of "global" more narrowly defined? The answer depends, to some extent, on whether one is thinking about functions having to do with what we have called the "management" of the international

339

economic system and the emerging global economy, or whether one is thinking about functions that have to do with giving some substance to the nascent sense of world community. But that distinction only begins to give some guidelines. It is necessary to look at roles and functions a little more closely to see what the answers should be.

The legs of our tripod that have most to do with rule-making and rule-enforcement functions at the global level are the IMF and our PTO (or, failing that, a much improved GATT cooperating closely with a much improved UNCTAD). Here the general principles should be that acceptance of some common rules should define the inclusiveness of the organization, but the rules which have to be accepted as a condition of membership must respond to the needs of all countries which importantly affect or depend substantially on the system concerned. The qualifying rules must not, however, be meaningless. And there should be flexibility so those who need additional rules or procedural understandings—whether stricter or simply different—can agree upon them, provided they do not infringe on the basic principles or injure other members. One of the weaknesses in today's GATT, and one of the main reasons for our PTO proposal, is that the qualifying rules are regarded by the LDCs—with some justification—as too tailored to the needs of the advanced industrialized countries. The fact that the GATT rules are today so widely honored in the breach by the countries whose needs they were primarily designed to serve—and disregarded partly because the developing countries do not accept them—also casts doubt on their validity as basic, qualifying principles.

As we explained in Chapter 5, we see ways of combining a large membership in the PTO "umbrella organization" with narrower memberships and stricter rule-systems in a number of semi-autonomous, code-related bodies. The general principles that we suggest should be accepted to qualify for membership in the overall organization are ones that not only the LDCs but also the command economies could accept without having to change the essentials of their economic systems. But it is very difficult to see the Soviet Union accepting the first principle, that is, that domestic actions which have external effects are legitimate matters of international concern. Nor is the Soviet Union likely to seek membership in an organization requiring so much information on domestic policies or one in which both the international staff and the panels that investigate complaints would have as much power as we envisage. Thus, to the question what does "global" mean when applied to membership in our proposed PTO, the answer would be that the "umbrella" organization should be potentially "universal," but it is unlikely to include the Soviet Union or, perhaps, the more doctrinaire Eastern European countries. Most other states should belong, although in some of the subordinate, code-related bodies membership would be limited—in some instances more limited than in today's GATT. If current trends continue, it seems probable that China would decide to join the PTO. There would be advantages both to China and to the trading system in having China become a member of the overall organization (and hence on the Trade Policy Review Board), although Chinese participation in many of the code-related bodies would be neither likely nor particularly advantageous either to China or to "the trade system."

The situation is somewhat different when one looks at the "money system." In the case of the IMF, there is not the same reason as there is in the case of the main global trade organization to seek to expand the membership or to think about modifying today's qualifying principles. Most countries that need to be members of the Fund, either in their own interest or for the good of the monetary system, already are members. Therefore, to the question what does "global" mean in the context of the Fund, the answer would seem to be, about what it does today. Probably a few more of the smaller Eastern European countries will decide to join—as Romania has already done. So, too, will more LDCs, as they find it useful to do so. The Soviet Union does not seem a likely participant in the foreseeable future. It is linked with today's money system through the Eurocurrency market and in other ways, but it is not an essential part of the money system. Nor is the PRC. But it has taken the "China seat," in part (one assumes) because this is a precondition of participation in the World Bank.

The situation is different, once again, when one looks at the World Bank Group. We have suggested that the requirement that members of the Bank must also be members of the Fund be changed. The argument against doing so is that membership in the Fund ensures at least a little financial discipline and thus helps guard against a waste of resources. Although this argument cannot be lightly dismissed, the general thrust of the changes we are proposing for the handling of resource transfers points to a breaking of the link, particularly as we are proposing to bring within the scope of the Bank Group some activities previously handled by the UNDP and other agencies, membership in which carried no commitments to Fund membership. Even if this were done, the Soviet Union is unlikely to want to join the Bank, but, as we indicated in Chapter 7, there might be advantages in associating it in some way with certain aspects of the Bank's work. The PRC has taken the "China seat" in the Bank, as in the Fund.

As we said in Chapter 4, our proposed Basic Support Program has been designed to acknowledge and to give tangible expression to a global responsibility for ameliorating some of the direst forms of economic misery and to deal with natural disasters that overwhelm governments. "Global" in this context does mean universal, and for this reason the Basic Support Program, which is in a sense the UNICEF concept expanded and carried further, would be (as is UNICEF) a part of the central U.N. structure. This does not mean, of course, that operating decisions would be reached by plenary bodies in which the one-nation, one-vote rule applied. Again like UNICEF, the UNBSP should be governed by a limited-member Board with much reliance on a strong, impartial staff for day-to-day administration.

THE TRIPOD AS CENTERPIECE

We are not suggesting that all the functions that need to be performed at the global level should be brought within the "tripod" and the new UNBSP. All the specialized agencies remain, as well as many special-purpose organizations, although some organizations in both categories could to advantage be slimmed down, and some might well be combined. We are looking to the "tripod" as the centerpiece of the system, and we are suggesting that priority be given to strengthening and modernizing this set of institutions. We are also proposing to bring together under the PTO quite a number of functions that some will argue should, instead, be dealt with by separate organizations—for example, the Commodities Board, discussions and codes on investment, discussions and conventions on business practices, and some of the work on structural adjustment now done in the OECD. We are also bringing additional functions within the ambit of the World Bank Group, including much of the work done by the UNDP. And we are suggesting that some of the coordination of macroeconomic policy that now takes place in the OECD might better be done by a small group within the context of the Fund.

Some people will argue that we are putting too many functions under too few hats and that the way to marry "participation" with "efficiency" in international organizations, that is, to give all countries an adequate sense of participation without organizations becoming unwieldy, and the way to keep issues from becoming overpoliticized is to have a multitude of issue-specific functional organizations with memberships varying with the issue. Other people will argue that the division of functions among the IMF, the Bank group, and the proposed PTO separates problems that must be looked at together and that some kind of World Economic Authority is needed to deal with this entire range of problems.

In a world where issues as well as states are increasingly interlinked, there is no perfect answer. Too much consolidation can be cumbersome and can politicize issues that could be handled more routinely and expeditiously if kept separate. But too much separation into issue-specific organizations accentuates problems of coordination and makes it harder to identify and exploit interrelationships. And, somewhat paradoxically, if some issues

343

are to be handled effectively, they will have to become more politicized. Only in that way will they receive the priority on national agenda and the high-level attention that is required.

As one moves from the realm of rule-making designed essentially to reduce friction and to eliminate restrictions on the operation of the market to the far more difficult task of fostering the development of a global economic system that provides certain "international public goods" and satisfies more fully the normative concerns discussed in Chapter 2, coordination across issue-areas becomes more necessary. The advantages of seeking to keep issues manageable by keeping them separate has to be weighed against the importance of paying more attention to how they interact. For example, the transfer of resources needs to be seen not simply in terms of the needs of poor countries for financial help if they are to develop, it also must be seen as a part of the process of managing the global economy to attain steady, noninflationary growth. Surplus savings generated in some sections of the world economy must be transferred, one way or another, to those places in which they can be invested productively if the system as a whole is to prosper. The total pattern of resource flows—concessional assistance, commercial lending, direct foreign investment, portfolio investment, debt-settlement arrangements, special balance-of-payments financing—is a matter of global concern and should be looked at as a whole. There must, as well, be a more conscious effort to look at the interlocking relationships between investment, shifts in comparative advantage, trade restrictions, and adjustments to new patterns of production. By improving each leg of the tripod and by strengthening coordination among the three, we think it should be possible to achieve the global oversight of the closely interconnected central issues that will increasingly be needed, without too much overloading of any one institution.

In our proposed PTO we may, indeed, be trying to bring too many functions within a single institution. A less comprehensive version can be imagined, although we think there are clear advantages in having commodity arrangements and discussion of investment rules and business practices come under the same "umbrella" as the tasks that are more directly concerned with trade rules and problems of adjustment to changing patterns of production. In the PTO, we have sought to diminish the hazards of comprehensiveness and to gain the advantage of looking at the most closely interrelated issues together by combining an array of issue-specific, limited-member, semi-autonomous groups with other bodies—like the Trade Policy Review Board—that do represent, although on a constituency basis, the whole PTO membership and are designed to look at the interconnections. Our proposed PTO also permits groups of countries to adopt special procedures and different substantive rules, but within a general framework of principles, surveillance, and complaints arrangements.

No division of functions is ideal. But the tripod, with each of the legs a strong one, with good coordination among the three organizations, some joint committees where problems clearly call for a closely coordinated approach, and with a considerable measure of autonomy for subordinate groups with diverse memberships within the most comprehensive of the three (the PTO), seems to us likely to be better than either more splintering or further consolidation.

"LEVELS OF MANAGEMENT"

Trying to decide how best to divide functions vertically, or functionally, is difficult enough, but cutting them horizontally and finding the right "level of management" for many problems is even more difficult. That is, it is very hard to identify and to agree upon which aspects of the "governance" of trade, money, resource transfers, investment policies, and so forth should be done at the national or subnational level, which at the regional level or among some group of states that share common problems or common attitudes, and which must be done globally or truly universally. In almost all cases, action is needed at several levels. We have focused on the action that seems to us to be needed at the global level, but one cannot think adequately about action at any level without reflecting as well on the action required at other levels. And, ideally, this book should have said much more than it has about the kinds of actions that should be taking place among groups of states (and also, transnationally, among non-state actors) at the regional and other levels.

In the years ahead, cooperative action at some of these other levels will be the most effective way of dealing with many problems. Yet, at the same time, action taken at these other levels will raise some of the most difficult questions and pose some of the hardest choices about the perspective from which to view problems—about the "right" level of management. In thinking about the tensions and the contradictions that may exist between "intermediate"-level, intergovernmental institutions and global-level institutions, one needs to distinguish among several rather different kinds of intermediate arrangements. Those that go very far down the road to genuine integration present problems that are not much different in kind from those that exist between many states and international institutions. That is, the problems of fitting a really unified European Community into a global rule-system for trade or money would not be substantially different from those of accommodating a large federal state, like the United States. And organizations that mainly deal with questions which only involve the group concerned—as is the case with certain kinds of regional cooperative arrangements, e.g., the development of river basins—are, again, not difficult to handle.

But many arrangements are not clear-cut. The European Community is, for example, very far from being a federal union. The potential for tension between the EMS and the IMF was commented on in Chapter 6. And one can already see that when the Community of Nine expands to Twelve, the needs of "its NICs" (Greece, Portugal, Spain) will inevitably have priority over "other" NICs, in that the terms of access of the new members to the markets of the older members of the Community will be more favorable. But beyond that inevitable preferment, will the fact that the rich, highly industrialized members of the Community have accepted the need to adjust to accept this competition make it very much more difficult to gain their cooperation for arrangements designed to encourage adjustment on the global level?

Easy assumptions about the benefits that might be derived from encouraging economic integration among groups of LDCs and the earlier enthusiasm for seeking to replicate the European Community elsewhere in the world have yielded to more realistic appraisals of the problems and limitations in transferring the European model to areas marked by very different conditions. Nevertheless, there is clearly much scope for many different kinds of cooperation among groups of LDCs, some linked by geography, others by common needs. The Andean Group and ASEAN both point to useful patterns and so, too, do some of the subregional arrangements in Africa. In the case of many small developing countries, a larger-than-national approach to investment and industrial development is desirable and can be helped by preferential trading arrangements as well as by a larger role for the regional development banks, as we urged in Chapter 7. But LDC regionalism, as well as European regionalism, may pose problems. It is not difficult to see that new regional powers might come to dominate some groupings, imposing patterns of development or trade that would be less in the interest of the poorer states in the region than more multilateral arrangements. And it is easy to see preferential arrangements being maintained long after they have served their legitimate purposes of encouraging investment and industrial development.

Part of the purpose behind the proposal for the PTO is to find ways to ensure that special arrangements are not made among any group of countries, developed or developing, that result simply in shifting trade and industrial adjustment problems onto other countries. But even if agreements could be reached on new guiding principles and on improved surveillance and complaints arrangements, problems would remain. Tensions and conflicts of interest *do* exist. Adjustments that are acceptable on a national basis are frequently not acceptable on a regional basis (even in as homogeneous a group as the European Community), and some which are politically acceptable on a regional basis or among a like-minded group of countries like the OECD are simply not acceptable on a more inclusive global basis.

In addition to problems of this kind, some particular problems arise when one thinks about the future role of the OECD. In our discussion of trade and production problems and of arrangements for the better management of money, we have suggested that some of the work now done among the advanced industrialized countries in the OECD might better be done in limited-member groups within the context of global organizations. And we suggested that the DAC (the OECD's Development Assistance Committee) might, in time, be superseded by a more broadly based advisory committee linked to the World Bank Group. No one would today create an economic institution with the particular membership of the OECD—it is the product of history not of deliberate planning.[14] For some purposes, like the coordination of macroeconomic policy, the membership is too large because about half its members—countries like Portugal, New Zealand, Iceland, and Turkey—are peripheral to the problem. For other purposes, like facilitating the process of adaptation to new patterns of production, it is too small because it does not include some of the most rapidly industrializing non-European countries, like Brazil, Mexico, and South Korea, that are essential participants in discussions about many aspects of this subject. However, although the OECD is not the ideal forum for many of the problems with which it is today concerned, it does include within its membership all the most advanced market-economy countries (as well as some others), and it has developed methods of consultation and patterns of cooperation that it would be foolish to abandon before alternatives exist. Many problems do tend to hit this group of countries first, and some questions are still of primary importance only to this group. But, to a rather greater extent than is now the case, the OECD should view its role as that of pathbreaker, experimenter, and gap-

[14]For further details on the history and operations of the OECD, see Camps, *"First World" Relationships*.

filler.[15] It should not seek to cling to functions once it is clear that the interests of other countries are deeply involved, provided, and it is an important proviso, an institutional alternative that more nearly matches the scope of the problem exists or can be created. Clearly, the transfer of functions from the OECD will happen, if it happens at all, in a gradual way. But rather than seeing in the IMF and other key global institutions a threat to its own existence and the transfer of functions to them as something which should be resisted, the OECD should regard the strengthening of these institutions and the eventual transfer of some of its present functions to them as part of its purpose. Its continued usefulness may, paradoxically, be closely related to how successfully it can, over time, work itself out of a role.

Looking to the future, somewhat similar points might be made about the Group of 77. Some people argue that the path to fairer and more productive bargaining lies through stronger organizations in North and South and better preparation on both sides of their bargaining positions. We doubt it. The Group of 77 undoubtedly improved the bargaining position of the LDCs at a time when too little attention was being paid to their needs. But the North-South dichotomy is becoming obsolete. Efforts to find common positions from which to negotiate will become increasingly difficult as the real interests of the LDCs become more divergent, and the ensuing bargaining process will be a brittle one. The best safeguard against unfair bargaining is to have it take place within an agreed framework of rules, with international staffs holding the ring, supplying technical advice and information to those less fortunately placed. If changes are made so that the key institutions are more responsive to the needs of the LDCs and if their role in the governance of the "tripod" is felt by them to be a fair one, the Group of 77 should diminish in importance.

[15]Organizations like the OECD are, of course, not independent actors but the creatures of the member states. Nevertheless, both international staffs and those parts of national governments most involved in the work of a particular organization do have views of where any particular organization fits into the scheme of things. These views are frequently at variance with views held elsewhere in member governments about the roles of competing organizations.

COMMON THEMES AND CONTINUING PROBLEMS

The need for change, the extent of change, and the timing of change is rather different in each of the four main areas we have concentrated on. And our suggestions for change range from fairly precise immediate steps to long-term "visions" that are intended more as frameworks within which to think about incremental steps than as programs of action. Certain common themes do run through much of our discussion, considerations that seem to us should guide any efforts to improve the global-level institutions on which we have been focusing: the need to adjust voting arrangements and staffing patterns to take account of shifts in economic power and to give more recognition to the fact that dependence on a system, as well as the ability to affect a system, deserves a "voice" in decision-making and in "management"; the need to find better ways to combine general rules and procedures that are widely applicable with special rules and procedures to meet special needs; recognition that different groups of countries need to cooperate in different ways and that they should be free to do so, provided they do not simply shift problems on to others; the need for the "steering" and the "leadership" that only a few countries can really provide, to be supplied continuously and within the context of key global institutions, rather than being supplied, if at all, spasmodically by Summitry or by unilateral actions (with that must go the acceptance of the legitimacy of "inner" groups); the need to discuss internationally issues that have been traditionally regarded as matters of purely domestic concern; the desirability of moving away from thinking and institution-building in terms of "separate worlds" and toward thinking in terms of a continuum or spectrum of states, recognizing that states occupy rather different positions on that spectrum, depending on the issue; the need to maintain the quality and the independence of international staffs, but, at the same time to strengthen the participation of national policy-makers in the key institutions; the importance of looking at the distribution of costs and benefits, powers, and responsibilities in the system as a whole, not in each institution separately; the desirability of trying to get a few essentials right—of concentrating on a basic support program and on the "tripod"—rather than scattering efforts and trying to improve everything that might be improved or assuming that the situation is hopeless.

One aspect of institutional improvement which needs thought, and which we are very conscious of neglecting, is how one should involve in institutions at the global level (as well as at other levels) the non-governmental entities that do so much to shape the changing economic environment—the banks and enterprises that treat the world as a single economy and other transnational groups that act across national boundaries in ways which both constrain governments and make some of their actions meaningless. If, as we believe, we live in a mixed system that is part "international" economy, part "global" economy, many of these groups are as "real" components of the global system as are the national units with which we have been mainly concerned. They must increasingly be involved, one way or another, in the process of multilateral governance at the global level. Some useful reflections on this problem are contained in another 1980s Project book.[16] It is a problem now: it will become a more important one in the future.

The biggest problem of all is how the needed shifts in perspective in national policies are to come about. Obviously, governments need to be organized to deal more effectively than they do today with problems that cut across traditional distinctions between foreign and domestic concerns. Beyond that, there are large questions about the capacity of modern democracies to define national interests in ways that transcend the too-frequent simple aggregation of parochial concerns and in ways that give systemic effects more weight in national decision-making. There are also questions about a democracy's ability to look at problems in a longer time perspective than that imposed by short-term electoral cycles. It is easier for an autocracy than for a democracy to take the long view, but the kind of society that gives birth to autocracy seldom concerns itself with concepts of

[16]William Diebold, Jr., *Industrial Policy as an International Issue,* op. cit., chap. 6.

351

welfare that extend beyond national frontiers. Nor is an autocratic government likely to welcome international scrutiny of domestic policies. It is even less well adapted than a democratic government to deal with many of the problems we have been discussing and to participate in the "collective management" the system needs.

The steps we have suggested would not take one very far down the road to "collective management," although some of our proposals may be beyond the realm of the possible. Better answers than ours will probably be found to some of the problems we have pointed to. But it is difficult to feel very confident that, in today's world, all the solutions that will be found will be ones that match the need.

As the world becomes more crowded and more interconnected, there will be new issues which will require both "collective management" and radical shifts in national perspectives if economic welfare is not to become hostage to political rigidity, short-sightedness, and lack of inventiveness. The dilemma that today plagues policy-makers will persist for many decades. It is easy to define, immensely difficult to resolve: how to gain support for policies which take the longer-sighted, systemic view, given political systems that are organized, structured, and expected to advance claims and satisfy needs defined in other ways. There *is* a lack of congruence between the economic world and the political world, and there is no easy way to overcome it. Unless the answer is found in hegemony (or a willing acceptance of hierarchy) on the one hand, or in an impoverishing (and perhaps impossible) reversion to a disintegrated economic system on the other, this lack of congruence will eventually make new perspectives and new forms of "collective management" inescapable. How long it will be before the "inevitable" becomes "acceptable" remains to be seen.

Selected Bibliography

GENERAL

Acheson, A. L. Keith, *et al.* (eds.), *Bretton Woods Revisited,* Macmillan, London, 1972.

Aspen Institute for Humanistic Studies, *The Planetary Bargain: Proposals for a New International Order to Meet Human Needs,* Report of an International Workshop Convened in Aspen, Colorado, July 7–August 1, 1975.

Bell, Daniel, *The Coming of Post-Industrial Society,* Basic Books, New York, 1973.

Bergsten, C. Fred, *The Future of the International Economic Order: An Agenda for Research,* A Report to the Ford Foundation, D. C. Heath and Co., Lexington, Mass., 1973.

Bhagwati, Jagdish N. (ed.), *The New International Economic Order: The North-South Debate,* The M.I.T. Press, Cambridge, Mass., 1977.

Brown, Seyom, *New Forces in World Politics,* The Brookings Institution, Washington, D.C., 1974.

Bull, Hedley, *The Anarchical Society: A Study of Order in World Politics,* Macmillan Press Ltd., London, 1977.

Camps, Miriam, *The Management of Interdependence: A Preliminary View,* Council on Foreign Relations, New York, 1974.

Cooper, Richard N., *The Economics of Interdependence: Economic Policy in the Atlantic Community,* McGraw-Hill, for the Council on Foreign Relations/Atlantic Policy Studies, New York, 1968.

———, "Worldwide vs. Regional Integration: Is There an Optimum Size of the Integrated Area?" in Fritz Machlup (ed.), *Economic Integration World-Wide, Regional, Sectoral,* Macmillan, London, 1976.

———, Kaiser, Karl, Kosaka, Masataka, *Towards a Renovated International System,* A Report to the Trilateral Commission, Triangle Paper, No. 14, 1977.

Cox, R. W., and Jacobson, H. K., *The Anatomy of Influence,* Yale University Press, New Haven, Conn., 1973.

Falk, Richard A., *A Study of Future Worlds,* The Free Press (Macmillan), for the World Order Models Project, New York, 1975.

Gordon, Lincoln, *Growth Policies and the International Order,* McGraw-Hill, for the Council on Foreign Relations/1980s Project, New York, 1979.

Halperin, Morton H., *Bureaucratic Politics and Foreign Policy,* The Brookings Institution, Washington, D.C., 1974.

Hoffmann, Stanley, *Primacy or World Order: American Foreign Policy since the Cold War,* McGraw-Hill Book Company, New York, 1978.

Keohane, Robert O., and Nye, Joseph S., Jr., *Power and Interdependence: World Politics in Transition,* Little, Brown and Co., Boston, 1977.

———— and ———— (eds.), *Transnational Relations and World Politics,* Harvard University Press, Cambridge, Mass., 1972.

Lewis, W. Arthur, *The Evolution of the International Economic Order,* The Eliot Janeway Lectures on Historical Economics in honor of Joseph Schumpeter, Princeton University, 1977.

Morse, Edward L., *Modernization and the Transformation of International Relations,* The Free Press (Macmillan), New York, 1976.

North-South: A Program for Survival, Report of the Independent Commission on International Development Issues (The Brandt Report), The M.I.T. Press, Cambridge, Mass., 1980.

Schachter, Oscar, *Sharing the World's Resources,* Columbia University Press, New York, 1977.

Shonfield, Andrew (ed.), *International Economic Relations of the Western World, 1959–1971,* 2 vols., for Royal Institute of International Affairs by Oxford University Press, 1976.

Tinbergen, Jan, coordinator, *RIO: Reshaping the International Order,* A Report to the Club of Rome, E. P. Dutton and Co., New York, 1976.

Vickers, Geoffrey, *Freedom in a Rocking Boat: Changing Values in an Unstable Society,* Allen Lane, The Penguin Press, London, 1970.

SPECIALIZED

American Society for International Law, *Re-Making the System of World Trade: A Proposal for Institutional Reform,* Studies in Transnational Legal Policy, No. 12, Washington, 1976.

Arad, Ruth W., and Arad, Uzi B., *et al., Sharing Global Resources,* McGraw-Hill, for the Council on Foreign Relations/1980s Project, New York, 1979.

Asher, Robert E., *Development Assistance in the Seventies: Alternatives for the United States,* The Brookings Institution, Washington, D.C., 1970.

Atlantic Council of the United States, *GATT Plus—A Proposal for Trade Reform*, Praeger, New York, 1976.

Bergsten, C. Fred, Horst, Thomas, and Moran, Theodore H., *American Multinationals and American Interests*, The Brookings Institution, Washington, 1978.

Bernstein, E. M., *et al.*, *Reflections on Jamaica*, Princeton Essays in International Finance, No. 115, Princeton University, Princeton, N.J., 1976.

Caldwell, Lawrence T., and Diebold, William, Jr., *Soviet-American Relations in the 1980s: Superpower Politics and East-West Trade*, McGraw-Hill, for the Council on Foreign Relations/1980s Project, New York, 1980.

Camps, Miriam, *"First World" Relations: The Role of the OECD*, Atlantic Institute for International Affairs, Council on Foreign Relations, New York, 1975.

Chenery, Hollis, *et al.*, *Redistribution with Growth*, Oxford University Press, New York, 1974.

Cohen, Benjamin J., *Organizing the World's Money: The Political Economy of International Monetary Relations*, Basic Books, New York, 1977.

Coombs, Charles A., *The Arena of International Finance*, John Wiley and Sons, New York, 1976.

Cooper, Richard N., *Economic Mobility and National Economic Policy*, Wicksell Lectures, May 15–17, 1973, Almquist and Wiksell, Uppsala, 1974.

———, "Prolegomena to the Choice of an International Monetary System," *International Organization*, Vol. 29, No. 1, Winter 1975, pp. 63–97.

Corden, W. M., *Trade Policy and Economic Welfare*, Clarendon Press, Oxford, 1974.

Crockett, Andrew, *International Money: Issues and Analysis*, Nelson, London, 1977.

De Vries, Tom, *On the Meaning and Future of the European Monetary System*, Essays in International Finance, No. 138, Princeton University, Princeton, N.J., September 1980.

Diebold, William, Jr., *Industrial Policy as an International Issue*, McGraw-Hill, for the Council on Foreign Relations/1980s Project, New York, 1980.

———, *The End of the ITO*, Essays in International Finance, No. 16, Princeton University, Oct. 1952.

Evans, John W., *The Kennedy Round in American Trade Policy: The Twilight of the GATT?*, Harvard University Press, Cambridge, Mass., 1971.

Fishlow, Albert, *et al.*, *Rich and Poor Nations in the World Economy*, McGraw-Hill, for the Council on Foreign Relations/1980s Project, New York, 1978.

Fleming, J. Marcus, *Reflections on International Monetary Reform*, Princeton Essays in International Finance, No. 107, Princeton University, Princeton, N.J., 1974.

Frank, Charles R., Jr., with the assistance of Stephanie Lewinson, *Foreign Trade and Domestic Aid*, The Brookings Institution, Washington, D.C., 1977.

355

Gold, Joseph, " 'Political' Bodies in the International Monetary Fund," *The Journal of International Law and Economics,* Vol. 11, No. 2, 1977, pp. 237–85.

————, *Uniformity as a Legal Principle of the International Monetary Fund,* reprinted from *Law and Policy in International Business,* Vol. 7, No. 3, 1975.

Golt, Sidney, *The Developing Countries in the GATT System,* Thames Essay No. 13, Trade Policy Research Centre, London, March 1978.

Gordon, Robert J., and Pelkmans, Jacques, *Challenge to Interdependent Economies: The Industrial West in the Coming Decade,* McGraw-Hill, for the Council on Foreign Relations/1980s Project, New York, 1979.

Green, Stephen J., *International Disaster Relief,* McGraw-Hill, for the Council on Foreign Relations/1980s Project, New York, 1977.

Guindey, Guillaume, *The International Monetary Tangle,* M. E. Sharpe, Inc., White Plains, N.Y., 1977.

Guth, Wilfried, and Lewis, Sir Arthur, *The International Monetary System in Operation,* The 1977 Per Jacobsson Lecture, Sept. 25, 1977, Washington, D.C.

Hansen, Roger, *Beyond the North-South Stalemate,* McGraw-Hill, for the Council on Foreign Relations/1980s Project, New York, 1979.

Haq, Mahbub ul, *The Poverty Curtain: Choices for the Third World,* Columbia University Press, New York, 1976.

Helleiner, G. K. (ed.), *A World Divided: The Less Developed Countries in the International Economy,* Cambridge University Press, Cambridge, England, 1976.

Hill, Martin, *The United Nations System: Coordinating Its Economic and Social Work,* Cambridge University Press, Cambridge, England, 1978.

Hirsch, Fred, *Money International,* revised edition, Pelican Books, Harmondsworth, England, 1969.

————, *et al., Alternatives to Monetary Disorder,* McGraw-Hill, for the Council on Foreign Relations/1980s Project, New York, 1977.

Hudec, Robert E., *The GATT Legal System and World Trade Diplomacy,* Praeger, New York, 1975.

Jackson, John H., *World Trade and the Law of the GATT,* Bobbs-Merrill, New York, 1969.

Johnson, Harry G., *Economic Policies Toward Less Developed Countries,* Allen and Unwin, London, 1967.

Kafka, Alexandre, *The International Monetary Fund: Reform without Reconstruction,* Essays in International Finance, No. 118, Princeton University, Princeton, N.J., 1976.

Kaplan, Jacob J., *International Aid Coordination: Needs and Machinery,* American Society of International Law, Washington, D.C., 1978.

Kock, Karin, *International Trade Policy and the GATT, 1947–1967,* Almquist and Wiksell, Stockholm, 1969.

Kostecki, M. M., *East-West Trade and the GATT System,* St. Martin's Press, New York, for the Trade Policy Research Centre, London, 1979.

Lewis, John P., and Kapur, Ishan (eds.), *The World Bank Group, Multilateral Aid, and the 1970s*, D. C. Heath and Co., Lexington, Mass., 1973.

Lindbeck, Assar, "Stabilization Policy in Open Economics with Endogenous Politicians," Richard T. Ely Lecture, *American Economic Review*, Vol. 66, No. 2, May 1976.

Mason, Edward, and Asher, Robert E., *The World Bank since Bretton Woods*, The Brookings Institution, Washington, 1973.

Morawetz, David, *Twenty-five Years of Economic Development*, The World Bank, Washington, 1977.

Mundell, Robert A., and Polak, Jacques J., (eds.), *The New International Monetary System*, Columbia University Press, New York, 1977.

Noreng, Øystein, *Oil Politics in the 1980s: Patterns of International Cooperation*, McGraw-Hill, for the Council on Foreign Relations/1980s Project, New York, 1978.

Preeg, Ernest H., *Economic Blocs and U.S. Foreign Policy*, Report No. 35, National Planning Associations, Washington, 1974.

Rangarajan, L. N., *Commodity Conflict: The Political Economy of International Commodity Negotiations*, Croom Helm, London, 1978.

Reid, Escott, *Strengthening the World Bank*, Adlai Stevenson Institute, Chicago, 1973.

Singh, Jyoti Shanhar, *A New International Economic Order: Toward Fair Redistribution of the World's Resources*, Praeger, New York, 1977.

Solomon, Robert, *The International Monetary System, 1945–1976: An Insider's View*, Harper and Row, New York, 1977.

Southard, Frank, A., Jr., *The Evolution of the International Monetary Fund*, Essays in International Finance, No. 135, Princeton University, Princeton, N.J., 1979.

Streeten, Paul, and Burki, S. J., "Basic Needs: Some Issues," *World Development*, Vol. 6, No. 3, March 1978.

Tapinos, Georges, and Piotrow, Phyllis T., *Six Billion People: Demographic Dilemmas and World Politics*, McGraw-Hill, for the Council on Foreign Relations/1980s Project, New York, 1978.

Tew, Brian, *The Evolution of the International Monetary System, 1945–1977*, Hutchinson, London, 1977.

Triffin, Robert, *Gold and the Dollar Crisis: Yesterday and Tomorrow*, Essays in International Finance, No. 132, Princeton University, Princeton, N.J., 1978.

Vernon, Raymond, *Sovereignty at Bay: The Multinational Spread of U.S. Enterprise*, Basic Books, New York, 1971.

——, *Storm over the Multinationals: The Real Issues*, Harvard University Press, Cambridge, Mass., 1977.

Warnecke, Steven J., (ed.), *International Trade and Industrial Policies*, Macmillan, London and Basingstoke, 1978.

Whitman, Marina v. N., *Sustaining the International Economic System: Issues for U.S. Policy*, Essays in International Finance, No. 121, Princeton University, Princeton, N.J., 1977.

Wilcox, Clair, *A Charter for World Trade,* Macmillan, New York, 1949.

Williamson, John, *The Failure of World Monetary Reform, 1971–1974,* New York University Press, New York, 1977.

Wriggins, W. Howard, and Adler-Karlsson, Gunnar, *Reducing Global Inequities,* McGraw-Hill, for the Council on Foreign Relations/1980s Project, New York, 1978.

Young, Oran, *Resource Management at the International Level,* Nichols Publishing Company, New York, 1977.

OFFICIAL PUBLICATIONS

(As will be apparent from the footnotes, much use was made of the annual reports and other official publications of all the organizations with which we were concerned. A very few reports of special interest are noted below.)

Blackhurst, Richard, Marian, Nicolas, and Tumlir, Jan, *Trade Liberalization, Protectionism, and Interdependence,* GATT Studies in International Trade, No. 5, Geneva, November 1977.

———, *Adjustment, Trade and Growth in Developed and Developing Countries,* GATT Studies in International Trade, No. 6, GATT, Geneva, 1978.

Gold, Joseph, *The Second Amendment of the Fund's Articles of Agreement,* Pamphlet Series, No. 25, International Monetary Fund, Washington, 1978.

International Labour Office, Tripartite World Conference on Employment, Income Distribution and Social Progress and the International Division of Labour, *Employment, Growth and Basic Needs: A One-World Problem,* 2 vols., ILO, Geneva, 1976.

Organization for Economic Cooperation and Development, *From Marshall Plan to Global Interdependence,* OECD, Paris, 1978.

———, *The Case for Positive Adjustment Policies,* A Compendium of OECD Documents, 1978/1979, OECD, Paris, June 1979.

———, Interfutures Final Report, *Facing the Future: Mastering the Probable and Managing the Unpredictable,* OECD, Paris, June 1979.

Selowsky, Marcelo, "Balancing Trickle Down and Basic Needs Strategies: Income Distribution Issues in Large Middle-Income Countries with Special Reference to Latin America," World Bank Staff Working Paper No. 335, The World Bank, Washington, 1979.

Singer, H. W., "Food Aid Policies and Programmes: A Survey of Studies of Food Aid," World Food Program, Rome, 1978.

United Nations, *A Study of the Capacity of the United Nations Development System* (The Jackson Report), DP/5, Geneva, 1969.

———, *Report of the World Food Conference,* E/CONF, 65/20, United Nations, New York, 1975.

————, *A New United Nations Structure for Global Economic Co-operation,* Report of the Group of Experts on the Structure of the United Nations System, E/AC.62/9, May 1975.

————, *Report of the Ad Hoc Committee on the Restructuring of the United Nations System,* Official Records, Thirty-second Session, UNGA, Supplement No. 34 (A/32/34), United Nations, New York, 1978.

United Nations Conference on Trade and Development, *The Balance of Payments Adjustment Process in Developing Countries: Report to the Group of Twenty-Four,* UNDP/UNCTAD Project INT/75/015, January 1979.

————, *International Monetary Issues,* Report by the UNCTAD Secretariat, TD/233, UNCTAD V, March 1979.

————, *Towards an Effective System of International Financial Cooperation,* Report by the UNCTAD Secretariat, TD/235, April 1979.

————, *Contribution of UNCTAD to the Preparation of the New International Development Strategy,* Report by the UNCTAD Secretariat, TD/B/758, September 1979.

United Nations Economic and Social Council, *Transnational Corporations in World Development: A Re-Examination,* Commission on Transnational Corporations, E/C.10/38, March 1978.

Index

About the Authors

MIRIAM CAMPS has been a part-time Senior Research Fellow with the Council on Foreign Relations since 1970. She was born and educated in the United States (Mt. Holyoke, Bryn Mawr) but now lives most of the year in Cambridge, England, where her husband is the Master of Pembroke College and she is a fellow of Wolfson College. She served at the American Embassy in London during the latter part of World War II and the early postwar period, and thereafter for several years in the Bureau of European Affairs in the Department of State. Later, during the 1960s, she was for two and one-half years on the Policy Planning Council of the Department of State, for much of that time as the vice-chairman of the Council. She has held research positions with the Center of International Affairs at Princeton University, Political and Economic Planning and the Royal Institute of International Affairs in London, as well as, most recently, and at an earlier period, with the Council on Foreign Relations. She has written extensively about European affairs and about international economic institutions. Among her publications are: *Britain and the European Community, 1955–1963; European Unification in the Sixties;* and *The Management of Interdependence.*

CATHERINE GWIN, who was on the staff of the 1980s Project from late 1975 through mid-1978 and its Executive Director from mid-1978 through the completion of the Project in January 1980, is now the North-South Issues Coordinator of the International Development Cooperation Agency. Mrs. Gwin has a Ph.D. from the University of California, Berkeley, has taught at Columbia University, and has written several articles on North-South relations. The views expressed by Mrs. Gwin are her own and do not necessarily reflect those of the United States government or any of its agencies or departments.